Summers Off?

New Directions in the History of Education

Series editor, Benjamin Justice

The New Directions in the History of Education series seeks to publish innovative books that push the traditional boundaries of the history of education. Topics may include social movements in education; the history of cultural representations of schools and schooling; the role of public schools in the social production of space; and the perspectives and experiences of African Americans, Latinx Americans, women, queer folk, and others. The series will take a broad, inclusive look at American education in formal settings, from prekindergarten to higher education, as well as in out-of-school and informal settings. We also invite historical scholarship that informs and challenges popular conceptions of educational policy and policymaking and that addresses questions of social justice, equality, democracy, and the formation of popular knowledge.

Dionne Danns, *Crossing Segregated Boundaries: Remembering Chicago School Desegregation*
Deirdre Mayer Dougherty, *Race and Place: School Desegregation in Prince George's County, Maryland*
Sharon S. Lee, *An Unseen Unheard Minority: Asian American Students at the University of Illinois*
Jason Mayernick, *Not Alone: LGB Teachers Organizations from 1970 to 1985*
Margaret A. Nash and Karen Graves, *Mad River, Marjorie Rowland, and the Quest for LGBTQ Teachers' Rights*
Christine A. Ogren, *Summers Off? A History of U.S. Teachers' Other Three Months*
Diana D'Amico Pawlewicz, *Blaming Teachers: Professionalization Policies and the Failure of Reform in American History*
John L. Rury, *An Age of Accountability: How Standardized Testing Came to Dominate American Schools and Compromise Education*
Kyle P. Steele, *Making a Mass Institution: Indianapolis and the American High School*

Summers Off?

A History of U.S. Teachers' Other Three Months

CHRISTINE A. OGREN

Rutgers University Press
New Brunswick, Camden, and Newark, New Jersey
London and Oxford

Rutgers University Press is a department of Rutgers, The State University of New Jersey, one of the leading public research universities in the nation. By publishing worldwide, it furthers the University's mission of dedication to excellence in teaching, scholarship, research, and clinical care.

Library of Congress Cataloging-in-Publication Data

Names: Ogren, Christine A. author
Title: Summers off? : a history of U.S. teachers' other three months / Christine A. Ogren.
Description: New Brunswick, New Jersey : Rutgers University Press, [2025] |
Series: New directions in the history of education | Includes bibliographical references and index.
Identifiers: LCCN 2025003006 (print) | LCCN 2025003007 (ebook) |
ISBN 9781978831759 hardcover | ISBN 9781978831742 paperback |
ISBN 9781978831766 epub
Subjects: LCSH: Teachers—United States—History | Teachers—United States—Social conditions | Work-life balance—United States | Career development—United States | Travel—Psychological aspects | BISAC: EDUCATION / History | BUSINESS & ECONOMICS / Education
Classification: LCC LB1775.2 .O37 2025 (print) | LCC LB1775.2 (ebook) |
DDC 371.100973—dc23/eng/20250614
LC record available at https://lccn.loc.gov/2025003006
LC ebook record available at https://lccn.loc.gov/2025003007

A British Cataloging-in-Publication record for this book is available from the British Library.

∞ The paper used in this publication meets the requirements of the American National Standard for Information Sciences—Permanence of Paper for Printed Library Materials, ANSI Z39.48-1992.

rutgersuniversitypress.org

In honor of Jurgen Herbst and Geraldine Clifford,
on whose shoulders I am privileged to stand

Contents

Summers Off?

Introduction

When New Jersey teacher Nicholas Ferroni began a campaign on social media platforms Twitter and Instagram in 2019 to debunk common misconceptions about how teachers spend their summers, he struck a chord. "Teachers are working multiple jobs, on top of having to pay for professional development, writing curriculum, going to conferences, workshops, presentations. . . . I was just trying to use my platform as an educator and influencer to expose all that," explained Ferroni.[1] The outpouring of #NoSummersOff tweets included social studies teacher Kevin Cline's expression of excitement and thanks for a seminar on the American Revolution, fourth-grade teacher Carrie Lillard's report from Mount Vernon that the tour had provided her with "More info about slavery!" for her classroom, and Coleen Curry's comment at the end of a four-week National Endowment for the Humanities program, "I don't have words yet to describe how amazing this opportunity was, but now it's time to go home and plan for Sept." Other teachers documented their engagement in manual labor and their fleeting attempts to unwind, and "@NEAToday" recapitulated, "Professional development, conferences, summer job, year long school, tutoring, night job, training, school maintenance, coaching, summer classes, camps, volunteering, all the #NoSummersOff jobs don't fit in a tweet!"[2] Such posts demonstrated what has been the case since the nine-month school year took shape in the United States a century and a half ago: Teachers have never really had "summers off," and their activities during the summer months have always supported their work during the school year.

While X (formerly Twitter) and Instagram are new media, the issues highlighted under #NoSummersOff are long-running. The modern school year with its long summer break was one result of widespread reform initiatives in the mid-nineteenth century to create common public schools with uniform curriculums, trained teachers, and standardized procedures. Before the common school reform movement, fledgling rural schools generally convened for two- to three-month terms: the winter term, usually taught by a man, and the summer term, increasingly taught by a woman. Meanwhile, many urban schools met year-round with occasional two-week breaks. As a result of calendar standardization, by the 1880s or 1890s in most cities and rural areas, teachers taught from September through May or early June.[3] This book focuses on the 1880s through the 1930s, a period that was both formative and distinctive regarding schoolteachers' summer pursuits. Formatively, during these decades education leaders identified, and teachers began to engage in, types of appropriate summer activities. The period was also distinctive in that teachers during these decades had a fair amount of flexibility due to invasive regulations and gender ideology. In particular, women teachers—whose numbers grew as longer school years and rising certification requirements repelled men from teaching—were subject to rules and cultural expectations barring them from homeownership and marrying through the early twentieth century and from being mothers through the mid-twentieth century, meaning that most teachers were free from immediate household responsibilities.[4]

Summer vacation was intended, historian Kenneth Gold explains, "to recharge weary school children and adults" as well as "to achieve individual and social purposes"—and it drew criticism from its inception.[5] U.S. commissioner of education Philander P. Claxton and *The Elementary School Teacher* editorial team headed by Charles Judd remarked in 1914 that "comparatively few" teachers "use the vacation months in any profitable way."[6] However, the summer activities of many teachers fulfilled individual and social purposes quite profitably. In Kansas from the 1880s into the twentieth century, sisters and country school teachers Amanda, Mary, May, and Maude Stewart returned for the summer to work on the family farm. Another sister, Nora, taught for a short time in the 1880s before she married. The Stewarts also attended local teachers' institutes, and Maude toured Europe during the summer of 1912. Farther north, Bess Corey similarly taught in one-room schools and devoted her summers to helping on her family's Iowa farm in the mid-1900s, after which she left to teach and homestead in South Dakota. Corey spent her summers in the 1910s and 1920s developing her claim as well as attending institutes and augmenting her small salary through service work in nearby Fort Pierre. And Beatrice Cramer, a junior high school teacher in White Plains, New York, devoted her summers in the 1920s and 1930s to summer school at the University of Rochester or the New York State Teachers College at Albany, or to extensive tours of different regions of the United States. Moved by a "grand and glorious feeling to be alive" and energized by "invigorating mountain air," Cramer found her travels to be rejuvenating.[7]

The engagement of teachers like the Stewart sisters, Corey, and Cramer in professional development and summer school, work to support their family or to make ends meet, tourism in the United States or Europe, and rejuvenation or rest, has largely been absent from the increasingly rich scholarship on the social history of U.S. teachers. These histories focus mainly on the school year and highlight the control and constraint of teachers' personal and professional lives in the wake of the mid-nineteenth-century common school reform movement and feminization of the teaching force. In rural areas, community pressure and longstanding rules dictated acceptable dress, behavior, and social activities for both female and male teachers, often stipulating that they were not to drink alcohol, smoke, dance, or play cards and that women teachers—especially those who were white—were not to marry. Even after rural residents had greater contact with urban commercial culture in the 1920s and 1930s, rural communities continued to enforce strict behavioral standards, which now also included prohibitions on bobbed hair and, for white women teachers who gained permission to marry, having children. Histories of teachers in urban areas, which focus for the most part on women, acknowledge restrictions on teachers' personal lives—especially marriage and motherhood bars—while paying particular attention to the constraints on teachers' professional lives that resulted from Progressive Era reform. New forms of school administration and bureaucracy dictated curricular content and "de-skilled" teachers; in the words of historian Nancy Hoffman, "the 'what' and 'how' of teaching were wrested away from teachers." One of the few works that look explicitly at male teachers during this period suggests that along with inadequate compensation, behavioral restrictions and deskilling turned many of the remaining men away from the profession; a male former teacher stated in 1908 that men viewed teaching as "a hireling occupation" that was "looked down upon in the community" and "usually belittles a man."[8]

In large cities and the urban as well as rural districts that followed their lead in the late nineteenth and early twentieth centuries, school leaders sought to shape teachers as cogs in a rationalized system, casting teacher professionalism as adherence to administrators' directives. In his 1936 analysis of "freedom of teaching in American schools," Howard Beale argued that "in teaching, 'cooperation' is usually the administrative euphemism for blind obedience." Thus, teacher "professionalization" during this period engendered, in the words of historian Jurgen Herbst, "the betrayal of the teacher." According to Diana D'Amico Pawlewicz, "Teacher professionalization initiatives were never about improving the stature, working conditions, or general circumstances of individual teachers." Instead, top-down, administrator-led professionalization required teachers to toe a rigid bureaucratic line and denied them the authority, the expertise based on esoteric knowledge, and, ultimately, the status of professionals. Historians describe teachers' agency in the face of administrative control—collectively through unions and individually behind closed classroom doors—but ever-present in their accounts are the constraining effects of professionalization on teachers. D'Amico Pawlewicz argues, "gendered and racialized assumptions about the nature of women workers and [middle-class] Whiteness as Americanism converged to yield a brand of Progressive Era professionalization reforms that, on the surface, promised stature and order, but in practice degraded teachers and their work."[9]

Gendered assumptions enabled the feminization of teaching, and gender discrimination was baked into administrators' approaches to professionalization. In the eyes of mid-nineteenth-century school reformers, teaching fit within the female sphere, as women's maternal, nurturing temperament made them ideal teachers of young children—not to mention that districts could save money by paying them less than men. By 1850, women were 60 percent of teachers nationwide and 80 percent in the Northeast, and by 1900 women were 74 percent of teachers nationwide and 85 percent in the Northeast, with women providing almost all elementary-level instruction. Feminization occurred more slowly among Black teachers, but over 80 percent of them were women by 1930 as well. And as late as 1930, 80 percent of all women teachers were unmarried.[10] The education bureaucracy that germinated in the common school movement and grew profusely during the Progressive Era rested on the assumption that female teachers, who were naturally docile, needed the direction of male administrators, who were natural leaders due to their inherent rationality and strength. While increases in training requirements, the standardization of a longer school year, and differentiation among teaching positions seemed to improve teachers' status and create an ordered path for career advancement, school bureaucracy functioned for teachers as "an 'inclined plane' where men governed 'the grade and the scale.'" As school bureaucracies became more factory-like and U.S. women increasingly challenged gender boundaries by the early twentieth century, some school leaders decried the "woman peril" in education in an unsuccessful effort to attract more men to teaching and to control women teachers. Historian Adam Fairclough adds that for Black women teachers, racism combined with sexism to create "an education bureaucracy of white men who generally ignored, belittled, or patronized them."[11] In the patriarchal regimes that governed Black as well as majority-white schools, professionalization required a higher level of commitment but provided little independence on the job as school leaders defined good teachers—both female and male—as those who dutifully followed their directions.

Professionalization also required that teachers balance subservience with "a certain level of class collateral"; historian Kate Rousmaniere explains that the teacher was to conduct herself as "a cultured middle-class woman." The quintessential cultured middle-class woman in the Victorian era, however, did not work, and most teachers' lower-middle or lower-class background and less-than-middle-class salary presented further challenges for their gaining class collateral. By the late nineteenth century in the United States, historian Burton Bledstein explains, "being middle class referred to the kind of person one was" in regard to not only domestic life but also cultural tastes, level of education, professional pursuits, and recreation. Daniel Rogers notes that the new "gospel of relaxation" excluded the working class, and Cindy Aron adds that being able to travel on vacation helped to define the middle class before the expansion of vacationing to the lower classes in the 1930s.[12] Teacher education provided some cultural capital while rules regarding teachers' dress, conduct, and social lives enforced middle-class standards of respectability, but the solidly middle-class status of independent professionals remained elusive for teachers. A 1913 study by the National Education Association (NEA) reported that low salaries made it difficult for teachers to fulfill expectations that they "live as gentle folks," and Beale remarked, "Custom requires teachers to dress far beyond the small-town teacher's salary." Fairclough captures a similar situation for Black teachers in the segregated South with the observation that they "received the equivalent of a laborer's pay but had to dress like ladies and gentlemen." In their 1929 Middletown study, Robert and Helen Lynd placed teachers in the "business" rather than the "working" class yet noted their low pay and "bitter comments . . . upon their lack of status," and, a few years later, teacher educator Marguerite Clark wrote that the inability to afford middle-class activities like country club sports and upscale travel made some teachers "feel inferior."[13]

Intertwined in professionalization's imposition of impracticable social class standards was the expectation that teachers live as *white* "gentle folks." Rousmaniere notes that the ideal cultured middle-class teacher's blond hair embodied her northern European heritage, and another historian lists "proper white womanhood" as a job requirement during this period. Education reformers conflated Americanized whiteness with teacher quality; in New York City, D'Amico Pawlewicz reports, administrators avoided hiring teachers of color and worked to erase the ethnic identities of those who did not fit the ideal. Black teachers were by definition excluded from whiteness, but it nevertheless undergirded professionalization in their ranks as well. In segregated southern schools, white philanthropists, school boards, and superintendents demanded that Black teachers conform to white cultural standards which isolated them from others in the Black community, yet also restricted Black teachers from teaching classical subjects and addressed them only by their first names in order to enforce white supremacy. In various ways throughout the country, top-down professionalization constrained and controlled teachers' work and personal lives.[14]

It makes sense that historians overlook the summer in their analyses of professionalization because teachers' contracts—and paychecks—covered only the school year. However, the fact that teachers were not actually employed during the summer months did not keep school leaders from attempting to regulate how they spent them. Claxton and Judd's editorial team prefaced their remark that few put their vacations to good use with the unsubstantiated declaration, "Whatever may be the terms of the contract, teachers are in fact employed by the year."[15] Based on this view, administrators regularly issued instructions for summer vacation, beginning with admonishments that teachers should rest. As the nine-month school year took shape in the mid-nineteenth century, Gold explains, education leaders subscribed to the prevailing medical view that teaching put one's health at risk and that women teachers especially needed a period of quietude to restore their fragile nervous system.[16] When the first summer school for teachers opened in 1878 on Martha's Vineyard, according to late nineteenth-century educator William Mowry, "the general voice in the country was in opposition" on the grounds "that the vacation was designed for rest and recuperation for the teachers and they should not employ their time in study and hearing lectures." Along the same lines, an 1890 article in *The Iowa Normal Monthly* stated that at the end of the school year, "Worn and wasted by the cruel canker of school-room care and weighted down with the heavy responsibilities of daily duty, the mind of the school teacher craves for rest and diversion." By this time, though, the range of prescribed summer diversions was growing, and for the next several decades teachers received seemingly contradictory advice on how to spend their summers. In paternalistic articles with titles such as "What Shall We Do with the Long Vacation?" or "Making the Most of Summer," school leaders directed teachers to rest, study, and engage in other middle-class activities including travel, all in the interest of professionalization.[17]

In "How Shall I Spend the Summer?" published in the *Texas School Journal* in 1889, the writer attempted to reconcile professional development and rest with the argument that a "good, live" monthlong training institute was best for teachers who were "broken down and need rest and recreation." In 1897, when *The Iowa Normal Monthly* reported that the "leading universities and the best normal schools are now conducting summer schools and they are being well patronized by the [high] class of teachers," tension remained over whether teachers should rest or study. A response to the *Monthly*'s report quoted a Boston newspaper's comment that "one must wonder at the numerous summer schools which have sprung up. . . . Not only the child, but the adult as well, should enjoy a period of absolute rest from intellectual exertion." Administrators continued to advocate rest well into the twentieth century; in 1914, the *Pennsylvania School Journal* printed the observation of the state superintendent of Illinois that "a considerable number of teachers should give up their entire vacation to quiet and rest." However, school leaders paid more attention to professional development as a summer activity for teachers. Before advocating rest, the Illinois superintendent reflected that it was a blessing that "the great majority of teachers will use their vacation for advanced study." Education journals celebrated high summer school enrollments, ran advertisements for all sorts of educational summer programs, and encouraged teachers to attend the summer meetings of their state teachers' associations and the NEA. *The Journal of the National Education Association* suggested in 1921 that during the three summer months, professional development was more important than rest for all but unhealthy teachers, stating that while the latter "may need that much time for rest and recreation," for most teachers, "the importance to the Nation of summer training is incalculable."[18]

While professional development remained the main summertime activity that education leaders prescribed for teachers, beginning in the early twentieth century administrators also advocated travel and tourism. Reflecting middle-class sensibilities, Illinois education journal *The Intelligence* celebrated teachers' "long vacations" as "a good thing for mind and body" and recommended that they take advantage of "large opportunities for travel, recreation, and for professional and culturing improvement." Every spring, this journal published Tour and Travel sections and/or a Summer Outing Number in which articles offered advice for travel and advertisements touted rail routes and possible destinations. The editorial opening the May 15, 1903, issue stated that its contents should be "most helpful and valuable" for teachers despite containing "no professional or pedagogical literature."[19] In education journals, ads related to travel—as well as for summer schools—mushroomed in the 1910s and 1920s and continued throughout the Depression; *Midland Schools*' Educational Recreation Travel section in April 1931 included an article on "Suggestions for Summer Touring" in the western United States and Canada and ads for travel in the U.S. and Europe. Some school districts rewarded teachers for approved summer activities. In the 1920s, Hammond, Indiana, structured expectations by providing a salary bonus for teachers who rotated in a three-year cycle among enrolling in normal school or college for at least five semester hours' credit, "travel of educational value," and "rest"—prompting one commentator to remark sarcastically that the district's paternalism would be "a great relief to the teachers of Hammond, for they are now freed from all thought concerning their periods of rest, study and travel" and that there was "still room to decree what teachers shall eat, what they shall drink, and wherewithall they shall be clothed."[20]

Although a bonus would have helped, many teachers struggled to balance further education, tourism, or rest with the need to earn money during the summertime. Encapsulating this dilemma, a cartoon on the cover of *The American School Board Journal* in 1905 titled "The Vacation Problem" showed a teacher puzzling over a ledger book with her salary and expenses listed on one side and "cost of vacation trip" on the other (figure 1).[21] As they came to grips with school leaders' heavy-handed advice for how they should spend their vacations, teachers did manage to shape their own summer experiences just as they found ways to forge a degree of agency over their work in the classroom. While historians tend to echo Beals's claims of "complacency and inertia" on the part of teachers, they also acknowledge ambiguity in teachers' work lives and their hidden efforts to exert a degree of control. During the school year, Rousmaniere explains, city teachers responded to their stressful work situations by "alternatively accommodating, adapting, and resisting" various aspects of administrators' instructions. Rural teachers, according to historian Margaret Nelson, similarly negotiated "the boundaries of these constraints" by finding ways to improve classroom conditions and simply ignoring some of the controls on their personal lives. And Black teachers, Fairclough explains, developed various forms of "accommodationism" to white control in the interest of advancing the education of their race. Historian Jarvis Givens adds that they eluded white surveillance through "fugitive

THE VACATION PROBLEM.

The American Schoolmarm:—Can I go, or must I remain at home?

FIGURE 1 "The Vacation Problem," *The American School Board Journal* 31, no. 1 (1905): cover. (Courtesy of HathiTrust.)

tactics" developed during slavery to incorporate Black history and combat anti-Blackness in their classes throughout the post–Civil War and Jim Crow eras.[22] While D'Amico Pawlewicz agrees that teachers "did not sit idly by" as top-down professionalization threatened what little control they had in the classroom, she also observes that "ordinary classroom teachers stand somewhat voiceless in this history" because their efforts were often furtive and left unrecorded.[23]

Many teachers did leave records of their summer activities, however, and the ways in which they spent these months reveal how teachers accommodated, adapted, and resisted the prescriptions administrators issued for their time "off." Collectively, their summer experiences substantiate *teachers'* version of professionalism, or a grassroots vision of professionalization from the bottom up. In their letters, diaries, and the articles they occasionally published on their summer experiences, teachers demonstrated how the time away from the classroom allowed them to reflect on and improve their skills as well as advance their knowledge of education as a field. While some resisted, most teachers accommodated administrators' directives that they devote part of the summer to enhancing their skills, but they adapted their experiences to also include engaging with esoteric topics in education and building support networks with other educators. Some teachers took advantage of opportunities to pioneer progressive techniques through teaching in nonschool settings or to immerse themselves in avocations that supported—or departed from—the subjects they taught in the nonsummer months. While studying academic subjects and touring the United States and other countries also enhanced their teaching as well as enriched their stock of cultural capital, teachers gained cultural knowledge and explored new places not simply to gain trinkets for their classes or to affirm their adherence to the standards of the white middle class, but to be more learned and cultured people, a key tenet of grassroots professionalization. For many, living as "gentle folks" also meant working to ensure their financial well-being or to support their family of origin. Thus, the geographical and psychological space that summer provided allowed teachers to assert their social class and professional legitimacy.

Summer also provided teachers with a reprieve from administrative and community surveillance, and many used it to act in resistance to the gender assumptions that shaped schools' patriarchal structures or, in the case of Black teachers, to hone their resistance to white supremacy in the schools in which they taught. Some male teachers engaged in labor or pursued other activities that asserted masculinity that the educational bureaucracy called into question. Women teachers, on the other hand, often used summer school, temporary employment, tourism, or even the need for rest and rejuvenation to break free of constraints by claiming what historian Virginia Scharff in her history of women as automobile drivers terms "the right to broaden their horizons." Jackie Blount asserts that while schools enforced gender conformity among their workers, the restrictions such as marriage bars that they imposed during this period also unintentionally enabled teachers to transgress gender boundaries. Kathleen Weiler and Geraldine Clifford argue that through living lives that were conventional yet "aslant" and by securing a "measure of psychological and economic independence," respectively, women teachers subverted the confines of separate gender spheres.[24] Blount, Weiler, and Clifford foreground the school year, but women teachers' accounts of their summer experiences especially demonstrate how they challenged gender conventions and thus infused women's independence into their view of professionalism. Similarly, Givens's compelling account of Black teachers' "fugitive pedagogy" focuses mainly on how Carter Woodson and the Association for the Study of Negro Life and History developed an insurgent curriculum and how teachers enacted it in their classrooms. Givens discusses Woodson's work with teachers' associations and summer programs, but focusing more explicitly on Black teachers' summer education demonstrates how they acquired the tools for fugitive pedagogy and insurgent professionalization.[25]

The version of professionalization that teachers forged through their summer activities between the 1880s and the 1930s fostered expertise based on esoteric knowledge, intellectual independence, authentic membership in the middle class, and agency for women and Black teachers. Individual teachers pursued different types of activities to varying extents, but the composite of teachers' summer experiences fortified them to make well-informed, authoritative decisions in the classroom. Bottom-up professionalization was not without costs to teachers, as their summer activities were basically unpaid contributions to the schools. And teachers' model of professionalism would remain latent in the presence of administrative control. Nevertheless, it subversively prepared teachers to act as independent professionals and was an important counterpoint to school leaders' approach. Grassroots professionalization was an underground benefit to the education system and the teaching profession.

The following five chapters trace teachers' vision of professionalization through in-depth examinations of teachers' summer professional-development activities, experiences in college and university summer school programs, summer work for wages as well as on behalf of family, tourism in the United States and Europe, and responses to the notion that they should spend the summer resting. The first two chapters demonstrate that teachers between the 1880s and 1930s had more training than historians have assumed. In chapter 1, "Professional Development in Institutes and Association Meetings: 'So Many Serious, Intensely Professional Teachers,'" I argue that these forms of professional development enhanced teachers' skills and understanding of the broader field as well as their social and cultural capital, even if they were not enough to earn them unequivocal professional status. Local summer institutes focused mainly on skill development and subject matter knowledge but also included other educational and cultural subjects. National programs including the Chautauqua Institution, the Martha's Vineyard Summer Institute, and the Columbian Catholic Summer School broadened teachers' educational and cultural horizons even further, and summer meetings of state teachers' associations and the NEA as well as the National Association of Teachers in Colored Schools allowed them to witness, and occasionally to participate in, discussions of esoteric topics while they benefited from fellowship with others in the field. Also at these meetings, women teachers incubated and asserted their independence, and Black teachers learned the content and methods of fugitive pedagogy.

Organized primarily for schoolteachers, summer sessions at institutions of higher education supplanted summer institutes in the early twentieth century. In chapter 2, "Studies at Normal School, College, and University Summer Sessions: 'Invaders' in Harvard Yard," I describe teachers' experiences as summer students at normal schools/teachers colleges, including the institutions in Emporia, Kansas, and Cedar Falls, Iowa; Black colleges, including Lincoln University in Missouri; flagship state universities, including the University of Iowa and the University of Tennessee; and elite private universities, including Harvard University and Columbia's Teachers College. Summer sessions at all of these institutions enhanced teachers' skills, knowledge, and cultural sophistication, while at Black colleges teachers had access to courses on Black history and culture, and at state flagships and elite private universities teachers were able to study with famous scholars such as John Dewey and Frederick Jackson Turner. Members of the National Association of Summer School Directors advised one another on providing scholarships, adapting men's dormitories for women, and inclusion, albeit limited, of Black teachers. Unacknowledged in the historiography of higher education, university summer sessions expanded access for unprivileged students, as many of the teachers who attended would have been unwelcome as regular students by virtue of their social class, gender, and/or race.

Chapters 3 through 5 add important new dimensions to the historical understanding of teachers' lives as well as aspects of their work in the classroom. In chapter 3, "Work for Family, for Supplemental Income, and for an Exit Strategy: The Center of a 'Crazy Calico Quilt,'" I explain that despite administrators' discouragement, teachers engaged in many forms of work during the summer months. Especially in rural areas, they enhanced the economic standing of their families of origin by providing critical help on the farm or in the home. In towns and cities, laboring for wages supplemented teachers' resources for meeting middle-class standards. Teachers who answered the wide range of advertisements in education journals recruiting them for summer work also augmented their finances as well as broadened their horizons and sense of independence. Teaching summer school was not an appreciable option until summer instruction in public schools became widespread in the 1920s, but teachers in earlier decades were able to hone their progressive teaching techniques and enjoy adventures as camp counselors or ranger naturalists. Summer work thus enabled teachers to maintain a middle-class standard of living, enhance their professional skills, and/or defy gender boundaries. In some cases, teachers' summer endeavors drew them to new vocations, or courtships drew them to marriage and away from the classroom, but most summer work supported and reinforced grassroots professionalism among teachers.

Although travel historians mention teachers only in passing, they were enthusiastic partakers in the cultural approach to tourism that helped to define the middle class beginning in the 1880s. Chapter 4, "Tourism: 'The Teachers Are the Greatest Traveling Class,'" illustrates how women teachers claimed their right to broader horizons through travel and how tourism strengthened teachers' position in the middle class and functioned as a form of professional development. The school leaders who encouraged teachers to travel provided little financial support, but teachers economized during the school year so that they could travel—frugally—in the summer. In the United States, teachers toured the natural landscape in the West and historic and metropolitan sites in the East and South as well as attended world's fairs. In Europe, generations of American teachers deepened their understanding of history, literature, and the arts through a grand tour of cultural highlights. While connections between sightseeing and teachers' day-to-day instruction in the classroom were not always evident immediately, tourism complemented grassroots professionalism by not only enhancing teachers' work with students but also making them more cultured and worldly.

Chapter 5, "Rest: Putting 'New Blood into My Veins,'" returns to the original prescription for how teachers should spend the summer. Beginning in the 1880s, the meaning of summer "rest" for teachers quickly evolved—along with the ideal of the middle-class vacation—from quietude to reinvigoration through fresh air and physical activity. Rural teachers expanded their physical capacities by engaging in agricultural work and participating in other outdoor activities, and urban teachers reinvigorated themselves by communing with nature, hiking, and "wheeling" on bicycles. Rigorous physical activities allowed men teachers to reinforce gender boundaries by enacting rugged masculinity and women to transgress boundaries by demonstrating a lack of frailty and the robustness of a "new woman."

Finally, in the epilogue, I briefly trace the evolution of teachers' "summers off" since the mid-twentieth century—when raising families emerged as a new activity—to argue that since the Second World War, the long summer break has continued to benefit the teaching profession and the schools. The "new blood" from summer rejuvenation and the knowledge gained through tourism and summer studies strengthened teachers' work in the classroom and, along with heightened middle-class identity, buttressed their standing as professionals. Teachers' pursuit of their version of professionalism, including women teachers' greater sense of intellectual and physical independence, surely enhanced the whole education system, even if—or perhaps because—it diverged from administrators' approach to professionalization.

1

Professional Development in Institutes and Association Meetings

"So Many Serious, Intensely Professional Teachers"

Sarah Gillespie Huftalen, a leader in the early twentieth-century rural education movement, grew up on a farm near Manchester, Iowa. When she was a teenager in the mid-1880s, she later explained, "There were Normal Training summer schools in Manchester each year of six or eight weeks and these I attended thus being in readiness to teach." Meanwhile, a country schoolteacher attending the Chautauqua summer assembly in western New York State told a reporter, "I feel as if I had come into a fortune; I've new methods to try in everything that I teach," and novice teacher Jessie Herrick noted in her journal during a three-week summer school for teachers in Glens Falls, New York, that she was "well pleased with all the work as they give 'a minimum of theory and a maximum of practice.'" Four decades later, experienced Portland, Oregon, teacher Nettie Mae Rankin wrote, "One of the most interesting phases of the National Education Association conventions is the meeting directly or indirectly with so many serious, intensely professional teachers, unselfish workers."[1] Although seldom acknowledged in histories of teachers and teacher education,[2] such summertime experiences were instrumental in these and many other teachers' professional education.

As school reformers from the mid-nineteenth century onward called for more extensive teacher preparation and higher certification standards, teacher education remained, as historian James Fraser explains, "a haphazard affair." Through the first half of the twentieth century, Fraser argues, "the majority of teachers had no formal preparation."[3] Considering teachers' summer pursuits, however, suggests that they may have had more, albeit haphazard, training than historians have assumed. By the 1880s, summer institutes at the local and national levels and summer meetings of education associations provided a range of educational options for teachers during their "off" months. While these approaches to professional development were less systematic and shorter than teacher-education programs in higher education institutions, they offered a degree of formal training during a time of the year when teachers had time to reflect and thus played an important role in shaping the teaching force. In fact, school leaders' encouragement of, and teachers' commitment to, summer education—even as it required a sacrifice of time and, often, money—was so strong that it would inspire institutions of higher education to begin offering summer sessions by the turn of the twentieth century.

Through participation in summer professional development, teachers gained pedagogical skills and deepened their understanding not only of the broader field of education but also of various cultural subjects. As historian Diana D'Amico Pawlewicz argues, administrator-led efforts to "professionalize" teaching generally aimed to socialize teachers to follow directions from above by excluding them from discussions of esoteric issues in the field and denying them a level of authority worthy of professional status.[4] While pedagogical skill development conformed to this approach to professionalization, teachers' exposure to abstract concepts in education and to culture more broadly through summer education did enhance their professional prowess and their social and cultural capital, supporting professionalization from the bottom up even in the absence of unequivocal professional standing. For Black teachers, summer provided the time and space to learn content and approaches to teaching that challenged white supremacy, or what historian Jarvis Givens calls "fugitive pedagogy." For women teachers, summer professional-development experiences also stoked what Geraldine Clifford in her social history of women teachers refers to as "psychological" independence and what Virginia Scharff in her history of women drivers terms "the right to broaden their horizons."[5]

Local summer institutes, or "normals," focused mainly on skill development and subject matter knowledge but also included elements of esoteric knowledge of education and white middle-class culture. The Chautauqua Institution and other freestanding national programs broadened teachers' educational and cultural horizons even further, and summer meetings of education associations including state teachers' associations (STAs) and the National Education Association (NEA) as well as the National Association of Teachers in Colored Schools (NATCS) allowed them to witness, and occasionally to even participate in, discussions of abstract topics while benefiting from fellowship with others in the field. In the process, grassroots teacher professionalization through institutes and association meetings also fostered Black teachers' understanding of fugitive pedagogy and incubated women teachers' sense of independence.

Local Summer Institutes, or "Normals"

School superintendent W. C. Rote of San Antonio told his fellow Texas administrators in 1884 that he was concerned about the large numbers of teachers in the state "who lacked the first requisite of a teacher—namely, scholarship." Because Texas's normal schools, high schools, and colleges did not have the capacity to close this gap, he advocated that "Summer Normal Institutes . . . be established on a broader basis, to fill up the rank of educated and skillful teachers."[6] Teachers' institutes had arisen in the mid-nineteenth century to provide much-needed training throughout the year for teachers already in service. Most institutes were local in the sense that they were planned by the state or county superintendent, featured local or state teachers and administrators as instructors, and served teachers in the immediate county or region. They met in schools, courthouses, or other available facilities, generally for a few or several consecutive days. Beginning in the 1880s, institutes that convened during the summertime grew to last two to eight weeks or, occasionally, even longer. The terminology was somewhat fluid, but these longer sessions were usually called "summer normal schools" or, simply, "summer normals"—although they were not affiliated with state normal schools, which were in their heyday during this period.[7] Summer institutes were widespread between the 1880s and the 1900s and persisted through the 1920s for teachers in remote areas and among African Americans in the South even as institutions of higher education became the main venues for other teachers' summer education. Throughout the decades between the 1880s and 1920s, summer normal schools enhanced teachers' skills and content mastery while fostering esprit de corps and a degree of independence in the teaching force as well as providing some access to more esoteric educational and cultural knowledge.

1880s–1900s

Summer normal schools touched the lives and careers of significant numbers of teachers before they gave way to university summer sessions. Current and aspiring elementary and rural school teachers dominated the enrollment; Kate Wofford observed in a 1935 study that, through the first decade of the twentieth century, the "summer normal school was perhaps the institution that best served the rural teacher."[8] In his 1911 report *Agencies for the Improvement of Teachers in Service*, William Carl Ruediger captured the spread of summer institutes throughout the country. In the Northeast, the state superintendents of Vermont and Maine organized summer normals that lasted two to four weeks. Supported by legislative appropriations, Maine's institutes met in four or more different locations each year and were free for teachers. By 1911, New York's institutes were generally just five days long and met immediately before the beginning of the school year, but between 1896 and 1907 the state offered three three- or four-week midsummer institutes that were free for all who planned to teach in the state during the following school year. The 48 men and 374 women who attended the state institute that convened at the Chautauqua Institution in 1897 had an average of over seven years of teaching experience. They and the five hundred to six hundred teachers who attended Chautauqua's state institute during each of the next ten years had access to all Chautauqua assembly events during their stay. Ruediger's summary suggested that other northeastern states did not offer summer normals on a consistent basis, perhaps because many independent summer institutes convened in this region.[9]

On the other side of the country, the Idaho legislature authorized a state board to establish three six-week summer normals and to charge an attendance fee of five dollars, while Utah county superintendents worked with the state superintendent to provide shorter summer institutes at the county level. Historian Melinda Spearman explains that in 1888 the Colorado legislature divided the state into six "institute districts," each of which offered a two-week course for teachers in July or August. Reduced rail fares facilitated attendance, and the largest institute met in Denver. Ruediger indicated that by 1911 Colorado had fifteen districts, the summer normals lasted six weeks, and teachers who attended earned a 5 percent salary bonus.[10]

Summer normal schools were even more common in the South than in the West or the Northeast. One exception was Maryland, where a speaker argued before the State Board of Education in 1890 that the "weight of opinion" was against holding institutes "during times of vacation," and later board reports indicated that Maryland did not conduct summer normals.[11] But in Tennessee, state- and county-level summer institutes lasting one to four weeks convened from the 1880s into the twentieth century; in 1886, fifteen hundred attended eight state institutes for white teachers and three for Black teachers, while three thousand teachers attended more than four hundred county institutes. With funding from the Peabody Education Fund, one of the state institutes met on the University of Tennessee campus in Knoxville each summer between 1880 and 1898.[12] Ruediger listed Tennessee, Arkansas, Florida, Louisiana, Oklahoma, South Carolina, Texas, and Virginia as offering summer normal schools lasting at least two and more commonly six to nine weeks, and Alabama, Georgia, Kentucky, and West Virginia as convening five-day institutes that met variously during the school year or the summer. Most of these southern normals and institutes received state funding and were organized by state or county superintendents. In Virginia, Ruediger explained, "the older type of teachers' institutes has been displaced by a system of summer schools supported in large part by the State.... In 1910, 19 were held, 12 for white teachers and 7 for colored teachers.

The total enrollment was nearly 5,000, which is approximately one-half of the number of teachers in the State." Ruediger also listed separate "white" and "colored" summer normals in Alabama, Florida, Mississippi, Tennessee, and Texas.[13]

In Texas, the legislature provided for a four-week summer normal for white teachers in each of its thirty-one senatorial districts and for African American teachers in each of its eleven congressional districts (except one that had few Black teachers) from 1881 through 1884. After Superintendent Rote argued for their expansion, an editorial in the August 1884 issue of the *Texas School Journal* noted that the summer's normal schools had been "uniformly successful" and argued, "It will be the duty of the next legislature to make appropriations to cover the expenses." Although the legislature curtailed funding, Texas's summer normals continued with county sponsorship, some support from the Peabody Fund, and tuition fees. In 1888, the *Journal* reported, "Twenty-one normal institutes for white and nine for colored teachers were held in different sections of the state. This is a less number than conducted by the state heretofore, but from reports received to date the aggregate attendance was considerably larger." A few years later, Texas State Superintendent James Carlisle said that he "regretted that the state withdrew its support" but that it was "to the credit of many teachers that they have organized institutes and employed conductors and assistants at their own expense, and have thus pushed forward this work." In 1893, the state's thirty-nine summer normals for whites enrolled 3,021 teachers and twelve summer normals for Blacks enrolled 827 teachers. Ten years later, a school superintendent stated that the number of summer normals had increased to more than one hundred and their enrollment had increased to over five thousand. The normals lasted five weeks, and the custom of lowering rail fares for teachers traveling to institutes continued. In 1911, according to Ruediger, Texas's seventy-three summer normals for 10,567 white teachers and forty-three summer normals for 2,398 Black teachers were "supported almost entirely by a fee of $5 required by each student."[14]

While summer normal schools thrived in Texas and other southern states, they were also widespread in the Midwest and the Great Plains. Historian Mary Hurlbut Cordier states that the teachers' institute, including the summer normal, was "the most common means of teacher education on the prairies and plains" until the early 1900s. In Illinois in 1890, State Superintendent Richard Edwards explained, "The regular institutes are mostly held during the summer vacation. They are conducted under the direction and authority of the county superintendents of schools," generally lasting "from two to four weeks." The situation was similar in Iowa, where summer normals were two to six weeks long and experienced their highest enrollments between the mid-1880s and the mid-1890s; nearly twenty-three thousand enrolled in 1896. Iowa teachers had to pay a small fee to supplement stingy state appropriations for summer institutes, a practice that State Superintendent Henry Sabin decried in the late 1880s. State law in Kansas stipulated, "The county superintendents of public instruction shall hold annually, in their respective counties, for a term of not less than four weeks, a normal institute for the instruction of teachers and those desiring to teach." Minnesota, Nebraska, and North Dakota also offered multiweek summer normals, while Indiana, South Dakota, and Wisconsin convened institutes of five or more days that met during either the school year or the summer. Nebraska developed a distinctive—or, according to Ruediger, "most promising"—approach to summer teacher training by the early twentieth century. Concerned that sparsely populated counties were unable to offer summer institutes, the state encouraged counties in the 1890s to join forces and convene "union normal institutes." This approach mushroomed until State Superintendent William Fowler took it a step further in 1903 and established "junior normal schools," which convened under his direction during the summer in selected high school buildings. By 1907, eight eight-week junior normals each provided free instruction for teachers from multiple counties. Attending teachers received subsidies for rail fares and the possibility of a pay increase for completing the entire course of study. The junior normals' course of studies was "progressive from summer to summer, identical with that leading to the elementary certificate in the normal schools."[15]

Throughout the country, summer normals' programs focused mainly on subject review and basic teaching methods but also fostered community among the teachers and provided some exposure to more esoteric educational and cultural topics. The *Texas School Journal* explained that the summer institute was "designed especially for that class of teachers which the regular normal school cannot reach; to such it furnishes valuable instruction in principle, matter and method," and advised teachers to include attending a normal in their summer plans as a "means of self-improvement and professional growth."[16] Math professor at the University of Colorado and future dean of the Harvard Graduate School of Education Paul Hanus conducted county summer institutes in Colorado in 1885 and 1886. He reflected later that he was "impressed with both the earnestness of the teachers in attendance and their dire need of help. It was necessary," he explained, "to give the teachers instruction in the studies they had to teach—English, history, geography, etc., of which their command was, in many cases, rudimentary." He structured the institutes so that "instruction in methods of teaching paralleled the instruction in subject matter." With "little time or opportunity to deal with the larger problems of education," Hanus "attempted a daily lecture on the subject at the opening of each session." He added, "As I myself was only beginning to organize my ideas about education, the lectures must have been superficial."[17]

While the rigor of studies varied, many summer normals offered structured sequences of courses that took a number of sessions over multiple years to complete, along the lines of Nebraska's junior normal schools. An 1884 manual for summer institutes in Iowa outlined a sequential "graded course of four years" aimed at teachers with progressively higher levels of experience and preparation. The first year included common-school subjects and "School Economy"; the next two years focused on academic subjects and teaching methods; and the final year covered "Civil Government, Algebra, Botany, Zoology, Mineralogy, Rhetoric and Literature, Art of Teaching, Science of Teaching, [and] Primary Teaching."[18] The heart of such courses, especially at the lower levels, was the subject review and instruction in methods of teaching that Hanus observed many teachers sorely needed. In Texas, Principal Lulu McCoy of the 1884 summer normal in Anderson reported that during each day's morning session, the teachers took "charge of different branches. . . . After each exercise given, the principal gave such criticisms and suggestions as was thought necessary and appropriate. . . . Theory and practice of teaching came under discussion." At the conclusion of the Mineola "colored normal" in 1892, teachers passed resolutions thanking "Prof. A. J. Criner for the manifest interest which he took in lecturing to us upon the methods of teaching"—which perhaps included subtle ways to challenge white supremacy—and "the Principal, Prof. G. W. Jackson, for the many noted lectures on school management and higher branches."[19]

In their correspondence during the summer months, rural teachers often discussed teachers' institutes. A friend named Eva wrote to fellow Kansas teacher Amanda Stewart in July 1881, "I wanted to attend the Institute this summer, they have a methods teacher from Ft. Scott, Miss Hoxie[;] they say she is good." P. C. Petherbridge wrote to Stewart in June 1885, "Well, it is almost Institute time now, and I suppose you folks [Amanda and her sisters] will be likely to attend." The following month, he reported from Oskaloosa, Kansas, "We have quite a large normal, 159 today." For subject review, he liked Professor Nihart, "a splendid teacher: he teaches advanced Arith. Gram. & History; also Penmanship." When it came to methods, however, Petherbridge was not as fond of Professor Heath, who, he said, "conducts, not teaches, the Methods class . . . a perfect 'bore.'"[20] May Stewart wrote to the "girls at home" in July 1906 at the conclusion of the summer institute she attended in Westmoreland, Kansas, "I enjoyed the Institute work. . . . I liked Prof. Bell quite well as an instructor."[21] At the summer normals young Sarah Gillespie attended in Iowa, she enjoyed refreshing her subject matter knowledge and learning more about how to teach it, noting in her diary on August 1, 1883, "Attending Normal. Like it." While attending the institute in August 1884, Gillespie mentioned "Arith., Read., Gram., Orthog., Penmanship, Didactics and Astronomy lectures," an evening talk on "Education for Citizenship," and that she was one of the leaders in her division. She also observed, "We had such good instructors. . . . Had a discussion in the reading class every day." Gillespie must have performed well, as she wrote during the second week, "Mr. Miller is much pleased with my recitations" and commented after the institute had concluded, "Examination was easy for me."[22]

Summer normal schools typically culminated in certification examinations covering subject knowledge and established teaching methods. In Texas, questions in 1884 focused on methods for teaching reading; general methods and school discipline; and content in geography, arithmetic, natural philosophy, algebra, geometry, English grammar, and U.S. history. Six years later, questions covered similar subjects, with the additions of Texas history, civil government, physiology, and physics. Questions on "theory and practice of teaching" ranged from "Give two rules that should govern a teacher in questioning pupils" to "What is a graded school? State one of its advantages; one of its disadvantages." In 1906, ten questions on reading included "Why is it that a successful professional elocutionist may not make a good teacher of reading in the public schools?" and "What good and what harm may arise if the teacher reads the reading lesson aloud for class?"[23]

High scores on summer certification exams did not come as easily for many teachers as they did for Gillespie. At Texas's summer normals in 1885, only 214 of the 1,844 white teachers and 34 of the 521 Black teachers in attendance earned first-, second-, or third-"grade" certificates—with the grade indicating the duration of certification rather than the level of instruction—and in 1906, 1,744 of the 3,253 white teachers and 112 of the 1,092 Black teachers who sat for exams earned first-grade, second-grade, or permanent teaching certificates.[24] Black teachers' scores probably were not entirely objective; A. K. Spence wrote in 1883, "It is quite a common rule never to give a first-class certificate, no matter what the scholarship, to a colored student." Regardless of whether they were fair, poor results apparently caused some summer institutes to devote time explicitly to exam preparation. At the 1889 normal for white teachers in Abilene, Texas, teachers spent their afternoons "reviewing the various subjects preparatory to the state examinations at the close of the school," and an advertisement for the 1902 normal for Black teachers in Liberty, Texas, touted "a six weeks' session [that] will prepare you for the examinations" and "thorough instruction in all branches required for temporary and permanent certificates."[25]

The normals' focus on the exams was not without its critics. Editors of the *Texas School Journal* reflected upon the conclusion of the 1893 summer normals, "It is to be regretted that teachers became so engrossed with their preparation for the examination as to neglect matters of general interest to the profession. Text-book knowledge is valuable. Yet the teacher who limits his range of reading and thought to the subject matter of school texts is but poorly equipped for his professional duties." The editors criticized teachers who attended the normals "with no other apparent purpose than to obtain certificates," arguing that "'cramming' very aptly describes the work many of them do."[26] The superintendent in Calhoun County, Iowa, intentionally held the 1900 institute after certificate examinations because, an article in *Midland Schools* explained, "the institute is not a place simply to prepare for an examination."[27]

Certification examinations were a necessary evil for teachers, however, and it was natural that exams commanded their attention—and induced anxiety. G. P. Randle wrote to a friend upon the conclusion of the institute he attended in Taylorville, Illinois, in 1887, "I received a first grade certificate . . . made a good average in the sciences but only fair in the common branches." Randle provided examples of exam questions including "Discuss the teeth" and "Describe the alimentary canal of the sea urchin." He added that orthography was "very tough" but reflected, "We had four weeks of very fair work and I feel repaid for my work."[28] Anxious about examinations as she prepared to attend the 1885 summer institute in El Dorado, Kansas, teacher Miranda Cather wrote to her friend and fellow teacher Nellie Covert that she anticipated "more rigid" questions. The following month, Vallie Williams wrote to Covert from El Dorado, "Normal is lively and full. . . . Miss Cather is here and a good many others."[29] Also in Kansas, a friend who had left teaching when she married wrote to Nora Stewart in July 1887, "I can imagine your feelings about now, so near your 'day of fate' but . . . so far you have always done so well. I am thankful I don't have to go through the same (Get married Nora + bid farewell to examinations)." May Stewart wrote to her sisters from Westmoreland, "The Institute and examinations are over. . . . I took the examination. . . . But my head and eyes nearly failed me, so my standing won't be much in some things for which I am sorry. But I got through the Algebra work enough to pass. The Arithmetic was hardest of all, and you know I usually get good grades in Arithmetic." Still, she added, "I enjoyed the Institute work."[30]

While the emphasis on subject review and instruction in methods, culminating in certification exams, served the "professionalization" goal that teachers be compliant workers rather than independent thinkers, summer normal schools also did allow for independent reflection on approaches to teaching and the larger field of education, as well as a sense of solidarity with other teachers. The *Texas School Journal* explained that the institutes "intended to aid and encourage teachers of every class, to arouse and interest the cold and indifferent, to stimulate those fainting ones, to refresh the weary, to cheer the sad and despondent and to give to each his portion of meat in due season, *to awaken thought*." Prominent Texas educator and institute instructor Anna J. H. Pennybacker reflected further that, although "the present status of teachers in Texas" generated "some necessity for institute drill in the ordinary branches," a "true institute" had "two main objects, *Instruction in the Philosophy of Teaching* and the *Cultivation of an esprit de corps* among teachers."[31]

Pennybacker suggested that a philosophical approach used "practice" to "season . . . theory," and reports on Texas summer normals commonly echoed Principal Lillie Shaver's statement that at the 1888 Hunt County Normal "the work was practical as well as theoretical." Normal conductors did not really explain what they meant by "theoretical," but it seemed to incorporate evaluation of accepted teaching practices and consideration of new methods as well as reflection on more esoteric topics in the wider field of education. At a "true institute," Pennybacker explained, teacher-students addressed questions including, "Is this plan true to Nature? Why does this plan succeed and that other one fail? What relation does this study bear to the child's mental development? When should it be taught? What is its underlying principle?"[32] The announcement for

New York State's three summer institutes in 1905 stated that they would each have a "department of professional training" as well as "drill and review." The former included courses not only in methods but also in psychology, child study, and other subjects that would have provided a more theoretical perspective on teaching and learning.[33]

The Calhoun County, Iowa, superintendent stated that the 1900 institute would be "progressive," and, at the county institute she attended in 1891, Gillespie learned about the new "Delsarte system of physical culture," a gymnastic approach to bodily movement gaining popularity in Europe and the United States. The ad for the 1902 Black normal in Liberty, Texas, promised "all the latest ideas in education and methods," and white teachers wrestled with "the 'New Methods'" as early as 1884 at the summer normal in Dallas, Texas. The conductor of the Dallas institute reported that one of the instructors shared some of what she had learned from a national leader in progressive education:

> We were fortunate to have with us a lady who had been for several years under the instruction of Col. [Francis W.] Parker. She took a class of little folks who had never been to school, and demonstrated to the skeptical, and there were not a few, with what ease and rapidity those tiny ones could be taught to read and write by the word method. . . . She had also a class in map moulding. On a small table covered with sand . . . she formed the State of Texas. . . . Those who had never seen geography taught in this way found it immensely interesting. . . . I do not believe there was a teacher who did not go home with energy renewed, and with a determination to do better work than in the past.[34]

The same child-centered topics appeared at the Tennessee institute in Knoxville, where, historian Clinton Allison explains, Professor Karns regularly introduced attendees to the word method of teaching reading through a model lesson with a group of children, and in 1892 "Miss Doak of Nashville" demonstrated progressive instruction in geography by constructing "a thirty square foot sand map of Tennessee." A Knoxville newspaper reported, "All the principal ranges of mountains and valleys were neatly moulded out as they exist . . . and the rivers and railroads were indicated by different colored strings of yarn and the whole was a very clever design." Karns and Doak were fulfilling another Knoxville paper's claim in 1881 that "new and more complete methods for the instruction of young people are being discovered continually, rendering the old system obsolete. It will be the object of the institute to make known these new discoveries in teaching."[35]

In addition to introducing teachers—and Knoxville's newspaper reporters—to cutting-edge methods, summer institutes exposed teachers to developments in their profession more broadly. At Knoxville, lectures on current issues in public education, such as tax support for schooling and the separation of church and state, allowed teachers to grapple with the wider context of teaching—and perhaps to raise concerns about opening each day of the institute with devotional exercises. Knoxville papers reported on "spirited discussions" among teacher-students at the institute, who were pursuing their own version of professionalization. Beyond teaching theory, the "department of professional training" at New York's 1905 institutes included the history of education, "school organization and management," and other subjects that would have involved reflection on the wider field.[36] Reports in the *Texas School Journal* described further ways in which teachers engaged with broader educational issues at that state's summer normals. Afternoon sessions at the 1884 normal in Anderson were "devoted to discussion of various subjects relative to the teachers' profession. A query box was provided at the opening of the school, and questions proposed for discussion were taken therefrom at the close of each day's exercises." At the 1886 Nacogdoches normal, the attending teachers considered "educational questions of vital importance," such as textbook laws and the introduction of graded classrooms in country schools, and the 1888 Bell County Summer Normal Institute in Belton featured "lectures in the evenings upon live educational topics."[37] In Illinois, Emma Wormwood reflected that she "thoroughly enjoyed" her week at the 1898 Carlinville institute, where one of the most "helpful" subjects was "school law."[38] Wormwood, like the teachers who attended summer normals in Texas, New York, Tennessee, and other states, deepened her engagement in "the philosophy of teaching."

The other object of Pennybacker's "true institute" was esprit de corps in the teaching force, cultivated through relationships and a shared mission: "Constant association, from year to year, reveals to us strong friends in our co-workers, makes us realize that we have about us men and women with great hearts and great brains. The mere knowledge that such is the case thrills us with pride for our vocation and stimulates us to aim higher."[39] The friendships and social capital they formed at institutes provided teachers with professional support as well as the enjoyment of companionship. The *Texas School Journal* advised teachers that acquaintances made at a summer normal "may be worth a great deal to you. You may meet some teacher who may aid you in materially, or you may make a good impression upon some visiting trustees." The "teachers' bureau" at the 1888 normal in Calvert, Texas, helped "nearly every" teacher who was looking for a position secure one. And, in a less formal approach to teacher placement, as G. P. Randle learned of openings in Illinois at the 1887 Taylorville institute, he shared the information with his friend who was seeking a position.[40]

While attending an Iowa institute in August 1884, Gillespie noted that she had "made the acquaintance of Miss Fannie Pooley, Primary Teacher of the Earlville School. She is my intimate friend." Six years later, Gillespie wrote of the normal where she saw her fellow teachers, "I do enjoy it so much."[41] Social events such as a "magnificent banquet" provided by a local citizen during the 1888 Bell County normal in Texas and a reception attended by more than four hundred at the 1903 New York institute at Chautauqua, allowed teachers to extend their social and professional networks.[42] In Illinois, a teacher named Mr. Walker attended a "walk around + social" and a "Walk Around and Reunion of Teachers" during the 1886 institute in Columbus, where he also accompanied fellow teacher Miss Terrell to two evening lectures. Randle mentioned "homely schoolmarms" in a letter to his friend at the beginning of the Taylorville institute but later reported, "We had a sociable last night at the residence of Supt Orr[;] had a fine time," and "I was very favorably impressed with . . . the young ladies. More ladylike and refined ladies I would not care to meet. One cannot but be better for having met such people."[43] Randle did not explain how he would be "better," but he likely felt inspired to be a better teacher. Echoing this sense of esprit de corps, the announcement for the 1900 Calhoun County institute in Iowa stated, "Teachers need the encouragement and inspiration that this agency gives that they may become better qualified to do the noble work of teaching."[44]

Randle's claim that he would "be better for having met such people" had a social class undertone. Indeed, wider intellectual and social dimensions—or, in the words of a Texas county superintendent, the "general culture"—of summer normal schools immersed teachers in forms of cultural capital associated with the middle class and learned professionals. In Texas, Principal McCoy reported that at the 1884 summer normal in Anderson, "one day of the week was devoted to recreation, in which the school and visitors were entertained with music, recitations, readings, addresses, essays, etc." Teachers at the summer normal in Calvert four years later organized a "literary and social club," which provided "weekly entertainments," and the advertisement for the Liberty Summer Normal for Black teachers touted "a lecture course by leading lawyers, doctors and educators," presumably on a range of intellectual and social issues and perhaps including challenges to racism.[45] Teachers attending the institute in Knoxville, Tennessee, viewed the moon through a telescope as well as traveled vicariously through "stereopticon" slide shows in the evenings. The reception at Chautauqua in 1903 featured music performed by the larger assembly's orchestra, and Vallie Williams wrote from El Dorado, Kansas, that she and her friends had enjoyed organ music and had attended services at the local Methodist and Baptist churches.[46]

In addition to gaining cultural capital in the arts and sciences, teachers who attended summer normal schools experienced middle-class mores in the host communities. Proper manners and appropriate conversation topics would have been features of the "magnificent banquet" at the 1888 Bell County normal in Texas. After the death of Ulysses S. Grant in July 1885, P. C. Petherbridge witnessed magnificence of a different sort when he attended what he described as "a grand affair" memorializing the former president hosted by the citizens of Oskaloosa, Kansas, where he was attending the summer normal. The local home hosting the memorial, Petherbridge wrote, was "nicely decorated with flowers, flags + mourning."[47] In Peabody, Kansas, the town's residents also welcomed visiting teachers into the local community; the newspaper's "Institute Souvenir

Edition" for 1901 noted that the residents had "greeted the visiting teachers with sincere cordiality. They have welcomed them freely to the hospitality of their homes, and placed at their disposal their fine public library, opera house, and high school building." And at the conclusion of the 1892 summer normal for Black teachers in Mineola, Texas, the attendees passed a resolution expressing their "sincere gratitude" to "the white and colored citizens" who "so carefully and bountifully cared for us while in their midst," astutely noting "that such kindness is a rare thing from both sides, and more especially the former."[48] While enlarging their world, cultural entertainment and social interaction with members of the host community signaled that summer normal attendees belonged in the middle class.

In the eyes of some teachers, the county summer normal fell short of creating useful esprit de corps or imparting helpful knowledge and restricted their exposure to the wider world. While attending the 1887 institute in Greenville, Illinois, a teacher named Armstrong wrote to a friend, "I am disgusted with these little one horse affairs." He complained about the other teachers' "quiet slumber of complete nothingness"; stated, "I am not 'dead in love' with the teaching fraternity, as we find it today"; and mentioned other career prospects. Using the byline "A Village School Ma'am" in an Iowa education journal in 1892, another teacher did not broach the idea of leaving teaching but complained that the requirement that she attend the local institute made her unable "to take advantage of the cheap excursion rates to visit other parts of the country." The teacher lamented that she had to "forgo the pleasures of the trip and remain at home to hear the second and third rate home talent drone over the effects of stimulants and narcotics, quibble over unimportant points in grammar and waste hours in discussing the question of whether George III or Lord North was to blame for the Revolutionary War." She asked rhetorically, "Is it just that a teacher who has complied with all the requirements of the law be obliged to lose her summer's vacation to satisfy the whim of a man who cannot himself teach an ordinary village school?"[49]

Within several years, some school leaders agreed with Armstrong and the "School Ma'am" that many county-level summer institutes were of dubious value; in Iowa, one even remarked that institutes served only "to *line* the pockets of the conductors and to *lighten* those of the teachers." Leaders generally maintained, however, that summer studies were important. A 1906 editorial in the Iowa journal *Midland Schools* argued that smaller numbers of teachers attending summer sessions at higher education institutions would better serve school districts than greater numbers of teachers attending local institutes.[50] By the mid-1900s, state normal school, college, and university programs for summer teacher education were proliferating, and education administrators were incorporating them into their expectations for teachers' professional development. Texas's "Regulations for Summer Normal Institutes" began to allow college and university summer sessions to serve as summer normal schools, and the *Texas School Journal* began to promote summer sessions at various universities. Ruediger noted that the state superintendent in New Hampshire began in 1908 to donate summer-institute funds to the summer session at the state normal school in Plymouth and that, by 1911, state-supported options for summer instruction for teachers in North Dakota included sessions "held in connection with the university, agricultural college, or a normal school."[51] Developments in Iowa encapsulated national trends: Beginning in the early 1900s, attendance at summer county institutes declined as attendance at higher education institutions' summer sessions increased, and then a 1913 school law mandated that county institutes be held only during the school term, with a possible exception for remote counties where the superintendent considered longer summer institutes to be "advisable."[52]

1910s–1920s

As local summer normal schools faded away in many regions, they continued through the 1920s to play an important role in professional development for teachers in sparsely settled areas as well as among African Americans in the South. Where summer institutes continued, they followed a pattern similar to that of the earlier normals. New Mexico's territorial legislature first authorized two-week county institutes in 1897, but counties did not offer them reliably and enrollment was low when they did meet. By the 1910s, however, institutes—now four weeks long—were held more consistently, and the incentives of reduced rail fares and, in some cases, a small stipend helped to boost attendance. Santa Fe County conducted four-week summer normals beginning in 1909. After an opening address and a song, morning sessions included reviews of the content of the public school course of study, occasionally with a model-class demonstration with young pupils of a lesson such as teaching reading through the word method. Most afternoons were devoted to preparation for certification exams, although teachers sometimes engaged in activities such as folk dancing or a spelling competition. Evenings at the Santa Fe institute brought a variety of lectures on education or cultural topics as well as social events ranging from a comedy performance at the courthouse to a reception at the home of the city superintendent. During World War I—by which time the normal lasted six weeks—curriculum review and exam preparation were less of a focus, and teachers instead heard lectures on the war and patriotism as well as learned how to teach canning and sewing in support of the war effort.[53]

While Santa Fe County moved away from test preparation, certificate examinations continued at institutes in other remote areas, to the chagrin of school leaders in at least one case. In Pennsylvania, where 104 six- to eight-week summer normal schools in rural counties enrolled 3,782 in 1916, an officer with the State Board of Education reported, "As to the need of such schools there is considerable doubt expressed by a very large number of superintendents." Instead of the normals thoroughly grounding teachers in "review of the common branches" and "the theory of teaching, school management and methods," he observed, "too often the work is of a very superficial character and students are encouraged to 'cram' for the superintendents' examination."[54] In Arkansas, summer institutes and certificate exams were topics in correspondence between Vivian Bullock and her teacher friends in the early 1920s. In 1921, Aula Tompkins reported in a letter to Bullock that she was attending the six-week normal in Ozark. "I decided to take the teacher examination for a first grade license. Then I began to study and have just studied, studied and then studied some more," she wrote. She had sat for the exam a couple of days earlier and was concerned about her performance: "I am sure that I shall make a third [a poor result]. If I do I will not have it!"[55] The certificate exam clearly motivated Tompkins to study at the summer normal school; less clear was whether this was an effective means of professional development or she was merely cramming.

Nebraska's junior normal schools thrived in the early 1910s, when Muirl Dorrough, a one-room-school teacher in the Sand Hills of the western part of the state, attended the Junior Normal at Alliance. During the summers of 1911 and 1912, when Dorrough was in her early twenties, she and her sister Bonnie traveled together and shared a room while they attended classes in Alliance's school buildings and churches. They studied hard despite heat that could be stifling. "The Normals do so much good," reflected Durrough as she weighed whether to return for a second summer. From Alliance in 1912, she wrote, "I like the Normal work real well. The teachers are excellent." Although she did not seem to focus inordinately on preparing for the exams, her goal that summer was to earn a first-grade certificate. To that end, she took exams in primary methods and algebra at midterm, after which the sisters returned home to be with their ailing other sister. During both summers, Muirl and Bonnie socialized with the other teachers and attended art exhibits and concerts that were not available to them in the Sand Hills; Dorrough remarked that one performance included "the best piece of music I ever heard." While her time in Alliance broadened Dorrough's horizons and sense of independence, she also noted that the five-dollar pay increase she received each of the two years was "great."[56]

Meanwhile, South Dakota one-room-school teacher and homesteader Elizabeth "Bess" Corey attended the local institute in Fort Pierre, across the Missouri River from South Dakota capital Pierre, nearly every summer between 1910 and 1918. Corey's experiences at the institute were similar to those of other teachers who attended earlier summer normals throughout the country. She also faced more—or was more open about—financial challenges. In 1911, she performed housekeeping chores to cover her room and reported to her mother, "It was quite a strain attending the institute and working too." She did not work during the 1912 institute but worried constantly about money. Although she was "living on tick," Corey wrote to her mother in mid-July that she was "so glad" not to be working, "for I don't feel extra good and there is more or less going on and of course there is the exams next week." In 1917 and 1918, Corey found new ways to save on room and board in Fort Pierre. She wrote to her mother before the two-week 1917 institute that was to begin on June 18, "Mrs Gordon wants me to come down the 14th or 15th and take care of the place while she goes [out of town]. . . . My board wont [*sic*] cost me anything if I do that." After the one-week 1918 institute, she wrote, "A bunch of us girls rented a furnished cottage and batched. We had *some time*."[57]

In addition to finances, Corey's struggles while attending summer institutes included balancing her desire to relax and socialize with her need to study and perform well on examinations. A couple of weeks after mentioning upcoming exams to her mother in 1912, Corey wrote, "I haven't heard about the exams yet and am worried about S D History. . . . I didn't study a lick during the two weeks and I surely had some fun. I know a good many of the teachers and was acquainted with all the instructors and I never entered a class or assembly room without a four inch grin on my phiz and I managed to keep every one around me going some, except during recitation." After receiving her grades, Corey expressed disappointment and remarked, "I thot that a *perfect* attendance and class record was enough after I'd taught all year . . . that was the only chance of a little fun in the whole year." After missing the 1913 institute in order to visit her family, Corey buckled down in 1914, explaining to her brother, "We recite from 8:30 in the morning till 12 and from 1:15 till 4 in the afternoon and prepare our work outside. Am afraid I won't have any time for cussedness this four weeks." Having worked hard and not simply crammed for the exams, Corey wrote ebulliently to her mother at the end of the session, "Surely these past few weeks have been busy ones yet I've enjoyed every minute almost and have gained more than from all the rest of the institutes I've attended put together. . . . Dr. W. F. Jones of the State University who was our instructor in Fundamental Principles of Teaching, Games, and Teaching Processes . . . [is] simply great." In 1916, she wrote of the second-grade exams, "I didn't think they seemed so hard."[58]

Corey also socialized outside of class at the Fort Pierre institute, often at educational or cultural events. In 1910, she enjoyed ice cream socials, a reception at a local school, and a tour of the state capitol. One afternoon, she wrote to her mother, "The teachers were taken in autos out to the buffalo pasture where we saw three hundred feeding—such fun we had." While not studying "a lick" in 1912, she explained, her "time was awfully filled. . . . Two mornings we got up and went down to Rev. Roberts to look at Saturn," and one evening, "we heard Rev Roberts lecture on 'The Dead Man in the Moon' illustrated by lantern slides." With lectures and social events, there was "something every evening." At a gathering hosted by the local Woman's Club, Corey reported, "There were a hundred or more of us in three large boats. We were out most of the afternoon and had a swell time."[59] Through such events, Corey and her fellow remote-school teachers built esprit de corps while broadening their intellectual and cultural horizons.

In the South, the General Education Board (GEB) underwrote the addition of a new position of "state agent of Negro rural schools" to each state's school leadership structure during the 1910s. Historian Adam Fairclough explains that these agents reinvigorated and expanded summer institutes for Black teachers in the interest of infusing industrial education along the lines of the programs at Hampton and Tuskegee institutes into Black public schools; some states even required attendance at these summer normal schools. In Alabama in 1913, eighteen hundred people—three-quarters of the state's African American teachers—enrolled in thirty-seven "colored teachers' institutes." The institutes' five-day sessions included instruction in farming, sewing, and sanitation, along with academic subjects. With financial support from the GEB, Black summer institutes throughout the South increased in length, and the numbers of teachers attending grew from five thousand in 1916 to more than twenty-three thousand—54 percent of the teachers in Black public schools—in 1928. It was common for teachers to attend year in and year out. Although GEB leaders were disappointed in the quality of many of the institutes and charged that they were merely "'cramming schools' for a teachers' exam," Fairclough argues that they provided relief from the isolation of teaching in rural schools, expanded teachers' intellectual horizons, and encouraged them "to regard themselves as professionals"[60]—likely with greater knowledge of Black history and culture. Black teachers in the South, like Bess Corey, Muirl Dorrough, and teachers in Santa Fe in the 1910s and 1920s, deepened their subject matter knowledge and grew professionally, culturally, and socially through attending local summer institutes.

Throughout the country in the 1880s–1900s and in remote areas for an additional two decades, summer teachers' institutes, or normals, enhanced teachers' work as well as their professional and middle-class identities by enabling them to strengthen their pedagogical skills, subject matter knowledge, social capital, and exposure to more esoteric educational and cultural topics. Still, in the eyes of Armstrong in Illinois, these programs were just "little one horse affairs." He, the "Village School Ma'am" in Iowa, and other teachers sought to broaden their horizons more widely than was possible at the local institutes. Before university summer sessions were widespread, independent national programs would support these grassroots professionalization efforts by providing teachers with a higher level of professional development, intellectual stimulation, and cultural enrichment.

Independent National Programs

W. W. Willoughby's 1894 *History of Summer Schools in the United States* celebrated a new "movement" for "summer schools as an element in the educational system of the country," beginning with Harvard zoology Professor Louis Agassiz's establishment of a program for science teachers and university students at an ocean-side laboratory on Nantucket in 1872. Within two decades, Willoughby argued, the few fledgling university summer sessions and a number of independent programs—most of which were "located at pleasure or health resorts"—were fostering "the increase of knowledge among the people" in various ways, including through enhancement of the work of schoolteachers: "Several of the schools are devoted purely to instruction in the art of teaching, and in all of the larger institutions are departments of methods."[61] While Agassiz's venture lasted only a few years, "the real genesis of the modern summer school," according to early historian of American teachers Willard Elsbree, "was the Lake Chautauqua Institute established in 1874."[62] As Chautauqua became a favored destination for middle-class Americans who desired that their vacations include cultural enrichment, professional development for school teachers remained an important mission of the institution throughout its first six decades. Many other programs that also operated independently of state education systems or institutions of higher education—including the Martha's Vineyard Summer Institute in Massachusetts, the National Summer School of Methods in Glens Falls, New York, and the Columbian Catholic Summer School in Madison, Wisconsin—focused more exclusively on teacher education. Independent summer schools featured national leaders in education, famous speakers on other topics, and, especially in the case of Chautauqua, a rich menu of cultural events. The teachers they drew from beyond their immediate region or even from throughout the country pursued bottom-up professionalization by improving their pedagogical skills and engaging in esoteric educational and social topics as well as in middle-class culture and causes including independence for women.

Chautauqua

The institution on the banks of scenic Chautauqua Lake in western New York State began in 1874 as a summer camp meeting and lyceum to train Sunday school teachers for Methodist churches and soon became a "national podium" where middle-class Americans gathered to soak up culture and learn about social issues. As "a place where leisure could be put to the purpose of education and self-improvement," historian Cindy Aron explains, the Chautauqua Institution—and the "daughter chautauquas" it inspired throughout the country—appealed from the outset to sober members of the middle class, who stayed in tents and modest dwellings. Chautauqua quickly grew into a small village with an open-air amphitheater, small gingerbread cottages, grand gabled homes, and the stately Athenaeum Hotel, attracting the upper middle class as well. Gwyneth King (later Roe), who first arrived at Chautauqua in 1887 as a nineteen-year-old college student from South Dakota and returned for several summers in the 1890s when she was a teacher of Delsarte and physical culture, wrote, "My first observation was the magnificent trees . . . [and] wide grass-covered streets. No vehicles. No horses were allowed within the gates. People, instead, walked freely, anywhere." During the six- and then eight-week summer "assembly" or "season," Chautauqua attendees immersed themselves in the arts, heard prominent speakers on a wide variety of subjects, and played recreational sports on land and in the water.[63]

As the Chautauqua Institution evolved, teacher education remained a priority and expanded far beyond the original focus on Sunday school. The Teachers' Retreat and the School of Languages became part of the assembly in 1879, and the two programs joined to create a formal summer school in 1880, when the NEA recognized Chautauqua's work on behalf of teacher education by holding its annual meeting there. Also in 1880, a "pilgrimage" on foot, with a horse and wagon full of camping supplies, to Chautauqua of two brothers, one of whom was a principal in New York City and the other a schoolteacher in Newark, New Jersey, preluded an influx of teachers at Chautauqua each summer into the 1930s. Texas educator Anna J. H. Pennybacker wrote in her state's education journal that she had "a delightful time" attending the 1891 Chautauqua assembly, commenting that "so many opportunities to enjoy the best instruction" left little time to rest. Pennybacker also reported that Colonel Francis W. Parker "was at the head of the 'Teachers' Retreat' of which he made a most striking success."[64] Ten years later, Illinois journal *The Intelligence* also urged teachers to head to Chautauqua, calling it "one of the greatest movements for popular education set in progress during this generation," "the largest summer school" in the country, and—somewhat contrary to Pennybacker's experience—an ideal "resting place for teachers."[65] *The Chautauquan* weekly newsmagazine exaggerated only slightly when it noted in 1907, "In this great concourse are literally thousands of teachers." More precisely, the registrar reported in 1923 that "more than 500 teachers from all sections of the country" attended that year's session of the summer school. These teachers benefited professionally and personally from what the *Chautauqua Assembly Herald* referred to as the institution's distinctive "liberal culture for professional training."[66]

Various policies and programs at the institution helped make Chautauqua accessible to schoolteachers, beginning with arrangements for reduced railway fares and inexpensive rooming and boarding options. In 1902, the *Assembly Herald* reported that not only were "transportation companies now engaged in an active campaign to boom Chautauqua," but the railways had granted even lower "excursion rates" to teacher attendees. Philadelphian Ann Haynes Jewett, a judge's wife and a former teacher, in 1886 donated a cottage that would house twenty-five or so women teachers each summer for five decades. Teachers selected through an application process to reside in Jewett House "free of expense" prepared their own meals and shared housekeeping duties.[67] Other "student club houses" and, later, dormitories also made Chautauqua affordable for teachers. The institution's president, Arthur E. Bestor, explained in 1924 that memorial donations for rooms in a new women's dormitory provided additional accommodations "at the minimum of expenses" and in 1925 that the remodeled Summer School Commons "provided excellent service on the cafeteria plan." *The Chautauquan* reported when the commons first opened in 1910 that Bestor "spoke briefly on the democracy of Chautauqua and the long felt need of a place where its privileges could be enjoyed at a minimum of cost. . . . The Commons has three slogans: simplicity, democracy, comfort."[68]

Part-time work and scholarships also supported teachers' attendance at Chautauqua. The "Dining Room Force" of women servers at the Athenaeum Hotel in 1909 included two New York City teachers, four teachers from other towns in the state, and a teacher from Warren, Pennsylvania—as well as college students.[69] Before the institution acted on a founder's call for formal scholarships for teachers, other organizations or individuals occasionally sponsored selected teachers. In the mid-1900s, the owner-editor of the journal of the Kentucky Anti-Saloon League provided a yearly free one-week stay at Chautauqua for Kentucky teachers who signed up new subscribers to the journal. During the early 1910s, an "unknown donor" in Pittsburgh (Henry Clay Frick) funded summer school at various institutions for dozens of the city's teachers; seven in 1910 and thirteen in 1911 elected to study at Chautauqua. *The Chautauquan* reported in 1911, "A very large proportion of those sent last year brought back valuable data [to Pittsburgh] and they have spread it among their fellow teachers with good results."[70]

Through the formal scholarship system that began in 1910, donations from "friends of the institution" provided "full" and "half" scholarships to aid selected public school teachers in attending Chautauqua. Full scholarships provided "a season gate ticket" to assembly events, three summer school courses, lodging, and board in the commons; half scholarship provided the same for a twenty-five-dollar fee. *The Chautauquan* regularly listed scholarship rules and recipients, clarifying in the first year that "a successful candidate must be actually engaged in public school teaching, at a salary not to exceed $600, and must not have been a student at Chautauqua within ten years past" in order to "assure the bringing of a deserving and desirable class of persons who probably would not come at all otherwise." The sixteen teachers whose "personal qualifications" earned them full scholarships for a six-week stay in 1910 were women from New York, Pennsylvania, and Ohio, and one of the twenty women who won full scholarships two years later was from Mississippi. Rules for scholarships in 1919 stipulated that recipients "shall have taken no course in Chautauqua for ten years, they must be bonafide teachers in the public schools with assured positions, their total income shall not exceed $750; they shall agree to pursue at least three academic courses, and must be in good health." The number of scholarship winners increased and the rules remained similar into the 1930s, when the maximum allowable income rose to $1,500. "The scholarship idea has taken hold at Chautauqua," trumpeted an institution publication in 1926.[71]

With scholarships and other financial support, generations of teachers at Chautauqua honed their pedagogical knowledge and skills, with a focus not on passing certification exams but on deeper learning. The article that referred to "liberal culture for professional training" reported that leaders of the Teachers'

Retreat aimed to provide "personal contact, small classes, laboratory work—'acquaintance with' and not mere 'knowledge about.'"[72] William Rainey Harper oversaw educational programming at Chautauqua beginning in 1883, when the institution also secured a charter and the power to grant degrees as Chautauqua University. It issued few degrees and abandoned the university title and aspirations in 1892, but Harper, who served—in addition to his work as a professor at Yale and then as president of the University of Chicago—until 1895, established a long-lasting tradition of academics who were leaders in education and other fields teaching in the summer school and speaking to the broader assembly on contemporary or esoteric topics.[73] Throughout each decade between the 1880s and the 1930s, teacher-students at Chautauqua gained "'acquaintance with' and not mere 'knowledge about'" their field under the tutelage of some its leading lights.

When Eva Moll, a single Kansas schoolteacher in her late twenties, first attended the Teachers' Retreat in 1884, she noted in her diary that she studied psychology with Professor John W. Dickinson, who was secretary of the Massachusetts State Board of Education and the former principal of Westfield State Normal School. Dickinson's instruction centered on "the principles on which all real teaching lies" and how teachers should "develop minds instead of erecting machines in their pupils," according to a review of the following year's Teachers' Retreat, which also noted that students came to the retreat in 1885 from twenty different states as well as Canada. Moll did not say much about Dickinson but remarked that she found his assistant, Mr. Kendall, "very pleasing." Kendall, according to the 1885 report, provided "ample illustrations" of how to put into practice the psychological theories that Dickinson explicated. It was also in 1885 that the country-school teacher told a reporter that she felt as if she had "come into a fortune" at Chautauqua. The experience—for which she had spent her limited savings and scrimped on lodging on the outskirts of the grounds—was "the best investment" she had ever made. "I have always believed I could make something out of my teaching if I only knew how to go at it," she said. "This work here has taught me how to work. . . . I have the most delightful plans laid way for those little folks of mine." Moll returned to Chautauqua for nine weeks in 1886, when she pursued academic subjects and studied education with Arthur Boyden, principal of Bridgewater Normal School in Massachusetts. Her sister also attended in 1886, and Moll reflected, "Oh Chautauqua is doing a grand work for such as she and I. May the good work continue."[74]

The "good work" continued into the 1890s and beyond. The *Chautauqua Assembly Herald* reported in 1890 that Dickinson and other instructors exposed teachers from throughout the country to "the most advanced methods in teaching" and "experimental lessons in instruction in all common branches." Under the guidance of Parker and several other instructors from the Cook County Normal School in Chicago the following year, the Teachers' Retreat offered "talks on psychology, pedagogics, and methods and lessons upon the principles and

FIGURE 2 "An Out-Door Class," *Chautauquan Weekly* 22, no. 34 (1923): 29. (Courtesy of the Chautauqua Institution Archives.)

methods of teaching" in several subjects—talks that Pennybacker viewed as a "striking success." Referring to the principles of progressive education that Parker and his colleagues were developing in Chicago, the *Assembly Herald* also reported, "All the teaching and training is concentrated upon the central subject of life and the laws of life, physical, mental and moral."[75] By 1895, the teacher-education component of the summer school was called the School of Pedagogy, and its eleven instructors included five—three men and two women—from another incubator of progressive education, Columbia University's Teachers College. In Teachers College President Walter L. Hervey's pedagogy course and his colleague John F. Reigart's psychology course, both of which met five times per week, students became deeply acquainted with current pedagogical and psychological theories.[76]

In the opening decades of the twentieth century, Chautauqua continued to expand its summer school infrastructure and curriculum for teachers. While some classes met outdoors on nice days (see figure 2), an enlarged Hall of Pedagogy provided additional classroom space, and new course offerings included agricultural education and nature study with instructors from Cornell University. A three-week course designed for rural school teachers in 1908 incorporated experiments relating "agricultural chemistry to practical garden work" as well as demonstrations in "horticulture, dairying, poultry and animal husbandry." Also in 1908, *The Chautauquan* encouraged teachers attending the June meeting of the NEA in Cleveland to make the short trip to Chautauqua for summer studies in "Educational Method and Theory."[77] Three years later, *The Chautauquan* reported that "the consistent development of courses especially for teachers has met with cordial and widespread response" and that elementary grades had been added to the well-established summer kindergarten to provide "an observation room for [elementary school] teachers engaged in theoretical work." In 1912, Chautauqua offered more than eighty courses emphasizing "Theory of Education"; among these, Psychology of Childhood enrolled 92, Methods for Primary Grades enrolled 153, and Public School Art enrolled 99.[78]

By the 1920s, Chautauqua billed its educational programs as "the Oldest Summer Schools in the United States." An announcement for the 1924 session listed as the first of various groups of student constituents, "*teachers* who desire to increase their professional skill and knowledge." Under the direction of John W. Withers, the Education Department was to offer thirty-two courses for which "properly qualified students" would earn credit from New York University, where Withers was dean of education; the arrangement with NYU would last for three decades. In keeping with the "liberal culture for professional training," the listings for academic departments in the 1924 announcement included courses that focused on teaching methods. Offerings in English included "Methods of Teaching English Literature in the High School," and in Mathematics, "Content and Teaching of Arithmetic in the Middle and Upper Grades." Arts and Crafts was to offer twenty courses in everything from drawing to metalwork, while the Music Department, which was to include "Practice Teaching," had the lengthiest description in the announcement, reflecting the beginning of a shift in Chautauqua's summer education toward a focus primarily on the arts.[79] Typical of teacher-students at the institution in the 1930s were New York City supervisory teachers of "thread and needle art" Fanchon Hayver and Louise Knowles. *The Chautauquan Daily* reported in 1934, "This is Miss Hayver's fourth summer here. The first three seasons she studied weaving in the local classes; this year she is producing Swedish tapestry." As Chautauqua transformed in the mid-twentieth century into an arts institution, teachers continued to enroll in its music, dance, theater, studio arts, and writing programs.[80]

Opportunities between the 1880s and the 1930s to acquire "'acquaintance with' and not mere 'knowledge about'" education extended far beyond the formal summer school curriculum at Chautauqua. Lectures and programs for the larger assembly—to which summer school students had full access—often focused on cutting-edge or even esoteric topics in education. Renowned philosopher and architect of psychology William James in 1896 delivered a series of lectures in Chautauqua's amphitheater. Later published as *Talks to Teachers*, the lectures related new psychological principles to educational theory and teaching practices. James was impressed with the amphitheater's acoustics and reported that the large size of the audience did not prohibit people from asking questions. He also noted that the audience was "mostly teachers and women, but they make the best impression"—even though "there is hardly a pretty woman's face in the lot."[81] Pioneering psychologist and Clark University President G. Stanley Hall made multiple visits to Chautauqua. In 1895, he presented five "Pedagogical Lectures" in the summer school on topics including child study and adolescence. In 1907, Hall again presented a series of talks on education to the summer school students, and during his five-day residence he also addressed the larger assembly on the subject of religion.[82] Interacting with prominent scholars such as James and Hall, in addition to taking classes with professors including Parker and Hervey, introduced ordinary schoolteachers to esoteric ideas and elevated their engagement in the field of education.

Teachers also considered broader issues facing the education profession through conferences that met on the grounds during the summer season. The long-running Chautauqua Education Conference was "a place in which principals and teachers and all others interested in educational problems may meet for the discussion of such problems," according to *The Chautauquan Daily*. The 1914 conference included Professor Earl Barnes's talk on "Failures of our Educational System," specifically, "the lack of men in the profession, the tendency toward overconcentration, and the overloading of the teachers with a great amount of institutional work which should be done by other organizations." After World War I, the summer school worked with the Women's Christian Temperance Union to organize conferences on Americanization, which the *President's Report* noted was "one of the pressing problems of the present day."[83] In addition, when the New York State teachers' institute met at Chautauqua between 1896 and 1907, teacher-students in the summer school were welcome to attend. One who availed himself of this opportunity was Otis M. Shackelford, a Black teacher at Lincoln Institute in Missouri, who wrote that he "took advantage of the discussions on pedagogy and school management" in the institute during his three successive summers at Chautauqua's summer school. Participating in such discussions enhanced Shackelford's and other teachers' professional sense; Shackelford explained that he "was strengthened intellectually, morally, and spiritually, and . . . endeavored to disseminate whatever of good I had learned, and thereby benefit the youths that chanced to fall under my guardianship."[84]

The article that characterized the approach of the Teachers' Retreat as "liberal culture for professional training" also emphasized "the opportunities for collateral study afforded by the College of Liberal Arts."[85] Indeed, teachers' studies in the Chautauqua summer schools extended far beyond the field of education, and their learning in traditional academic areas supported grassroots professionalization by deepening their understanding of a range of subjects and familiarizing them with the culture of learned people. As in education, leading academics often taught liberal arts courses. Gwyneth King wrote that in the late nineteenth century, Harper; Richard T. Ely, then a professor at Johns Hopkins University; and Edward Olson, president of the University of South Dakota, were the core members of the faculty; "friends laughingly referred to them as 'The

Triumverate.'" The faculty also included George Vincent, who would later serve as president of the University of Minnesota, and Melville Dewey, who was developing his library classification system. A professor from Lewis Institute in Chicago taught higher math; Professor Robert Cumnock of Northwestern University taught literature; and William Anderson of Yale University, Alonzo Stagg of Yale, and Eliza Mosher of the University of Michigan taught physical education. King had some "foreboding" about working with such an esteemed faculty but soon "couldn't help feeling that founding a new kind of educational center on the edge of a Lake, in the Cultured East, was not too unlike founding a town on the bank of a River in the wild uncultivated West. I, somehow, felt at home with them."[86]

Teacher-students also had access to state-of-the-art equipment at Chautauqua. Facilities in 1895 included a chemistry laboratory "supplied with a full stock of chemical glassware," a physics lab with apparatus on loan from Kenyon College, and a well-stocked zoological lab. Principal T. E. Hollingsworth, who came to Chautauqua in 1898 with a party of educators from Washington, Georgia, reported, "We find that we can get more out of the course here than we expected. . . . I am studying physics and chemistry, which are my specialties, and my teachers are taking mathematics, physical culture, clay modeling, and nature study."[87]

In addition to studying education, Eva Moll enrolled in the English department in the College of Liberal Arts during her second summer at Chautauqua, and Shackelford studied "Latin, German, French, higher English, Arithmetic, Algebra, and Geometry" and "did work in the School of Expression" during his three summers at the institution. Moll also read dozens of literary works at home in Kansas through the Chautauqua Literary and Scientific Circle (CLSC) before and after her time at Chautauqua, where she also attended CLSC ceremonies. Pennybacker began pursuing the CLSC self-study course while teaching in Missouri in the early 1880s and founded a CLSC club and completed the course while teaching in Tyler, Texas, in the late 1880s.[88] While "collateral" studies through the CLSC and at the institution undoubtedly enhanced teachers' work in the classroom, they also inspired them intellectually in a broader sense. The *Herald* quoted a schoolteacher's reflection: "What the place seems to me to do particularly is to teach people to take an interest in everything. . . . Before you know it you find yourself interested in something you have always ignored." And Shackelford observed that at Chautauqua, "one can sit with folded hands and breathe the intellectual air, and thereby become inspired to do great things."[89]

In his history of Chautauqua, Jeffrey Simpson remarks on the "social fluidity" at the institution, where members of the upper middle class became more grounded and "schoolteachers and local business proprietors went to the opera."[90] This fluidity was especially meaningful for teachers, whose studies at Chautauqua elevated both their professional identity and their exposure to the liberal arts. Beyond the summer school program, Chautauqua offered teachers a smorgasbord of activities that imbued a wealth of additional cultural capital of the learned middle class. In addition to the opera, teachers attended music and drama performances, lectures on cultural subjects and social issues, and recreational activities. Moll noted that during her first summer at Chautauqua in 1884, she found "a lesson, lecture or concert for nearly every hour of the day," including "Stereopticon views" of the British Isles and a talk entitled "Chaucer and Shakespeare Compared." She wrote about her second summer, "The season was full of rich things of course. Heard some fine violin and harp playing by two Italians. I never expect to hear 'Nearer my God to Thee' sweeter on this earth, than it was played by the violinist." She "met many grand people . . . heard some excellent sermons and lectures, and music—both instrumental and vocal—[and] saw some beautiful sights." King commented, "I doubt if there was a single speaker of note in the United States . . . who was not heard at some time in this Amphitheatre, all Presidents included," and summarized, "In the evenings, there was entertainment—the N.Y. Symphony, the Philharmonic, a violinist, a singer, or a dramatic reader." The country teacher who called Chautauqua her "best investment" exclaimed, "I never had such a glorious time in my life."[91]

The schedule for each summer season continued throughout the opening decades of the twentieth century to abound in opportunities for intellectual and cultural enrichment as dozens of nationally prominent speakers and performers appeared in Chautauqua's now-iconic amphitheater, the open-air Hall of Philosophy, and other venues. The 1908 program included lectures on Shakespeare, theater in Salzburg, chemistry, "Reconstruction in Germany," and "The New Africa." Educator John Erskine, suffragist Carrie Chapman Catt, reformer Maude Ballington Booth, and Eleanor Roosevelt delivered addresses; and the institution's president, Arthur Bestor, spoke on "Contemporary Problems in Ancient Capitals." The New York Symphony Orchestra and John Philip Sousa with his band were headliners in the 1908 musical program. The Coburn Players appeared during multiple seasons at Chautauqua; in 1912, they presented *The Merchant of Venice* and *The Taming of the Shrew*. Symphonic music was especially prominent by the 1920s and 1930s, when Chautauqua had a resident symphony orchestra, but notable speakers continued to appear in the amphitheater. At a reception following President Franklin Roosevelt's address in 1936, a teacher from England asked him for a message to share with her students the following fall.[92]

Engaging freely in intellectual and cultural activities and studying with leading scholars not only imparted cultural capital but had great potential to stoke women teachers' sense of their right to broader horizons and independence. Some activities and talks on social issues addressed women's rights directly. Pennybacker focused in her account of the 1891 assembly on "Dress Improvement" for women, praising Col. Parker's wife Mary for convincing many Chautauquans through lectures and examples of the need for reform. "Of the prominent women at Chautauqua," she explained, "*every one* dressed sensibly; Miss [Frances]

Willard, Mrs. Mary Livermore, Mrs. Julia Ward Howe, Rev. Anna Shaw, Mrs. Zerelda Wallace, Miss Grace Dodge, Mrs. Emily Huntington Miller, Mademoiselle Decca—not one of them wore corsets, tight shoes, high heels, heavy skirts or trailing street dresses." Women teachers who heard Parker speak or witnessed these sensibly dressed, strong women on the grounds would have been, as Pennybacker stated, "carried away" by the movement for dress reform.[93]

King went to Chautauqua to assist her mentor and family friend Emily Mulkin Bishop, superintendent of public schools in Rapid City, South Dakota, teacher of Delsarte, and advocate of dress reform. In a series of talks presented each summer for several years, Bishop schooled Chautauquans on the "right use of the body," proper relaxation and stretching, and a system of gymnastic exercises that did not require apparatus. Implicitly and at times explicitly, Bishop's lessons emphasized women's rights; King explained that her approach to gymnastics "was revolutionary" for women because it enabled them to strengthen their bodies without using gymnasium apparatus, which at the time was a male domain.[94] Before Chapman Catt delivered an address in 1908, she visited Chautauqua in 1900 with fellow suffragists Susan B. Anthony and Anna Howard Shaw; the three would most certainly have presented their arguments for the vote as crucial to women's independence.[95] New York City teacher Anna Williamson asserted her independence and literally expanded her horizons in 1913 when she won an airplane flight at Chautauqua for submitting the winning name of "Bumble Bee" in a contest to name the plane. She said that she was "rather surprised and a trifle frightened" to win the flight but felt "enthusiastic and delighted" after she landed.[96] Such experiences broadened teachers' worlds, affirmed their position in the middle class, deepened their knowledge, and thereby enhanced their confidence in the classroom.

Throughout the country, teachers also gained some exposure to "liberal culture for professional training" at smaller "daughter chautauqua" summer assemblies. By 1880, the New England Chautauqua Assembly in a wooded area of Framingham, Massachusetts, and the Bay View Assembly near Petoskey on the shore of Lake Michigan, attracted teachers and other upright members of the middle class with courses in the liberal arts and education, usually taught by faculty members from colleges in the region. New England, where the session was only a couple of weeks long, in 1882 included an "Advanced Grade Normal Department" and a "Primary Teacher's Department." At Bay View, Richard T. Ely—now a professor of economics at the University of Wisconsin—directed the 1892 summer school, and an advertisement in *The Intelligence* for the 1901 session listed a five-week "College and School of Methods" with instruction in "School Organization and Management" and subjects ranging from botany to Greek. By the early twentieth century, 150 "independent chautauquas" included one convened by Booker T. Washington at Tuskegee Institute and other assemblies for African Americans in the South and Midwest; a Jewish summer assembly in Atlantic City; and the Texas-Colorado Chautauqua established by Texas educators near Boulder, Colorado, "closely patterned after the parent Chautauqua of New York," with a series of lectures by G. Stanley Hall in 1907. Like the New York institution, these assemblies provided opportunities for cultural improvement and stoked women's sense of independence. Politicians and reformers spoke in New England's Hall of Philosophy; the ad for Bay View boasted that it combined "vacation pleasures" with "an Assembly where some of the greatest scholars of the day, the finest music and entertainments, can be heard"; and among the speakers at the Texas-Colorado Chautauqua in 1908 were Hull House founder Jane Addams and writer and suffragist Marjorie Benton Cooke. Before many "daughter" assemblies succumbed in the 1920s to competition from the more entertainment-oriented circuit, or "tent," chautauquas and other forms of recreation, they provided many teachers with a taste of the original Chautauqua.[97]

Other Independent National Programs

In addition to "the great experiment at Chautauqua Lake," Willoughby's 1894 history of summer schools documented programs "devoted purely to instruction in the art of teaching," including the Martha's Vineyard Summer Institute and the National Summer School of Methods—as well as university summer sessions. While the Columbian Catholic Summer School and other independent national programs beyond the scope or date of the 1894 study also provided teachers with opportunities for professional development and broader educational and cultural horizons, from Willoughby's perspective the program on the Massachusetts island of Martha's Vineyard was "one of the leading and most flourishing institutes for summer instruction in the United States."[98] Col. Homer B. Sprague, headmaster of a girls' high school in Boston, established the institute in 1878 and served as its president until 1882. Sprague later explained that during his tenure and beyond, the five-week session's mornings were devoted to "class exercises, the afternoons and evenings to public lectures and entertainments, Friday and Saturday evenings to receptions, and the whole of Saturdays to excursions and recreation." Students, who were encouraged to focus on just one subject at a time, studied with instructors from institutions ranging from the Boston Latin School to Cambridge University. The institute added a new main building in 1882 and two additional buildings for music instruction soon thereafter.[99]

As at Chautauqua, teacher-students at Martha's Vineyard honed their knowledge and skills under the guidance of leading lights in education and other academic fields. Col. Francis W. Parker headed the "didactics" department in 1882 and 1883, when he was completing his term as superintendent of Boston's public schools. The following summer, H. H. Straight from Parker's new professional home and a breeding place for progressive ideas in education, Cook County Normal School in Illinois, directed Martha's Vineyard's pedagogy department. Also in the mid-1880s, Principal F. Louis Soldan of the St. Louis Normal School and future U.S. commissioner of education William T. Harris deepened teachers' understanding of the philosophy of education, while leading scholars in academic subjects, including Charles Adams in history, W. A. Brownell in mineralogy, and Hermann B. Boisen in German, helped teachers to deepen their knowledge of these fields.[100]

New England educator William Mowry accepted an invitation to present lectures on American history at Martha's Vineyard in 1887, although he believed that teachers should spend the summer resting rather than studying and that summer studies were superficial. "I was surprised to find," he later wrote, "on the one hand a class of very earnest teachers, thirsting for knowledge and wisdom, and on the other hand, a faculty composed of some of the best teaching material in the country." He served as president of the institute for the next nineteen years, during which time Martha's Vineyard expanded its "school of methods for elementary studies," added a "school of methods for high-school studies," and broadened its other academic offerings. Instructors included education scholars William Payne of the University of Michigan and John Dewey of the University of Chicago, leaders in practice Principal J. C. Greenough of Westfield Normal School and school Superintendent Will S. Monroe of Pasadena, and editor of *Primary Education* Eva D. Kellogg. Philosopher and historian Josiah Royce of Harvard University and former president of Wellesley College Alice Freeman Palmer also served on the faculty. The hundreds of teachers who had the privilege of attending Martha's Vineyard learned from these and other nationally prominent faculty members as yearly enrollments during Mowry's tenure increased to nearly seven hundred.[101] A 1903 advertisement for the institute highlighted its pleasing location and range of studies for teachers, stating simply, "Out in the Atlantic. Cool and Healthful. Courses in Oratory, Academics and Methods."[102]

The National Summer School of Methods in Glens Falls, near the Adirondack Mountains in New York State, was not as old as Chautauqua or Martha's Vineyard and could not boast of a location on the water, but it was significant to Willoughby as "the first school of methods" and the result of a merger in the late 1880s of four separate methods-oriented summer institutions in New York State. The original summer school in Glens Falls was the Glens Falls Training School, established in the early 1880s by Superintendent Ballard of Jamaica, New York, and Superintendent Williams of Glens Falls. More than a local summer normal but not yet quite a national institution, the training school focused on methods of physical training and primary teaching and soon grew into a three-week summer program that drew students and instructors from a large region. One of those students was twenty-three-year-old Jessie Herrick of the south-central New York town of Horseheads, who appreciated learning "a minimum of theory and a maximum of practice" when she attended the Glens Falls Training School in August of 1887.[103]

The school provided practical material and knowledge that Herrick desired as a novice teacher while it also exposed her to some more theoretical ideas.

Attending sessions in the Union School building with one hundred other teachers, she deepened her understanding of methods of teaching drawing, physical education, and general primary-level lessons. She noted in her journal early on that "Prof. Smith of Brooklyn, the Drawing teacher is doing excellent work," and later that she had "copied the forms used in 1st year work in drawing," "cut forms for future drawing work," and observed an advanced drawing class. Herrick also remarked that Professor Ballard's instruction in physical training was "very interesting." During the third week, she wrote that her studies were "getting more interesting. Today Miss [Harriet] Morris of School (39) Brooklyn gave a talk on Primary teaching." Herrick also appreciated the practical advice that another instructor provided in a "fine discourse": "Do not study to [*sic*] many different subjects. Know some one thing thoroughly and be content with a general knowledge of things."[104]

Although she purported not to be as interested in theory, Herrick also engaged at Glens Falls in lessons on broader, somewhat more esoteric topics related to education. After Professor Allen's psychology lectures, she reproduced in her journal his "diagrams showing the sensibilities and will" of people of different ages and recorded her "good" scores for "the four temperments [*sic*]." She also noted that one of Allen's talks was followed by a lesson on the history of grammar and that another professor "gave a very interesting talk on Civics." Herrick quoted Professor Love's conceptual lecture on manual training at some length, including his observation that, without proper instruction, "scholars leave our high school without knowing how to get a living." After enhancing her practical skills and her understanding of some broader issues, Herrick gained a long-distance support system when Morris invited the training school students "to write to her on any subject we liked."[105]

Through her experience in Glens Falls, Herrick also expanded her cultural knowledge, geographical horizons, and middle-class sociability. She attended services at different churches and enjoyed exploring the "beautiful village" of Glens Falls, where she learned about local culture in the "French portion" of town and about paper-making at the local mills. After an "Entertainment at the Opera House," she noted that the building was "tastefully decorated—and in the latest styles." Near Glens Falls, she saw a cave said to have been a hiding place for a character in Fenimore Cooper's *The Last of the Mohicans* and enjoyed "a delightful row down the glorious Hudson" River. Short excursions took Herrick to Ulysses S. Grant's cottage—a historic site that was "just as he left it"—and to Lake George, where she saw Fort William Henry and Sagamore, "an elegant summer resort." On the way home from Glens Falls, she stopped in Albany to see "the new State Capitol," observing that the building "presents a very imposing appearance." Herrick found her fellow boarders to be "an interesting lot, jolly and witty." One evening, she and her new friends conformed to local mores when they went to downtown Glens Falls "without hats, which," she explained, "seems quite the style here." A highlight of her stay was a reception for the training school in a local home, where she "visited with a number of pleasant people who made us feel perfectly at home" and danced to "delicious strains of music."[106]

After three weeks at the training school, Herrick was more skilled in teaching and a little more worldly and independent when she assumed her role as a teacher in Hornellsville, sixty-five miles east of her family home. She had noted on the opening page of her journal that the 235-mile trip to Glens Falls was "the first time I ever went away from home any distance," and the experience clearly broadened her sense of her professional and personal horizons. "Glens Falls are grand," she reflected. "What can Niagara Falls be like?"[107] Soon after Herrick's summer at Glens Falls, the training school increased its ability to expand teachers' horizons when it merged with the other New York institutions and took the name of the one that had been housed in Saratoga: the National Summer School of Methods. Within a few years, the school employed more than thirty instructors from various normal schools, universities, and school districts in the Northeast and Midwest, and each summer enrolled as students nearly five hundred teachers from country schools to high schools and even colleges, and from close to three dozen different states. "This comingling of teachers of all grades and from all sections of the country has of itself proved to be of great value," wrote Willoughby.[108]

Like Chautauqua, the most prominent independent national programs were in the Northeast. Yet, like "daughter chautauquas," independent programs appeared in other parts of the country as well. For example, a two- to three-week "School of Methods" that was more advanced and enrolled teachers from a broader area than a summer normal convened periodically in Texas. Announcements for the 1888 Summer School of Methods in Fort Worth promised "the most notable effort yet made in Texas to bring to the State the attractions which have drawn teachers to Saratoga," "eighteen departments and a model school," and "experienced instructors," including five who had taught at Saratoga. In 1896, the school convened in Austin and the faculty included school superintendents and professors from across the state and Kansas City. Between 1903 and 1907, the School of Methods thrived in San Antonio under the direction of Superintendent Lloyd E. Wolfe, who used his national connections to bring in prominent educators and spread child-centered, hands-on methods. Attendees listened to lectures, watched demonstrations, and took field trips to sites related to the industrial arts. Renowned educational theorist Charles A. McMurry of Illinois lectured on the Herbartian pedagogical principles of student-focused lesson planning at the school in 1904 and 1905; in a 1904 ad for the school, Wolfe stated, "There is no one in this country who can handle the selection and organization of subject-matter better than Dr. McMurry."[109] One of the largest national programs was the Summer School of the South, which attracted thousands of white teachers from every southern state and beyond to Knoxville, Tennessee, from mid-June through July beginning in 1902. "Country school teachers who had never been to high school . . . listened to lecturers whose voices carried across the continent," reflected Philander P. Claxton three decades after directing the school.[110] (While the Summer School of the South was officially an independent organization, it was embedded in the University of Tennessee and therefore is featured in the following chapter.)

A different type of independent national institute served primarily women religious who taught in Catholic schools but also attracted some lay teachers, including veteran Chicago public school teacher of Irish Catholic heritage Margaret Haley, who was hungry to engage with esoteric ideas and aspects of her profession. Beginning in the 1880s, the most common form of summer education for teaching sisters was local institutes organized in response to calls for higher certification standards for teachers in Catholic schools. Women religious would return from the branch houses where they lived during the school year to the motherhouse community for further instruction and fellowship; three hundred Dominican Sisters returned in July 1897 to the Sinsinawa motherhouse in southwestern Wisconsin to study Shakespeare, psychology, and "biblical science" with visiting professors and priests.[111] In the 1890s, Catholic educators also organized national summer programs in response to a liberal movement within the American Catholic church for Catholics, including parochial as well as public school teachers, to engage more deeply in contemporary social and intellectual issues. Haley attended the Catholic Summer School on Lake Champlain in Plattsburgh, New York, in 1896 and the Columbian Catholic Summer School in Madison, Wisconsin, in 1897. Organized by the Dominican Sister leaders at Sinsinawa, the Columbian school especially satisfied Haley's desire for what she called a "widening view." "It was a raging place to get into," she remarked.[112]

The Columbian Catholic Summer School convened at the Fuller Opera House on Madison's isthmus for six weeks each summer from 1895 through 1897. Yearly attendance exceeded one thousand, and each day opened with hundreds of voices joining in song. In morning, afternoon, and evening lectures, bishops, priests, and professors from seminaries and universities such as Notre Dame, Saint Louis, and Louvain addressed subjects including psychology, labor relations, ethics, church and state, "Historical Development of Catholic Popular Education," and "Science and Dogma." The school also included Sunday services, and receptions in the opera house and other Madison venues. In 1895, two receptions took place in the state capitol, and progressive archbishop John Ireland addressed the assembly on "Patriotism" in a University of Wisconsin gymnasium. A notable addition to the Columbian faculty in 1897 was the Reverend Dr. Thomas Edward Shields, who presented a course on "(1) Three Phases of Mental Life; (2) Fundamental Qualities of the Student Life; and (3) Laws of Mental Development."[113]

Haley, who had studied with Col. Parker at Cook County Normal School, found Shields to be especially inspiring. With a PhD in biology from Johns Hopkins, Shields taught biology, physiology, and psychology at a seminary in

St. Paul and, later, at the Catholic University of America, while also lecturing extensively throughout the country on educational issues. A member of the Sinsinawa community described him as "a dynamic personality" who "challenged his audiences rather than cajoled them." Shields argued that "there should be in every school a correlated curriculum which would have a core," and "teaching should be related to all other subjects taught. The objective of education was not to cram a lot of information, useful or useless, into a student's mind. The objective should be the making of a good citizen." While Shields stated that the curricular core in Catholic schools should be religion, Haley easily discerned the usefulness of his progressive message for the public school context, reflecting later that he "seemed to grasp educational truths with a vision" and that the Dominican schools that adopted his ideas were "years away ahead of the public school system." Immersion in the intellectual and social-reform discussions in Shields's and other courses at the Columbian school helped to shape the core of Haley's view of teacher professionalism: "The fundamental issue in the unending war for academic freedom: the right of the teacher to call his soul his own." As historian Kate Rousmaniere argues, Haley's "vision of the school as the center of a progressive welfare state" was also inspired by the leadership and commitment she witnessed in Mother Superior Mary Emily Power and the Sinsinawa sisterhood as professional development during the summertime helped to launch her work in educational politics and leadership of teachers' unions.[114]

In addition to Catholic summer schools, Haley attended fledgling normal school and university summer programs in the 1880s and 1890s. "The early summer schools outside of colleges and universities" had proved "once and for all the availability of summer weeks for collegiate study," according to Professor Joseph Avent, and summer sessions at institutions of higher education became widespread at the turn of the century. As a result, many independent national summer schools, like local summer institutes, ceased operations. The directors of the Martha's Vineyard Summer Institute in 1905, Mowry explained, "came to the conclusion that, as there were now so many summer schools in all parts of the country, this particular institute was no longer needed," and they closed shop. Taking a different approach, it was out of concern about rising competition from university summer sessions that Chautauqua's trustees in the 1920s arranged the affiliation with New York University, through which teachers and other summer school students at Chautauqua could earn academic credit. Although many schoolteachers continued to spend their summers at Chautauqua, they focused on the arts rather than on education and teaching.[115] The success of independent national teacher-education programs precipitated their demise by inspiring higher education institutions to move into the market. Another form of summer professional development for teachers was not as affected by the rise of university summer sessions: summer meetings of state and national associations.

Meetings of State Teachers' Associations and National Education Associations

In his 1911 report *Agencies for the Improvement of Teachers in Service*, Ruediger wrote, "The type of work that is done at the National Educational Association and at the State teachers' associations is so familiar that no space need be taken here for its discussion."[116] Within a half century, however, these associations would transform into teachers unions, and their earlier work in the area of professional development would become less familiar and largely disappear from histories of teacher preparation.[117] STAs and the NEA began in the mid-nineteenth century as platforms for leaders in education, who were mostly men, to communicate with teachers and other administrators. Although the NEA was established as the National Teachers' Association in 1857, classroom teachers and women had little voice in the organization for decades. The NEA also remained a quasi-segregated white organization until well into the twentieth century; while not barred officially from membership, Black teachers were often unwelcome in the North, and state chapters in the South were exclusively white. Black teachers and administrators founded the National Association of Teachers in Colored Schools (NATCS) in 1904 as a parallel organization to the NEA. While STAs—including separate organizations in Southern states for Black and white educators—were more welcoming of teachers, their state-level leadership mirrored that of the NEA. Teachers were encouraged, though, to attend annual meetings of STAs as well as the NEA and NATCS as a form of professional development.[118] Most STAs met over the winter holidays, but a handful met during the summer in the late nineteenth and early twentieth centuries, when general membership meetings of the NEA and NATCS always took place in the summer months. The many teachers who devoted a portion of their time off from the classroom to attending state and/or national association meetings were able to reflect on teaching practices and issues facing the schools and society while they enjoyed camaraderie and cultural entertainment that fostered grassroots professionalization.

State Teachers' Associations

A June 1880 editorial in *The Maryland School Journal* encouraged teachers to attend the upcoming July meeting of the Maryland State Teachers Association in Ocean City. The editors reported that the governor and other prominent Marylanders would speak on educational topics, that railroads would provide reduced fares for attendees, and that the schedule would "give large liberty for recreation and social enjoyment." Also among the small number of STAs that met during the summer, the Pennsylvania STA, the Texas STA, and the Texas Colored Teachers' Association (CTA) regularly met for three or four days in June or July from their founding in the 1870s or 1880s through the turn of the twentieth century (when they moved their meetings to late December). The associations and hosts in the various cities where they convened secured reduced rail fares and inexpensive or even free room and board for attending teachers. For the Pennsylvania STA meeting in Williamsport on July 10–13, 1883, the *Pennsylvania School Journal* reported, the "local committee" did "everything in its power to give the teachers of the State a grand welcome," including lining up reduced rates at four local hotels and free return rail fares.[119] Before the Texas STA meeting in Waco on June 29–July 2, 1897, the *Texas School Journal* devoted more than a page to instructions for reaching Waco by rail at a discounted fare, and also reported that the CTA would meet there as well "because it will be possible to obtain cheaper rates on account of the meeting of the white teachers' association at Waco at that time." The *Journal* also campaigned often for a large attendance at Texas STA meetings. In an 1884 editorial on the upcoming meeting in San Antonio, STA President John Collier proclaimed, "Every teacher in the State is entitled to a seat," and promised, "The subjects presented at the Association will be deeply interesting."[120]

Efforts to encourage teachers to attend the meetings seemed to pay off. After the 1881 Pennsylvania STA meeting in the town of Washington's Town Hall, the *Pennsylvania School Journal* noted that while most of those in attendance were from the area, "a majority of the counties in the State were represented by their leading teachers and school officers." In other years, the *Journal* listed the "Members in Attendance" at the Pennsylvania STA meeting, who totaled 488 in 1882, 620 in 1886, and 495 in 1891. Between 30 and 45 percent of the names were women's; the lists did not include the attendees' titles or positions.[121] After the 1884 meeting of the Texas STA, the *Texas School Journal* reported that in San Antonio, "nearly two hundred teachers, from the sweet eighteen-year-old maiden, with her bewitching smiles and flowing curls, *down* to ex-Governor O. M. Roberts, though twice a governor, and now a *teacher*, joined in the discussion and formed plans for elevating the youth of the greatest of states."[122] Over six hundred teachers attended the 1886 Texas STA meeting in Austin, where "several papers full of thought were read" and the governor hosted a reception for the teachers at the executive mansion. Between 850 and 900 teachers, "many from remote sections of the state," attended the 1889 meeting in Galveston. The Texas CTA attracted over fifty teachers from eighteen different counties to its second meeting, in 1886 in Galveston, and 105 attended its meeting the following year in Dallas.[123]

In describing the summer STA meeting as "no picnic excursion, but a meeting for work, for consultation with reference to the best methods of instruction, and the best system of school government," the *Texas School Journal* suggested that attendees gained ideas for improving their own day-to-day work with students and considered broader educational issues. Discussion of methods of instruction involved how to teach as well as more esoteric questions of what subjects were most effective in the curriculum. At the 1880 Pennsylvania STA meeting, Jennie Johnston stressed in her paper titled "Moral Training" that teachers must focus on setting "a proper example" while keeping their classrooms "free from all sectarian teachings," and J. D. Pyott presented a paper on how common-school teachers could make room for the study of astronomy by eliminating ineffective math and grammar lessons. In her paper on "Primary Work" at the 1886 Pennsylvania STA meeting, E. Jessie Llewellyn emphasized, "The attention of young children should be *attracted*, not *forced*" and sought to clear up confusion around object teaching by stating that its purpose was "a thorough development of all the child's faculties and their proper employment in the acquisition of knowledge." The same meeting included a plea by a state geologist for the inclusion of geology in the school curriculum.[124]

Similarly, the 1885 Texas STA meeting program included "A New View of Geology," as well as talks titled "Religion and the Public Schools," "The Newspaper as a Factor in Education," "Industrial Education in its Relations to Common Schools," and "The Moral Influence of the Public School," each followed by "Discussion." Four years later, when Texas State Superintendent O. H. Cooper's paper on the elementary course of study went past the allotted time and the STA president ordered him to stop speaking, the *Texas School Journal* reported, "a howl" arose "from the convention, who wanted to hear Supt. Cooper out." He was allowed to finish, and the association passed a resolution endorsing his paper. The 1892 Texas STA meeting included Miss Stout's argument for utilizing Froebelian methods in elementary-level teaching and Principal John W. Hopkins's report on the high school course of study.[125] At the Texas CTA meeting in 1886, C. J. Anderson's paper called for more industrial education "among the colored people." CTA secretary H. T. Kealing, in "Are Our Methods of Teaching Practical?" expressed opposition to the classical course of study and, the *Journal* reported, "made a strong plea in favor of devoting more time to the study of science and all that tends to fit students to the practical work of life." Kealing was president of the CTA three years later when papers presented at the Houston meeting included "Training the Sensibilities," "The Relation of the Teacher and Pupil," and "Mental Culture."[126]

Complementing the papers at the 1889 CTA meeting was an exhibit with displays related to higher education, graded schools, country schools, industrial education, art, and "bound Pedagogic literature, school journals, etc." During informal interactions in the exhibit hall and elsewhere behind the scenes at Black teacher association meetings, participants were able to tap into the "insurgent intellectual networks" that historian Givens argues operated away from public view. He and Fairclough detail how, by the second decade of the twentieth century (when most state teachers' associations no longer met during the summer), many southern Black teachers became familiar with the Negro history movement through their association meetings—as well as through summer schools—when founder Carter G. Woodson and members of the Association for the Study of Negro Life and History openly exhibited books and teaching materials.[127]

Exhibits also added an important dimension to consideration of teaching practices at majority-white STA meetings. The *Pennsylvania School Journal* reported that at the 1882 meeting, "the exhibits of specimens of drawing, both map and industrial," were a "great credit" to the schools and "showed very clearly the grand possibilities of the art." And the *Texas School Journal* stated that "a most creditable display of drawings, language and composition work, specimens and examination papers" at the 1889 meeting demonstrated that "more can be learned from seeing what other schools have really done and comparing results and methods as shown in the work represented than in any other way."[128]

While exhibits and papers on methods and curriculum deepened teachers' engagement with teaching practices, other addresses at the state association meetings heightened their awareness of broader issues that shaped and challenged school systems. For the Pennsylvania STA, Hon. J. Q. Stewart spoke on "Needed Legislation . . . in developing and perfecting the growth of the Free School System" in 1881, and Col. Brainard Case addressed "Defects in the Pennsylvania School Laws" in 1886, arguing that local school boards, chosen "without the slightest regard for their fitness or unfitness for the office," wielded too much power. Speakers in Texas also addressed school laws and legislation. At the 1887 CTA meeting, J. D. Davis's paper in favor of compulsory education provoked extensive discussion in which one member supported his argument by pointing to successes in Germany, while another countered that "such ideas on education were communistic" and would violate parents' rights. The 1888 CTA meeting included a paper titled "National Aid for Education," and at the 1889 meeting of the Texas STA, J. M. Carlisle reflected on the role of the state superintendent and "the present inadequacy of the state school fund."[129]

Other broader issues that were popular topics at state association meetings included teacher education and the demands of the profession. In his paper on "Teachers' Studies and Degrees" at the 1880 Pennsylvania STA meeting, E. O. Lyte argued that more extensive teacher education was necessary in order for teaching to join the ranks of the learned professions: "Considering the fact that so little special preparation is made by many teachers, it is remarkable that the calling is regarded as high as it is," he reflected. In 1882, Pennsylvania State Superintendent E. E. Highbee's address considered "how shall we secure and keep active . . . the best qualified class of common school teachers?" and ten years later, the Pennsylvania STA president discussed "the discouragingly low rate of increase in teachers' salaries."[130] Papers presented at the Texas CTA included "The Wide Awake Teacher" in 1886 and "The Teacher's Profession" in 1889. Narnie Harrison's paper on "The Teacher; the Demands which the Schools Make Upon Him" was so well received at the Texas STA meeting in 1889, according to the *Texas School Journal*, that "all eagerly rose to their feet as a mark of tribute to the gifted lady."[131]

Support for Harrison's address reflected the sense of camaraderie that teachers developed not only through hearing and discussing formal papers but also through the cultural elements of association programs and the meetings' less formal middle-class activities. Meetings commonly included devotional exercises and music as well as other forms of entertainment. For the Pennsylvania STA, the Conservatory Orchestra of York performed several times during the 1880 meeting in York, and members of the local Musical Institute presented instrumental and vocal solos during the 1881 meeting in Washington, which also included an evening illustrated lecture on Yellowstone National Park.[132] Daily sessions of the 1887 Texas CTA meeting in Dallas opened with songs, organ music, and a prayer, and the final day ended with a "citizens banquet given for the benefit of the teachers," who no doubt enjoyed each other's companionship. "When the teachers separated" after the 1892 Texas CTA meeting in Fort Worth, the *Texas School Journal* reported, "there was a better interest and a higher degree of enthusiasm for the work of teaching than ever known among the colored teachers." Teachers attending the 1889 Texas STA meeting in Galveston enjoyed orchestral music, a reception with lemonade, and an excursion by barge. Camaraderie was so important to teachers—and the summer heat was so oppressive—at the 1895 and 1896 STA meetings in Dallas and Austin, respectively, that the editors of the *Texas School Journal* lamented, "Teachers do not listen to the proceedings at these summer meetings" and broached the idea of holding only a winter meeting (which the STA adopted in 1902).[133] Even if their attention occasionally lapsed, for many teachers, summer meetings of state associations provided an opportunity to reflect on their craft and the wider field of education while enjoying cultural entertainment and fellowship.

National Education Associations

Beyond individual states where association meetings provided professional development during months when school was not in session, the annual convention of the NEA functioned as a sort of national summer institute, mainly for white teachers, and the NATCS did the same for African American teachers after its founding in 1904. The summer NEA meeting, according to historian Edgar Wesley, was in many ways "the greatest educational show on earth," beginning with the 1884 meeting in Madison, Wisconsin. NEA President Thomas Bicknell undertook an unprecedented publicity campaign for the Madison meeting, placing information about the program, speakers, and exhibits—as well as promoting Madison and excursions in the area—in publications such as the *New England Journal of Education*. In order to facilitate attendance by classroom teachers, Bicknell also arranged for inexpensive accommodations and negotiated reduced rail fares. According to Bicknell, the Madison convention was the biggest to date with more than seven thousand in attendance, and most meetings after 1884 were much larger. He later reflected that at Madison, "the immense significance of women's work in education was recognized for the first time. . . . Two women were elected as vice-presidents," and the "names of twenty-three women educators were recorded as speakers or officers of the N. E. A."[134] Women and classroom teachers remained outside the upper echelons of NEA leadership until the 1910s, but from 1884 onward, the summer meeting was an opportunity for them to take part in grassroots professionalization by learning about new methods and pieces of apparatus, witnessing and occasionally joining discussions of broader topics with national experts and renowned figures, and communing with other teachers.

The NEA's commitment to facilitating and promoting teachers' attendance continued long after 1884. NEA staff members in Washington, D.C., arranged for reduced railroad and, when appropriate, steamship fares to and from each gathering. They also published hotel rates and even lined up rooming and boarding places for visiting teachers. In advance of the 1890 meeting in St. Paul, a blurb in a local newspaper explained that the NEA's "clerical force is working from early morning until 10 o'clock at night to complete work of assigning teachers to their boarding places. . . . Cards are sent to the people who entertain the teachers, telling them who has been assigned to them and when they will arrive. Cards are also mailed to the teachers, telling them the names of their hosts, with street and number, and stating what car to take."[135] A flyer for the 1896 convention in Buffalo promised, "The finest residence portion of Buffalo has been districted by a committee of the teachers, and a competent person placed in each district, to make a thorough canvass for suitable homes in private families for our guests." At the state level, education leaders who served as NEA "directors" promoted the meeting and arranged transportation and housing for groups of teachers. In advance of the 1898 convention in Washington, D.C., "Director for Kentucky" E. W. Weaver distributed a four-page brochure with information on a special train for Kentucky teachers, accommodations, and side trips, as well as the assurance that "ladies traveling alone will have the protection of chaperones, who will afford them every care and attention." A similar brochure for Kentucky teachers regarding the 1901 meeting in Detroit provided the same type of information and noted, "The program is exceptionally strong and a great meeting is confidently expected."[136]

The NEA in 1920 established a "representative assembly" of delegates from state associations, including some teaches, and the assembly convened at each summer gathering thereafter. Beginning with the 1924 meeting in Washington, D.C., the organization provided funding to help pay the rail fares of state delegates who traveled long distances to attend. At least one school district also subsidized teachers' travel to the national convention: Through an arrangement initiated by the local teachers' federation, the Evansville, Indiana, district awarded a fifty-dollar "bonus" to each of thirteen Evansville teachers who attended the 1930 NEA meeting in Columbus, Ohio.[137] To combat the financial challenges of the Depression, the NEA also offered a new option for accommodations in Columbus; the *Pennsylvania School Journal* explained, "A large tourist camp will be established on the Ohio state fair grounds for the many who come by auto. This provision assures an economical as well as unusual way to attend this great professional gathering."[138]

Education journals throughout the country printed NEA meeting programs, listed discounted railroad fares and hotel rates in the host city, and explained how attending would foster professional development. A short blurb in the May 1885 *Texas School Journal* promoted the July 14–18 meeting in Saratoga: "It promises a rich treat to all educators. Low excursion and entertainment rates are assured. . . . Texas was largely represented at Madison last July and should be well represented at Saratoga." *The Iowa Normal Monthly* told teachers in 1889 that they would benefit by attending the upcoming meeting in Nashville: "It gives us great heart when we learn that others are thinking our thoughts, are meeting our difficulties, are sharing our successes."[139] At a meeting of the Michigan STA the following year, Grand Haven superintendent E. L. Briggs recommended the upcoming NEA convention in St. Paul, stating, "Its discussions are upon the most advanced educational topics that are forcing themselves upon the attention of the world." Published in the association's *Transactions*, his comments would have reached teachers throughout the state. Illinois journal *The Intelligence* devoted an entire issue each spring from the late 1890s onward to the upcoming meeting. The May 15, 1899, issue contained a plethora of photos of and articles about attractions in host city Los Angeles, listed rail routes between various points in the Midwest and LA, and devoted three pages to programs for the general session and various departments. "From the preliminary program," an article summarized, "our readers will see what may be anticipated in the way of addresses from prominent speakers."[140]

Journals' promotion of the summer NEA convention as an accessible professional-development opportunity for teachers continued into the twentieth century. Before the 1907 gathering in Los Angeles, *The Iowa Normal Monthly* touted the NEA meeting not only for "stimulating, co-ordinating, and unifying the educational thought and practice of our country" but also for "the valuable education of travel which it has provided for fifty years for the teachers of the United States." The *Texas School Journal* promised "an opportunity for teachers . . . to hear the latest and best . . . from among the most progressive educators from all sections of our country" at Cleveland in 1908, and *Midland Schools* noted before the Des Moines meeting in 1921, "What congress and the departments are to national politics the N. E. A. is to national education."[141] Not surprisingly, *The Journal of the National Education Association* promoted the summer convention extensively. Before the 1923 meeting, the *Journal* published the program along with articles on the host city of Oakland, California. Afterward, it reported on the newly organized Department of Classroom Teachers sessions in Oakland. The following year, the *Journal*'s coverage of the Washington, D.C., meeting reflected change in the organization: One article focused on the new representative assembly, and another reported that the topics of tenure and the single salary schedule prompted the "liveliest" discussions in the Department of Classroom Teachers. Even in the midst of the Great Depression, the May 1935 issue of the *Journal* promised both a full program and that "a thousand vacation delights await teachers who attend the 73rd annual convention" in Denver.[142]

Due at least in part to exhortations in education journals, many teachers traveled to NEA meetings. The 1887 gathering in Chicago attracted upwards of 1,700 teachers from Illinois; 1,100 from Iowa; 900 from Kansas; 600 each from Nebraska, Minnesota, and Missouri; 500 from Ohio; and 400 from Indiana. Disappointed that only 272 Michigan teachers went to Chicago, a Detroit principal reported these numbers to the Michigan STA and pointed out that farther-away Massachusetts made a better showing with 275. From Iowa, more than 500 teachers attended the 1891 meeting in Toronto, approximately 700 attended the 1896 meeting in Buffalo, and 1,146 attended the 1897 meeting in Chicago. From Texas, nearly 300 educators attended the 1895 meeting in Denver and more than 500 attended the 1907 meeting in Los Angeles.[143] In the 1920s, the *Pennsylvania School Journal* listed the names—but not the titles or positions—of Pennsylvanians who attended various NEA conventions; 12 men's and 47 women's names appeared on the list for Oakland-San Francisco in 1923, and upwards of 400 names appeared on the list for Washington, D.C., in 1924. The *Journal* listed as "registrants" at the state's headquarters hotel 51 men and 28 women for the 1929 meeting in Atlanta, and 74 men and 48 women for the 1930 meeting in Columbus, where it is likely that additional Pennsylvania educators found other accommodations, such as at the campground.[144]

For the many teachers who were able to attend, the summer NEA convention was in many ways "the greatest educational show on earth." They gained new ideas for their classrooms in the exhibit hall and at the meetings of individual departments. An NEA document listed as the purpose of the exhibit "to promote 'the stimulation of educational thought and the improvement of educational practices.'" At Madison in 1884, an extensive educational exhibit in the Wisconsin capitol covered everything from kindergarten to technical education; William T. Harris observed that it was as complete as the educational exhibit at the Centennial Exposition in Philadelphia. The showcase at Madison featured mainly materials produced by school pupils, but commercial exhibits soon joined and then eclipsed school-based displays. In advance of the exhibit at the 1930 meeting, the NEA *Journal* explained, "This great educational fair repeated at each annual convention has for years stimulated thousands of teachers to the development of more effective methods, and widely modified teaching practices," and promised, "Every nook and corner of the convention exhibit hall at Columbus will be filled with aids to learning." After she attended the 1936 meeting in Portland, teacher Anna Dwyer wrote in a published letter, "The exhibits were most educational in value."[145]

NEA departments that focused on particular areas of teaching—including vocational education, established in 1875; kindergarten and primary education, 1884; business education, 1892; science, 1895; rural education, 1907; and social studies, 1925—met as part of the summer gathering, allowing teachers to explore practices specific to their subfield. After its establishment in 1913, the Department of Classroom Teachers soon became one the biggest and most helpful departments for teachers in the NEA. Department president Eula Hunter wrote in 1930, "Many times we have seen small groups of teachers assembled in the headquarters room of the Department of Classroom Teachers to discuss some specific problem ... and have later heard some one of the group say, 'This alone is worth my trip to this convention.'" It was in the Department of Classroom Teachers' *News Bulletin* that Nettie Mae Rankin wrote of meeting with "serious, intensely professional teachers" at Minneapolis in 1928. She continued, "a great many classroom teachers were recognized by the convention ... many filling prominent places on the program."[146]

Beyond exhibits and department programs, association-wide speeches and discussions as well as the general presence of men and women to whom Dwyer referred in her published letter as "the celebrities of our profession" made the NEA meeting "the greatest educational show." Prominent educators as well as political and social leaders discussed a wide array of developments in education and big questions facing the field and the country. Speakers at Madison in 1884 included U.S. commissioner of education John Eaton, Booker T. Washington, Frances E. Willard, Alice Freeman (later Palmer), G. Stanley Hall, Col. Francis W. Parker, and William T. Harris. Samuel C. Armstrong spoke on Indian education and Alexander Graham Bell spoke on "Deaf-Mute Education as Related to Public Education." In Michigan, Superintendent Briggs promised that at the 1890 meeting "the strongest educators of the country will discuss the most interesting and vital questions."[147] Conrad Selvig was a twenty-five-year-old rural school teacher and principal in Minnesota when he attended the 1902 NEA convention in Minneapolis. After a long career in education and in the U.S. Congress, he wrote that the meeting was "the most impressive gathering." Speeches by a "galaxy of great men and women"—including William Rainey Harper, Harvard President Charles W. Eliot, John Dewey, Archbishop John Ireland, and Carrie Chapman Catt—left "imperishable impressions" on him. "The world is not the same after one has been moved emotionally or broadened and lifted, intellectually, by a great speech," Selvig reflected. After Philadelphia teacher Clement Foust attended the 1928 meeting, also in Minneapolis, he wrote about seizing the opportunity to "meet the king pins of the profession.... In the lobby of a hotel we met Dr. [George D.] Strayer, Dr. [Thomas E.] Finegan.... Invigoration goes forth from contacts like these." Foust further explained that the meeting provided the opportunity to "hear known authorities frankly speak their minds.... Such a privilege inevitably enlarges a teacher."[148]

One area in which hearing known authorities enlarged NEA attendees was new developments in teaching practices. Superintendent Briggs emphasized that the NEA was "progressive"; whenever there was "a new idea or a special inspiration," prominent educators discussed it at the convention. A Texas educator's report on the 1907 Los Angeles meeting emphasized that the NEA was "rapidly . . . abandoning the traditional idea that education has for its only purpose the mastery of books. . . . This democratizing of education was shown [at the meeting] in the emphasis given to manual training, agriculture and domestic science and art; in the discussion of the exceptional child." Pennsylvania educator F. Theodore Struck similarly reported that a "high spot" of the 1925 Indianapolis meeting was "the emphasis placed upon the need for a more scientific basis for education, and the equally important need of making public education a service that aims to give *equivalent*, as distinguished from *equal* educational opportunities." Pennsylvanian Calvin Hogg was impressed with a speech he heard at Columbus in 1930 on one rural school's "progressive uses of the spirit of adventure" in creating "experiences for the worthwhile developments of its children," and R. W. Robinson of Greensburg, Pennsylvania, described the sharing of ideas by "many leaders in the field of rural education" at Los Angeles in 1931 as "epoch-making."[149]

"The greatest educational show" also allowed teachers to deepen their understanding of more esoteric issues of school governance and, increasingly, teacher welfare. The editors of the *Pennsylvania School Journal* reported that in his address at the 1916 meeting in New York City, U.S. education commissioner Philander Claxton made a case for a "national system" of education headed by a "Federal bureau," and that at the 1923 convention in Oakland, George Strayer spoke on "Financing of the American Schools" and in support of a federal cabinet-level department of education, while Missouri teacher Mattie Montgomery "appealed to all" in the Department of Classroom Teachers "to lend support in the cabinet fight." Pennsylvania teachers Fred Diehl wrote about what he learned from a speech on school consolidation in Philadelphia in 1926 and Walter Douthett explained that "lobby conferences" in Los Angeles in 1931 revealed agreement on necessary reform in school financing. The program in Indianapolis in 1925 convinced Pennsylvania teachers Margaret Lowman and D. A. Kline of the classroom teacher's "vital place in every phase of the school organization."[150] By the 1930s, issues directly affecting teachers' working conditions and livelihood were prominent at NEA conventions. A variety of speakers addressed academic freedom at the 1934 meeting in Washington, where Willard Givens, then–school superintendent in Oakland, framed his address to answer the question, "Are Teachers Citizens?" Two years later, Dwyer listed "teachers' oaths, the *Little Red Rider* of the District of Columbia, tenure, academic freedom, equal opportunity for teachers, [and] adequate compensation" among "the problems in which we are all interested" that were discussed at Portland.[151]

Even more broadly, NEA meetings enabled teachers to engage in the larger political arena through the appearance of political issues and actors on the programs and the podiums. "Nearly every president of the United States, from Buchanan to F. D. Roosevelt, spoke to one or more of the conventions," reports historian Wesley. After Claxton advocated a federal bureau of education, others at the 1916 meeting spoke to the context of the war raging in Europe. Former U.S.

President William Howard Taft promoted the League to Enforce Peace, populist leader William Jennings Bryan argued against schools becoming "breeding places for armies"—and in favor of women's suffrage—and University of Wisconsin President Charles R. Van Hise addressed "The Place of the State University in a Democracy."[152] A decade after the war ended, Nettie Mae Rankin reflected that her "most lasting impressions" of the Minneapolis meeting "perhaps were the forceful declarations made by so many speakers for Universal Peace through world citizenship created by a newer and broader educational system." The address of then–President Calvin Coolidge was the "climax of the convention" in 1924, according to the *Pennsylvania School Journal*: "Enthusiasm went wild" when the president announced that he supported a federal department of education without "interference with local control and dignity." Dwyer wrote that at Portland, she most enjoyed a political debate between the Democratic governor of Indiana, a Republican professor from Miami University, and a Socialist candidate for president in the 1936 election; she "came away from the convention with a feeling of satisfaction and with the realization that at least we were headed toward sound educational advancement." Another teacher, Mildred Babcock of New York, was most moved at Detroit in 1937 by Secretary of Agriculture Henry Wallace's speech on "Education and the General Welfare," Congressman Brooks Fletcher's advice that "educators must become more politically-minded," and author Mary R. Beard's argument that "if more women of a humanistic bent were permitted to exert their wit and intelligence in all the ranges of American education, America might be more secure."[153]

Dwyer also noted the importance of the "social side" of the Portland meeting, and Babcock wrote that communing with other teachers was one of the "most enjoyable features" of the Detroit meeting: "The social contacts made bring you more closely in touch with those whose interests and field of work are similar to yours than do the formal meetings." Indeed, the many opportunities to form professional connections through social interactions and cultural entertainment at NEA conventions fostered esprit de corps as well as agency among the teachers who attended. A reception for teachers in 1916 occupied an entire floor of New York's Biltmore Hotel, and at a free barbecue during the 1929 meeting in Atlanta, attendees consumed nearly seven thousand pounds of meat and an untold amount of Coca-Cola. The Department of Classroom Teachers held an annual banquet; the three hundred who attended in 1925 enjoyed "good fellowship" as well as "songs, tableaux, and stunts," and the one thousand who attended in 1929 listened to "Negro spirituals sung from the balcony" and a speech by a prominent sculptor. For Helen Hunt—who won a free trip to the 1934 meeting for teaching at the farthest rural school from Washington, D.C.—it was a "real thrill" at the banquet "to look into a sea of 700 faces [and] to view the decorations" in the Mayflower Hotel's grand ballroom.[154] State delegations also gathered for group meals during NEA meetings; the 232 Pennsylvanians who partook in their state dinner at Washington in 1924 enjoyed toasts and songs, and the eighty-one Iowans who attended their state breakfast at Portland in 1936 appreciated table decorations provided by Oregon teachers. Teachers "fortunate enough" to experience the social and other aspects of the NEA meeting—as well as tourism in the host city and region, as discussed in chapter 4—"return to their homes with new inspiration, broadened outlook, and enlarged friendships," reported the NEA *Journal*. Philadelphia teacher Euphemia Mann was impressed by "the earnestness, the enthusiasm, [and] the ideals" of her fellow teachers in the NEA, and rural Pennsylvania teacher Mary McAndrew testified to the "great spiritual force" and "contagion of true professionalism" at the 1926 meeting.[155]

Teachers at the Iowa breakfast at Portland celebrated their successful campaign to have Iowa superintendent of public instruction Agnes Samuelson elected NEA president for 1936. They no doubt felt a sense of agency within their profession, fostered especially by their involvement in the Department of Classroom Teachers and the Representative Assembly. One of the aims set forth in the department's constitution was "to secure teacher participation in school management," and the NEA *Journal* declared that the assembly made it "possible for each of the hundreds of thousands of teachers of the Nation to have a voice in the management of the National Education Association," which meant that "every teacher now has a part in shaping education policy." McAndrew reported that "a young lady attending the national convention for the first time . . . marveled" at the "spirit" of the assembly—"the fairness of the business proceedings, the good fellowship among the delegates."[156]

It is also significant that the first-time attendee and Samuelson were women. After women struggled to have a voice in the early decades of the NEA, Margaret Haley—now the leader of the Chicago Teachers Federation—and other prominent women educators claimed their and classroom teachers' right to participate fully in upper levels of the organization. They organized the National Federation of Teachers during the 1899 meeting in Los Angeles and met on the same dates and in the same city as the NEA for several years thereafter in order to call attention to issues of teacher rights and welfare. Haley upended NEA gender dynamics by speaking from the convention floor in 1901, spearheading the defeat of a proposal to restrict the participation of floor members in 1903, and delivering an address on "Why Teachers Should Organize" in 1904. Other women assumed her mantle by the late 1900s and saw to it that Ella Flagg Young in 1910 was the first woman elected to the presidency of the NEA and that the Department of Classroom Teachers was established in 1912 to give women more of a voice. The NEA endorsed women's suffrage in 1912 and elected a woman president every other year from 1917 onward.[157] These activists and actions—along with speeches like teacher Mattie Montgomery's at the 1923 meeting and Mary Beard's at the 1937 meeting—provided potent examples of psychological independence for women teachers who attended NEA conventions. Milwaukee teacher Lotta Fowler wrote of the Representative Assembly at Denver in 1934, "It was gratifying to note the number of classroom teachers who participated in these discussions. . . . If some of those ancient educators, who honestly believed with Saint Paul that women should be silent in meetings, had returned that night, what a shock they might have received!"[158]

Attending the summer NEA gathering made a strong impression on Fowler, Babcock, Dwyer, Rankin, and other women—as well as men—teachers. For Black teachers who did not have access to the NEA, the summer meeting of the NATCS played a similar role while also preparing them as fugitive pedagogues. The NATCS's eighth annual meeting, the largest to date, took place in 1911 at Sumner High School in St. Louis and also featured speeches in the city coliseum by the Missouri state superintendent and Booker T. Washington. The NATCS *Bulletin* announced before the organization's July 1920 annual meeting in Baltimore, "The teachers of Maryland, Pennsylvania and the District of Columbia will spare no pains to make all arrangements for the pleasure and profit of the teachers of the country who attend. . . . We hope we may have—we ought to have—a large attendance from every State where there are people—white people and colored people—who are working in colored schools."[159] The association arranged for reduced rail fares to meeting locations and inexpensive board and lodging, including in local homes. When the meeting convened at Hampton Institute in 1922, Tuskegee Institute in 1923, and at the Black state college in Petersburg, Virginia, in 1930, attendees were able to stay in college residence halls for a small fee. The "Proceedings" for 1923 stated that the NATCS meeting "brought educators from seventeen different states and the District of Columbia together to discuss and help solve matters as they relate to education." The NATCS president reported at the 1928 meeting in Charleston, West Virginia, that fifteen hundred teachers from nineteen states and the District of Columbia had attended the previous year's meeting in Nashville, and a group photograph of the "Twenty-Seventh Annual Session" in 1930 showed approximately two hundred men and women assembled outdoors (see figure 3).[160]

FIGURE 3 Group photo, annual meeting of the National Association of Teachers in Colored Schools, Virginia State College, Petersburg, Virginia, July 22–25, 1930. *The Bulletin* 11, no. 1 (1930): cover. Rare Book Collection, Wilson Library, The University of North Carolina at Chapel Hill.

Like teachers who attended NEA conventions, those who attended annual meetings of the NATCS gained ideas to enhance their work with students. The program for the 1919 meeting in Orangeburg, South Carolina, included a round-table on "Elementary and Rural Schools" and papers on high schools' relationship to local industry and the role of "habit" in education, and at the 1920 gathering two speakers addressed "Educational Tests and Measurements," Mrs. W. T. B. Williams of Tuskegee presented "Some Ideas for Teachers," and Commissioner Claxton discussed "Educational Problems in the United States."[161] "Conservation and Americanization through the Teaching of Geography" and "Problems and Problem Making in the Teaching of Arithmetic" were two of the addresses in 1922. The following year, principals from North Carolina spoke in the Department of High Schools on examination procedures and career education, while members of the Elementary Grade Section discussed "Developing a Cotton Project," "Games and Devices for Teaching Spelling," and a student project on George Washington. Departments that convened at the 1924 meeting in Dallas included High Schools, Elementary Schools, Vocational Education, and Professional Education.[162]

Beginning in the late 1910s, NATCS meetings also functioned as "a crucial extension of the black counterpublic sphere," according to Givens, as programs included talks on the state of Black education, Black history, and race relations, while exhibits displayed materials that would help teachers to represent Black culture in the classroom. According to historian Linda Perkins, Black teachers' status and training as well as conditions in Black schools were common topics. "Reports from the field" by school supervisors, college presidents, and Rosenwald school agents at the 1923 meeting provided a synopsis of current issues in the South's system of Black education, and a speaker began his address titled "Comparative Costs of Public Education White and Colored" at the 1930 meeting with a discussion of the "problem of inequality in educational opportunity." Professors addressed "Negro History in the Schools" and the Urban League before Claxton spoke at the 1920 meeting in Baltimore. "Those who attended the annual meeting of the Association at Hampton last July," the NATCS *Bulletin* reported in April 1923, "doubtless recall with interest the splendid collections of books, pamphlets, periodicals and music by and about Negroes. It is planned, this year, to extend the scope." And an article in *The Bulletin* marking the twenty-fifth anniversary of the founding of NATCS stated, "The question as to where the Negro history can be authentically obtained is another reason for the existence of the National Association as in this Association information can be given as to sources of references needed for the teacher whose cry is to know."[163]

Speeches at NATCS meetings by leading educators and Black intellectuals further familiarized teachers with broader, more esoteric topics related to education for African Americans and connected them with efforts on behalf of fugitive pedagogy. *The Bulletin* announced that among the "big men" who would speak in Baltimore were the deans or presidents of several Black colleges and James H. Dillard, a leader of philanthropic foundations that supported Black education. Carter Woodson of the Association for the Study of Negro Life and History also spoke at the 1920 meeting on "Changes in Education During the Past Century." In 1922, James Weldon Johnson, secretary of the National Association for the Advancement of Colored People, addressed the association, and Lucy Laney, principal of Haines Institute, spoke on "The School as a Center of Community." The following year, president of Daytona Institute Mary McLeod Bethune highlighted "the splendid growth" of Tuskegee Institute—and was elected president of the NATCS. Labor leader and civil rights activist A. Philip Randolph addressed the NATCS at the 1939 meeting in Atlantic City on schools' role in shaping relationships between employers and employees. If Mississippi's governor and state superintendent of education painted rosy pictures of segregated education when they spoke at the 1929 meeting in Jackson, Howard University President Mordecai Johnson, Dillard, and Woodson would have presented better-informed views during their turns at the podium.[164]

In Woodson's frequent appearances at NATCS meetings, Givens explains, he "urged teachers to hold themselves and their colleagues accountable for ensuring that 'Negro children study Negro history in the schools'" and emphasized that "teaching of black life and history could not be by happenstance and sporadic; it was worthy of coordinated and intentional action." Incorporating Woodson's ideas into their view of teacher professionalism, NATCS attendees collectively asserted their support for Black history and other civil rights. At the close of the 1918 meeting in Harper's Ferry, they recommended that states provide "adequate facilities for Negro education" and equal pay for Black and white teachers and commended President Woodrow Wilson "for his outspoken attitude on lynching." They passed resolutions at the 1920 meeting endorsing National Negro Health Week, supporting "better trained teachers for colored schools" and declaring "that the length of school terms for colored schools be made the same as for white schools" and "that our colored teachers be urged to introduce the systematic study of the history and literature of the Negro race in their schools, in order that our youth will acquire pride of race." Five years later at the meeting in Durham, North Carolina, a committee recommended "the increased study of Negro history" and suggested textbooks for use in elementary and high schools. Widening their focus, attendees at the 1933 meeting in Louisville collectively sent a telegram to President Franklin Roosevelt urging him to use his "power and influence . . . to prevent discrimination because of race, color, or creed."[165]

Finally, as at NEA conventions, social and cultural events at NATCS meetings fostered esprit de corps and reinforced teachers' professional and personal agency, while the smaller size of the NATCS facilitated more interaction among educators who worked at different levels in the school system. *The Bulletin*'s announcement in 1920 stated facetiously that "great teachers of the country" would "condescend to 'mix' once more with their coworkers in Baltimore," where the meeting included a boat trip on Chesapeake Bay. At Tuskegee in 1923, NATCS members enjoyed a "lawn fete." They also prayed together in the chapel and enjoyed several performances by the institute's choir. In Dallas the following year, one evening's performances included "Lift Every Voice and Sing," or the "Negro National Anthem," which the assemblage then sang together during the closing ceremony, and "entertainments" at the 1930 meeting included a pageant titled *Light*, which "depicted the progress of the Negro from his landing as a slave in America to the present time." While singing the anthem and watching the pageant would have stoked Black teachers' self-respect, convening at Howard University and touring the White House and Library of Congress as part of the 1931 meeting in Washington would have further empowered them as citizens.[166] Social gatherings and cultural events, like collective actions, exhibits, and speeches by leading Black educators and intellectuals, undoubtedly enhanced NATCS attendees' work in the classroom as well as bolstered their resolve against a racist society.

By the opening decades of the twentieth century, organizations other than the NEA and NATCS provided teachers with additional options for professional development during the summertime. Meetings such as the American Classical Conference and the Conference on Elementary Education convened in conjunction with the NEA. After meeting jointly with the NEA in 1923, the World Federation of Education Associations convened separately on a biennial basis throughout the rest of the 1920s and 1930s, in cities including Edinburgh, Toronto, Geneva, Denver, and Tokyo.[167] Throughout this period in the United States, however, the NEA summer meeting—and, for Black teachers, the NATCS annual meeting—remained in many ways the "greatest educational show on earth," at which teachers honed their vision of professionalism.

As indicated by the size and popularity of NEA and NATCS conventions, STA meetings, independent national programs, and local normal institutes, the market for teachers' professional development during the summertime had great potential. Institutions of higher education soon became aware of this market and began to establish their own programs, often touting the attractiveness of their natural settings to compete with the likes of Chautauqua. In the 1890s, advertisements for university summer sessions began to appear in education publications, and an editorial in *The Intelligence* referred to the "advantages to be gained" by merging summer institutes and freestanding programs into "the summer terms of the regular universities and normal schools."[168] The editorial was prescient, as summer normals, most national summer schools, and summer STA meetings disappeared during the early twentieth century, and the NEA's focus shifted to teacher welfare as it morphed into a union and merged with the NATCS in the mid-twentieth century. These programs were such important sources of teacher education that they inspired colleges and universities to co-opt their functions.

2

Studies at Normal School, College, and University Summer Sessions

"Invaders" in Harvard Yard

The July 7, 1933, issue of the *Boston Post* included a photo of Lillie Fortman as she prepared to attend Harvard Summer School for the twentieth successive year (figure 4). A short article explained that Fortman, "a teacher in the public schools of Jersey City, looks forward each year to coming to New England to spend six weeks in the study of advanced English literature, history or higher mathematics."[1] During her summer studies, Fortman may have resided in a residence hall in Harvard Yard, decades before this male bastion would admit women as undergraduates. A middle-aged woman studying at Harvard was certainly unusual in the early twentieth century, but her experience was far from unique.

Following in the footsteps of the local summer institutes and independent national summer schools discussed in the previous chapter, U.S. normal schools, colleges, and universities began by the 1890s to organize summer courses primarily for schoolteachers, who attended in increasing numbers as summer sessions expanded in the early twentieth century. In 1922, Columbia University, the University of California at Berkeley, and the University of Chicago had the highest summer enrollments: 12,567, 9,697, and 6,463, respectively. "The majority of the 300,000 summer-school students on the college campus are teachers," reported Dean Raymond Walters of Swarthmore College in 1926. These "invaders," he continued, "stream across the Yard at Harvard; they file from Teachers College

Her Twentieth Year at Harvard School

TWENTY YEARS A SUMMER STUDENT

Miss Lillie Fortman, Jersey City school teacher, shown as she registered for her 20th consecutive year at the Harvard summer school.

FIGURE 4 Photo of Lillie Fortman in the article "Her Twentieth Year at Harvard School," *Boston Post*, July 7, 1933. (Courtesy of the Harvard University Archives.)

to the Library at Columbia; they pour into Hutchinson and Noyes Halls at Chicago; they pause to hear the chimes of the Library Tower at Cornell; they sit on the Oak Knoll at Minnesota; in the cool of the evening they stroll along the serpentine brick walls that Thomas Jefferson built at the University of Virginia."[2] Nationwide, the number of summer school students in 1931 was more than

425,000, of which the number who enrolled in education courses was over 273,000—equal to 28.6 percent of the country's teachers.[3] Like the local and national programs that preceded them, summer sessions between the 1900s and the 1930s played a crucial, though largely unacknowledged, role in furthering teacher education and grassroots professionalization.

Historians of teachers and their education have not explored fully Fortman's and other "invaders'" yearly migrations to college campuses, and historians of higher education have written little about them.[4] Yet the spread of summer sessions served the interests of both administrators endeavoring to professionalize the teaching force and university leaders seeking to strengthen their institutions. Led by U.S. Commissioner of Education William T. Harris and Harvard President Charles W. Eliot, representatives of both groups made up the Committee of Ten appointed by the National Education Association (NEA) to consider the future of high schools. In its 1893 report outlining a vision for the secondary curriculum, the committee acknowledged that "to carry out the improvements proposed more highly trained teachers will be needed," and advocated for expanded summer sessions—"a reasonable service which the colleges and universities may render to their own communities"—as a feasible solution.[5]

School leaders on the Committee of Ten would have been pleased with the growth of summer sessions that followed the report as individual states heightened educational requirements for teacher certification. After the Iowa legislature raised requirements in 1914, the director of the University of Iowa summer school asked for more funding, writing to the university president that similar legislation had recently "meant a large increase in summer school attendance at the state institutions of Illinois and Ohio." In Pennsylvania, a 1921 state law mandating that by 1927 all public school teachers complete at least two years of post–high school coursework resulted in dramatic increases in the enrollments of the state's teachers in summer school sessions not only in Pennsylvania but as far away as the Universities of Illinois and Wisconsin; seven hundred Pennsylvania teachers attended Columbia University's Teachers College in the summer of 1921.[6] By the 1930s, historian James Fraser observes, the movement was well underway to require that all teachers hold a bachelor's degree. A 1933 survey of teacher education revealed that providing "provisions for securing the bachelor's degree" was "one of the principal functions of summer sessions." Similarly, department head E. C. Denny reported in 1935 that during the summer at Iowa State Teachers College, "many teachers who have not yet graduated from college earn credit toward the degree or complete the final work for graduation," thus satisfying administrators' expectation that they achieve higher levels of education in the interest of professionalization.[7]

The expansion of summer sessions was also beneficial to colleges and universities. To attract teachers as students—and to accrue the resulting proceeds—during months when campus would otherwise have been idle, institutions increasingly placed advertisements in education journals and distributed materials to publicize their summer sessions. An ad for the 1920 summer term at the State Normal School in San Diego, California, promised "professional improvement, cultural studies and recreation" in an "ideal" climate, and one for the 1929 summer school at Tuskegee Institute, a Black college in Alabama, was addressed "To the Ambitious Teacher Who Wants to Keep Up."[8] Private universities and public flagship institutions were especially prolific promoters. Alongside ads for 1902 summer sessions at Cornell and the Universities of Illinois, Wisconsin, and Michigan, a blurb for Valparaiso College's program touted "especial advantages to teachers." A booklet promoting Harvard's 1905 summer school likewise listed courses "designed primarily for teachers" in two dozen fields, and stated that the university's museums and recreational facilities would be available for students. During the Great Depression, the University of Denver advertised "lectures on today's social, economic, and educational problems" at its 1936 summer session. A multipage, state-by-state detailed list of hundreds of college and university summer sessions planned for the coming summer appeared every spring during the late 1920s in *The Journal of the National Education Association*. Meanwhile, throughout the 1920s and 1930s, the University of Iowa sent yearly mailings—produced with an "addressograph" machine—on summer offerings to a long list of teachers and administrators in fifteen different states. It's no wonder that *Midland Schools* in 1939 included a poem that began, "The postman is staggering wearily, / . . . His bursting brown burden drags drearily," and continued, "For catalog time is here again, / And summer school beckons once more."[9]

Promotion paid off; as historians Geraldine Clifford and James Guthrie explain, summer tuition and state support for summer teacher education were important sources of revenue for institutions, many of which struggled financially. One observer wrote in 1930 that offering summer instruction "substantially helps the university to meet the annual salary budget. When universities boast of the numbers attending their summer sessions, it is usually with one eye on the university treasury." State funding flowed primarily to public institutions, while some school districts paid teachers' summer tuition at all "recognized colleges and universities" through "special funds." A 1911 report noted that it was "only by means of" these funds that scores of teachers in Indianapolis and Pittsburgh were able to attend summer school—benefitting both the teachers and the institutions they attended.[10]

Summer sessions marketed to teachers also earned goodwill for colleges and universities through their service to public education. An observer of the Summer School of the South at the University of Tennessee in 1902 remarked that the teachers who attended would return "to their little school-houses in the towns and in the woods, to give out what they have learned and to stimulate, each in her own neighborhood, to new educational enterprise." Two decades later, Dean Walters of Swarthmore wrote that, through their summer programs, colleges and universities helped to place in "every classroom in America a well qualified, professionally trained teacher." He elaborated on this idea in his 1926 article with a description of "Miss Smith, the mild young woman who teaches your Mary in the third grade" and in the summer "delights in the atmosphere of Teachers College," where she gains "a zeal for technic as a means to an end, and a scorn for intellectual looseness and bluff. She is becoming a professional." Walters reflected, "It probably is fair to say that the most far-reaching effect of the summer school, its great social significance, lies in the betterment of the professional training of its teachers."[11]

For teachers, summer school was more than merely a means to satisfy directives from above. Some were undoubtedly motivated by the opportunity to increase their salaries, as a 1922 study found that nearly half of school districts offered bonuses or salary increases for summer study, and a 1932 study found that nearly two-thirds of districts did so while others imposed financial penalties for not attending. But, as the NEA *Journal* reported, "the tens of thousands who attended summer schools with no assurance that they will receive any additional reward" demonstrated teachers' "genuine desire to become better trained for their chosen work."[12] In keeping with their view of professionalism, teachers seized opportunities to wrestle with abstract concepts in education, to deepen their cultural knowledge, and to exercise independence—or, as teachers put it, to relish "the mental friction that results from rubbing two ideas together," to "enjoy elective courses," and to acquire "a broad outlook on life." At summer school, one teacher wrote in *Midland Schools*, "I could feel myself growing intellectually" and "my horizon had been extended."[13] Summer sessions at state normal schools/teachers colleges and Black colleges, like local summer institutes, augmented teachers' skills and deepened their understanding of more esoteric educational and cultural topics, in accord with these institutions' missions to enhance the teaching force and extend higher schooling to previously excluded students. Like freestanding national programs and meetings of education associations, summer school at private universities and state flagships broadened teachers' horizons even further as teachers asserted through their attendance that people from their humble backgrounds belonged among academic and professional elites.

State Normal Schools/Teachers Colleges

After the failure of her father's business in 1878, sixteen-year-old future union organizer Margaret Haley began her teaching career in a one-room country school near her family's Illinois home. In 1882, she was able to attend a four-week summer program conducted by the faculty at Illinois State Normal University (ISNU). According to historian Kate Rousmaniere, the opportunity to focus on her professional education was "cathartic" for Haley. Although some of her fellow teacher-students were intimidated, she was awakened intellectually by exposure to cutting-edge Herbartian approaches to teaching and by studying with progressive economist Edmund Janes James, who made compelling connections between education theory and practice. The readings he assigned "opened up to her a 'wide world' of economic restructuring for social improvement." Haley's experience was also cathartic because it involved boarding away from home for the first time and meeting teachers from throughout the state, further broadening her world and sparking her interest in farther ventures for summer studies.[14] Beginning in 1890, a program similar to ISNU's called the California School of Methods convened for three weeks each July in the normal school building in San José. The 1891 session included instruction in more than two dozen subjects, eight evening lectures, and excursions to Lick Observatory and Stanford University; teachers from fourteen different counties in California earned certificates of attendance.[15] Although neither Haley nor the California teachers received official normal school credit for their studies, this policy would soon change as these programs morphed into institutional summer sessions.

At ISNU—where President David Felmley believed that the return of active teachers made summer the most important time of the year at normal schools—the summer term became a regular, credit-bearing part of the academic program in 1900. By that time, a number of other state normal schools had also added summer sessions. "In response to the demands of teachers" who were "unable, for financial reasons, to give up their schools and attend during the regular year," Kansas State Normal School in Emporia and Iowa State Normal School in Cedar Falls first offered summer classes in select subjects during the early and the mid-1890s, respectively. Their success prompted the inauguration of a full-blown six-week summer session in 1894 at Emporia and in 1897 at Cedar Falls. More than a quarter of all state normal schools, including at least one in each of twenty-six states, offered a summer session by the late 1900s—in Texas, the school year at the State Normal School in San Marcos included a full summer session from the time of its opening in 1903–1904; and in Minnesota, a 1909 law mandated that each of the state's five normal schools offer a twelve-week summer session—and virtually all did so by the late 1910s.[16] This growth in summer offerings occurred just as state normal schools were beginning to transition into teachers colleges offering four years of college-level work and bachelor's degrees. As normal schools, these institutions provided coursework and activities that centered on their formal mission of teacher preparation while also fulfilling their unofficial mission of welcoming students from marginalized backgrounds into intellectual life and the middle class. But newly christened teachers colleges placed less emphasis on both missions as they diversified their coursework and adopted football- and Greek-oriented student life. The needs and interests of the schoolteachers who occupied these campuses during summer sessions, however, upheld distinctive normal school missions at teachers colleges into the 1930s, albeit outside the standard school year.

Like normal school students—and Margaret Haley—teachers who attended summer sessions were generally women from financially challenged, often rural, backgrounds who had limited access to higher education. Based on a study of students attending five teachers college summer sessions in the mid-1920s, Joseph Avent reported that 88 percent were women and that among students' fathers, 63 percent were farmers, 23 percent worked in industry or trade, and only 6 percent engaged in "professional service." One-third of the students had attended normal school/teachers college, and one-fifth had attended liberal-arts college/university, but only 15 percent had graduated from the former and 6 percent had a degree from the latter. Also like normal school students, those in Avent's study tended to be older than typical college students and to have teaching experience. Their median age was twenty-three and the oldest was sixty-two, while 13 percent were married or widowed and more than 30 percent supported dependents. Over three-quarters of these students had already taught, primarily in rural schools, for a median of 3.4 but as many as 38 years.[17] Regarding summer students at Iowa State Teachers College (ISTC) in Cedar Falls, the student newspaper *College Eye* reported in 1922 that they arrived from "every nook and corner of the state, from other states, from city and hamlet" and were "old and young, teachers and would be teachers, tall and short," and in 1930 that the men ranged in age from fifteen to sixty-nine and the women from sixteen to fifty-six, and that one-third of the men and 80 percent of the women had taught school.[18] While neither the *College Eye* nor Avent mentioned race, it is likely that these summer-school students, like those who attended normal schools, were primarily white, with an appreciable number hailing from minoritized ethnic or racial groups. A Black man from Kingfisher, Oklahoma, Daniel W. Lewis, earned a two-year certificate from Kansas State Normal School in 1922 and then taught in his hometown and then in Kansas City, Kansas, returning each summer to Emporia for further study. He earned a bachelor's degree there in 1928—and would undertake further graduate study at several universities and complete a master's degree.[19] Like Lewis, generations of teachers from unprivileged backgrounds pursued advanced education through normal school/teachers college summer sessions.

The persistence of these teacher-students required state teachers colleges to sustain in their summer sessions the unofficial normal school mission of welcoming students from marginalized backgrounds, and an important first step was securing state funding and other forms of support. After lobbying by the institution's president and board, the Iowa legislature appropriated funding for the summer session at Cedar Falls each year from 1900 onward, allowing for "a generous reduction in tuition," according to the student newspaper. The Illinois legislature resisted initially but followed suit in 1903, after which ISNU did not charge summer tuition. The Kansas legislature also declined the first requests for support, but by 1901 summer students at Emporia paid only a five-dollar "matriculation fee" if they were Kansas residents or a ten-dollar fee if they resided elsewhere.[20] Lobbying for state support for summer sessions at state normal schools in Pennsylvania and Maryland began with their inauguration in the 1910s, and the schools were able to offer "free tuition" while charging small registration fees by the 1920s. Meanwhile, the State Normal School in San Diego advertised "No Tuition Fees."[21]

In addition to low tuition, the publications of these institutions focused on the overall affordability of summer study. Teacher-students in the 1900s were able "to live in Emporia more cheaply and comfortably than elsewhere" and qualified for reduced railroad fares to and from summer school in Cedar Falls. Two decades later, expenses at ISTC were "most reasonable," the normal schools in Pennsylvania offered "reasonable rates for board and lodging," and the purpose of the summer session at Maryland State Normal School (MSNS) at Towson was to furnish professional training at a "very low cost." The information bulletin for the 1934 summer session at what was by then Kansas State Teachers College (KSTC) in Emporia listed "the small cost" as its first attraction, and a flyer for the 1937 summer session at KSTC acknowledged a small increase in fees but added, "the cost of attending Teachers College is still remarkably small."[22] These statements assured teachers with limited resources that they could afford to attend summer studies at normal schools/teachers colleges.

Summer sessions at these institutions also sustained into the 1930s a curricular focus on teaching methods and academic subjects relevant to teachers, contributing to the supportive atmosphere and enabling teacher-students to fill gaps in, as well as to widen and deepen, their professional and academic knowledge. Taught primarily by members of the regular faculty but also by instructors from other normal schools/teachers colleges, administrators, or high school teachers, credit-bearing summer programs included all or most of the teacher-education courses offered during the school year.[23] At Emporia in 1905, teachers who had not completed normal school or who wanted to brush up could enroll in "Child Study," "History of Education," "Philosophy of Education," "Psychology," "School Law and Management," "General Methods," "Primary Methods," or methods courses on particular subjects. In Cedar Falls, ISTC added courses for "those engaged in teaching country schools" in 1911 and courses for elementary teachers in home economics, agriculture, and manual training in 1914, when the college also began operating its training school during the summer session in order to provide opportunities for observation and practice teaching. San Diego advertised "professional studies" in "psychology—pedagogy—tests and measurements—the problem-project method—classroom methods—all illustrated by the work of the training school and special demonstration lessons" in 1920.[24]

The San Diego ad also promised professional seminars "for advanced students," reflecting the shift toward more differentiated offerings in education and higher-level summer-session courses as teachers' general level of training increased throughout this period. In 1927, MSNS added to its lineup of courses in methods and educational psychology "Measuring the Results of Teaching," in which students learned "how to make good tests . . . how to give and make use of the results of standard tests, and how to note objective evidence of growth in habits and attitude." By 1930, KSTC offered methods courses in a dozen different academic departments and more than two dozen courses in the education department, ranging from "Kindergarten Play and Games" to "High School Curriculum Problems." Various courses in history, sociology, and philosophy of education focused on more abstract concepts, while "School Finance" and "City School Administration" considered education from different angles—and perhaps paved a way out of the classroom. KSTC by 1930 also maintained a "graduate division . . . for students who desire to work for the degree Master of Science in Education" during the summer. And by 1932, eleven of Pennsylvania's teachers colleges added to their summer "courses for the preparation of elementary and secondary teachers" one or more "special curricula" in music, art education, commercial instruction, health education, home economics, industrial arts, kindergarten, and/or library science. Edinboro State Teachers College added art education while Mansfield added both music and home economics. Slippery Rock State Teachers College offered instruction in health education as part of its Nature Study and Health Education Camp, established three miles from campus in 1925.[25]

When retired Pennsylvania teachers reflected on conducting small country schools early in their careers, they described how most of their training took place in summer sessions at the state's normal schools. Tressa H. Jones began teaching after taking a crash course with her high school principal and earning a provisional certificate in 1913, when she was eighteen years old. Jones spent four summers in the mid- to late 1910s at Clarion State Normal School, where her studies enabled her to earn a permanent certificate. During these years, she taught in a one-room school with forty-five pupils in "all grades." It was hard work, but, perhaps due to her summer training, she wrote that she "did accomplish more than I expected." Evelyn Genberg enrolled in Clarion's summer session after her high school graduation in 1924 and, with a provisional certificate, commenced teaching the following fall. When she returned to Clarion in the summers of 1925 and 1926, Genberg "chose the courses which I knew from my teaching experience would help me most. The good old course, 'School Efficiency,' helped me a great deal." Anna Fetterolf followed a similar path, enrolling at East Stroudsburg in 1926 after her first year of teaching and attending other Pennsylvania normal-schools-turned-teachers-colleges during subsequent summers. "I believe going to school each Summer and then putting into practice what was taught as I went back to the classroom each Fall was the most valuable experience," she wrote. "When discussing the problems of children in psychology, when examining textbooks for evaluation, learning the difference between purposeful activity and 'busy work'—all were situations already experienced, and gave me an opportunity to understand and use them. . . . How enlightening those Summer classes were and how appreciative the instructors were to have students who had teaching experience and were eager to learn and improve!"[26]

On the other side of the country, California teacher Grace Canon Pogue made good use of summer school to extend her understanding of teaching methods. Having taught for four years before marrying in 1910 and becoming a mother in 1916, Pogue returned to teaching in 1923 when her superintendent requested that she take charge of a small school on Ash Spring Mountain. For three years, she and her son spent school terms at Ash Spring and vacations with her husband at their ranch near Woodlake in the San Joaquin Valley. Then, the opportunity to teach at the local school in Woodlake propelled Pogue to enroll in her first of what would be many summer sessions at California state teachers colleges. She later wrote in her memoir that the 1926 summer course on Americanization was "helpful" preparation for "the most interesting work" of her career. Pogue attended another summer session in 1928, and, after the death of her husband in 1932, she headed to San Francisco State Teachers College for the summer of 1933, establishing a pattern of attending a summer session "every three years, in order to keep abreast of educational trends." At San Francisco, she appreciated Dr. Gifford's "practical" instruction in "teaching children who have speech difficulties," and, at San José in 1936, she "loved the story-book campus" and found that "President MacQuarrie was an inspiration and the esprit de corps of the whole school was wonderful." After attending Fresno State Teachers College in 1942—when she was in her mid-fifties—Pogue reflected, "Miss Brewster's curriculum class and Miss Hamilton's reading course tipped the scales favorably and made me glad I was there." White Plains, New York, teacher Beatrice Cramer assessed her classes during the summers of 1936 and 1937 at the New York State Teachers College (NYSTC) in Albany similarly. After three courses in school guidance in 1936, she felt "properly 'guided,'" and her courses in adolescent psychology, philosophy of education, and mental hygiene the following summer were beneficial "even though we all 'fussed' about the assignments."[27]

In addition to enhancing their professional skills and knowledge, summer courses enabled teachers to fill gaps in their understanding of subjects they taught or, increasingly, to stretch themselves further intellectually. The 1897 summer offerings at Cedar Falls included English, political economy, Latin, French, mathematics, physics, natural history, and more, and the 1905 program at Emporia similarly included a wide range of subjects such as English literature, "History and Law," Latin, algebra, chemistry, and physics. The ad for the 1920 San Diego summer session promised "Cultural Studies" in "history, literature, sociology, geography, Spanish, etc.," and a blurb on offerings at San Francisco State Teachers College in 1923 listed many science courses—including chemistry, physics, astronomy, geology, biology, physiology, bacteriology, nature study, and psychology—as well as math, the social sciences, literature, and philosophy. KSTC's 1930 summer session offered over two hundred courses in twenty departments in addition to Education. History courses ranged from "History of England and British Empire from 1603" to "American History Since 1876," and offerings in physics included "Mechanics, Sound, and Heat" and "Light, Magnetism, and

Electricity." The emphasis on science and math encouraged women students to stretch not only their knowledge but gender boundaries as well. In keeping with the proliferation of noneducation courses, the bulletin announcing KSTC's 1932 summer session noted that students could work toward a Bachelor of Arts degree or the customary BS in Education.[28]

Ruby Dresselhouse was a young teacher in a country school in southeastern Michigan when a supervisor informed her in 1928 that she would have to take an extension course and attend summer school in order to qualify to teach again the following year. In response, Dresselhouse enrolled in spring and summer extension courses and headed to Ypsilanti for the summer session at Michigan State Normal College. From late June through early August, she lived on campus during the week and attended daily classes in math, English, and music. Outside of class, Dresselhouse studied a lot, including during her weekends at home. When her music class did not meet on July 3, she noted in her diary that she "studied instead" before traveling home to celebrate Independence Day. On July 9, she went to math class and music class, heard a piano "lecture recital," and then "studied as usual." Dresselhouse noted on July 18 that she had taken "a good hard test in Music" and on July 19 that she had taken a math test, "got A- on English test," and "had to sing a song in Music."[29] Dresselhouse's summer studies filled gaps in her knowledge of math, English, and music, surely enhancing her teaching in the country school.

While Dresselhouse stuck to basic subjects, Cramer challenged herself by taking a world history course alongside her education courses at NYSTC in 1937. She wrote, "Whew! What a summer! The weather was not only sweltering; the courses were super-sweltering! Tried to crowd all that had ever happened in Russia, Germany, Italy, Great Britain, France, Denmark, China, Japan and Mexico into 'six weeks.' By the time I began readings on Russia's educational system, the class . . . was working on Germany's social development. When I began working on Germany, the class was ready to discuss Italy's past, present, and future political developments." She also remarked that she "enjoyed the course very much." Pogue, who had dreamed of attending Stanford University, also studied liberal arts subjects along with education. At Fresno in 1942, she found a modern poetry course with Paul Haines, a visiting professor from Boston, "most amazing." "My 5000 word criticism at the end of the six weeks," she wrote, "was only a small part of what I said to Paul Haines and a smaller fraction of what I thought of the modern trend." At San Jose three years earlier, Pogue relished the opportunity to audit academic classes in addition to those she took for credit. She "went up and downstairs from 7:30 in the morning until mid-afternoon drinking in usable information"—and worked so hard that she had to be admitted to the hospital.[30]

Dresselhouse, Cramer, and Pogue were not the only teachers who took their summer studies at teachers colleges very seriously. At Cedar Falls, the campus paper remarked in 1897 on the "unusual quietness on Normal Hill" and reported that the 1898 summer session attracted "an intensely earnest lot of students" for whom "studying was the principal occupation." "All were on the jump every minute," stated the *College Eye* in 1920, as a "great many of the students had been out teaching during the past year and had a chance to see the value of lots of knowledge." During a stretch of hot weather the following summer, the "reading room of the library was very warm especially when it was full of students as it was most of the time." The library evidently was more popular than the YMCA's recreational space; a 1933 article titled "Summer School Students Are More Studious Than Regulars" quoted the manager of the YMCA "rooms" as likening their atmosphere in the summer to that of a funeral parlor. Two years later, "In Summer School, Life Is Just A Bowl of 'A' Students" explained that the presence of schoolteachers "who believe that life is real and life is earnest" raised academic standards, forcing "the year-round student" to work harder in summer courses. In the same vein, a survey of ISTC faculty in 1937 revealed a common belief that summer students were "better." One professor said, "I get much better results from those who have taught. I enjoy the more mature group." Another added, "The summer school people come to learn. They have a more scholarly approach." While one instructor remarked that teacher-students lacked creativity, another emphasized that they "are eager for materials and more alert. They ask for more than is given." Finally, the *College Eye* reported in 1939 on a year-round student's observations that summer-school students "responded more in class, that there were more students in the library . . . and that they were not so noisy in the dormitory after quiet hours."[31]

Teacher-students did pull themselves away from their books, however, for lectures on education and academic topics, cultural events, and recreation with other teachers. All-campus education lectures engaged teachers in wider issues and bolstered the teaching-focused ambience of summer sessions. At Cedar Falls, "four members of the regular faculty" presented "evening lectures" in 1900, and President Homer Seerley spoke on "Rural School Problems" in 1911. At KSTC in 1926, the director of teacher training presented a "series of informal lectures" on "methods to improve teaching in the intermediate grades," and a math professor discussed his research on elementary math instruction. Both outgoing Iowa superintendent Henry Sabin and his replacement, Richard C. Barrett, appeared on the rostrum at Cedar Falls in 1898, and Sabin returned the following summer to present a series of lectures on "educational problems and practice." Ruby Dresselhouse heard Michigan superintendent Webster Pearce speak at Ypsilanti in 1928. She also mentioned other talks and "illustrated" lectures in her diary but did not elaborate on their content.[32]

Normal school/teachers college summer sessions also occasionally featured speakers from farther afield, encouraging teachers to consider education beyond their states' borders. *Journal of Education* editor E. A. Winship of Boston and the presidents of both Northern Illinois and Northern Alabama state normal schools were among the speakers at Cedar Falls in 1900, and the school superintendents of the city of Milwaukee and the state of Pennsylvania were among the "noted educational lecturers" there in 1912. Berkeley, California, Superintendent H. B. Wilson, Johns Hopkins University psychiatric researcher Ester Richards, and Columbia University Professor J. Montgomery Gambrill were visiting lecturers at MSNS in Towson in 1924, 1925, and 1926, respectively. In 1927, MSNS welcomed Professors Mable Carney and Fannie Dunn of Columbia, as well as Superintendent Edwin Broome of Montgomery County, Maryland, all of whom spoke on issues in rural education. Along with local KSTC lecturers, speakers at Emporia included child psychology professor John Douglas of Northwestern University in 1930 and commerce professor Ann Brewington of the University of Chicago, who in 1931 reprised the talk she had presented to the NEA on financial education in elementary and secondary schools. Brewington, Dunn, Carney, Richards, and other speakers who were women would have also served as examples of women shaping education. Meanwhile, the *Pennsylvania School Journal* announced that the state's teachers colleges' summer sessions in 1931 would feature "nation-wide lecturers" and "talking films" of "leaders in the field of education," which would enable "teachers enrolling in these summer courses . . . to hear for the first time outside of the classroom master teachers from all parts of the United States."[33]

While lectures and even films on education immersed summer-session students in the field, talks on other academic and cultural topics, performances in the arts, and organized activities engaged them in the intellectual and cultural life primarily of the white middle class. Leaders in education occasionally spoke on other subjects, demonstrating their scholarly acuity. One of Sabin's addresses at Cedar Falls was on historical figure Aaron Burr, and Gambill spoke at Towson on "Our Changing World and Its Civic Problems."[34] Other lecturers' topics further widened teacher-students' horizons and perhaps challenged some of their assumptions. "Illustrated lectures" at ISTC included "The African Hunt" in 1912 by a field naturalist who had accompanied Theodore Roosevelt on safari, and, in 1925, "Chinese Life" by a professor who had just returned from a year in that country and "Other Worlds than Ours" by a noted astronomer from the University of Chicago. Before Chief Red Fox of the Sioux Nation appeared on the lecture stage in 1925, the *College Eye* reported that he would "put on a program of dances, songs, and historical Indian stories that promises to be of unusual interest. . . . Here is a man who can tell of early America from a native standpoint. He is a true Indian interested in the welfare of the Indian of today."[35] Avent reported that the median number of "extra-class lectures" per institution in the mid-1920s was 15.5, and KSTC surpassed that total. In 1926 at KSTC, "foreign talent" included Professor H. H. Newman of University of Chicago, who presented "four lectures on various phases of eugenics and biology"; Professor C. A. Elwood of the University of Missouri, who delivered four talks on anthropology and sociology; and Professor Rollo Walter Brown of Harvard, who presented three lectures on "The Creative Spirit in America." Local speakers included

English faculty members on books and authors, and social science instructors on "different economic and social subjects of current interest."[36]

Performance venues were busy during these summer sessions, as plays and concerts provided further opportunities to acquire middle-class cultural capital. Dramatic performers included campus groups—such as the academic year students at ISTC who in 1911 staged a repeat performance of their commencement play *School for Scandal*, and the Gibson Players at KSTC, who staged *The Old Soak* and *The Merchant of Venice* in 1930—and, increasingly, touring professional troupes. The International Operatic Company presented scenes in costume from well-known operas at ISTC in 1912, and the Chicago Art Theater Group presented plays at KSTC in 1930 and again in 1932. Three dramatic companies—Coburn, Cotter-Miller, and Devereux—appeared on stage at so many institutions that Avent included them on his list of "literary and cultural opportunities" at summer sessions. ISTC's *College Eye* reported in June 1925, "Next week Wednesday and Thursday, the old favorites, Clifford Devereux and New York Company, will appear in the auditorium in three plays." And before Cotter-Miller appeared in 1938, the paper explained that the "duo-dramatists" were "well-known because of their performances throughout colleges and universities. . . . Their skits, written by themselves, are taken from scenes in history; their costumes are done by Chicago costumers."[37]

Touring and local musicians also entertained summer school audiences. In 1925 alone, students at ISTC were able to hear the famed piano duet of Philip Manuel and Gavin Williamson, the Vassar College organist, and a joint recital of a Swedish contralto and an American baritone as well as multiple performances of the Cedar Falls Concert Band. The Aita Trio featuring Italian tenor Enzo Aita and the Russian Cossack Chorus performed at KSTC in 1930 and 1932, respectively, along with the student group The Madrigalians and other students and faculty members who presented "Twilight Musicals."[38] When she was not studying, Dresselhouse attended several recitals and concerts at Ypsilanti in 1928. In the auditorium on July 10, she "heard a concert by 4 negroes from Alabama" and noted that they were from Tuskegee Institute and were "very good." Two days later, she enjoyed a concert by pianist Grace Emery and violinist Emily Mutter, who, she remarked, was "simply wonderful." And on July 25, she saw the Rockford Players' performance of *The Vikings*, accompanied by a "color organ," which was also "wonderful."[39] These experiences would have not only complemented Dresselhouse's music class but also increased her sophistication as a patron of the arts.

Summer inhabitants of normal schools/teachers colleges were not just passive observers of others' performances. After noting in 1898 that studying was the "principal occupation" of summer students, the Cedar Falls paper also reported, "Bugology, plantology, surveying, fruit gathering, and tennis courting drew many from the library of books into the larger library of nature, but perhaps the most interesting as well as instructive of pastimes was the weekly meetings of the Panthugalarian literary society." Avent's list of "organized group activities for students" in the mid-1920s included literary societies, a variety of academic clubs, publications, band, and chorus, while bulletins announcing the summer sessions at MSNS mentioned "opportunities for community singing" and urged students to bring their musical instruments so that they could "develop both a glee club and an orchestra during the six weeks." By 1926, ISTC summer students formed five "glee clubs": the Euterpeans, Cicilians, and Bel Cantos were all women, whereas the Minnesingers and Troubadours were all men. Meanwhile, students at KSTC participated in "community sings" and formed a band and symphony orchestra. Summer students at MSNS in the late 1920s went on "excursions" to Gettysburg, Richmond, and the Baltimore Harbor, and at ISTC in 1930 organized a "stunt night" in which twenty groups of students from different regions in Iowa prepared and performed skits.[40]

Other activities were athletic and/or more social in nature, further belying the *College Eye*'s suggestion that campus was overly quiet during the summer. At the turn of the century, Emporia catalogs stated, "Boating, bathing, fishing, wheeling, open air evening band concerts, and driving, added to golf and tennis on the Normal campus, give sufficient variety of exercise and amusement." Avent listed ten different "athletic activities," and men at ISTC in 1925 organized intramural baseball, track and field, and a tennis tournament; by 1934, ISTC offered "a program of men's and women's intramural sports." Providing both exercise and camaraderie, "the Y. W. hikes have been very successful so far this year," reported the *College Eye* in June 1925. "There were forty girls who went the first Saturday morning, and thirty-five last Saturday, despite the rainy weather. . . . There is a spirit of sociability and friendliness among the groups that makes every one feel at home." The all-campus picnics that were common throughout these decades and the dances that became popular in the 1920s were, as the *College Eye* explained, another "great chance to get acquainted." During her first week at Ypsilanti, Dresselhouse wrote in her diary, "Went to Campus Mixer in Gymnasium. Had some time." As her social circle expanded, she often noted who her companions were at various meals.[41]

Considering teachers' lower-class backgrounds, Avent viewed their social and cultural activities in summer school as important vehicles for establishing a "common culture," or adherence to middle-class norms. "Dormitory life," he added, "presents certain opportunities for training in conventionalities and cultural customs of home and school."[42] Teachers who attended teachers college summer sessions undoubtedly did enhance their class cachet, but doing so in the normal school milieu with other teachers enabled them to incorporate it as an aspect of grassroots professionalism. Dresselhouse's diary entries on her dinner companions and social adventures as well as her academic progress and the concerts she enjoyed reflected her deepening understanding of the many facets of her identity as a teacher. When Grace Pogue wrote that she and her apartment mates in San Francisco had a "wonderful time" and Beatrice Cramer wrote that she "met several fine girls" in the residence hall in Albany "and had some fun in spite of the general pouring in of work and more work," they indicated that they found enjoyment in sharing their summer school experiences with others.[43] By engaging deeply in their classes, in lectures on education and academic topics, in cultural events, and in campus social life, teachers who attended normal school/teachers college summer sessions expanded their own intellectual and professional horizons.

Black Colleges and Universities

"Once upon a time I taught school in the hills of Tennessee. . . . I was a Fisk student then," wrote W. E. B. Du Bois in *The Souls of Black Folk*. Like many of his Fisk University classmates, in the mid- to late 1880s, Du Bois spent the summer teaching in a country school in order to support his studies during the rest of the year. As historian Michael Fultz explains, many rural public schools for Black students in the South continued through the 1890s to convene during the summer months rather than in the spring or fall so that their pupils were available to help with plantings and harvests. In a crude log hut, Du Bois met young students with "eyes full of expectation," and they "read and spelled together, wrote a little, picked flowers, sang, and listened to stories of the world beyond the hill." Du Bois also wrote that Black colleges and protocolleges shared a mission of "giving teachers and leaders the best practicable training; and above all, to furnish the black world with adequate standards of human culture and lofty ideals of life."[44] While Du Bois's summer teaching supported this mission by both funding his own education and helping to spread knowledge and culture to remote areas, teacher preparation was crucial to the mission and thus a central function of Black institutions from their founding until well into the twentieth century. Only some Black colleges included "Normal" in their name, but all prepared teachers for Black schools with the goal of race uplift.[45] Like primarily white state normal schools, the campuses that Du Bois and other students vacated for stints as rural teachers increasingly hosted summer programs for practicing teachers, and these programs grew in the early twentieth century into full-fledged summer sessions.

Some of the local summer institutes described in chapter 1 met on the campuses of Black colleges. State-controlled Alabama State Normal School for Colored Students (ASNSCS) in Montgomery hosted a ten-week institute in 1890 at which President William Burns Paterson, who was white, presented lectures "on education and the importance of moral training" to the seventy-five Black teachers who attended. At this and later institutes—which drew teachers mainly from the region surrounding Montgomery—Paterson likely emphasized the liberal arts over industrial training, as he did during the regular school year.[46] Hampton Institute in Virginia held a yearly summer "school of methods" by the late 1890s that drew Black teachers from more than a dozen states. Like national institutes primarily for white teachers, the approach at Hampton to academic subjects, methods, and new developments in education had, in the words of *The Southern Workman*, "broadening influences." The 316 who attended in 1899 mixed with educators from a variety of schools and studied with faculty from Hampton as well as the Washington, D.C., public schools and Cook County Normal School in Chicago. A professor from Stanford University conducted Saturday roundtable discussions of methods, textbooks, citizenship, and school discipline; and lectures by a child-study researcher generated a great deal of enthusiasm. *The Southern Workman* also reported that "history was made attractive by Miss Maria L. Baldwin, the successful and well-known colored principal of the Agassiz School in Cambridge," and that attendees left with an "increased knowledge of race problems." Baldwin—who at home in Massachusetts hosted literary gatherings for Black Harvard students and joined with other Black professionals, including Du Bois, to denounce racial violence and advocate for civil rights—undoubtedly helped to foster this knowledge of race issues.[47]

As the summer programs at Black colleges transformed into credit-bearing summer sessions, they expanded opportunities for Black teachers to "broaden their scholarship and increase their efficiency as teachers," as stated in mid-1900s summer session catalogs for the Lincoln Institute in Jefferson City, Missouri. Established by formerly enslaved people, Lincoln opened in 1868, began receiving state support for normal instruction in 1879, became the state's Black land-grant institution in 1891, and began to offer a yearly summer session of seven weeks in 1902. Lincoln's summer enrollments totaled sixty or more before trailing off in the early 1910s; then, after a six-year hiatus, summer sessions resumed in 1919 with enrollments of over 100 by the late 1920s and over 150 in the 1930s—by which time the institution was called Lincoln University.[48] Meanwhile, ASNSCS inaugurated a credit-bearing summer session in 1914 that enrolled 748 in 1924 and over 900 in 1925; these teacher-students hailed from more than three-quarters of the counties in the state. Also in Alabama, the summer school at Tuskegee Institute began in 1910 and enrolled eight hundred teachers from as many as fourteen different states in its ten-week session by the mid-1920s. Tuskegee, ASNSCS, Lincoln, and many other Black colleges had by this time instituted a quarter system, incorporating the summer session into what a 1920 advertisement for Fisk referred to as "an all-year college." "The summer school . . . has made a special contribution to the improvement of Negro teachers in service," reported Black U.S. Office of Education officer Ambrose Caliver in 1933. "Most of the work done toward graduate degrees by Negro teachers has been done during the summers."[49] Black colleges' summer sessions remained focused on teacher education—and often incorporated Black history and culture—in service to the institutions' larger goals of increasing Black people's access to higher learning and strengthening teaching at all levels for Black students. Through this important summer work, Black teachers enhanced their professional skills, academic knowledge, and cultural understanding not only to meet state certification requirements but, often, to shape a professional approach to teaching grounded in what historian Jarvis Givens calls "fugitive pedagogy."[50]

Meeting the institutions' goals and teachers' needs required Black colleges, like state normal schools, to secure financial support and offer assurances that summer sessions were affordable. Northern philanthropies including the John F. Slater Fund and the General Education Board (GEB) focused on Black summer schools from the 1900s into the 1930s. GEB funding reached its highest point in 1922, when it supported ninety-four different summer schools in thirteen states.[51] State appropriations also enabled ASNSCS and Lincoln to keep costs down for summer students. After the Missouri legislature began in 1905 to provide appropriations for the summer school, Lincoln catalogs stated, "Tuition is free." Catalogs also listed low costs for room and board as well as a small "incidental fee" by the mid-1920s. Even then, as Lincoln history professor William Savage stated in his 1939 history of the university, "the expense of [attending] the summer school was very small." Also emphasizing affordability, a 1929 advertisement for the Morehouse-Spelman Summer School in Atlanta listed "Reduced Railroad Rates" along with "Strong Experienced Faculty" and a "Wide Range of Courses in Education."[52]

The wide range of courses extended far beyond methods of manual and industrial education, which, Fultz points out, were the main target of philanthropic support. Knoxville College, a Black institution in Tennessee, in the early 1900s offered manual training and basketmaking but also American history, chemistry, physiology, and other academic subjects. Lincoln catalogs listed courses in manual training and basketry in the 1900s, manual training and agriculture in the 1920s, and manual training and home economics in the 1930s; but they also included increasing numbers of courses in other aspects of the education field as well as in literature, history, math, science, and the social sciences. A 1921 bulletin invited teachers to come to Lincoln during the summer "for good standard courses in education—for a school that maintains high standards throughout—for an atmosphere of culture and refinement—for all that is best in the making of manhood and womanhood."[53] The 1920 Fisk ad that boasted "an all-year college" listed summer-quarter courses in manual arts, home economics, and school gardening as well as education, school administration, economics, languages, business, history, sociology, and "sciences." Similarly, an ad for Tuskegee's 1923 summer session touted "splendid opportunities to teachers to carry courses in" not only "Agriculture, Mechanical Training and Rosenwald Schools" but also "Academic Subjects" and "Professional Subjects."[54] In the education and academic courses that overshadowed manual training, Black teachers were able to acquire requisite knowledge for fugitive pedagogy.

Like the Tuskegee ad for "the ambitious teacher who wants to keep up," Lincoln's *Summer School Bulletin* targeted teachers "who wish to keep growing" in the 1920s and "who desire to keep abreast of the best and most recent methods in education and community uplift" in the 1930s. Commensurately, summer offerings in the field of education increasingly differentiated and incorporated advanced knowledge that would strengthen teacher autonomy. By the mid-1920s, the Lincoln *Bulletin* listed more than a dozen education courses including primary and high school English methods, educational psychology, history of education, and educational measurement; "School Administration" utilized Elwood Cubberley's well-known text, *Public School Administration*. In the 1934 *Bulletin*, the description of "Elementary School Organization and Management" stated that the course aimed to provide teachers "with a review of some of the major researches in the field" and to introduce "knowledge of the organization, curriculum, support and control of school systems and understanding of the social and political principles of education." Lincoln's summer faculty included members of the regular faculty, a few of whom had master's or even doctoral degrees from universities including Harvard, Columbia, and Chicago, and "a number of eminent educators from other institutions," such as Sherman Scruggs, PhD, supervisor of Negro Elementary Schools in Kansas City, Kansas, in 1936.[55]

Several of Scruggs's summer colleagues held undergraduate degrees from Black institutions including Virginia State College, Lincoln University in Pennsylvania, Howard, and Fisk—where the summer offerings in education expanded by the late 1920s to include methods in art, music, math, secondary English, and physics as well as educational psychology, "Educational Tests and Measurements," and "Administration and Supervision of Teaching."[56] When Septima Poinsette's parents could not afford to fulfill their desire to send her to Fisk in 1916, she commenced a forty-year teaching career in her native South Carolina. By the late 1930s—when she a widow with a son who resided mainly with his grandmother—Septima Clark was teaching in Columbia, South Carolina, and taking summer and extension courses. "Curriculum was the big word" then, she remembered, so she headed to Atlanta University for the summer of 1937 to study "curriculum building and rural sociology" and interpersonal relationships with Professor W. E. B. Du Bois. Inspired by her work at Atlanta, she continued summer and extension studies in Columbia, earning a bachelor's degree from Benedict College in 1942. Clark went on to earn a master's degree at Hampton University during the summers of 1944, 1945, and 1946. Although her Hampton experience was "too strenuous—literally all work and no play," her summer studies must have helped to empower Clark to deepen her involvement in education and community advancement in Columbia and, beginning in 1947, in Charleston through organizations including the National Association for the Advancement of Colored People, for which she was fired from her teaching position in 1956. Clark's studies must also have provided inspiration for her to enact overtly the ideals of fugitive pedagogy during summers at Highlander Folk School in 1954 and 1955 and, after her firing, year-round involvement with Highlander and the Civil Rights Movement.[57]

Although she did not mention them in her memoir, Clark's summer studies likely also included academic subjects that were proliferating in Black summer sessions during this period. A Tuskegee administrator noted in 1929 that summer sessions at "leading colored schools and colleges" offered "an astonishingly wide range of professional and general cultural subjects." Through pursuing "degrees undergraduate and advanced," teachers extended themselves intellectually and, in some cases, learned about Black culture. Savage reported that at Lincoln's first summer session, the "subjects offered were English, civics, geometry, algebra, arithmetic, physiology, physics, and Latin," and that attending teachers showed "unusual enthusiasm and interest." History soon joined the list, and catalogs in the mid- and late 1900s specified "all work in science must be done by the laboratory method; all work in literature and history by the source, or library method." Beginning in 1919, summer students at Lincoln could work toward a bachelor's of arts or science (or a "BPh" degree indicating completion of the normal course), and the 1920 Fisk ad stated, "Most courses entitle you to regular college credit."[58] Lincoln's summer bulletins by the 1920s listed a wide range of liberal arts courses. In 1926, "English Literature" covered "from Chaucer to Browning"; "The Westward Movement" emphasized "Missouri's place in the growth of the West"; "French II" took up where "French I" left off; "Principles of Sociology" treated "social concepts" and provided "practice in reasoning about society"; "College Algebra" focused on "linear equations determinants and quadratic equation[s]"; and two physics courses provided instruction in mechanics, sound, light, heat, and electricity. Fisk in 1929 included subjects from "Art Appreciation" to philosophy to both "Invertebrate Zoology" and "Vertebrate Zoology"; and Lincoln's offerings expanded by 1936 to also include "Contemporary Thought and Literature of France," inorganic chemistry, differential calculus, Shakespeare, and "Current Social Problems."[59] In such courses, teacher-students gained knowledge of prestigious subjects in a setting supportive of Black achievement.

The Black-college setting and student body may have inspired professors to incorporate discussions of Black experiences and race issues. At Morehouse-Spelman in 1929, Professor Frederick Detweiler of Denison University taught sociology; having authored *The Negro Press in the United States*, he likely paid attention to civil rights and race. The course description for "Current Social Problems" at Lincoln mentioned "minority groups, poverty, [and] unemployment," and other titles and descriptions left no doubt that summer courses helped to build a foundation for fugitive pedagogy. Among the liberal arts courses that Lincoln offered in 1926 were "Negro Literature"—"a comprehensive survey of Negro authors and their contributions to the world of literature"—and "Negro History"—"a survey of the influence of the [N]egro on the history of the United States from 1619 to the present." Six years later, "History of the Negro in America" aimed "to show the influence of the Negro in the history of the United States, first as a slave and later as a freeman"; and in 1934, "The Negro in American Literature" focused on "prose and poetry written by and about American Negros," with an emphasis "on recent authors." Summer offerings at Lincoln in the late

1930s included Professor Lorenzo Green's courses "The Negro in Africa"—which emphasized "the interplay of the Negro upon the peoples of the world and their contributions to the general stream of civilization"—and "The Negro in America"—which endeavored "to integrate the Negro into the stream of modern world history." Greene had been mentored by Carter Woodson, the director of the Association for the Study of Negro Life and History, with whom he corresponded from Jefferson City to request materials on Black history for his students.[60] Courses like Greene's equipped Black teachers to infuse elements of Black culture into their classroom instruction.

Like teacher-students at predominantly white normal schools/teachers colleges, summer students at Black colleges also extended their learning and enjoyed themselves at lectures and cultural events. Education was a common lecture topic. Lincoln catalogs promised in the 1900s, "Lectures will be given from time to time by President B. F. Allen, and by others who are eminently qualified to speak on Pedagogical and Literary subjects," and in the 1920s and 1930s that "several leading scholars from neighboring points" or "lecturers of note and members of the faculty," respectively, "will deliver lectures" on education and other topics "of special interest to the summer students."[61] Knoxville College capitalized on the presence of the Summer School of the South across town and invited scholars who were scheduled to speak there to make an additional stop. Visiting lecturers at this Black summer school in 1903 included George Washington Carver, who presumably spoke on agricultural science, and Du Bois, who presented a series of six lectures on the "history of education of the American negro." At ASNSCS in 1920, Alabama State Department of Education officer and future president of ASNSCS George Trenholm presented a lecture on physical education and teacher training, and two faculty members spoke on anti-illiteracy work in the state. Four years later, a federal education agent urged teacher-students at ASNSCS "to study vocation and agricultural training as outlined in the Smith-Hughes Act and to seek to connect the schoolroom with the farm and workshops," and another speaker discussed "the sociological problems of teachers." While these lecturers at ASNCSC did not necessarily address race issues directly, Afro-Latino scholar Arturo Schomburg did when he presented his vision of "a course of study in Negro History and achievements" to inspire "racial identity, racial preservation and racial unity," in a lecture advocating for Black history as a discipline during the 1913 summer session at Cheyney Institute, a Black college in Pennsylvania.[62]

Other lectures and activities enriched summer students' stores of the cultural capital that marked high status in white society as well as helped them to establish Black cultural capital. At Lincoln, Allen spoke on "True Refinement" in 1903, and the literary society named for him soon began meeting on Saturday evenings during the summer session, providing each student "an opportunity to debate, to read a paper, to sing or to perform on some musical instrument." While the Allen Literary Society did not appear in Lincoln *Bulletins* during the 1920s and 1930s, the announcements did list lectures covering "a wide field, including science, art, literature, health, education, and religion" and "a number of concerts" and even "moving picture shows." Meanwhile, summer students at Howard went on excursions to John Brown's Fort in Harper's Ferry, the Gettysburg battlefield, and Cedar Hill, the historic home of Frederick Douglass.[63] Before joining the faculty at Lincoln, Greene visited the 1930 summer session at ASNSCS—now Teachers College—as a representative of the Association for the Study of Negro Life and History. Greene lectured and disseminated educational materials on Black history, noting in his diary, "Speak in classes. . . . Sell books in hall." Along with classroom studies, cultural activities and lectures at Black colleges' summer sessions helped teacher-students to blend "the 'best practices from schools of education and the best thinking of the black intellectual elite on issues related to black advancement,'" as Givens explains.[64]

When they weren't acquiring cultural capital through classes and activities, summer school students were able to build social capital with other Black educators through recreation and social events. At Lincoln, they visited the nearby state capitol building and grounds, were welcome in local churches, and enjoyed all-campus picnics. "Definite arrangements are made for social meetings of students; in this way, opportunity is offered for cultivating new friends," stated *Bulletins* in the 1920s, which also encouraged students to play tennis and croquet. "There are well-furnished recreation rooms in each of the dormitories," added *Bulletins* in the 1930s. "Other items on the recreation program include golf, tennis, baseball, hikes, picnics . . . and many social entertainments all of which foster a spirit of comradeship."[65] This spirit of comradeship was professional as well as social; as teachers engaged in social life, cultural activities, and their studies at Black-college summer sessions, they were able to hone their use of fugitive pedagogy in the execution of their professional duties.

Private Universities and Public Flagship Institutions

After Margaret Haley attended the 1896 NEA meeting in Buffalo (and before she attended the Catholic summer institutes discussed in chapter 1), she stayed on for the two-week Summer Institute for Teachers at the University of Buffalo's School of Pedagogy. Established the previous year with the intention of replicating Columbia University's Teachers College, the school capitalized on the presence of the NEA convention to attract both teacher-students and visiting faculty to the summer session. Haley—now thirty-four years old and having recently moved out of her family home—relished the opportunity to further expand her horizons. At the summer school, she was able to learn from School of Pedagogy Dean Frank McMurry and Columbia professor and advisor to the school's trustees Nicholas Murray Butler. But it was visiting scholar William James who made the biggest impression on Haley at the school. While Butler held forth as if sharing "the opinions of God," she explained, the Harvard

University philosopher "was the indicating numeral which determined the value of the school. . . . James was a mighty wind whirling through dark corridors, clearing out cluttered corners of the mind. . . . Because of him I came away from Buffalo thrilled with pride of my profession." Haley did not earn university credit, and the School of Pedagogy closed within a few years.[66] But its star-studded 1896 session was one of several short-lived university-connected summer programs aimed primarily at teachers that paved the way for credit-bearing summer sessions by the turn of the twentieth century.

As early as 1871 and 1873, Harvard Professors Asa Gray and Louis Agassiz offered summer programs primarily for science teachers in botany and in natural history and zoology, respectively. Other independent efforts by Harvard faculty soon led to a proliferation of summer programs that were also loosely affiliated with the institution. According to a report on the 1876 courses in chemistry, botany, and geology, a "good proportion" of the students who enrolled were "teachers who already occupy good positions." As Harvard programs continued in the 1880s, the University of Pennsylvania (UPenn) experimented with a four-week summer session, and the University of Wisconsin (UWis) offered "review courses for teachers," primarily in science. Although taught by UWis professors, the courses had only tenuous ties to the larger institution and did not grant university credit.[67] Meanwhile, as explained in the previous chapter, many university faculty members were involved with independent national summer schools including the program at the Chautauqua Institution. The success of Chautauqua likely inspired Harvard President Charles W. Eliot and others to move further into the market for summer education. Eliot tasked geology professor Nathaniel Shaler in 1887 with organizing and enlarging Harvard's summer offerings, and Eliot's letter appointing Paul Hanus as the university's first professor of education in 1891 listed as one of his five duties "the conduct of a summer school for teachers at Cambridge, giving instruction in your own subjects, and being in service of the considerable number of teachers who come to Cambridge in the summer." Hanus organized the Harvard Summer School of Arts and Sciences, in which his education courses were so well received that he soon realized that "the summer courses could probably be counted on to extend the influence of my department both within and without the university."[68]

Other universities soon followed Harvard's lead. When the University of Iowa (UIowa) experimented with summer sessions in the 1890s, President Charles A. Schaeffer noted, "The teachers of the state . . . are already fully alive to the importance of further study." UIowa began in 1900 to offer a regular six-week summer session administered mainly by the dean of the College of Education, and a university publication announced, "The primary object in organizing the Summer Session has been to give to teachers in the public schools of Iowa the opportunity to come in touch with the State University and to see something of the methods of work followed in the different departments of instruction."[69] By 1900, the University of Chicago (UChicago), Cornell University, Teachers

College at Columbia (TCC), Indiana University, and the Universities of California, Illinois, Iowa, Michigan, Minnesota, Wisconsin, and Texas all offered regular summer sessions, in most cases for university credit. In Texas, the summer institutes described in the previous chapter morphed into the state university's summer session, as an 1897 article in the *Texas School Journal* noted that summer normals had "awakened a desire for more knowledge" and inspired some teachers to head in the summer "to the great schools of the North and East." The next year, the *Journal* announced, "the State School of Methods and the University Summer School [are] to be held in the University buildings, Austin." A decade later, Catholic universities also began to provide summer schools aimed at teachers; after Marquette University established the first one in 1909, twenty other Catholic universities added yearly summer sessions by 1920.[70] Many smaller private colleges also offered summer studies. In Iowa, for example, Morningside College inaugurated a regular summer school just after the turn of the century, and Coe College and Iowa Wesleyan soon followed suit. Raymond Walters—himself a dean at Swarthmore College—noted, however, that for "numerous smaller, privately endowed colleges . . . it would be uneconomic to try to operate all year round." In the summer, he added, small colleges "cannot compete with the large institutions in attracting students."[71]

In 1917, a group of private universities and public flagship institutions consolidated their advantages in attracting summer students by founding the National Association of Summer School Directors (NASSD) "for the purpose," according to its constitution, "of considering matters of common interest relating to the university summer sessions, particularly with regard to graduate study." Although the group's concerns and discussions at its annual meetings ranged far beyond graduate study, its members were research universities, most of which were located in the North: Boston University, UChicago, Clark University, Columbia, Cornell, UPenn, George Washington, Harvard, Johns Hopkins, New York University, Northwestern, Syracuse University, and the state universities of California, Colorado, Illinois, Indiana, Iowa, Kansas, Michigan, Minnesota, Missouri, Montana, Nebraska, Oklahoma, Oregon, Texas, Virginia, Washington, and Wisconsin. Ohio State University and Iowa State College were also members, and the University of Toronto was the only non-U.S. member. During the next two decades, the University of Buffalo, the "Los Angeles Branch" of the University of California, George Peabody College for Teachers, Pennsylvania State College, the University of Pittsburgh, and Rutgers University joined while a few institutions discontinued their membership. Most of these institutions appeared on a list Walters compiled of the fifty university summer schools with the largest enrollments in 1922. The College of the City of New York and Ohio University were the only non-NASSD members in the top two dozen, and many of the other nonmembers on Walter's list were southern white universities, including Tulane and the state flagships of Georgia, North Carolina, West Virginia, and Tennessee. The Summer School of the South (SSS) at the University of Tennessee (UTenn) enrolled thirty-two thousand white teachers from throughout the South between its founding in 1902 and 1919, when it completed its conversion into a standard summer session. Clark in Massachusetts remained in the NASSD but did not appear on Walters's 1922 list, perhaps due to the retirement of President G. Stanley Hall two years earlier. Established by Hall in the 1890s, the Clark summer school had included his course on "the study of children." Teachers were among his intended audience, although, as historian Ellen Lagemann explains, Hall generally aimed to "avoid close contact with teachers."[72]

Unlike state normal schools and Black colleges, private universities and state flagships were often reluctant to embrace teacher education due to its low prestige—which was linked with the low status of teachers' backgrounds and the field. Like Hall, leaders at these institutions wrestled to reconcile their aversion to teacher education with the benefits of enrolling teachers during the summertime. Historian Lawrence Cremin and his coauthors explain that at TCC, this "friction" arose from "the hostile attitude of some members of the University Faculty toward Teachers College itself, toward all courses in education, and toward the presence of women in higher education." In their history of UWis, Merle Curti and Vernon Carstensen observe that before the turn of the century, summer instruction for teachers "was slow in finding complete acceptance as in integral part of the University." And, even with the backing of President Eliot, Hanus found a "largely unsympathetic atmosphere" for teacher education at Harvard; in time, his success with the summer school "buttressed" regard for the field.[73] Belying their reluctance to educate teachers, however, universities' summer programs provided teachers with remarkable opportunities to deepen their knowledge of education and academic subjects and to broaden their cultural and social horizons. With higher status than normal schools/teachers colleges or Black colleges, private universities and public flagships offered more rarefied instruction and greater exposure to the wider world, enabling the teachers who attended to refine themselves personally and professionally and, by doing so and by making themselves at home on campus, to challenge the nonelite status of their work and social position.

Teachers, including most of those who enrolled in university summer sessions, did not fit the general profile of private and flagship institutions' academic year students. Although even Harvard did enroll some poor students, most were middle- or upper-class as well as white, and institutions including Harvard and the University of Virginia admitted only men as undergraduates.[74] Summer sessions were thus valuable in widening access to higher education for people whose socioeconomic status, race, and/or gender otherwise limited their ability to attend—albeit during a time of year when most traditional students were not on campus. Private benefactors and foundations, state governments, and universities themselves took various steps to make summer school affordable on a teacher's salary and limited family resources.

Industrialist Henry Clay Frick anonymously established an endowment in 1910 to fund summer school for Pittsburgh teachers selected by their principals on the basis of the teachers' interest in "social and physical betterment." The 65 scholarship winners in 1910 and 125 in 1911—most of whom were women—chose to attend universities including Harvard, TCC, Cornell, Dartmouth, the University of Pittsburgh, and Pennsylvania State, as well as Chautauqua.[75] In Philadelphia, several organizations—including the German-American Alliance, the New Century Club, and the Pennsylvania branches of the Congress of Mothers and the Women's Christian Temperance Union—provided scholarships in 1913 for teachers at UPenn's summer school. Such aid apparently dried up by the Depression, as UPenn's representative reported at the 1930 NASSD meeting, "Our summer session has now no provision for scholarships of any kind." Frustrated, he continued, "I feel very strongly that scholarships are needed in the summer school. . . . A fairly large proportion of the winter students are sons of rich parents who can afford to send them through college, whereas a very large proportion of the summer school students are young teachers struggling along on very meagre salaries and to whom it is a financial hardship to come and pay fees and many of whom are compelled to do that by state law."[76]

Various scholarships funded by states or host universities facilitated the attendance of teachers of particular subjects or who worked in the local community. The state of Tennessee and UTenn's agriculture department worked together to provide annual scholarships to SSS for two teachers from each county, appointed by their superintendent of education on the condition that they study "agriculture and methods of teaching it"; 106 students attended the 1910 session with the support of these scholarships. By 1912, county as well as city superintendents in Tennessee were also able to designate teachers for scholarships in manual training and domestic science. Harvard by the late 1920s provided scholarships for teachers selected by school districts in the Boston area. In a typical form letter, the summer school director notified the university's bursar, "In accordance with the arrangement between Harvard University and certain schools in the vicinity Miss Marion Barnes is entitled to the remission of the tuition fee."[77]

Rather than provide scholarships to individuals, some subsidies to university summer sessions reduced or even eliminated tuition for most or all students. SSS director and UTenn education professor Philander Claxton raised money from foundations, textbook companies, and Knoxville residents to ensure that teacher-students paid only a small registration fee at SSS. The General Education Board provided $10,000 for each of the 1903–1905 sessions after other contributors satisfied the contingency that they match the board's donation. When he wrote to the GEB in the fall of 1905 to offer thanks and request more support, Claxton explained, "Thousands of teachers have attended this school, who could not pay the expense of a summer in the schools of the North. . . . Our teachers have had less opportunity for education and professional training than in other sections, and their annual salaries are so very small." Although Claxton's appeal to the

GEB was not successful—the board had begun to support summer sessions at Black colleges and other southern universities—contributions continued from companies including Houghton Mifflin and Macmillan, as well as Knoxville residents. A visitor to SSS in 1909 was able to report that he observed "faces, on which are written stories of toil. These persons have spent years in the school room, educating the youth of the land. The Summer School offers them the opportunity, to a certain extent, of a college education, for which, perhaps, they one time longed, but which they had to give up, forced by stern necessity."[78]

Summer sessions at many public flagships received appropriations from the state. Such funding enabled the University of Texas (UTexas) to advertise in 1907, "Tuition is free; registration fees are nominal," and UIowa to announce throughout the 1900s and 1910s that summer school students paid only "a nominal tuition of five dollars" and no "contingent expenses of any kind." Pennsylvania State's summer session received legislative appropriations managed by state department of public instruction from 1903 onward; a 1917 report stated that the institution continued to enjoy "special aid" for the summer school. In Virginia, university summer schools at both white and Black institutions were "supported in large part by the State," according to a 1911 report. Virginia teachers who attended summer school at the University of Virginia during the late 1920s paid only a $10 registration fee, while nonteachers and nonstate residents paid both tuition and registration fees. And when the representative of the University of Illinois announced at the 1931 meeting of the NASSD that Illinois provided funds to cover tuition for "all teachers in the state," other members peppered him with questions. After UWis's representative asked, "How do you determine an Illinois teacher?" he replied, "We make a liberal interpretation" and later noted the great value to teachers of "free tuition" in "hard times."[79]

Other efforts also reduced the financial burden of summer school attendance for teachers. It was common, for example, for the schools to secure reduced rail fares for teacher-students. An advertisement in the *Texas School Journal* for the 1903 summer quarter at UChicago touted "reduced rates from Texas," and Edwin Slosson reported several years later, "Every year the Texas students charter a special train for the University of Chicago. . . . This is the same geographically as if 150 Italian students came every year to Oxford." An announcement of the 1904 summer school at UTexas noted, "The railroads will provide special rates for those wishing to attend," and a 1905 Harvard publication explained that summer school administrators had applied to "Railway Passenger Associations for reduced rates" for those traveling from nearby states, and that students from more distant locales could travel to cities from which they could secure the lower fares.[80]

Even with subsidies and scholarships, attending a university summer school presented financial challenges for teachers, and they worked with institutions to line up campus jobs to help them meet the costs. Emily Morley of Pensacola, Florida, wrote to an SSS administrator in March 1903, "I would like to attend the 'Summer School' this year and write to know if there is any way in which I could work and so earn enough to pay my expenses while there. I found last summer that the amount which I am able to save during the year is not enough." Hattie Kent of Mosheim, Tennessee, was especially persistent—and particular—in advance of the 1903 session, writing in April, "I am very anxious to attend the summer school and want to do some dining room work for my board. I prefer to set the table but if I cannot get that task let me wait on tables." On May 12, she sent a list of references, asked again to set tables, and requested that her friend be hired for the same job. Kent clarified on May 14 that she would rather wait tables than set tables *and* wash dishes. A week later, an SSS administrator assured Kent, "You are first on the list of applicants. . . . By working five hours a day, you will therefore be able to pay all expenses." Kent accepted "gladly," but it is not clear whether she had to wash dishes. Another prospective SSS student—a man—wrote, "I would be glad to get some work that would not take up too much of my time or would distract from my reputation as a teacher." The reply letter suggested that he seek work as a publisher's representative or as a ticket-taker in the dining hall, which would not interfere "seriously with the class work you wish to take."[81]

At UIowa, the campus newspaper reported in June 1922, "The office of the dean of women has had no difficulty in finding jobs for women who desired to work. . . . Housework and taking care of children are the kinds of work that get the most calls," and summer session catalogs in the late 1930s invited students to "avail themselves of the opportunities afforded by the University Employment Services." Meanwhile, the *Harvard Summer School News* reported that the school's "unsung heroes" were men and women "student aids," who did odd jobs ranging from delivering messages to moving furniture to folding copies of the *News*. Led by schoolteacher John Gilmore, the "brigade" included several teachers, and members worked between 30 and 150 hours during the summer session.[82] They, like the many other teachers who took advantage of job opportunities and scholarships at other universities, became integral members of the summer community at these elite institutions.

In order to reduce students' living expenses during summer school, institutions commonly arranged for accommodations in local homes and/or campus dormitories. Because enrollment in SSS during its early years far exceeded the capacity of UTenn's five residence halls, Claxton also secured rooms in one thousand Knoxville homes. UIowa did not have dormitories or commons at the turn of the century, but the summer school announcement explained that board and lodging in private homes were reasonably priced, and that students often formed boarding clubs. By the 1910s, UIowa summer session catalogs listed "very moderate" rates for single and double dormitory rooms. Similarly, Harvard advertised low rates for board and lodging until 1915, when the university provided furnished rooms for the first time. Summer students resided in dormitories along the Charles River until 1931, when rooms in Harvard Yard became available. Columbia University, which included TCC, by the 1920s provided "wholesome food at moderate rates" during the summer in the university's "cafeteria dining rooms . . . open to men and women alike," along with lodging in several residence halls, two of which would have been especially welcoming to teachers: Thompkins Hall was reserved for "women over twenty-four years of age," and Whittier Hall was managed by TCC for "women registered primarily in education."[83]

In a novel approach to reducing living expenses for summer students with families, UWis and UIowa established campgrounds on campus. UWis's "tarpaper town" was in the woods on the shore of Lake Mendota just west of campus. It began in 1911 with eighteen wooden tent platforms, added fifty more by the 1930s, and remained in use through the 1950s. The University of Iowa Summer Camp began in 1925 with twenty sites, grew by 1929 to include ninety sites, and flourished in the 1930s. The comment by UWis historians David Cronin and John Jenkins that "the tent colony made University study possible for many teachers who otherwise could not afford to relocate to Madison" also applied in Iowa City. Both camps housed teachers, principals, and school superintendents, along with their families, although only UIowa's camp was restricted to educators. In addition to wooden platforms and tents for rent, the camps included kitchen and bathroom facilities, lighted study halls, mail delivery, and organized play for children—seventy-seven of whom lived at the UIowa camp in 1928. Both camps had civic councils headed by elected mayors; at UIowa in 1930, mayor Lowell Cockrill—the school superintendent in Livermore, Iowa—led a council of three men and three women, while Hale Quandt—a teacher from Beloit, Wisconsin—served as baseball commissioner. Most of the teachers who resided in the UIowa camp were men; Quandt shared a tent with just his wife, and Cockrill's tent housed his family of six. While it was unusual at the time for women teachers to have families, teachers Lessie Alderhold of Oklahoma City, Helen Everson of Duluth, and Emily Mayne of Plankinton, South Dakota, also lived in the camp in 1930—Alderhold and Everson with their husbands and one and two daughters, respectively, and Mayne with another woman.[84]

UIowa was coeducational throughout the school year, but attendance by married women with children was a new phenomenon, as were the high percentages of women among summer session students at most public flagships and private universities. At UTenn, where women had gained admission only in the 1890s and remained "a curiosity" during the regular school year, nearly 70 percent of SSS students were women. Similarly, the ratio of women to men at Pennsylvania State's 1922 summer session was approximately four to one, the inverse of the ratio during the academic year. This summer influx coincided with an early twentieth-century wave of negative reactions to women students' success at coeducational universities during the academic year, which led UWis to seriously consider separate classes for men and women and UChicago to institute sex-segregated classes for a short time. Wesleyan College in Connecticut discontinued the admission of women, Stanford and the University of Michigan enacted strict quotas to restrict their numbers, and institutions including the University of Rochester segregated women in "coordinate colleges."[85] Women's numbers in summer sessions, however, overwhelmed any hostility toward their presence, and they demonstrated that they belonged by thriving on campus. An observer at SSS in 1902 remarked that the women students "had a nonchalant and very independent air, and seemed perfectly at home" as they "gathered here and there or walked boldly up and down the walk." To better serve these women, UTenn by 1909 expanded its women's residence hall, and, twenty years later, one of the topics of discussion at the NASSD meeting was "adaptation of men's dormitories to use of women."[86]

Beyond universities that were officially coeducational, summer sessions welcomed women to institutions that were otherwise nearly or exclusively all male, serving as "the opening wedge of coeducation," in the words of Clifford and Guthrie. TCC's summer courses were under the umbrella of Columbia University, which admitted only men as undergraduates. Although TCC enrolled women year-round, its outsized role in the summer school, along with the larger university's admission of women to this session only, meant that women constituted more than half of the student body on campus during this part of the year. UPenn, which admitted women only to its School of Education and only beginning in 1913, advertised in 1925 that at its summer session "all instruction is open to both men and women" with "attractive dormitories for all." All-male Harvard made similar concessions, announcing in a March 1931 press release that "for the first time in history" women—who had attended the summer school from its beginning—were "to be lodged in the Yard," and that the common rooms in two of the halls would be "reserved to the women as reception rooms for teas or entertaining callers." Another press release two years later stated, "Once again the historic Harvard Yard will be turned over to the summer school, and women students"—perhaps including Lillie Fortman of Jersey City—"will be admitted to some of the famous old dormitories." Summer credits could count toward graduate degrees by the 1920s at Harvard, and among the hundreds of teachers who completed their master's in education were the first women to earn Harvard degrees.[87]

Students of color, especially Black teachers, also used summer session attendance to demonstrate that they belonged at elite universities, although they did not enjoy unlimited access. Faculty from UTexas's summer school in 1905 presented lectures at the "State School of Methods for Colored Teachers," which convened simultaneously in Austin. Southern institutions remained segregated, however; the UTexas representative reported at the 1930 NASSD meeting that in his state, "I do not think there is any institution that takes colored students." Thus, southern Black teachers not only attended Black colleges but increasingly headed to northern universities for the summer. So many attended UChicago and TCC that a 1915 GEB report noted their contribution to "the formation of a better teaching staff" in Black schools. Septima Clark spent the summer of 1930 at TCC (before attending Atlanta and Hampton later in the decade), and

Virginia teacher Patricia M. Ewell attended TCC the following summer on a scholarship that she earned by recruiting new members to the National Association of Teachers in Colored Schools. Anna Julia Cooper, the principal and Latin teacher at the M Street School in Washington, D.C., pursued graduate studies in romance languages at Columbia for six summers between 1914 and 1921, and Black Indiana teacher Jane Dabney Shackelford enrolled at TCC during successive summers in the mid-1920s and completed her master's degree in 1927, when she was in her early thirties.[88]

GEB records, historian Linda Perkins explains, list a large number of other Black women teachers who attended summer sessions at "some of the leading universities in the nation," including Harvard, Cornell, UIowa, UWis, and UPenn. The latter institution's representative to the 1930 NASSD meeting indeed acknowledged the attendance of "some" Black students, but he also stated, "We have no way of keeping them out. We have not made any attempt to encourage them; for every one that comes in, three white students are probably driven away." Such hostility probably did "keep out" some Black teacher-students at UPenn and elsewhere. Nevertheless, in TCC summer courses during the 1930s and 1940s, according to Perkins, "it was not uncommon for a third of the student body to be Black." Also at Columbia, visiting professor from the University of North Carolina Edgar Knight noted among the students "a few brothers and sisters in black, principally from the South, reveling in their golden opportunity."[89]

Not just Black students reveled in the opportunity to study at an elite institution. Dean Walters described summer school students—commonly high school teachers from unprivileged backgrounds, the majority of whom were women—as "mature and professionally ambitious," with "tortoise-shell spectacles and leather portfolios stuffed with books"; and Knight wrote that they were "eager for information. . . . They read ahead of the class" and "bombard the instructor with questions . . . and in his office they consult and pump him until his tongue hangs out from sheer exhaustion. And among themselves they discuss their work constantly" (see figure 5). Meanwhile, residents of the UIowa summer camp in 1930 passed an only somewhat tongue-in-cheek resolution "that a branch of the college of education library be established on the grounds as a further aid to residents" who wanted to study in the evening.[90] Summer students at private universities and public flagships, like those at normal schools/teachers colleges and Black colleges, clearly took their studies very seriously. At universities, they enjoyed the added benefits to their pursuit of professionalization of guidance through a wide range of substantial subject matter by faculty members who were at the top of their field.

Knight mentioned "first-rate professors," and Walters quoted an eminent British Shakespearean scholar who observed after spending the 1923 summer quarter at UChicago that the university did not "provide only its own professors but scholars of high standing from all parts of the world." Such was also the case at

FIGURE 5 Teachers College main building, stairs inside the entrance, showing students studying, Summer Session 1920. Part of the material used in a campaign to get a new library and practical arts buildings. (Courtesy of the Teachers College, Columbia University.)

public flagships. The Universities of Illinois and California touted courses "by the regular instructors of the University, assisted by leading educators from other institutions" and "by members of the regular faculty and by men of letters and science from Eastern Universities and Europe," respectively, while the University of Colorado advertised in a 1906 issue of the *Texas School Journal* "an exceedingly strong regular summer staff" and "a series of ten lectures from Professor

Paul Hanus of Harvard, on educational topics, and a series of five lectures by Professor Alber[t] Bushnell Hart of Harvard, on historical biographies."[91] At SSS, about one-third of the faculty were UTenn professors, and others were faculty from universities or normal schools throughout the South as well as other regions, or were superintendents of large school systems. Luminaries such as John Dewey of TCC and Liberty Hyde Bailey of Cornell taught and presented lecture series; it is not surprising that Claxton later reflected that SSS had allowed schoolteachers to learn from "lecturers whose voices carried across the continent."[92]

Guided by leading scholars and practitioners through professional courses in education, teacher-students at universities studied roughly the same subjects offered at other summer schools but at a higher level. An announcement of plans for UWis's 1902 summer session stated, "Courses in the history of education, mental development, teaching and management, educational psychology, and allied subjects will be offered by members of the regular faculty, and in addition eight of the most eminent educators of the country," including G. Stanley Hall and University of Nebraska chancellor and former superintendent of Chicago schools E. Benjamin Andrews. The student newspaper at UIowa reported in 1903, "In nearly all cases, the heads of the departments will be in charge of the summer session in their branches," and in 1908, "A large number of the heads of departments will remain for the Summer Session, thus assuring the summer students of the very best the University can offer." Meanwhile, at Harvard Summer School, Dean Paul Hanus taught school "organization and administration," and Harvard Professors Robert Yerkes and Josiah Royce taught courses tailored for teachers in psychology and philosophy, respectively, while UTexas's summer school added "more advanced courses" and brought in nationally known Herbartianist Charles McMurry to present a series of lectures.[93]

At SSS, University of Missouri Education Dean W. W. Charters presented a short course in 1914 focusing on motivation and methods. But it was in the mid-1900s that teacher-students at SSS especially learned from renowned education scholars. Hall presented a series of lectures on child study and other topics each summer, praising "the spirit of the students" and reflecting after the 1907 session that his experiment with doctoral-level lectures had been "successful." Ellen H. S. Richards of Massachusetts Institute of Technology addressed questions in her home economics course including, "How much 'science' must the teacher know?" and "How shall the fundamental facts be presented to the child in school so as to influence his whole life?" while Edward L. Thorndike of TCC in his psychology course described research on "the inheritance of mental traits." In the first of his ten lectures on "the Educational Aspect of Psychology" during the 1908 session, Dewey "defined the process of thinking as that of relating the known with the unknown," according to a Knoxville newspaper. Another paper reported after Dewey's July 1 talk, "He closed his remarks with an appeal to the teachers to interest their pupils in each other and not so much in the teacher." It is fitting that a school superintendent reflected in 1908 that at SSS, the teacher-student "is all the time in an atmosphere of more or less advanced thinking and feels the influence of the higher life which is pulsating all around her."[94]

Dewey and Thorndike also taught summer school courses at their home institution: Dewey presented "Aims and Principles in Education" and "Foundations of Method," while Thorndike taught various educational psychology courses. Teacher-students at TCC were also able to study with several of Dewey and Thorndike's colleagues who were on the cutting edge of education theory and methods. Throughout the 1910s, Paul Monroe taught history of education; William Heard Kilpatrick taught history of education with Monroe and philosophy of education and "Foundations of Methods" on his own; Frank McMurry taught elementary supervision; and George Strayer taught school administration. Willystine Goodsell likely brought her feminist perspective to "The Education of Women," a course rarely available elsewhere. Rounding out the TCC summer faculty, visiting instructors included Charles Prosser of the Society for the Promotion of Industrial Education and Professor Ellwood Cubberley of Stanford. Cubberley wrote to the TCC dean that many of the students in 1914 "expressed warm appreciation" for his teaching, and he returned in 1916 to teach "Public Education in America."[95] Enrollees in these courses at TCC, like those who studied with visiting and regular faculty members at other private universities and public flagships, often learned directly from the researchers and scholars who had written the textbooks and shaped the field of education.

The *Harvard Summer School News* reported that one of the most popular courses during the 1939 session was "Learning and Teaching," taught by Professor Herbert Espy of the famed UChicago Laboratory School. The summer curriculum at Espy's home institution, like that at many universities, incorporated tasks in an actual school. UChicago advertised in 1904 that a "model school representing different phases of elementary work will be open for observation . . . during the forenoon of each day"; SSS included "model schools" at the kindergarten and primary levels "under the direction of expert teachers"; UIowa's Observation School was in session for at least part of each summer session; and UPenn's summer School of Observation, as described by the *Pennsylvania School Journal* in 1913, was "a public school attended by pupils from many parts" of Philadelphia, with teachers who "were experts from various parts of the country." The representatives of Cornell and the University of Missouri reported to the NASSD in 1927 that they operated rural demonstration schools, and TCC's School of Demonstration met daily at the Horace Mann School, the university's laboratory school. A description of plans for the second and fifth grades during the 1916 summer session reflected the Mann School's progressive approach: "The purpose is . . . *not* to demonstrate *methods* of teaching the usual school subjects, but rather to exhibit certain phases of school work in which topics selected from real life are substituted for the traditional subjects."[96] Septima Clark reflected that during her summer at TCC, she learned "how to use the expressions of the children to teach them the words that they used every day" and, as a result, "was able to bring the test scores of those kids up." Beatrice Cramer took leaves of absence from teaching in White Plains in order to attend TCC for selected semesters in the late 1920s. She also enrolled for the summers of 1928 and 1929 at the University of Rochester, where she took "interesting courses" and observed at Washington Junior High School.[97]

Perhaps inspired intellectually by these summer school experiences, both Clark and Cramer would go on to earn graduate degrees, as the advanced nature of summer studies in education at these institutions manifested in the growth of graduate-level work. As early as the 1900s at UChicago, "MA students were particularly prevalent during the summer" and Education enrolled more students than any other department, according to a recent history of the university. In the early 1910s, the TCC "Summer Session Announcement" directed graduate students in education to "have their programs approved by Professor Monroe," and the course list included many above the undergraduate level. NASSD members discussed graduate study regularly at annual meetings; faculty supervision of large numbers of master's theses in education was a prominent topic at the 1930 gathering.[98] One teacher who earned a master's degree mainly through summer study was Margarete Bohle, who taught elementary school in Milwaukee for forty-two years after completing her initial training in 1932. Beginning in 1936, she enrolled in a few courses each summer at the Marquette University Graduate School, studying teaching methods, educational measurement, "problems in education," and more. She also took two evening courses during the 1939–1940 academic year completing her degree in 1941. Surely Bole's advanced studies enhanced her work in the classroom; they likely also increased her professional confidence.[99]

Bohle additionally challenged herself intellectually by enrolling in courses in world, European, and U.S. history at Marquette, while Fortman studied history, English, and higher math at Harvard. They and scores of other teachers tackled substantial academic subject matter beyond the field of education, often under the guidance of faculty members who were at the top of their field. In the process, teachers further widened their intellectual and cultural horizons and demonstrated that they belonged at elite universities. At UWis in the 1910s, teacher-students were able to study history with Frederick Jackson Turner, who helped to expand the summer school in an effort to improve history teaching in the public schools. At Harvard, courses in Roman, European, and American history, Shakespeare, and both eighteenth- and nineteenth-century English literature were among the offerings in 1905; Dean Charles Homer Haskins taught medieval history and "historical bibliography and criticism" in 1917; and the most popular courses in 1939 included "History of Renaissance and Modern Art" with Professor Everard Upjohn of Columbia and "English Fiction Since 1890" with Theodore Spencer of Harvard and Cambridge Universities. Among the visiting instructors at SSS were Vassar College Professor Lucy Maynard Salmon, who taught "History of the Colonial Period of the United States" in 1906, and UWis

Professor Charles Foster Smith, who taught "Masterpieces of World Literature" in 1910. And at Pennsylvania State in 1926, a wide range of English courses included "Composite Course in the Modern Aspects of English," in which Zona Gale and five other authors each led a one-week unit. Cincinnati teacher Lena Beatrice Morton, who was Black, enrolled in summer (and evening) courses in English at the University of Cincinnati throughout the 1930s. In order to maximize her time and preserve her health during the summer of 1937, she adhered to a schedule of "reading and study hours" in the mornings and evenings.[100]

The scope of academic summer school offerings extended far beyond history and English; the UIowa catalog for 1917 promised "nearly all of the lines of study of the University which are included in the work of the rest of the year," taught mainly by "the regular staff of instruction." The *Pennsylvania School Journal* in 1925 highlighted Lehigh University's summer plans for "valuable courses in History and Social Science" taught by "men who have attained distinction in authorship in these fields," and advertisements for the University of Minnesota (UMinn) in 1921 and New York University in 1925 listed among other courses Americanization, anthropology, government, political science, psychology, and sociology. Social science courses at UIowa included "Elements of Politics" and "Elements of Economics" in 1900; "Social Amelioration" and "The Industrial Revolution in Its Social Aspects" in 1902; and "Women in Industry," "The World War," and "Social Democracy in Europe" in 1918. The UIowa *Summer Session News* reported in 1920 that the Americanization course offered that term combined the fields of American literature, government, history, economics, and education to equip teachers "to combat the influence of the 'reds' in Iowa and to help the foreign-born residents of the state to become true Americans." While the catalog description of "The Negro in America" at UIowa in summer 1923—"A study of the Negro in America, with attention to the fundamental mental and temperamental traits of the black man and to the problems which his presence creates in American life"—similarly suggested that it was not taught from the point of view of the group under study, social science courses had the potential to broaden teachers' perspectives on social issues and world events.[101]

The natural sciences and mathematics were also well represented in summer session curriculums. An ad for Cornell's 1900 summer session listed math, physics, chemistry, botany, geology, physical geography, and physiology among the "named subjects" to be offered. Rural teacher Conrad Selvig headed to UMinn for laboratory courses in chemistry and botany in 1900 and a math class—in which he was "consoled" to earn a grade of 85—in 1901, in order to enhance his teaching with an eye toward moving into a principalship. When science teacher J. H. Voris of Huntington High School in Indiana wrote in July 1900 to Huntington math teacher Eva Lewis to congratulate her on her appointment as principal of the school, he reported that he was studying bacteriology "under Dr. Lyons of the State University" and that he found it "intensely interesting." Harvard's 1905 summer offerings included calculus and multiple courses in physics, chemistry, botany, and geology, while UIowa offered similar courses plus astronomy and zoology, the latter supported by the university's "large and valuable natural history collections." Announcements for UIowa summer sessions in the early 1900s also promised "those electing work offered in experimental and observational science will be able to avail themselves of the resources of the various laboratories."[102]

An observer of SSS wrote that UTenn's chemistry and physics departments were "admirably equipped, for a Southern institution." The facilities at SSS were acceptable enough for well-known horticulturalist Liberty Hyde Bailey to teach nature study and agriculture there in 1903, and the students at SSS exceeded the expectations of University of Georgia Professor A. H. Patterson, who wrote to Claxton after teaching physics at SSS in 1905 and 1907 that he was "impressed both times with the earnestness displayed by the students," who convinced him to add evening instruction in astronomy. More high school teachers signed up for and did well in Patterson's advanced course in electron theory than he had expected.[103] California teacher Margaret Wythe took botany with Bailey at the state university at Berkeley, where he also served as a visiting summer instructor. Wythe taught science courses from botany to zoology at Oakland High School throughout the 1890s and 1900s, spending many summers studying at Berkeley or at the marine laboratory operated by Stanford. While Wythe's summer studies were advanced work in the high school subjects she taught, elementary school teacher Septima Clark took a course in astronomy in addition to her work in education at Columbia in order enhance her general knowledge. Her students, Clark said, were "looking at the skies every day and every night, and it's good to be able to talk about it."[104]

Summer science courses like those at Stanford's marine laboratory took teacher-students into the field. In a five-week "intercollegiate" course titled "Geology of the Appalachian Region" in 1905, five professors—from Johns Hopkins, Harvard, Syracuse, Western Reserve, and Yale—taught in five different locations from Maryland to Connecticut. The course was restricted to men, who were instructed to bring a clinometer, hammer, and small bags for specimens. Most other summer field experiences were open to women as well as men. SSS courses in geology and geography included excursions to local mines and quarries; instructor Frances Warren took her geography class to a marble quarry on the belief that "first hand knowledge of the leading industries is one of the essentials of the teaching of usable geography today." Both UMinn and Columbia offered a field course in Glacier National Park in 1917, and the University of Wyoming's summer quarter—billed "the coolest summer school in America"—included field courses in geology, botany, and zoology in the 1920s.[105]

After her sixth year of teaching science at Elmira Free Academy, a high school in New York State, Lillian Herrick spent two months during the summer of 1900 at Cornell University's field camp. One of only three women in the group, she learned to use a tripod and magnetic needle to find directions "according to magnetic variations" and to plot her fieldwork according to mathematical calculations. On a typical morning, students set out with "baskets, chisel, hammers" to collect fossils in "the 'cut.'" Finding a trilobite filled Herrick "with enthusiasm," and another specimen that she chiseled out of a rock measured more than four inches across. "I knew this was excellent," she wrote to her family, "but I was glad when Prof. V. said, 'that is the find of the morning.'" In the afternoons, Herrick and her classmates examined and classified their finds, which she looked forward to using in her high-school geology classes. She also wrote enthusiastically about social activities and the field camp's "little colony of six white tents," where she felt at home with the Cornell students and the occupants of the tent that flew "the blue + white of Yale."[106]

UIowa opened a field station on Lake Okoboji in western Iowa in 1909, where professors such as future UIowa president Thomas Macbride taught summer courses in botany, geology, and zoology while conducting field research with students. Called the Lakeside Laboratory, the station included a laboratory building, a "main cottage," a boathouse, tents, and, later, a dormitory. Macbride listed among the lab's intended students, "teachers of biologic sciences in academies and high schools everywhere . . . who may find in the service of the laboratory occasion to acquaint themselves with Iowa conditions and thus better equip themselves for serving the children of the schools," and a report on the lab in its twenty-fifth year reiterated the biology teacher's need for "a genuine familiarity with the species of plants and animals inhabiting the region in which he lives, as they occur in nature." An observer praised the station's hands-on, interactive approach to learning, noting, "With scientists at their sides and with books merely as reference, these students go directly to nature for their information" and share "good meals" with faculty. Maude Brown reported of her fellow students, "Ornithologists with bird-glasses swinging over their shoulders were enthusiastic over the newly-found nest of young bitterns. Another group laden with baskets talked learnedly of agarics and slime molds, while down the hill came a lone enthusiast boasting of twelve species of grasses." Through their studies, Brown observed "something down deep in their natures that has been renewed and refreshed, and from which life-giving currents will flow throughout the year."[107]

Summer studies of foreign languages, sometimes also including a residential component, further enabled teachers to renew their passion while deepening their knowledge. Institutions from Harvard to UIowa and SSS offered Latin, Greek, French, and German; Spanish was also offered at Harvard and SSS, Italian at Harvard, and Scandinavian at UIowa. German teacher and principal of Huntington High School A.U. Crull found his studies of German at UWis during the summers of 1899 and 1900 to be "inspiring." While taking classes on the history of the language, Middle High German, and German dramatic poets in 1899, he wrote to Eva Lewis, "I shall never get nearer to a complete life in the flesh than I have right now." From Madison in 1900, Crull congratulated Lewis on her principalship and wrote, "I am having a very helpful summer, and am feeling buoyant."[108] French was one of Mary Lockwood's passions. She taught in West Virginia in the 1910s while maintaining strong ties to her mother's family of rural Kansas teachers, the Stewarts. In a reference letter that the family saved, one of Lockwood's summer session professors at UWis in 1918 complimented her "command of spoken French," elaborating, "her pronunciation and intonation are excellent as well as her vocabulary and knowledge of grammar. . . . She would be a valuable addition to any teaching staff." Three summers later, Lockwood wrote to her Stewart aunts from Quebec that she was enjoying "living with people who speak almost nothing but French." Meanwhile, New York City high school teacher Samuel Baker immersed himself in Spanish during an "intensive" summer program at Middlebury College. Morning classes covered Spanish language and literature, and evening lectures focused on Spanish and South American geography, art, and architecture. "The use of Spanish language was retained even during our recreation periods," Baker explained, "and after six weeks of reading, talking and eating in Spanish, one finally found oneself dreaming in Spanish." At UIowa during the 1920 summer session, residential options included "French House," where fifteen women teacher-students lived together and spoke only French. They took regular summer school classes but also watched French plays and played French games at the house, under the charge of a French instructor.[109]

Beyond language programs, myriad events and activities outside the classroom reinforced what teacher-students learned in their courses, acquainted them with elite intellectual and cultural life, and greatly expanded their horizons. Scholarly lecturers and prominent performers appeared even more regularly during summer sessions at private and flagship universities than they did at normal schools and Black colleges. UChicago advertised "Open Lectures, more than 100 in number, on subjects in History, Music, Languages, Literature, Science, Art, and Education from a series of popular lectures on the highest order" in 1903, and among the weekly lectures "on subjects of general interest" at UTexas in 1904 were "Law, Culture, and Utility" by UTexas law professor and former judge John C. Townes and "Glimpses of Ancient Life and Art" by UTexas classics professor D. A. Penick. SSS by the 1910s did not schedule any classes at 10:00 A.M. so that all students were free to attend a daily lecture "of general interest." Among the morning lectures in 1914 were three on philosophy by a Florida Supreme Court justice and three on American literature by a University of Virginia English professor. Frequent "public lectures" at UIowa included "International Relations in Public Health" by U.S. Surgeon General W. A. Evans and "The Moral Obligations of Citizenship" by University of Minnesota President L. D. Coffman in 1924, and speeches by U.S. Secretary of Agriculture Henry A. Wallace and architect Frank Lloyd Wright in 1939. Among several UIowa "Campus Forums" in 1937 and 1938 were "The Problems of Organized Labor," "The Problem of Judicial Reorganization," and "The Threat of Dictatorship," led by UIowa professors. The calendar at Harvard was similarly loaded; after "a week in which the lectures have zig-zagged giddily from Renaissance to Hitlerism," reported the *Summer School News* in July 1938, upcoming lectures would progress in a more orderly fashion from politics to science to the arts. Science lectures included a talk by Gloria Hollister of the New York Zoological Society and explanations of "the nature of meteors, stars, and galaxies" by "three of Harvard's leading astronomers" during evening open houses at Harvard's observatory.[110]

In addition to lectures, music and other arts events on campus provided a rich array of cultural capital. Claxton explained that typical of "musical entertainments" at SSS were performances in 1907 by "Maude Powell, America's great violinist; Daniel Beddoe, tenor; Henry Witherspoon, basso of the American opera; Janet Spencer, contralto; Violet Waterhouse, soprano . . . Henri Ern, great Swiss violinist, and Lillyn Sheila Powell, Celtic Ballad singer." Beholding such musical talent for the first time, SSS teacher-students gained "feeling if not understanding of the best," which, Claxton argued, was crucial to "forming tastes and ideals." Professional soloists, orchestras, and bands similarly graced the stages at university summer sessions throughout the country. TCC featured organ recitals and, in 1917, staged performances from eight operas directed by Edoardo Petri of the Metropolitan Opera Company in which professionals sang the principal roles and students formed the chorus and orchestra. At UIowa, the student chorus and orchestra performed regularly, and the 1928 "summer session artist series" consisted of five concerts by outside performers. At Harvard ten years later, the Federal Music Project presented five concerts and Puccini's *Madame Butterfly*, the Library of Congress's Coolidge String Quartette played pieces by Haydn and Brahms, and the very active student orchestra and chorus performed Beethoven's Ninth Symphony.[111]

Drama troupes commonly made the rounds of university summer sessions. The Coburn Players appeared regularly at SSS, where they performed *Twelfth Night* and two other plays in 1909. The Devereux Company performed five plays at TCC in 1917; from Plautus's *Fisherman's Rope* to Ibsen's *League of Youth*, the series illustrated "the development of modern drama." Rather than professional troupes, student groups at UIowa staged as many as five plays each summer in the 1920s and 1930s; Wilde's *The Importance of Being Ernest* and Shakespeare's *As You Like It* were among the productions in 1933 and 1936, respectively. And while the *Harvard Summer School News* recognized "amateur as well as professional talent" in summer performances, it highlighted Ethel Barrymore Colt's appearance in a Jitney Players' production on campus in 1937. While some dramatic performances undoubtedly contributed more to a "feeling if not understanding of the best" than others, the movie of a French stage production of a Moliere comedy and showings of other French and German films at Harvard in 1937 provided a new type of exposure to elite culture.[112]

For the many teachers who attended university summer sessions far from home, the experience also enriched their cultural capital in a geographical sense by familiarizing them with and introducing them to people from cities or regions of the country that were new to them. *The Iowa Normal Monthly* noted of Harvard Summer School as early as 1897, "One is struck by the number of western teachers who gather there," and the *Texas School Journal* listed over one hundred members of the "Texas contingent among the summer students at the University of Chicago" in 1905. Residents of forty-seven different states, the District of Columbia, Hawaii, the Philippines, and eleven countries enrolled at UIowa's summer school between 1927 and 1930, and the list grew to include two additional states, four additional countries, and the Canal Zone by 1934. A visiting professor at SSS reflected in 1908, "By no means least of the benefits conferred by the School has been the broadening influence resulting from the meeting of representatives from so many different States." The annual Independence Day celebration at SSS featured a parade of delegations from three dozen or so states and countries. A "barbarian"—the nickname for students from the North—wrote in 1911 that the delegations' "enthusiastic expressions of state and local pride" were full of "trust, affection, [and] good fellowship," as well as "truly educational" (see figure 6). State organizations and the Southern Club formed during TCC's summer session in 1910. Thirteen years later, thirty organizations for individual states, a few for regions such as the Far West, and even one for the British Empire, continued to attend to "the interests of those who were attending." In the late 1920s, the Southern Club's executive committee had members from sixteen different states and its "Annual Reception and 'Stunt' Night" included skits such as "A Yank's Impression of North Carolina" and songs such as "Dixie."[113]

Although Cremin and his coauthors pointed out in their history of TCC that "some Summer Session students regarded the College as little more than a headquarters for a summers' visit to the big city," being in New York—or the Boston area, or an unfamiliar region—for many teachers was like taking an additional summer class. Summer students at Columbia paid reduced or no entrance fees at museums including the Metropolitan Museum of Art and the American Museum of Natural History and participated in various "Summer Session Excursions" organized by the university with introductory lectures and guidance from "experienced local authorities and specialists." The Stock Exchange and the Financial District, the Brooklyn Navy Yard, Tarrytown and Sleepy Hollow, Ellis Island and the Statue of Liberty, the lower East Side and a tenement, and "New York City at night" including Chinatown were among the two dozen destinations each summer in the 1910s and 1920s. During one of her summers at Columbia in the mid-1920s, Jane Dabney Shackelford ventured on her own to the Harlem public library that housed the newly acquired Arthur Schomburg collection of African American and African materials. Moved by the scope of Black experiences represented in the collection, she was inspired to begin writing a book on Black history for elementary students.[114]

SUMMER SCHOOL SPECTATOR

Vol. III UNIVERSITY OF TENNESSEE, KNOXVILLE, SATURDAY, JULY 8, 1911 No. 1

CELEBRATING THE FOURTH

FIGURE 6 Summer School of the South: "Celebrating the Fourth," *Summer School Spectator* 3, no. 1 (1911): cover. Summer School of the South Collection, University of Tennessee, Knoxville—Libraries.

The article that mentioned the large number of "western teachers" at Harvard also noted that nearby historical landmarks—such as Bunker Hill, Lexington and Concord, and Salem and Marblehead—made it "particularly attractive," and the summer school soon offered excursions to these sights as well as guided tours of the Museum of Fine Arts; general tours of Boston; and "Industrial Excursions" to Athenaeum Press, Lever Soap Company, and other manufacturers. From SSS, large groups of students enjoyed excursions to Asheville, North Carolina; Mammoth Cave in Kentucky; and Chattanooga, Tennessee along with Chickamauga battlefield in Georgia. And at UIowa, "the students who visit the Amana Colonies . . . will see a community radically different from any in which they may have chanced to live," promised the *Daily Iowan* in June 1922. Guided by the head of the economics department, they learned about the communal society's religion, government, and residential arrangement. Excursions to the Amanas, the U.S. Arsenal at Rock Island, Illinois, and the Iowa State Penitentiary at Fort Madison were regular items on the UIowa summer calendar throughout the 1920s and 1930s.[115]

At other events and lectures, teacher-students further expanded their geographical horizons by learning more about the world and their potential to influence it. Travel and other countries were common lecture topics. At SSS, the *Summer School Spectator* reported that a 1909 talk "gorgeously illustrated with pictures" caused the audience to imagine that they were traveling to India and that a 1910 talk on Paris was delivered in French. Speakers at UIowa in the mid-1920s described a scientific expedition to Hawaii and "New Zealand and Its People," and speakers at Harvard in the late 1930s addressed current events in Spain, Central Europe, Russia, and China.[116] In a sweeping address at SSS in 1904, G. Stanley Hall argued "for the uncivilized and savage to be let alone commercially and religiously," encouraging listeners to consider other cultures from an anticolonialist yet paternalistic point of view. Members of SSS acted to pass a declaration of support for "the movement toward universal peace amongst the nations" in 1907 and to establish the Southern Branch of the American School Peace League in 1909, after which the *Spectator* suggested, "Every teacher should attach him or herself to this organization." Southerner and pioneering psychologist Celestia Parrish in a 1903 address at SSS highlighted women's "liberty to refuse marriage" and to "enter the professions," encouraging her listeners to broaden their conceptions of women's roles. Finally, the "Interracial Meeting" during TCC's 1929 summer session, which included talks on "Race Relations in the New South" and race issues in other parts of the world, as well as spirituals and "The Negro National Hymn," would have empowered Black teacher-students and encouraged others to consider how they might work to reduce racial boundaries. Edgar Knight was hardly exaggerating when he claimed that the university summer school was "probably the most effective institution in American education for putting provincialism and narrowness of view to rout."[117]

Reflecting on racism, women's rights, and world peace, along with seeing new sights and gaining exposure to elite cultural and intellectual life, would have stoked teachers' senses of agency in the world and of belonging in the professional class, increasing their confidence in the classroom. University summer sessions often also featured exhibits of educational materials that further enhanced teachers' work with students. In a typical description of such an exhibit, the SSS announcement for 1903 stated, "In a large hall there will be exhibits of text-books, school apparatus and all kinds of school work. There will be a special exhibit of scientific and psychological apparatus. Teachers will thus have an opportunity to see and study the best school books and apparatus and typical work from some of the best schools in this country and abroad." When NASSD discussed such displays in 1928, representatives reported that the University of Washington reserved rooms in the education building "for exhibits of textbooks and school supplies," and that Indiana University hosted "rather an elaborate exhibit for one week," after which the materials were displayed at the state's normal schools. Hanus later explained that the Harvard Summer School had a long tradition of inviting publishers to send books for teachers to examine, with the understanding that "there must be no solicitation by salesmen." Rather than requesting that they be returned, many publishers donated the samples, forming the basis of Harvard's extensive textbook library.[118]

As at normal schools and Black colleges, all-campus, education-focused lectures and events at university summer schools additionally deepened teachers' engagement in their field—and the university speakers were likely to be leading scholars. UTexas featured weekly roundtable discussions in which faculty members "freely" discussed "educational problems"; topics in 1904 included elementary mathematics, high school science, manual training and domestic science, and "Some School Legislation Much Needed in Texas." SSS and UIowa held similar forums—for example, on "practical problems that are met within the field" in 1914 and on "The Problem of Financing Public Education" in 1937, respectively—and hosted lecturers including Dewey, Hall, Richards, and rural-school expert Mabel Carney at SSS, and Massachusetts Commissioner of Education David Snedden and UChicago President Robert M. Hutchins at UIowa. Wellesley College President Mildred McAfee opened Harvard's summer 1937 lecture series, which continued with six "public discussions" on various aspects of adult education led by experts from TCC, UMinn, national organizations, and the Works Progress Administration (WPA). Dr. Eduard Lindeman of the WPA was especially critical of the U.S. school system, warning that political control, which made teachers the world's "most timid and frightened group of educators," brought the risk of totalitarianism. Two years later at Harvard, TCC professor and social reconstructionist George Counts again called teachers to action with his speech on "How to Save Democracy." Even the annual Independence Day celebration at SSS included lectures on education; in 1910,

Civil War veteran, peace activist, and minister Jenkin Lloyd Jones addressed "The Three R's, or a Plea for Better Education," and, in 1911, president of the University of Cincinnati and former UTenn President Charles William Dabney presented an argument for "The South Rationalized by Education."[119]

As part of the July Fourth festivities each year, students at SSS issued a "Declaration of Principles," most of which regarded education in the South. Their ten-point declaration in 1902 included support for "the Bible in our public schools"; local taxation to support education; school consolidation; professional status for teaching; and "a public school system, State supported and State directed, in which every child may have the open door of opportunity." They passed similar resolutions in 1914, adding "ample support" for Black schools and "higher pay for teachers."[120] NASSD recognized the importance of events like SSS's celebration, discussing ways to "meet the need for play and fellowship" including sports, clubs, dances, and other entertainment. Indeed, such activities abounded at university summer sessions, facilitating teachers' development of geographically diverse informal professional networks. Summer students commonly played recreational sports such as, at UIowa, basketball for men and tennis for both men and women. "Lawn tennis," a Knoxville newspaper noted in 1904, "continues to be the past-time of quite a large number of the students" at SSS. Ten years later, the campus courts were still "occupied every afternoon and in the early morning hours" by students playing this genteel sport. Partners for the annual tournament, which included mixed doubles, were "determined by drawings," and the winners' names were inscribed on the championship cup. The representative of the University of Missouri reported to the NASSD in 1927 that 90 percent of summer students at his institution participated in men's baseball or women's tennis. Rowing, a sport especially associated with elite universities, was a feature of Harvard's summer session, with annual "regatta" races for men and women in various classes of boats on the Charles River beginning in 1930.[121]

The Charles and the rivers that flowed by UTenn and UIowa also served as venues for swimming and more relaxed socializing among summer students. Harvard offered an annual "moonlight sail," SSS students enjoyed "steam-boat excursions" with dancing, and UIowa students headed to the river for "picnic parties and canoeing parties." On land, students socialized in their residences—Beatrice Cramer enjoyed the company of "swell girls" in the "Eastman dorm" at the University of Rochester—and at numerous receptions and parties. In the 1900s and 1910s, Harvard held "informal Friday evening receptions" with dancing in its Hemenway Gymnasium, while SSS had grand marches with orchestral music, punch, and "pleasant conversation." In the 1920s and 1930s, UIowa had all-university men's and women's dinners as well as dances in the Memorial Union, while Harvard hosted dances and garden parties.[122] An observer at SSS in 1909 summarized well the ties that teachers formed through summer school social events and recreational sports as well as in their classes: "They can receive here an inspiration and an outlook into a world that they might otherwise never have seen. . . . Here they can meet others like and unlike themselves, who have mutual interests and congenial experiences with themselves. Delightful friendships are formed here . . . which will make happier a whole lifetime of service."[123]

By the late 1920s and 1930s, increasing numbers of regular university students also attended summer sessions. Walters mentioned in 1926 that the largest group of "non-teacher elements" among summer students was "the undergraduate group"; Cronin and Jenkins wrote that "unexpectedly, significant numbers of regular students" began enrolling in UWis summer courses, "though teachers continued throughout the inter-war years to be the largest component of the summer student body"; and a chronicler of UIowa's summer session noted that by 1940 it "was catering to a very wide range of student interests."[124] But teachers continued to form informal professional bonds, and some social activities and events in these decades were geared toward their interests specifically. The University of Michigan's representative to NASSD in 1927 described the Men's and Women's Education Clubs there as "vital forces in the Summer Session," explaining that while they placed "some emphasis upon serious things, a good deal of the time is given over to social activities." William Kilpatrick was the featured speaker at TCC's Southern Club reception in 1928, and the Cambridge Union of University Teachers hosted a tea in 1937 for all teachers attending the Harvard Summer School so that they could "become acquainted with one another." Indeed, the presence of regular students on campus did not inhibit teachers from making themselves at home on an elite campus and deriving "much benefit . . . from their contacts with leaders in their professional fields from other sections of the country," as explained in UIowa's 1930 *Summer Session Report*. For many teachers, the opportunity to study with professors who were at the top of their field, to broaden their geographical horizons, and to enjoy refined cultural and social events, made summer school at a state flagship or private university, as Knight observed at TCC, "the means of a new birth" both personally and professionally.[125]

Summer sessions at state normal schools/teachers colleges, Black colleges, and private and flagship universities enabled practicing teachers to meet administrators' expectations that they earn higher-level degrees. Like Daniel Lewis, who returned each summer to Kansas State Teachers College in Emporia to complete his bachelor's in 1928, more than sixteen hundred of Pennsylvania's teachers who enrolled in 1928 summer sessions were earning credits toward bachelor's degrees. Iowa teacher Mildred Smith spent ten consecutive summers at the State Teachers College in Cedar Falls, where the student newspaper reported in 1935 that she expected to complete her degree the following summer—and that her brother and sister, who were both teachers, had enrolled at Cedar Falls for four and seven summers, respectively. Clarence Turpin, a Black teacher in Missouri, completed his BA through summer studies at Lincoln University. Turpin graduated in August 1936—one year after Lloyd Gaines, whose Supreme Court case would later compel Lincoln to establish a law school for Black students, graduated from the same institution during the summer session. A Pennsylvania math teacher identified in her oral history as E. Louisa K. enrolled at a university every summer from 1916 to 1938, earning a bachelor's in history and geology at Pennsylvania State College, followed by a master's in geography at Clark University. And, after Harvard began to count summer credits toward graduate degrees, hundreds of summer teacher-students completed their master's degrees there. Reports of rising numbers of bachelor's and master's degrees among the teaching force reflected their accomplishments as much as the enactment of higher requirements for new-teacher certification. But teachers used their experiences to reach far beyond the mere acquisition of credentials; they also pursued their own version of professionalization by sharpening their knowledge and skills, expanding their professional networks, and broadening their intellectual, cultural, and geographical horizons. E. Louisa K. reflected, "To be able to teach a learner I had to be a learner myself, so every summer . . . I went to summer school and learned something that I didn't know too well."[126] Of course, paying for summer school, not to mention living on a teacher's salary, presented challenges that compelled teachers to also earn money during the summertime.

3

Work for Family, for Supplemental Income, and for an Exit Strategy

The Center of a "Crazy Calico Quilt"

When nineteen-year-old Minnesota rural school teacher Gertrude Black (later La Due) returned to her parents' farm in the summer of 1901, she reported in her diary that the family dog was "so tickled" that he jumped into the buggy to greet her. During the weeks that followed, Black hoed, picked gallons of berries, cleaned "from one end of the house to the other," and sewed a block for "mamma's crazy calico quilt." Her mother's plan to place the block at the quilt's center symbolized the magnitude of Gertrude's contribution to the farm and household during her summer "off" from the classroom.[1] In urban New Haven, Connecticut, a dozen years later, a teacher quoted in a National Education Association (NEA) report on teacher pay said that she found it "absolutely necessary to go out as a waitress or something of the sort for the summer," and when North Dakota music teacher Merle Janice Schroeder also supplemented her earnings through service work in the 1930s, she made it an adventure by spending summers as a housekeeper at Canyon Lodge in Yellowstone National Park. Meanwhile, Wisconsin biology teacher Herbert Lystrup deepened his knowledge of wildflowers and wildlife as a seasonal ranger-naturalist at Yellowstone. Lystrup would have drawn upon the work of Denver teacher Alice Eastwood, who devoted her summers off in the 1880s to cataloging alpine flowers and discovering new plant species in the Rocky Mountains.[2] For these and countless other teachers, summer work related in various ways to their roles as educators, and they returned to school in the fall with enhanced knowledge and professional skills.

Although teachers commonly engaged in many forms of summer work from the 1880s onward, the topic was absent in most education journal articles that provided advice on how to spend these months, and some districts even forbade the practice; most summer work did not fit with school leaders' restrictive vision of teacher professionalization.[3] However, administrators' expectation that teachers "live as gentle folks" and teachers' own desire to achieve a middle-class standard of living created a need to engage in labor and earn additional income. "How Shall I Spend Vacation?" in the May 1890 issue of the *Texas School Journal* offered an uncommon acknowledgment of this need with the somewhat qualified statement, "If the support or credit of yourself or family make it imperative that you work to enable you to supply their wants or maintain your credit then you could not be expected to fail to do something to make money during the vacation months." The article went on to argue that the most important summer activity was "professional growth" through attending a multiweek summer teachers' institute.[4]

Ignoring teachers' need to support their families or to supplement their meager salary, an 1878 article on summer vacation in *The Iowa Normal Monthly* included a heavy-handed directive against manual work, cautioning that sewing would "be just as confining, as exhausting and as trying to the nerves as your school room labors." The Seattle school board went so far in the 1910s as to forbid teachers to take on any outside employment. Historian Doris Hinson Pieroth explains that, after arguing during the 1918 influenza pandemic that the "ban on summer jobs was intended to 'protect teachers from contagion,'" the Seattle board relented slightly in 1919 before denying all women teachers' requests for permission to work during the summer of 1920. In its rejections of Rebecca Knight's and Lulu Brown's requests, the board noted dismissively, "Nearly everybody, in the vicissitudes of life, has some relative to assist," and "that an additional increase in earnings is needed . . . is true to a certain extent of every teacher." While maintaining that "to compete with workers in other fields of labor is generally unwise, unfair, and unprofessional," the school board by the mid-1920s began to allow outside work during the summer but not the school year.[5]

Most administrators did not forbid teachers to work during the summer but endorsed only work that they thought would directly enhance teachers' efforts in the classroom, without openly acknowledging teachers' need for additional income. Likely written by an administrator, a short blurb in *Midland Schools* in 1911 stated, "A change of work is frequently better than conventional loafing," provided that teachers strike "a happy medium." Rare articles addressing summer work in other journals clarified that the best "change of work" was that which would improve instruction. To restore "the mental and nervous resources of teachers," the *Pennsylvania School Journal* reported in 1914, "A little excursion into other fields of work gives the teacher a touch of practical affairs, of which he or she is accused of being woefully ignorant." The *National Education Association Journal* in 1935 elaborated, "A teacher of business works in an office; a journalism teacher on a newspaper; an English teacher in a theater or at a soda fountain studying the moving panorama of life; a science teacher in a shop or on a farm; a sociology teacher in a settlement."[6] Although the 1913 NEA report acknowledged that "inadequate salaries force many teachers into outside work" and that opportunities for teaching summer school were increasingly available, the report's treatment of summer activities prioritized teachers' physical over their financial health. "Considering the extremely heavy nervous strain of teaching it is even doubtful whether much outside work of a gainful character is desirable during vacations unless it is manual labor in the open air," the report concluded.[7]

While school leaders' approach to professionalization constrained teachers' options, teachers' own view of professionalism incorporated a wider range of summer work. Providing critical help at home, as Black did in Minnesota, enhanced the economic standing and bonds between members of their family of origin, ensuring a stable foundation for their work during the school year. Laboring for wages, like the New Haven teacher, furnished resources for meeting middle-class standards and, in cases like Schoeder's, broadened teachers' horizons and stoked their sense of independence in life as well as in the classroom. Other paid employment, such as Lystrup's work as a park ranger, allowed teachers to deepen their knowledge of the subjects they taught and, in some cases, to try out progressive approaches to instruction. While indulging their intellectual passions through summer occupations enhanced many teachers' work during the school year, some used their time "off" to turn their avocation into a new vocation; the knowledge and reputation that Eastwood established during her summers as a botanical researcher facilitated her exit from teaching to head a herbarium in California. In other cases, summer allowed women teachers to occupy themselves with courtship, and marriage opened the door for their exit from the profession. Although pursuing new vocations or marriage clearly undermined some teachers' commitment to teaching, summer work for the most part supported and reinforced teachers' version of professionalism, to the benefit of the education system.

Supporting the Farm and One's Family of Origin

Historian Geraldine Clifford argues that, during the Victorian era, teaching "harmonized" women's engagement in an occupation with their traditional family roles because working with children fit squarely within the female sphere and it prepared young women for future family responsibilities including motherhood. While Clifford and other historians acknowledge that it was not uncommon in the late nineteenth and early twentieth centuries for married Black women to teach, they generally portray women teachers as having *concurrent* family responsibilities only after the mid-twentieth century, when shifting gender ideology and the disappearance of official marriage bars cast the ideal teacher as a married woman.[8] Examining teachers' summer activities between the 1880s and the 1930s, however, reveals that white as well as Black women teachers faced challenges in negotiating family and career even before school leaders sanctioned married women in the classroom. While married Black women teachers and the small number of married white women teachers looked after their own families, many single women teachers bore responsibility for supporting their family of origin. When their family needed help with farmwork and housework as well as emotional care, the seasonal structure of teaching enabled these women, as well as male teachers, to return periodically to the family fold. The summer vacation supported both family life and teacher professionalization by enabling teachers to shift their focus from the classroom to their family's standard of living and quality of life for a defined period of time. Shoring up their family's economic and emotional well-being during the summer months allowed teachers to focus on teaching for the remainder of the year.

Even before the common school reform movement instituted the nine-month school year and the feminization of the teaching force, men teachers routinely combined farming with teaching. The few men who remained in teaching in rural areas after the mid-nineteenth century often continued this practice. As a young country school teacher, Jas Turner lived on his parents' Illinois farm and, as he explained, "assisted in the crops." After he married in 1874, he maintained his own farm while also teaching in rural district schools. When he became head teacher in Stonefort, Illinois, in 1880, Turner rented out the farm and bought a house in town, renovating it during his summer breaks into "a most beautiful and comfortable home." But Turner maintained ties to his farm and reclaimed it later in his long career as an educator in order to pass it along to his sons. In rural Wisconsin in the mid-1880s, young teacher B. H. Meyer boarded with a local family and spent summers on the family farm. After his father retrieved him from his boarding place at the end of the 1885–1886 school year, when Meyer was twenty years old, he enjoyed visiting friends but spent most of the summer working on the farm. In his diary, Meyer described the challenges of an early harvest during a drought; his labor helped to save the year's crop.[9]

Like Meyer and Turner, many women teachers provided summer labor to improve the financial health of the family farm, generally in gender-appropriate roles. An only child, Gertrude Black was responsible for a wide range of tasks on her family's northern Minnesota farmstead during the summer—as well as on occasional weekends—in the early 1900s. After her father met her train in Thief River Falls and took her home, she quickly settled into the routine of "work around the house and farm." In the house, she cleaned, churned butter, made cheese, baked bread, and sewed clothing and quilt blocks, noting in her diary in 1902, "I do most of the housework this summer." Outside the house, Black cultivated flowers, hoed, and spent hours picking juneberries, strawberries, blueberries, and cranberries; she remarked in her July 17, 1901, diary entry that she was "tired and lame from yesterday's work." On August 21, 1902, Black "took the cattle to the meadow a couple of hours . . . picked cranberries . . . stacked a load of hay for father and milked two cows." As she packed later that month to return to her boarding place for another school year, Black's musings in her diary, "Is my vacation really gone? What has been accomplished in my home?" demonstrated the weight of the responsibility she felt to help her parents on the farmstead.[10]

Elizabeth "Bess" Corey likewise felt responsible for her family and the farm. After her father died in 1905, when she was seventeen years old, she began teaching and boarding around, spending summers on the family farm in western Iowa. She took care of her younger siblings, helped with farmwork, and even managed the farm while her mother was hospitalized during the summer of 1908. After she left in 1909 to teach and homestead in South Dakota, Corey stayed in close touch with her family and supported one of her brothers, who joined her and established an adjacent homestead.[11] Unlike Corey, sisters and teachers Amanda, Mary, Maude, and May Stewart remained anchored to the family farm in Millwood, Kansas, as they boarded near their schools and returned to "Stewart Hill" to contribute requisite labor for at least part of each summer. Amanda wrote to one of her sisters in June 1885 that May was weaving a rug while "Pa and Maude are planting potatoes and Ma and I are going to wash." Maude reported in June 1887 that they had finished weaving another carpet and that some of the potatoes were "as large as goose eggs," and May wrote in June 1892 that after "weeding and hoeing in the garden," she and Mary had "carried off two big baskets of weeds to the porkers." As their parents aged and then passed away in the 1890s, the unmarried sisters assumed ownership and full responsibility for Stewart Hill while they continued in their teaching careers.[12]

The seasonality of teaching also helped Grace Canan Pogue to navigate family responsibilities throughout her unconventional teaching career in California's San Joaquin Valley. Unhappy on the family ranch after her 1906 high school graduation, Grace Canan asked the county superintendent for "a position in a school just as far from the center of my particular circle" as possible. He placed her at a remote school in Yokohl, but her parents and sister came to live with her in the house provided by the district for the eight-month term. Canan then taught at the elementary school she had attended until she married John Lee Pogue in 1910. The Pogues established a ranch and Grace gave birth to their son Richard in 1916. Upon the request of her superintendent, she returned to teaching in 1923, and, for the next three years, she and Richard boarded near the school and spent the summer on the ranch with John Lee. After that, they all lived at the ranch while Grace taught in a local school and, when not attending college summer sessions, devoted her vacations to the family ranch business. John Lee's death from a stroke in 1932 challenged Grace's balance of teaching and family, but she and Richard were able to maintain the ranch after selling part of the land. After attending summer school in 1933, Pogue went to her "first and only cattle auction," at which she purchased a Guernsey cow. When Richard spent part of the summer of 1934 at scout camp, Pogue found that she "could stay alone and take care of the ranch,—after a fashion." "The summer passed rapidly," she wrote. "We packed figs in six pound crates and shipped them to San Francisco early in the season when the price was good. The second crop made good feed for the pigs." When Richard went away to college a couple of years later, Pogue hired a caretaker for the ranch, moved to town, and continued to teach and enjoy long summer visits with her son and, later, her daughter-in-law and grandchild.[13]

Sarah Gillespie (later Huftalen) also contributed to the economic health of the family farmstead when not attending the local normal institute during her summers off from teaching country school and boarding around in Iowa, but much of her energy went toward dealing with family strife and caring for her enfeebled mother. In the summer of 1884, she did a lot of housework—including washing, ironing, and sewing clothes—and picked berries, took up honey, and trimmed trees. Her cursory diary entries included, "Ironed & do house work. am tuckered out"; "worked hard all day"; and "Melons are ripe. work. am tired." Although the physical labor was taxing, Gillespie's exhaustion was likely also due to strife in her family. She noted in her diary entry for July 31, 1884, "Pa has been so ugly to Ma all summer." The 1885 summer normal provided Gillespie with a welcome break from housework, family stress, and nursing her mother, whose health, she noted, was "very poor. 90 lbs is all she weighs." After seeing her parents in February 1886, she wrote, "If it is in my power this summer I'll get away from that man." Throughout the spring, she worried constantly about her mother, writing in late April, "Ma is just dying for want of care. I'm almost [of] a mind to give up my school." Summer provided the time she needed, and she devoted herself to caring for her mother as well as protecting her brother Henry from their father's abuse. For the end of the following school year, she wrote that she was "not thankful for my own sake as much as Ma's and Henry's." Gillespie again devoted the summer to nursing her mother and did not return to teaching until after her mother's death in March 1888.[14]

Sarah Gillespie was no longer teaching when she married William Huftalen in 1892, but she returned to the classroom twelve years later in Oneida, Iowa. In 1905, the summer break again provided her with much-needed time and breathing space to attend to her brother and manage her father. After Henry had a hernia operation, she went to the family home to care for him. While there, she "cleaned the cupboards etc & straightened up pa's rooms," noting in her diary, "It kept me very busy to get the meals & do that which I did from 4:30 A.M. to 3 P.M. & so little rest." She added, "Pa is very weak minded and it is pitiful so pitiful—he talked so cruelly of Henry. . . . Pa is a terrible man." "So glad to get back to Oneida" after this stressful visit, Huftalen mustered her energy for the new school year. Having the summer off enabled her to balance stress in her family of origin with her responsibilities in the classroom. Soon after her father died with her by his side in 1909, Huftalen embarked on a new phase of her career as a highly successful county superintendent of schools.[15]

Teachers from small towns and urban areas also used the summer break to help their families, although rarely were they in as dire straits as the Gillespies. A New Haven teacher quoted in the 1913 NEA report on teacher pay said that she regularly spent "two months in summer, with relatives, helping a little," while a Denver teacher stated that she lived with her parents when not attending summer school. Following their father's death, thirty-two-year-old single twins Lillian and Millian Herrick—who taught at Elmira Free Academy and Binghamton Central High School, respectively—devoted the summer of 1904 to comforting their grieving mother at her home in Horseheads, New York. Lillian noted in her diary in June, "Mamma + Millie + I together all summer," and in July, "Summer passes away here with Millie and Mamma. We do for her alway[s]." As the summer ended, she reflected that it had been "filled with beautiful memories. Papa was with us in spirit-form but . . . Mamma misses him more than we can realize." In the spring of 1906, Lillian agonized over whether to travel with Millie to Europe or to fulfill her "duties . . . at home with Mamma." "I am not enthusiastic on going abroad," she wrote in early May, "tho she thinks I am foolish about it as she will be comfortable in her own home." Herrick did take the trip and wrote in September, "I shall never forget how rested + sunny Mamma looked when I came home! . . . How glad I was to be home—my own loved ones. None in the world like my own loved ones + home."[16]

Beyond her sense of duty to her widowed mother, family ties were clearly important to Herrick, and the seasonal structure of the school year enabled teachers like her to have a career without sacrificing extended stays with their family of origin. Herrick expressed appreciation for family time in Horseheads in late summer 1901, writing her diary that her sister "Jessie came up + [her brother] Fred followed + with Millian, Mamma and Papa we had such a sweet happy day. We all felt so bright + funny. Blessed family life."[17] While the Herrick siblings did not have to travel far to reach Horseheads from the towns where they taught, many of Seattle's women teachers had ventured far from home to work in the growing Emerald City. The extension of the Chicago, Milwaukee, and St. Paul Railroad to Seattle in 1909 enabled them to return fairly easily to their family homes for extended summer stays; according to Pieroth, "School district lore credits a railroad timetable with setting school schedules." NEA *Journal* editor Joy Elmer Morgan acknowledged teachers' family obligations when he listed "restoring family ties" as one of several recommendations in an editorial on "Making the Most of the Summer." Reflecting middle-class sensibility, Morgan wrote, "The rapid changes which have taken place in America have tended to separate families and to weaken home ties. The summer vacation offers for many the only free time to relive old memories and to renew one's companionship with his family and relatives."[18]

While the summer break enabled teachers to contribute to their family's financial and emotional health, their family's claim on their time away from the classroom could challenge their sense of independence. Even Lillian Herrick remarked in her diary in early fall 1901, "I have my own life to live." Unlike Herrick, Nellie Covert insisted on living her own life during the summer rather than returning to her parents' Kansas home. When she was in her late thirties and early forties and teaching in Colorado and then in Arizona, Covert's parents implored her often to come home. Her father wrote in late June 1895, "Wonder if you care anything about us . . . I hoped you would come home but it seems Providence willed other wise." He really laid on the guilt in spring 1900, writing to Nellie, "I hoped you would stay with us [to] be our support and comfort in our old age but you can use your pleasure about it our time in this world according to the nature of things cannot be very long then you will have no Parents to visit or sympathize with you." But she apparently remained away, as he wrote on July 4, "If it could have been possible for you to have been here to go to the celebration I would have been very glad." And he lectured in July 1903, "You are old enough to know the duties Parents and Children owe to each other and it is painful to point them out to you as though you were ignorant of them. . . . If you think enough of us to come and comfort and soothe our declining years come we will make you welcome." Finally, after A. J. Covert died on August 1, 1904, his obituary noted, "His daughter Miss Nellie came back from Arizona and was with him the last few months of his life."[19] When all was said and done, even Nellie Covert returned home to support her parents; the summer break enabled her and other teachers to attend to the family that had launched them into adulthood and their work in the classroom. Teachers' summer work for family enhanced the family's emotional and financial well-being but could infringe on teachers' independence. Other forms of summer work contributed more directly to teachers' own economic well-being and could be an adventure as well.

Agricultural Labor and Wage Work

Historian Adam Fairclough points out that Black teachers farmed, dug ditches, barbered, and washed clothes in order to augment their meager salaries.[20] Although historians who do not focus primarily on Black teachers say less about side jobs, such work was quite common throughout the teaching profession. Especially during the months when they did not receive a paycheck from the school district, teachers supported themselves financially through various forms of labor that were more blue-collar than their work in the classroom. They tended crops on others' farms and on their own homesteads and worked in factories, sales, and consumer services. Although engaging in manual labor and other work outside the white-collar realm had the potential to undermine teachers' precarious cultural membership in the middle class, the benefits to teachers' financial well-being outweighed the risks to their social standing. In addition, their approach to the work often carried a middle-class patina and occasionally provided opportunities to broaden their horizons, while at times also allowing men teachers to assert their masculinity and women teachers to step beyond gender boundaries. While it violated school leaders' view of professionalization, summer labor from the teachers' perspective had the potential to improve their work in the classroom by buttressing their financial well-being and independence.

Agricultural work was clearly manual labor, but, as the 1913 NEA report acknowledged, "manual labor in the open air" had health benefits, which the middle class valued. Occupations "carried on out-of-doors in the summer, may be to the advantage of the teacher physically as well as financially," stated the NEA committee.[21] Although men teachers who hired themselves out as farm workers in the summertime likely benefitted from the exercise and fresh air, their main objective was financial. When not studying or attending church or the local teachers' institute, a rural Illinois teacher named Walker worked during the summer of 1886 for farmers named Bates and Jessup in order to pay for board. He tended to Bates's oats and corn in June and July, helped Bates "put up hay" and "cut corn" in August, and worked "at hay on Jessup's place" in September. Afterward, Walker noted in his diary that the $17.25 he had earned through "service as a laborer" just covered his $17.14 bill for the board. When future school superintendent and NEA executive secretary Willard Givens was in his early twenties and needed to supplement his income from teaching in a one-room school in Indiana in the late 1900s, he worked on neighbors' farms and at one point dug ditches, using, he later explained, "just spades and shovels and good strong backs." Givens further asserted his masculinity in 1909 when he and a friend "rode like hobos on a freight train" west, in search of work. On a farm in Nebraska, they hauled manure into the fields from 4:00 A.M. until the dew dried in the midmorning and then cut wheat until the sun went down. He later reflected that the hard agricultural labor had provided "quite a handsome income, we thought." Givens and Walker supplemented their income with agricultural labor that, unlike their work in the classroom, confirmed their masculinity.[22]

When the *Minneapolis Tribune* reported in August 1878, "Schoolma'ams run reapers during vacation in Douglas county," the newspaper did not note whether the women teachers were working on their family's farm or had hired themselves out.[23] Their agricultural labor was likely noteworthy because it challenged both gender norms and the genteel image of the woman teacher. Some women teachers further stretched gender boundaries—and improved their financial well-being—by establishing their own homestead and devoting their summers to living and farming on it in order to "prove up" and become the owner. At the end of the school term in 1904, Gertrude Black moved into a small house on her own claim near her parents' farm in northern Minnesota, noting in her diary that the plaster was not yet dry. "Well, here I am on my own claim. Seems all so queer," she remarked. Black grew more comfortable as she spent the summer helping her parents while also settling into her own house and growing her own vegetables. It seemed "natural" to return to teaching and boarding in August, but she would return to her homestead for future summers and whenever possible during school breaks.[24] In Wyoming between 1880 and 1930, nearly 12 percent of homestead patents went to single women, many of whom were teachers. Soon after earning the certificates of ownership for their properties, Laramie County teachers Minnie Hidy, Bessie Fox, and Blanche Lyons sold them to local ranchers for a sizeable profit. Another teacher who remained on her homestead only long enough to "prove up" was Cynthia Yost (later Andrews), who had taught in her native Maryland, in Florida, and in Kansas before filing for a homestead adjacent to her brother's in Colorado in 1917. For three years, Yost taught in a mountain school. She boarded near the school during the snowiest months but lived for most of the year in a "dugout" home on her land, commuting to school by horse and then in a Ford Model T. She devoted her summers to raising cattle, cultivating crops, and fighting off a grasshopper invasion and the occasional rattlesnake. Although she appreciated the coolness of her dugout during the hot summer months, Yost was happy to put it behind her after she received her deed in 1920—and married Dr. George Andrews.[25]

Other women took a more long-term approach to balancing teaching and farming on their homestead. After twenty-one-year-old Bess Corey moved to South Dakota in 1909, she spent the next decade and a half as both a rural teacher and a homesteader (see figure 7). Corey devoted the first summer to securing a tract of land and a teaching job, writing to her brother Fuller, "Gee I wish you were out here to drive away the men—darn 'em. The wemon [*sic*] say 'You'll have to let 'em love you up a little or you'll never get along in Dakota' but I can't bring myself to it." After returning from a visit with her family in Iowa in June 1910, she reported to her mother, "My potatoes and the rest of my garden looks fine." Corey worked in subsequent summers to improve her land and her little house as well as to support Fuller, who had established a homestead adjoining hers. In June 1916, she wrote to her mother about trouble with a horse and calf's getting loose, and added, "We've just scads of tomato and cabbage plants [and are] almost ready to put in the corn field. . . . The hens are doing pretty well. We get five eggs most every night." Corey "proved up" later that summer and would own the land for thirty more years. Her letters to family members in 1918 celebrated her hard manual labor and defiance of gender norms during summers on her farm. In July, she wrote to her sister, "This morning I heard a chicken squall out by the barn. I ran out there in my bed room slippers and there was a big rattler coiled up. . . . Believe me! That snake was soon a deader." She continued, "The Tuesday before the Fourth one of the neighbors told me they'd be over in the morning to start to plow so I hurried home and moved the manure pile. . . . The first load made me tired, the second made me ache, and the third made me numb, then it went better." She also reported that after "range cattle broke into the potato patch,"

FIGURE 7 Elizabeth Corey's drawn map of the location of her homestead (1910). (Courtesy of the South Dakota State Historical Society.)

she "built [a] fence" with "every post hole over two feet deep. The neighbors brag on it. It looks good and is solid." In August, Corey wrote to her mother, "This has surely been a great summer. . . . Wouldn't you like to see me on a water wagon? Or riding a plow? Or a mowing machine? I can just make my little five foot mower hum." Corey signed her letters "Bachelor Bess," further signaling her sense of independence.[26]

Corey often boarded away from her homestead, both during school sessions when her position was too distant and during portions of summers that she spent attending the teachers' institute and/or working as a housekeeper or cook in Fort Pierre. While this time away from the homestead delayed her in earning the deed to her land and the status of the work was lower than that of teaching, it enabled Corey to make ends meet financially. She kept house and babysat for various families intermittently, writing at one point to her mother, "I'm tired of this working around and taking care of other folks [*sic*] kids." While housekeeping for Mrs. Holland in 1911, Corey wrote in June that she had her own "dandy room" and the "easy" work included cleaning and canning fruit. After she had continued working for Holland while attending the institute, she reported in August that she had strained herself cleaning under the stove and felt like she was "going to drop in my tracks." When Corey worked as a boardinghouse cook before attending the institute in the summer of 1912, she wrote to her mother that she liked the situation. She also acknowledged the low status of the work but suggested that her identity as a teacher distanced her from it. "The boarders are so nice to me," she explained. "They show me as much consideration as if I was one of them and they always call me Miss Corey tho they called the last cook 'Mary[.]' I don't know why unless it is because I'm a transplanted schoolmaam and they happen to like my cooking."[27]

Corey was hardly unusual, as many teachers supplemented their income from teaching through manual, service, or factory work. Despite *The Iowa Normal Monthly*'s caution that sewing was "exhausting," women teachers commonly did a lot of this gender-appropriate work during the summer, both for themselves and as a form of piecework. Kansas teacher Miranda Cather wrote to her friend Nellie Covert in late June 1885 that she was staying on for a couple of weeks with the family with whom she had boarded during the school year. "My school closed last Sat. but I am still at Andover doing some sewing. . . . The family still plan to keep me with them, by having me do my sewing," she explained. Three decades later, the NEA salary study quoted an Atlanta teacher who reported, "I am compelled to spend my vacation period sewing to make summer expenses," as well as the New Haven teacher who said that she needed to take on a job such as waitressing. Long before she became a civil rights activist, Septima Poinsette (later Clark) "always found some work" during the summer. She later wrote that while at her family home in Charleston, South Carolina, in the late 1910s, "I'd get up at 6 o'clock in the morning, and I'd be going down to Miz Gordon's boarding house. . . . I'd serve three meals a day, and in between I'd wash the table napkins and iron them." Male teachers engaged in more masculine forms of manual labor. In June 1888, Kansas teacher J. C. Petherbridge wrote to Amanda Stewart that he was "working in the carpenter's trade" in Kansas City. Petherbridge reported that he liked the work "very well" and was "gathering $2.50 per day" but would be able to remain for only a month due to steep competition for carpentry jobs. Four decades later, Lemuel Garrison balanced teaching at the high school in Haines, Alaska, with summer work as a seasonal fire guard in Alaska's Chugach National Forest.[28]

After the turn of the century, some women teachers stretched gender boundaries through short stints in factories. Irene Lindahl (later Krumpelmann) earned extra spending money in the Clear Lake, Wisconsin, pea-canning factory near her family's farm. Between her graduation from River Falls State Normal School and the commencement of her teaching career in Clayton, Wisconsin, in 1926, she worked in the can loft until the supervisor commented, "I hear you soon will be teaching" and moved her to the factory office. Canning work during the following two summers enabled her to purchase cosmetics and "Real Silk stockings" in 1927, visit relatives in Seattle in August 1928, and save a little money. Rural California teachers, according to historian Kathleen Weiler, occasionally worked in canneries or, in the case of her own mother in the late 1920s, in fruit-packing houses. While housekeeping, sewing, forestry, and factory work were not white-collar, these summer jobs provided teachers with additional resources for meeting middle-class standards, did not significantly undermine their social standing, and could even enhance their status. When Lindahl's train departed for

Seattle, she later wrote, "a gang at the factory waved a fare-well from the spur track as we chugged by."[29]

Other types of summer work had a white-collar or middle-class patina. Like Lindahl in the factory office in 1926, some of New York City's Jewish teachers took clerical jobs, and a woman teacher in Atlanta reported to NEA researchers, "When the school term is out I do office work for three months."[30] Although articles in education journals generally discouraged teachers from working for wages, the journals printed increasing numbers of advertisements recruiting teachers for summer positions. Some ads were as simple and vague as an offer of "Profitable Employment" in an 1889 issue of the *Texas School Journal* or the blurb "100 Teachers Wanted for vacation work. Straight salary of $50 a month," in a 1902 issue of *The Intelligence*. But the ads were mainly for sales positions and often reflected middle-class values in their promises of more than just financial returns. Working for a nursery would allow teachers to "make money and gain health traveling and selling our trees and plants," selling "household chemicals" was a "pleasant summer activity out of doors," and "life insurance work" was "one of the most profitable and philanthropic of all lines of human effort."[31]

Most of the sales opportunities related in some way to education, placing the work within teachers' professional realm. The Globe Furniture Company in 1896 sought an "agent in every county in Texas for School Desks, Blackboards, School Apparatus, etc."; the Smith System Heating Company in Minneapolis in 1911 promised "pleasant, profitable, dignified work" selling the "greatest single room heater in the world for heating and ventilating country and village schools"; and the Mobly Company in Kansas advertised in 1925 for teachers to "demonstrate and sell our wonderful new gravity-propelled Merry-Go-Round to village schools." Another company assured teachers as early as 1890 that selling its "subscription books," which were "strictly high grade works," would maintain "their reputation and standing in communities where they reside." The National Home and School Association advertised frequently during the 1920s in journals including *Midland Schools* and the *Pennsylvania School Journal*; teachers who sold "'Visualized Knowledge' charts—the latest adaptation of visual education," the ads explained, found the work to be "interesting," "educative," "broadening," and a "service to their fellow-men." When Givens and his friend headed west in the summer of 1909, they intended to sell maps in Iowa but continued on to Nebraska after a big flood washed away their market. Their plan may have been a response to an education journal advertisement, as map-selling was in keeping with the work these ads promoted.[32]

Especially prominent throughout the 1920s and the 1930s were ads recruiting teachers to spend the summer selling encyclopedias or textbooks, often including opportunities to broaden their horizons through travel. Selling *The World Book Encyclopedia* promised the "satisfaction of representing the newest and best" as well as a "trip to places you have always wanted to go" in 1921, and the "glamour of a delightful summer, seeing new places and new faces" in 1934.

While most ads did not target teachers of a particular sex, Geographical Publishing Company sought "school men" interested in selling atlases and texts for "liberal commissions," and publisher of encyclopedias and other reference works F. E. Compton Company headlined a widely distributed ad with the declaration, "Wanted: Women Teachers for Summer Work," under which it asked, "Would You Like to Travel All Summer Long—engaged in a work that capitalizes on your teaching experiences and offers unusual financial returns?" A 1932 recruitment ad for Compton stated, "For 37 years we have employed from 100 to 200 teachers each Summer," many of whom "have returned Summer after Summer. . . . Only successful teachers between 25 and 40 years of age, who have had two years or more of Normal School or college training and three years of successful teaching experience, can be considered." One ad reported that summer work for Compton had enabled Ione Hertzer "to travel with other congenial teacher companions, prepare herself for promotion in her teaching profession, and earn real money while she was doing it." Another ad quoted English teacher Elizabeth James on the many benefits of her summer with Compton. She stated that the experience had helped to draw her "out of my one-sided view of life . . . yet keep me in touch with my ideals of education. . . . Returned to my schoolroom after a delightful summer on the lakes, with a wonderful store of new knowledge and experiences, and . . . a nice bank account."[33]

The opportunity to travel also enhanced the middle-class patina of summer jobs that were not necessarily related to education. An advertisement that focused on travel without mentioning the actual work to be done began, "Hundreds of other women teachers have done it" and asked for teachers "between the ages of 25 and 40, willing to learn, ambitious to do big things, free to travel extensively," and possessing some advanced education. "Good health is very essential," the ad continued. "We will carefully train those selected, furnish them with everything needed, free of charge, and pay all railroad fare."[34] Ads such as this may have intended to recruit waitresses for the series of restaurants founded by Fred Harvey along the Santa Fe Railway beginning in 1883. Although waitressing was a working-class occupation, "Harvey Girls" had higher status because the Harvey House system hired educated, almost exclusively white women, housed them in attractive quarters, enforced strict regulations of their behavior, and served worldly transcontinental railroad passengers. Harvey management established a system that allowed waitresses from farming families to return home for the summer, when schoolteachers on temporary contracts took their places. These teachers spent their summers not only as workers whose classy reputation overshadowed their blue-collar tasks but also as Western travelers; some may have even worked at the Grand Canyon's Harvey House.[35]

A 1928 ad promoted working for F. E. Compton Company as a better way to combine travel with earning money than "waiting tables at the large summer resorts or working in the great National Parks," but summer work in vacation destinations enabled teachers—especially white teachers—to augment their finances while enjoying adventures in middle-class territory. Vacation historian Cindy Aron explains that by the early twentieth century, it was common for teachers to spend their vacations "working as waitresses, cooks, baggage boys, and chambermaids at camps, ranches, and summer hotels. The benefits of fresh air, lovely scenery, and fine weather allegedly offered sufficient compensation for the hard work."[36] After working in the canning factory in the late 1920s, Irene Lindahl spent two successive summers in the resort town of Hayward, Wisconsin, where she worked in the laundry at the Giblin Hotel in 1930 and as a waitress at Goulett's Confectionary in 1931. As a guest of her boss at a new nightclub one evening during the first summer, she experienced the "sophisticated company" of vacationing Chicago business elites and caught her "first sight of people mixing drinks from their bottle under the table." She liked the nightclub's orchestra but had "much more fun" dancing with friends at a lakeside pavilion on other evenings. She danced with many different partners again the following summer, when she also enjoyed golfing—a sport she had tried only once before, when her father was the groundskeeper at the course in Clear Lake.[37] Lindahl's leisure activities belied the social status of her service jobs during her summers in Hayward.

National parks by the late nineteenth century were sought-after destinations not only for middle- and upper-class tourists but also for summer workers, and teachers found the short season of Yellowstone National Park especially to be compatible with the nine-month school year. As railroad service opened Yellowstone to tourists in the early 1880s, Bozeman teacher and, for a short time, Montana superintendent of schools William Wallace Wylie published a guidebook and began devoting his summers to leading tours through the park. Although he later reflected that his entry into the tourism business was "accidental and unintentional," the Wylie Camping Company's economical six-and-a-half-day stage-coach or wagon tour was soon very popular, providing friendly service, informative entertainment, and economical meals and accommodations in "moveable camps" or, later, "permanent camps" made up of large canvas tents on platforms. Proud of the educational nature of his tours, Wylie hired many teachers to drive wagons, staff the camps, and guide tourists through the park's wonders. One of his guests noted, "The attendants are all people of refinement—many of the men being college fellows, and the girls being school teachers," and a historian described the staff as "spirited." Even in 1910, after Wylie had sold the company, a Wylie brochure touted the "character of our lady employees—teachers, students and young ladies from private homes, all drawn into Yellowstone for a summer's outing." Working for Wylie infused summer work with both middle-class respectability and the opportunity to broaden one's horizons.[38]

Married couple and Indiana natives David and Jennie Curry led tourists on Wylie-style tours through Yellowstone after they moved with their three children in 1891 to Ogden, Utah—where she was a teacher and he the principal at an academy—and then in 1895 to Redwood City, California—where she taught math and he was the first principal of Sequoia High School. The seasonality of their teaching positions allowed them to spend part of the year working in the outdoors, which they both loved. In 1899, they established an informal and inexpensive "hotel-camp" named Camp Curry in California's Yosemite Valley, their new summer home and workplace. During breaks from making beds, packing lunches, and coordinating other guest services, they hiked throughout the valley. Both had left Sequoia High by 1917, when David died suddenly and Jenny continued to run Camp Curry full time.[39] Also married with children, Irene and Leon Evans both taught school in Idaho and spent the summers of 1930–1933 at Yellowstone's Cooke City Entrance Station, where Leon worked as a seasonal ranger while Irene watched their children. After Leon stayed in Yellowstone during the winter of 1933–1934 as a permanent ranger while Irene returned to Idaho with the children, the entire family began to stay at the park year-round, and Irene's class consisted of only her own children.[40]

The Evanses may well have known Lois and Frank Kowski, who staffed various Yellowstone ranger stations in the early 1940s. Before her marriage, Lois had been a teacher and summer worker—or, in park slang, a "savage"—at the Yellowstone Lake Hotel. Summer service positions at Yellowstone and other parks enabled her and many other single, primarily white, women teachers to assert their independence and right to have an adventure. Beulah Brown (later Sanborn) graduated from college and taught high school in Ohio before moving west in the mid-1900s, after which she taught in Dear Lodge, Montana, in Ogden, Utah, and then in Spokane, Washington, while working at Yellowstone during the summer. After two summers as a "potato peeler" and dishwasher in a Wylie camp, she worked in a curio shop, which, she later said, "was the only job in my life that I didn't like, because here I was, caged in, walking back and forth behind these counters." When not in the shop, she began "taking people out to look at the Canyon, with no thought of remuneration." This led to a position as a guide; Brown escorted visitors down a trail to the Lower Falls in the morning and to Artist Point in the afternoon, before performing readings and skits for them in the evening. "And never in all my life have I ever enjoyed every solitary moment of the day," she reflected. After seeing her in action in 1920, the mayor of Ogden observed, "She is a remarkable girl in that she is as much as [*sic*] home on the brink of the gorge where a misstep would launch one into eternity as she is in a class room teaching oral expression."[41] Also a lover of the outdoors, Herma Albertson (later Bagley) highlighted nature study as an elementary school teacher in Montana and then majored in botany at the University of Idaho. Following her 1926 graduation, she spent summers at Yellowstone and school years as a high school science teacher in Montana. In a unique arrangement at the park, during her first summer Albertson worked in the mornings as a housekeeper—or "pillow puncher"—in guest cabins near Old Faithful and in the afternoons on a crew developing a nature trail through the geyser area. The team constructed the trail and erected interpretive signage describing the flora, hot springs, and other

FIGURE 8 Merle Janice Schroeder (likely third from right) and five other "pillowpunchers" at Yellowstone, 1936. (Courtesy of the National Park Service, Yellowstone National Park, Merle Janice Schroeder Papers, 1936–1939, YELL 133749.)

natural phenomena along its path. The creative and informative placards reflected Albertson's deep knowledge and enthusiasm for nature study.[42]

Another single white woman, North Dakota music teacher Merle Janice Schroeder, spent the summers of 1936–1939 as a pillow puncher at Yellowstone's Canyon Lodge (see figure 8). The sheet of instructions attached to her employment contract acknowledged how common teachers were among park savages with the statement, "TEACHERS!!! HAVE YOU MADE THE NECESSARY ARRANGEMENTS TO REMAIN TO THE CLOSE OF THE PARK SEASON AS YOUR CONTRACTS CALL FOR? THIS IS VERY IMPORTANT." The sheet also gave a nod to the outdoor adventures that summer workers enjoyed: "General Suggestions" included "You will like a hiking suit of some kind for hikes and horse-back riding" and "Employees may like to bring their own bathing suits." Further instructions reflected the informal duty that savages often performed on top of housekeeping and food service: "If you play musical instruments of any kind, we shall be glad if you will bring them with you, or anything else that will help in entertaining our guests." Schroeder apparently put her skills as a music teacher to good use, as coworker Margit Fetveit wrote in her memory album for 1939, "Have enjoyed your lovely voice somuch [*sic*] and your very able way of conducting community sing." Other coworkers who signed Schroeder's albums also praised her singing and referred to enjoyable social gatherings, and Missie Howell wrote, "I will remember us making beds together, dancing together and singing in the dorm." Fetveit and others in 1939 wished Schroeder success in her new teaching job in Alaska, a venture that would further nurture her independence and broaden her horizons.[43] The summer experiences of Schroeder and other teachers who worked in middle-class vacation destinations, who took positions in sales or factories, or who did agricultural or other manual labor buttressed their financial well-being without damaging their middle-class standing and, in many cases, stoked their sense of independence. Schroeder and Albertson also drew upon their expertise as teachers of music and science, respectively. Other teachers' summer work honed their subject matter knowledge and teaching skills.

Teaching in Various Settings

Continuing to engage in their craft during the fallow months was an obvious way for teachers to earn additional money without joining the ranks of blue-collar workers; as Bess Corey understood, a "schoolmaam" had higher status than a cook. Schoolteachers' opportunities for formal teaching in public schools during the summertime were short-lived between the 1880s and the 1930s, however. As historian Kenneth Gold explains, schools did not begin to offer summer academic instruction for course credit until the 1910s, and summer school offerings were among the "fads and frills" that declined precipitously during the Great Depression.[44] Nevertheless, teachers provided instruction in a variety of informal settings during the offseason throughout this period. They offered lessons and classes independently, guided students in vacation schools and organized playgrounds, and worked as camp counselors and ranger naturalists. These summer work experiences not only reinforced or, occasionally, extended teachers' knowledge of the subjects they taught but also deepened their exposure to and facility with progressive teaching methods. Historian Larry Cuban demonstrates that while child-centered progressivism became popular as an ideology by the late nineteenth century, public school teaching remained teacher-centered for the most part.[45] Examining various forms of summer instruction reveals that to some teachers who may have used traditional methods in their regular classrooms, progressivism was more than just an ideology. The informal nature of their summer instructional work allowed them to utilize child-centered approaches and, especially in the case of park rangers, enabled them to deepen their knowledge of the natural world while widening their horizons.

Some teachers hung out a shingle to work independently during the summer. Historian Ruth Jacknow Markowitz writes that New York City's Jewish women teachers offered voice and musical instrument lessons as well as English instruction for the many immigrants in their community. The fees they collected were especially helpful during the Great Depression.[46] The first and longest-serving Black teacher in Little Rock, Charlotte Andrews Stephens, did not need to advertise for summer pupils. After the conclusion of her first year as a classroom teacher in 1870, two mothers separately directed their daughters to "take your book and go up to Miss Lottie's and tell her I said for her to hear your lesson." Thus began the informal summer school that met in the mornings at Stephens's home—except when she left town to attend summer school herself—throughout the early decades of her seventy-year career as an educator. Her wide front porch or a storehouse in the yard served as the classroom, and she collected a small fee from those whose families were able to pay.[47] Familiarity with their students and the lack of a larger institutional structure enabled Stephens in Little Rock and the Jewish teachers in New York to tailor their lessons to the students' interests and abilities.

Teachers also enacted child-centered methods when they worked within the new institutional forms that arose for informal summer instruction during this period. After the nine-month school year took shape by the 1880s, vacation schools spread gradually in urban areas, primarily as a form of progressive innovation to keep poor children off the streets. Gold explains that most early vacation schools did not offer formal course credit and were run by reform organizations that hired people from a variety of backgrounds to teach in innovative ways. In Chicago, the Civic Federation established the first vacation schools in 1896, and the Chicago Women's Club put them on firmer footing when it assumed direction in 1898. The Women's Club hired more teachers from outside than from inside the public schools in the early years, but the chair of the Vacation School Board reported in 1905—two years after the program had begun to receive public financial support—"At present the teachers in the vacation schools are all taken from the Chicago public schools and are chosen with the greatest care." In New York City, the board of education in 1899 assumed full control of the vacation schools established by a philanthropic organization five years earlier. By 1901, sixteen schools in Manhattan, Brooklyn, and the Bronx enrolled over 15,400 pupils and employed close to three hundred teachers. As these numbers doubled within a couple of years, the Board of Examiners began selecting teachers from among multitudes of applicants based on "a system of requirements . . . like that used in the regular schools" that presumably favored public school teachers, the vast majority of whom were white women. Also among the nearly two dozen cities that established vacation schools by the turn of the century were Baltimore, Philadelphia, Cleveland, Kansas City, and Milwaukee.[48]

Beulah Douglas, who taught in Minneapolis during the school year, was a beloved vacation-school teacher in Milwaukee. In describing her summer teaching, historian William Reese explains, Douglas "sounded like a devotee of John Dewey when she asserted in 1902 that the 'work is experimental; what is considered best one year may not be feasible the next. This elasticity is of great value, for when methods become cut and dried, growth ceases.'" In the same vein, Superintendent William Maxwell wrote in 1899 that New York City's vacation schools could "be regarded as experiment stations that will supply valuable suggestions as to work in the regular schools." He commended "particularly the work done in these schools in nature study, in water colors, in sewing, and in woodwork." Maxwell's observations would have applied to many cities' vacation schools, which typically ran in the mornings for six weeks. As Gold explicates, while there was variety among vacation schools, their teachers customarily had a great deal of autonomy and focused on "cutting-edge" topics and approaches such as nature study, manual training, recreational activities, and field trips. Maxwell's 1902 report mentioned classes' "frequent excursions . . . under the leadership of their teachers to the parks and to places of historic interest," and the board chair in Chicago stated in 1905, "Weekly excursions into the country are among the most important features of vacation schools. There the children study nature at first hand, collect material for classroom work, and try their hands at reproducing the scenes with colors or pencil." Vacation schools also emphasized Americanization; teachers in Buffalo began and ended each session in 1899 with patriotic songs and the recitation of a pledge to be "true citizens of our great country and our beloved city," and teachers in New York added English classes after superintendent of vacation schools Evangeline Whitney reported in 1907 that "many little foreigners pleaded for language lessons."[49]

The English classes were a move toward offering more formal academic work, which soon became common in vacation schools. Instruction in English expanded quickly; Whitney reported that 484 pupils enrolled in these classes in 1908, and their "teachers were of high grade." At the same time, new "coaching classes" in New York allowed elementary pupils to earn academic credit for subjects they had failed during the school year. Supervisor Mary Brady observed in 1909, "No activity of the summer school ranks in importance with that of the work of the classes in common branches" due to its potential to mitigate "the retardation of children and the expense involved in carrying them twice through a grade." Brady also noted, "Drill was the main work of the summer school," and Whitney focused on the role of the "industrial branches" in preparing children for trades. In light of the success of the elementary coaching classes, Superintendent Maxwell recommended summer high school sessions to give "backward pupils an opportunity to make up work" and "bright pupils a chance to advance more rapidly."[50]

Developments in New York echoed in other cities as public school systems absorbed vacation schools and turned them into formal academically oriented summer schools. In Chicago, the board of education assumed full control of vacation schools in 1909 and added "academic review classes" and high school work in 1911. In most cities, summer education "had clearly shifted to regular schoolwork" by 1912, according to Gold. Instead of a site of "educational experimentation," Reese argues, the vacation-turned-summer-school was "a place for students to repeat failed subjects or to do advanced work and for regular teachers to augment their salary." Four thousand teachers in 1917 and more than fourteen thousand teachers in 1929 engaged in this respectable form of summer work before the Depression reduced their numbers to just over three thousand in 1934. These teachers benefited from the opportunity to earn more money but rarely honed their progressive methods.[51]

Vacation schools and supervised summer playgrounds, Gold reports, were "often conceptually, developmentally, and organizationally interwoven, and one program usually led to the other." Beginning in Boston in 1885, organized playgrounds appeared in cities mainly in the Northeast and Great Lakes regions. In Cambridge, Massachusetts, the Mother's Club established a system of playgrounds in 1902 and handed them off to the municipality in 1911. Chicago's playgrounds flourished until the Depression, but the heyday of supervised playgrounds was the late 1900s and 1910s. New York City served 112,000 children in 246 playgrounds during the summer of 1909, and the 1913 NEA report on teacher pay listed "playground instruction" as one of the most common sources of outside income for teachers. Not all playground workers were schoolteachers; some organizers preferred to hire social workers, and Whitney reported that New York's playgrounds in 1909 were "fortunate in securing many fine college men and women of marked ability to direct the summer activities." Still, those teachers who did work on playgrounds were able to immerse themselves in active teaching strategies. In Cambridge, programming focused on baseball and other sports for boys and crafts and dancing for girls. New York's "Daily Program" for 1907 listed marching, singing, and saluting the flag in assembly; "organized games"; "organized free play"; gymnastic and military drills followed by folk dancing and "occupation work" including clay modeling and scrapbooking; basketball; and "Good Citizens' Club." Only the note that "children attend the library and game room in half-hour periods; boys and girls alternately" made a gender distinction. A highlight of New York's 1909 playgrounds was a Fourth of July parade for which children built patriotic floats depicting historical events.[52]

Camp counseling also allowed teachers to engage in informal progressive teaching in the outdoors, through which some women teachers stretched gender boundaries. The first camps in the 1880s enrolled middle- and upper-class boys. Camps proliferated in the early twentieth century, especially in the Northeast, as campers diversified yet remained segregated by class, gender, and race: private camps served privileged white boys or girls; camps sponsored by agencies including the YMCA, Boy Scouts, Girl Scouts, and Camp Fire Girls enrolled middle-class white children; separate agency camps served Black or Jewish children; and, like vacation schools and playgrounds, camps sponsored by social service agencies focused on exposing poor city children to nature. Private camps often hired teachers from private schools, and other camps hired teachers as well as college students to work as counselors. Markowitz lists camp counseling as a popular "extra" job for New York City's Jewish women teachers in the interwar period, when large numbers of Jewish parents sent their children to camp as a means to foster both assimilation and connections with other Jews. Camp directors looked to new understandings of child psychology, having campers engage in "Indian play" to enact G. Stanley Hall's recapitulation theory. But "the single most influential theorist in summer camp circles," according to historian Leslie Paris, was John Dewey as interpreted by William Heard Kilpatrick. Under the direction of "progressive education enthusiasts," counselors put theory into practice as they facilitated nature study and handicrafts and socialized campers as members of "miniature communities."[53]

New York City high school teacher Laura Mattoon founded Camp Kehonka in New Hampshire in 1902. Paris explains that Mattoon and many other women who directed new girls' camps were college-educated outdoor enthusiasts and "new women" who "tacked between traditional and emergent notions of femininity." Camp brochures included photographs of girls firing rifles and building log structures. At Camp Kehonka through her death in 1945, Mattoon's efforts to instill "a practical and spiritual appreciation of the outdoors, physical prowess, and greater independence" surely broadened campers' as well as counselors' views of what women could do.[54]

Serving as a seasonal ranger naturalist in a national park was another way in which teachers engaged in informal progressive outdoor instruction as well as widened their horizons in middle-class territory and, in the case of women teachers, transgressed gender boundaries. Inspired by the educational impact of Wylie's and other early guides at Yellowstone—including teachers like Beulah Brown—the National Park Service in 1920 created the position of ranger naturalist to offer informal instruction to park visitors of all ages. When teacher Mary Rolfe worked during the summer of 1921 as a ranger naturalist at Yellowstone, she presented three lectures—at the auto camp, a hotel, and a lodge—each evening. Park superintendent Horace Albright wrote that Rolfe was "a fine enthusiastic girl" but that her lectures were overly "technical." And after dividing her time between pillow-punching and trail development in 1926, Herma Albertson worked as a seasonal ranger naturalist for the next three summers. While Albright supported women's employment, the National Park Service's all-male heritage was so powerful that through the mid-twentieth century, few women were able to follow the path that Rolfe and Albertson broke.[55]

Unlike women, it was quite common for men teachers to secure positions as seasonal ranger naturalists in the 1920s and the 1930s. When J. M. Johnson, head of the biology department at a New York City high school, wrote to Albright to inquire about summer work as a "nature guide," he said, "I want to get to the Rockies again and I feel that I must earn some money while doing so. . . . Of course I am familiar with most of the plant and animal life in your territory." Johnson spent the summer of 1923 as a naturalist at Rocky Mountain National Park. Summer naturalists at Yellowstone in the 1930s included Frank Oberhansley and Willis Smith, a geology and biology teacher and the biology department head, respectively, at Ogden High School in Utah; John A. Thompson, a science teacher and coach at Park County High School in Montana; Philip Fix, a geology and biology teacher at Bozeman High School in Montana; F. Howard Brady, a high school science teacher in Sheridan, Wyoming; and Herbert Lystrup, a biology teacher at Eau Claire High School in Wisconsin. Brady served as a seasonal naturalist at Rocky Mountain and Grand Canyon National Parks prior to working at Yellowstone, and several teachers returned to their Yellowstone positions year after year; Lystrup served for thirty-eight summers, often with his family in tow.[56]

The seasonal ranger naturalist position was ideally suited for teachers; a 1929 National Park Service manual stated that naturalists were "responsible for public contact in conducting field trips, delivering lectures and acting as museum attendants," as well as writing educational material, and were "chosen for their training in the sciences and their experience presenting information to the public." Teachers serving as naturalists were frequent contributors to *Yellowstone Nature Notes*, a monthly or bimonthly educational publication. Herma Albertson published both scientific observations of coniferous trees and personal reflections on their beauty, and Willis Smith wrote about the behavior of beavers and ground squirrels. While Albertson's and Smith's work for *Nature Notes* honed their knowledge of science subjects they taught during the school year, one of Lystrup's many contributions to the publication reflected his enthusiasm for active teaching as a ranger naturalist. "One of the highlights of my Nature Walk," he explained, "is to show members of my group a tree which has flowers. After having shown them both the staminate and the pistillate flowers I cannot help but note that this very obvious part of a pine tree is something they have never witnessed before. . . . Only one person had seen the flowers before!"[57]

Minnesota teacher Mildred Ericson in 1939 was one of a small quota of women who were able to attend the summer Field School of Natural History at Yosemite National Park. The Junior Explorer Nature Program that she went on to conduct as a seasonal ranger naturalist at Yellowstone epitomized progressive instruction. Ericson reported on one day's activities, "The kids were still talking about their ant lion discovery from the previous day and wanted to show their 'find' to the new boys and girls so we again . . . observed the ant lions. . . . While walking in the vicinity we flushed a night hawk sitting on her nest containing one egg. . . . This proved to be an excellent nature study trip." When they came across road construction the following week, a supervisor "talked to the children and explained what they were doing and how the crews worked." On a visit to a swamp, "each child gathered a bunch of cattail leaves. We brought them back to the museum back porch where we did weaving. The boys and girls made some very nice trays and mats." And, later in the summer, Ericson led the children in making "plaster of paris animal tracks."[58] Ericson's summer work as a seasonal ranger naturalist—like that of teachers who were camp counselors, instructors in playgrounds or vacation schools, or taught independently—allowed her to employ child-centered methods while deepening her subject matter knowledge and broadening her horizons. For many teachers, the opportunity to pursue their passions through summer work enhanced their instruction and may have strengthened their commitment to teaching; like Ericson's students, the generations of students who studied biology with Herbert Lystrup during his long career in Wisconsin would have benefited from his enthusiasm and ever-deepening knowledge of Yellowstone's flora and fauna. For some teachers, however, exploration of new territory during the summer facilitated their exit from the profession.

Working for an Exit Strategy: Establishing a New Vocation or Marriage

Geraldine Clifford points out that many women who pioneered routes into new fields or professions for their sex in the late nineteenth and early twentieth centuries were former schoolteachers. Among the first women journalists, office workers, religious leaders, lawyers, and doctors were many who had taught when they were younger. Clifford also explains that while marriage usually debarred women from teaching, the role of matrimonial status in determining teaching careers was complex.[59] Although Clifford does not acknowledge how the seasonality of teaching contributed to women—and men—teachers' movement into new lines of work or marriage, the extended summer break from the classroom played an important role by providing teachers with psychological and/or physical room for immersion in avocations, searches for new vocations, or opportunities to meet suitors. For some teachers, their avocation or a new relationship developed unintentionally into a new vocation or marriage proposal, while other teachers worked consciously to establish an exit strategy from the classroom. In both cases, the summer break hastened these teachers' departure from the profession.

Late in his life, William Wylie wrote of his "accidental and unintentional" role as a major tour operator at Yellowstone National Park, "It was at least ten years after this work began, before Mrs. Wylie and I realized that we were drifting into a tourist business." By the late 1890s, his summer avocation had become a full-time vocation, and he spent the nonsummer months not in a classroom but lobbying Congress to continue his lease of a route through the park and on speaking tours to promote the "Wylie Way." After they sold the Yellowstone company, the Wylies ran a camp-style resort at Zion National Monument in Utah.[60] The success of Camp Curry at Yosemite National Park similarly inspired Jenny and David Curry to turn their summer passion into a year-round pursuit, although that was not necessarily their original plan. Irene and Leon Evans's departure from the classroom to spend the full year at Yellowstone also seemed to take shape organically, just as Lemuel Garrison decided to leave his school in Alaska only after realizing that his newfound passion for his summer work in the national forest could lead to a full-time career with the National Park Service.[61]

Beulah Brown's enjoyment of her summers at Yellowstone also led unexpectedly to a new career. In the early 1920s, she was contently balancing working as a guide during the summer and teaching in Spokane during the school year when the owner of the Yellowstone Park Camps Company came to Spokane and asked her to manage one of the park's lodges for the summer. "Manager," she replied. "I have no ambitions along that line." He assured her that she could do it, and, she later explained, "So I did, and I was at Mammoth [Hot Springs] for two [summers] as manager, and later at Old Faithful for five." She continued for several years to teach school in Spokane—aside from 1922–1923, when she remained at Yellowstone to tutor the children of a "winter keeper," and 1924–1925, when she traveled internationally. But Brown's success overseeing housekeeping, kitchen, and dining room staff during the summer—an article on "Summer Savages" in a 1926 issue of *The Outlook* noted that Brown was "the friend, confidant, as well as the director, of many hundreds of girls"—ultimately gave rise to a new role that left no time for teaching. At Yellowstone in 1926, she met the owner of the new hotel soon to open at Death Valley, who offered her the position of manager. For the next two years, she managed Yellowstone's Old Faithful Lodge during the summer and, instead of heading back to school, managed Death Valley's Furnace Creek Inn during the remainder of the year. After marrying in 1928, she and Henry Sanborn managed a resort hotel in California and then the Mammoth Cave Hotel in Kentucky, where they earned a reputation as outstanding national park concessionaires.[62]

Before the national parks and their concessions were well established, Denver teacher Alice Eastwood's summer immersion in her avocation not only led unintentionally to a new career but also helped to establish the knowledge base upon which future ranger naturalists would draw. After graduating as valedictorian of her East Denver High School class in 1879, Eastwood began teaching at her alma mater. Over the next decade, she taught a wide range of subjects including Latin, composition, literature, history, and drawing as well as her favorites astronomy and natural science. She saved as much of her small salary as she could in order to devote her summers to botanical exploration and collection in the Rocky Mountains. "As soon as the school term was over," explains biographer Carol Green Wilson, "she packed up her old clothes and well-worn shoes. Then, with her new [botany] *Manual* in her hand, she headed for the high Rockies." Staying in primitive accommodations, she was "off on the trial, unconcerned with anything except myriads of flowers as she skirted glistening lakes on the short walks to the jutting peak." As she accumulated plant specimens, Eastwood established a herbarium at her school and began to earn a reputation for her extensive knowledge. In 1887, her principal introduced Eastwood to renowned English naturalist Alfred Russel Wallace, whom she guided on an excursion to Gray's Peak during the summer's alpine flowering season. While Eastwood expanded her collection, Wallace dug up plants to mail back to England. Eastwood likely never imagined that she could work as a botanist full-time but decided to devote herself completely to her avocation when she received a windfall from selling property that she owned with her father during a real estate boom in Denver. She headed to California in 1890 and soon began traveling extensively on collecting expeditions, publishing hundreds of articles, and naming hundreds of plant species while overseeing the herbarium at the California Academy of Sciences for fifty years.[63]

Far from the western mountains, Gertrude Black's religious devotion grew into an avocation that pulled her away from teaching. Before returning to her family's northern Minnesota farmstead for the summer of 1901, she spent several days at a camp meeting of the Free Methodist Church. She wrote in her diary upon her arrival that it was "good to see the tabernacle" and a few days later that she had accepted an "invitation for seekers for sanctification. I felt as if I must go and as soon as I did my heart was melted. I laid my ease before God and received the blessing." After joining her family, she noted that it was "nice to be home but strange not to be at church" due to the remoteness of the farmstead. During breaks from housework and quilt-making, she read religious texts and engaged in "secret prayer"; the berry patch, she wrote, was "a good place to talk to the Lord and meditate." The following summer, Black noted in her diary that she "read and prayed," was "leaning on Jesus," found "comfort in reading F. M. [Free Methodist] paper every week," and was "stirring" herself "to know more of God." By August 1903, Black was conducting Sunday school classes in homes near her parents'. Having the summer off from rural school teaching allowed her to study religious texts and prepare lessons. On Sundays, she celebrated high Sunday school attendance and reflected, "I feel like praising God so much. It is the means for bringing about a better feeling in this neighborhood," and "God was with me." After writing at the end of the following summer that she felt "very little ambition" to return to her regular teaching responsibilities, Black combined them with attending camp meetings, teaching Sunday school, and even preaching in the local church during the school year. In the fall of 1906, she did not return to rural school and instead attended a church conference and pursued other religious activities. Black would soon marry Samuel La Due, whom she met through religious work, and become a minister in the Free Methodist Church.[64]

While Wylie's success as a tour operator, Brown's enjoyment of her work at Yellowstone, Eastwood's love of botany, and Black's religious devotion pulled them away from classroom teaching, in other cases teachers' discontent with teaching pushed them to use the summer break to search for a new line of work. After he worked briefly as a carpenter in 1888, J. C. Petherbridge wrote to Amanda Stewart in Kansas, "I'm going to teach one more school, and that is all. School teaching is the smallest business in the world for a young man of any ability whatever. No honor, no money, no nothing!" He used the following summer to finalize his exit strategy, reporting to Stewart in August that he had sent his tuition payment "to Ann Arbor," apparently for law school at the University of Michigan. Five years later, it was J. C. Petherbridge, attorney and counselor at law, who provided legal advice to the Stewart sisters as they assumed ownership of the family farm. Discontent with teaching was hardly limited to men, although they had more options outside of education. Leavenworth teacher and Stewart friend Elizabeth "Libbie" Burbank wrote to Amanda in June 1887 that she wanted to concentrate on bookkeeping that summer: "Do you know, I have a notion to go to Evans and take a thorough course of bk. keeping. I think I would like that business. I hate teaching—only the pay and short hours being the attractive features." Burbank continued teaching for at least a few more years, writing in February 1888, "I wish I never was coming to school again. I am so tired and cross." She would have been attracted to an advertisement in the *Texas School Journal* several years later for the "great summer discount" at Draughton's Practical Business College.[65]

Future school administrator and congressman Conrad Selvig's discontent with rural school teaching in the late 1890s stemmed less from dislike of the work and more from ambition to make his mark in the world. After graduating from a southeastern Minnesota high school in 1895, Selvig's experiences working on a farm and laying steel railroad tracks propelled him to secure a teaching position in a nearby country school the following fall. For the next several years, he taught in a succession of rural districts and devoted his summers to various attempts to realize his higher ambitions. In the summer of 1896 he earned a nomination from his congressman and borrowed money to travel farther than he had ever been from home and sit for entrance examinations at the U.S. Military Academy at West Point and the U.S. Naval Academy in Annapolis. At West Point, he took a preparatory course and was awed by the academy's graduation ceremonies and meals in the dining hall. But Selvig failed both entrance exams, writing to his cousin, "Well, the worst has happened. . . . I found out Saturday night that I was not to become a cadet and since then I have felt so blue that I have hardly spoken." He reported that algebra was his downfall and implored his cousin, "Please do not tell anybody." Thus, Selvig explained several decades later, "It was to be country school teaching again." At least, he wrote, "I had a richer background now and felt surer of myself." The following summer, he took a civil service exam and explored government work but returned to teaching in the fall. Then, as soon as the school term ended in 1898, he enlisted in Company F of the Minnesota Volunteer Infantry and headed south for military training to defend U.S. interests in the Spanish-American War. The declaration of peace sent him back to the classroom, and studies and attending an NEA meeting during subsequent summers helped him to make his mark through a career in education and the U.S. House of Representatives.[66]

In the 1920s, advertisements like the one for Draughton's Practical Business College abounded in education journals, offering exit strategies to teachers who disliked teaching or harbored ambitions that fostered discontent. An ad for Franklin Institute's preparation for "U.S. Government examinations" promised "thousands of permanent, life, positions" and that teachers could "during vacation get a big paid permanent position." Ads recruiting teachers to sell school apparatus or books also commonly mentioned that it was possible to move from a summer position into a year-round one. In addition to an "Attractive Vacation Position," the National Home and School Association offered an "opportunity for promotion and growth if you should be desirous of a permanent position at the end of the summer," while the S. L. Weedon Company promised teachers that a successful summer as a "Weedonite" could be "a stepping-stone to a pleasant, profitable, permanent business career beginning next fall!" An ad recruiting teachers to sell *The World Book Encyclopedia* reported that hundreds of educators had left the schools to join the company when they "discovered after one or two summers' experience that they were fitted for a bigger field of service and income," and F. E. Compton Company touted "permanent salaried positions" for women teachers, boasting, "many of them have given up teaching to enter our business permanently." One Compton recruitment ad included Mrs. M. C. Cummins's testimonial, "I joined the House of Compton after spending years as a teacher. . . . I have enjoyed my relations with my co-workers, and know of no position open to women which has the opportunity for earning and for service equal to the one offered by the House of Compton."[67] Such advertisements would have been enticing to teachers who desired to leave the classroom.

For Herma Albertson, dislike of teaching and devotion to her avocation operated in concert to launch her into a new vocation. Like Petherbridge, Burbank, and Selvig, she was not content—in fact, she was downright unhappy—in the classroom. And like Brown and Eastwood, she relished exploring the natural world during the summer. When the opportunity arose to make her summer avocation a year-round vocation through a graduate fellowship and then a position as a park naturalist at Yellowstone, she later wrote, "I accepted the offer as quickly as I could run home from the post office, type out my acceptance, and get it into the mail again. That is the extent of my love for high school teaching." As Yellowstone's first woman full-time ranger naturalist in the early 1930s, Albertson worked year-round to educate herself, other park staff, and visitors on

Yellowstone's plant and animal life as well as geothermal features. She told a reporter, "Now that I am in this work, I'm the happiest girl in the world." She also fell in love with and married chief ranger George Baggley and went on to raise their daughter in the succession of parks to which George was assigned, publish two editions of a book on the plants of Yellowstone, and spearhead efforts to improve housing for national park employees.[68]

Herma Albertson Baggley, like Beulah Brown Sanborn and Gertrude Black La Due, met her husband-to-be through her avocation-turned-vocation; her new line of work pulled her away from teaching and then offered a path to marriage. For other women teachers, the summer break facilitated courtship more directly by providing a change of scenery or simply time away from surveillance by school administrators and the community. When courtship resulted in marriage between the 1880s and the 1930s, it was rare for women teachers to remain in the profession. For the few who did continue to teach—Clifford and Markowitz acknowledge instances in which Black, Jewish, and other women remained in the classroom[69]—or who, like Grace Canan Pogue and Sarah Gillespie Huftalen, returned to teaching several years after marrying, the seasonality of the profession helped them to balance their work and family responsibilities. More commonly, courtship served as an exit strategy when women teachers—especially those who were white—resigned upon marriage, either by choice or because their district enforced a marriage bar. Although marriage was an entirely gender-appropriate goal for women, school leaders' casting of the ideal woman teacher as unmarried meant that engaging in courtship transgressed the tenets of professionalization. Education journals occasionally published not-so-tongue-in-cheek cautions against "sweethearting"; the *Texas School Journal* noted in 1889 that while weddings were "in the air," the schools could not "afford to have too many of our teachers carried off in that way" and warned teachers in 1891 to interact with potential suitors only "on the veranda where all the rest of the people are."[70] However, many teachers did not see a conflict between courtship and their professional role and, during the summer especially, exerted their right to shape their own romantic relationships, wherever those relationships might lead.

"Teasing one's friends about their respective marital states was habitual in teacherdom," writes Clifford.[71] But such teasing and more serious discussions of suitors and courtship were also assertions of teacher agency in the face of administrators' expectation that they remain single. Libbie Burbank mentioned in a letter to Amanda Stewart at the end of the school year in 1881 that she had heard about a male acquaintance who had become "spliced," or married, and asked, "Now, Amanda, why didn't you 'set your cap' for him?" Another friend reported the birth of her second child to Stewart a few years later and quipped, "Don't you wish you were <u>well settled</u> like your humble friend?" During the summers of 1920 and 1921, friends of Russellville, Arkansas, home economics teacher Vivian Bullock (later Scarlett), who was in her mid-twenties, wrote constantly about courtship and marriage. Nelle wrote from Little Rock, "Three of the teachers from our school are going to get married so there has [*sic*] been several parties for them"; Joanne jested from St. Louis, "Have you found you a 'handsome man'? ha ha"; and Bess wrote from Ozark, "I don't know how you keep from catching matrimonial fever. . . . If you do be sure to let me know. I don't think there's a gleam of a chance for me." Also writing from Ozark, another friend quipped, "How have you been spending your vacation? has it been a thrilling romance, from one end to another?" Acknowledging women teachers' assertion of their right not to remain single, a short 1927 article in *Midland Schools* began, "School teachers may take vacation, but Don Cupid does not" and listed several "vacation marriages" in Iowa.[72]

Stories of various white women teachers' courtships leading to marriage demonstrate how the summer break played a role in this exit strategy. While teaching high school in Eau Claire, Wisconsin, in the early 1880s, Nellie Williams (later Brown), who was in her mid-twenties, corresponded frequently with Charles Brown, who was establishing a law firm in Madison. They discussed her boarding place, his progress in his practice, and their love and possible marriage. But it was during the summers, when she stayed at her family home in Madison, that they tested and really forged their relationship. In Madison in July 1882, Williams wrote to apologize to Brown for an "injustice," asking, "Can you take me back again?" He did, and she wrote to him excitedly from Eau Claire in June 1883, "One week from today I shall be home." She reported that she had turned down an opportunity for summer teaching in Eau Claire in order to spend the summer in Madison, and Brown replied, "I am glad to get the last letter from you and glad to write this last letter to you. Glad because the necessity for writing doesn't exist." She resigned her teaching position the following November, and they married early in 1884.[73]

Two decades later, Lillian Herrick made space for courtship during the summers that she spent supporting her family in Horseheads, New York. Among the several men whose letters and visits she mentioned in summer diary entries was Mr. Chapman. After she returned from a trip to the Pan American Exposition in Buffalo in July 1901, she wrote that a "fine letter" from him was waiting for her and that a palmist at the "Pan-Am" had predicted that she would be married within three years. She took pleasure in visiting and getting ice cream with Mr. Chapman a couple of weeks later but also mentioned how much she enjoyed another man's company and agonized over a friend's criticism of Mr. Chapman. He remained a fixture in her summers in Horseheads, though. Herrick wrote during the summer after her father's death in 1904 that "evenings spent with Mr. Chapman" were "blessed in so many ways. . . . We plan to plan together." She mused, "Love emanates from him to me. Can I reflect it?" The palmist's prediction came true, albeit belatedly, when they married and she left teaching in 1908.[74] By 1923, Vivian Bullock apparently had also caught a variant of the "matrimonial fever" that her friend had mentioned, and the summer break would enable her to treat it. Medical student William Scarlett wrote in March to say that he would spend the summer in Russellville. "It has been a cheer to me to think of being with you this summer," he said. Scarlett also suggested that the time together would allow them to do some serious planning, writing, "Vivian, it would make me happy to know that you really wish to prepare nice things in the future for me and 'ours.'" In the middle of their summer together, he wrote to Bullock that she was "wonderfully sweet" and he wanted to be with her "every night." His wish soon came true; they married in September and she did not return to teaching.[75]

With a steady boyfriend in the small Wisconsin town where she taught in the late 1920s, Irene Lindahl declared, "The notion that teachers taught because nobody would marry them and they were made neurotic by starved love instincts didn't apply to me!" But it was spending the summer working in the resort community of Hayward that paved the way to marriage for Lindahl. In 1930, she dated a couple of tourists from Chicago, one of whom corresponded with her throughout the year. In 1931, a friend introduced her to Louis Lee, Hayward's new undertaker. She was not interested at first due to his profession and the fact that he was a widower but agreed to a date when he stopped by the confectionary shop where she was working. From then on, she later explained, "every day Louis found reasons to cross the street . . . to Goulette's—for a coke, or cigarettes, or to try the slot machine." In their free time, they enjoyed golfing, swimming, and dancing together. Of the evening rides in Lee's Pontiac she later wrote, "I savored these hours in sight of these supremely indifferent stars," when he held her hand and paid her compliments. After Mrs. Goulette counseled her that a man in a second marriage would be "more mature, thoughtful, and responsible," Lindahl decided that her "original picture of Prince Charming needed only a bit of touching up" and ended the summer with "a boy-friend to call my own." During the 1931–1932 school year, they saw each other occasionally, spoke on the telephone, and wrote often. She savored letters such as one in which Lee wrote, "I shall just tell you that the undertaker in Hayward is very very much in love with a teacher in Frederic named Irene and how he wants her to know it." They discussed marriage in the summer of 1932 but decided that Lindahl should teach for another year in order to save some money. Then, she later explained, when school closed in 1933, "vacation would be for good. I knew I'd never be teaching again for the simple reason that married women did not work." She enjoyed the wedding shower that her teacher friends threw for her, including her roommate's josh that she would be taking a "chance with this next room-mate!" The chance took her to St. Paul, where he took over the family mortuary business and together they ran a boardinghouse.[76]

For Ruth Jensen (later Hamilton), who taught fourth grade in Colfax, Iowa, the summer break enabled her not only to meet suitors but also to get a taste of married life. While attending summer school at Iowa State College in 1919, she became enamored of Bob, who was playing professional baseball in Des Moines. Jilted when he announced that he was going marry someone else, Jensen resolved to become "a dedicated spinster and a devoted teacher at age 21." During the very next summer, however, she fell in love with Carter Hamilton, a high school acquaintance who was pitching for a semiprofessional baseball team in order to pay for his medical education at the University of Iowa. They were together whenever he had time off or a game near where Jensen was staying with her parents, and in August he presented her with his medical fraternity pin. Called to play with the Cleveland Indians for the summer of 1921, he came to her school in late April and proposed that they marry and keep it a secret so that she could continue teaching. They married the very next day, but, as she later explained, she was "not good at lying and confessed." Instead of firing her, the school board deleted the clause prohibiting marriage from her contract, freeing the Hamiltons to acknowledge their marriage publicly. She took the train to Rock Island, Illinois, where he was playing for a minor-league team affiliated with the Indians. "My new life had begun and I loved every second of it in the dingy, shabby apartment that I tried so hard to beautify," she wrote. When he was transferred to another league, in Pennsylvania, they made an adventure of it before she returned to her fourth graders and he to medical school in the fall. The seasonal nature of teaching enabled Ruth to combine teaching with her marriage to a baseball player. She missed his medical school graduation ceremony in 1923 because it fell on her last day of school, but after that they moved together for his internship and then his medical practice, and she never again had a permanent teaching position.[77] Even though the school board had made an exception for her, marriage led Ruth Jensen Hamilton to leave teaching just as it did Nellie Williams Brown, Lillian Herrick Chapman, Vivian Bullock Scarlett, and Irene Lindahl Krumpelmann. While challenging professionalization ideals, their summer romances were not necessarily an intentional exit strategy like a search for a new vocation; like other teachers' love for their summer avocation, marriage pulled these teachers away from the classroom.

Schoolteachers' summer work between the 1880s and the 1930s was a patchwork of different experiences. Although administrators viewed most summer work as detrimental to professionalization efforts, and some pursuits precipitated teachers' exit from the classroom, on balance teachers' summer work benefited the education system. Historian Johannes Westberg argues that in Sweden, "livelihood diversification" by teachers enabled the nineteenth-century expansion of mass schooling.[78] Examining teachers' summer work in the United States suggests not only that American teachers similarly subsidized the development of the education system but that in many cases summer work enhanced their efforts during the school year. Supporting their family of origin, laboring for wages with an element of adventure, and teaching in various settings dovetailed with teachers' vision of professionalism by shoring up the economic and emotional well-being of their family, augmenting their salary without threatening their middle-class standing, deepening their understanding of progressive teaching methods, and broadening their horizons. An activity that further widened teachers' horizons, tourism garnered both approval from administrators and enthusiasm from teachers, although not necessarily for the same reasons.

4

Tourism

"The Teachers Are the Greatest Traveling Class"

The Maryland State Teachers College at Towson Alumni Association's 1945 biographical statement on Lillian Compton '04 reported that she had earned a master's degree from Teachers College at Columbia University, held teaching positions at the elementary and high school levels, and served in various administrative roles. The statement provided the most detail, however, on Compton's activities as a tourist:

> Miss Compton has spent her summer vacations in extensive travel, having visited every state in the United States except North Dakota and Colorado. Four summers—1928, 1929, 1930, 1931—were spent in New England visiting the White Mountains, Lake Champlain, Cape Cod, and Boston; one summer, 1933, Canada, Montreal to Quebec; one summer, 1934, Niagara Falls; one summer, 1935, Kentucky, Mammoth Cave, North Carolina, Shenandoah Valley and Luray Caverns, Virginia; . . . three summers, 1926, 1927, 1940, New Orleans and vicinity; one summer, 1940, Mexico City, Guatemala and Honduras, and Southwest United States; one summer of three months in 1936, St. Louis, Cleveland, Cincinnati, and the Middle West to the Pacific Coast . . . visiting every National Park and the Canadian Rockies; two months, 1938, Ireland, Scotland, Holland, Germany, Switzerland, Italy, and France.[1]

Similarly, following a reception honoring Beatrice Cramer upon her retirement in 1967 after four and a half decades in the schools of White Plains, New York, the local newspaper noted as one of her accomplishments, "An inveterate traveler, Miss Cramer has seen not only the 50 states, Canada, Mexico, and Central America, but has visited throughout Europe, South America, Africa, Asia, Australia, and the South Pacific."[2] While Compton's and Cramer's travels were exceptionally wide-ranging, many of their predecessors and contemporaries shared their enthusiasm and ventured to new places as they were able. In 1901, a Chicago principal observed, "The teachers are the greatest traveling class nowa-days.... The teachers—practically all of them—are going somewhere." And each summer during the interwar years, 10 to 20 percent of teachers engaged in tourism, with high school teachers being more and elementary teachers being less likely to travel.[3]

Considering teachers' enthusiasm for travel, it is not surprising that tourists who were schoolteachers made frequent, albeit fleeting, appearances in travel writing of the 1880s–1930s. In the newspaper account of his 1888 trip to Yellowstone National Park, one traveler mentioned that his party included "a lady teacher," and, in the story of her family's experience at Yellowstone in 1903, another described camping near a group of "very pleasant people, mostly schoolteachers," with whom they "spent a happy evening getting acquainted."[4] Henry James's *Transatlantic Sketches* included the story of "Four Meetings" with teacher Miss Caroline Spencer, "a touching specimen of a type with which I had had other less charming associations." Spencer, James wrote, was afflicted with "the great American . . . appetite, morbid and monstrous . . . for the picturesque and the romantic." She pored over guidebooks and saved dutifully for a visit to Europe. After finally arriving in France, however, she fell for a swindle that brought her trip to an abrupt end.[5] Even as James portrayed Miss Spencer as profoundly naive, his and other accounts confirm that tourism was a popular and impactful summer activity among U.S. schoolteachers.

Tourism resonated with teachers, the vast majority of whom were women whose positions in the middle class and as professionals were precarious although they were responsible for fostering citizenship and educating their charges about the nation and the wider world. Leisure travel, including tourism, emerged in the United States early in the nineteenth century as an activity of the elite. By the 1880s, as guidebooks proliferated and the first travel agents hung out their shingles, vacation trips also became a defining feature of middle-class life. Historians of travel report that both men and women could be tourists, and some women used travel to transgress middle-class gender boundaries. Cindy Aron explains that tourism's focus on visiting inspiring sites particularly satisfied the middle class's need to purposefully pursue self-improvement even while on vacation. At the same time, as Shelly Baranowksi and Ellen Furlough explain, tourism conferred status by providing "the cultural capital of cosmopolitan modernity";

it "created new forms of knowledge, defining what 'ought' to be seen."[6] In the nineteenth century, Americans toured both their own country and Europe from a cultural or heritage perspective, taking in natural sights and historic sites as if pursuing self-enrichment in a museum. Hal Rothman argues that more recreational approaches to tourism took hold in the U.S. West as a wider cross-section of Americans began to travel in the 1910s, while Harvey Levenstein explains that upper-middle and upper-class American tourists in Europe adopted a more leisure-based, recreational approach at the turn of the twentieth century. Both historians also note that the cultural approach to tourism persisted among more sober members of the middle class; according to Levenstein, some middle-class Americans became frenetic consumers of the sights in Europe.[7] Although travel historians mention teachers only in passing, cultural tourism was especially suited to their societal circumstances and pursuit of grassroots professionalization.

Foregrounding teachers as summer tourists during this period reveals that women teachers asserted independence through travel, that tourism strengthened teachers' position in the middle class, and that tourism functioned as a form of self-directed professional development for teachers. On the assumption that tourism during the summer months would enhance teachers' work with students during the academic year, school leaders encouraged them to spend their summers traveling but provided little financial support. The teachers who found the means to engage in tourism flourished in ways that administrators intended as well as in ways that they probably did not intend. Travel in the United States allowed women teachers to exercise their independence and their right to adventure. Through cultural tours of the natural landscape and of historic and metropolitan sites, as well as attending world's fairs, teachers shored up their position in the middle class. Journeying overseas was another avenue for women teachers' assertions of independence and adventurousness. Europe was the most popular international destination; there, generations of teachers completed a grand tour of cultural highlights that conveyed high-status knowledge and also deepened their understanding of history, literature, and the arts. While teachers traveled on their own terms and rarely made connections during their journeys to day-to-day instruction in the classroom, they also used their tourist experiences to enhance their work with students. A valuable activity in their lives and careers, summer tourism was a central component of teachers' view of professionalism.

Encouragement and Financial Challenges of Tourism

Touting the professional benefits of tourism, educational leaders as well as travel companies increasingly encouraged teachers to sightsee during their summer vacations, even as teachers were more concerned with how to finance travel than with administrators' articulation of why it was worthwhile. In the 1901 article in which he called teachers "the greatest traveling class," Principal W. E. Watt stated that a teacher's work "is much enhanced by the results of such traveling," making "her much more valuable in the eyes of superintendent or board of education." Addressing teachers directly, Watt added, "All the great scenic and historic points in this country are offered you this summer." In a 1925 issue of *Midland Schools*, Professor Charles Payne observed, "If any folks owe it to themselves to travel, they are school teachers. I know of nothing which so successfully makes good teachers into better ones"; and Professor Stephen Bush added that tourism "puts more life into the work of teaching, no matter what the subject." Even during the Great Depression, *Midland Schools* reported that travel was "a specific part of the preparation of the teacher for her duties" and that "teachers each summer now become *crusaders* . . . to capture and bring home first-hand knowledge" that makes the teacher "a new creature. Something has happened to her that may be discerned even by the pupils."[8]

The National Education Association (NEA) promoted tourism extensively as part of its campaign to attract more teachers—specifically, white teachers—to its annual meeting each summer. Before the 1884 meeting in Madison, the association worked with education journals throughout the country to publish information not only on the meeting program but also on tourist opportunities in Wisconsin and throughout the West. In advance of the 1891 NEA meeting in Toronto, *The Iowa Normal Monthly* stated, "Many Iowa teachers have never been East. The Falls of Niagara, the Great Lakes and the St. Lawrence River are all worth a month's salary to see."[9] In the spring 1899 issues of the Chicago education journal *The Intelligence*, a travel agent told teachers that the upcoming NEA meeting in Los Angeles was "an opportunity to travel to the most interesting part of our continent," imploring, "SEE ALL THAT YOU CAN," and a dozen pages were devoted to descriptions and photos of California's "Points of Interest to N. E. A. Visitors."[10] Soon after it began publication in the 1910s, *The Journal of the National Education Association* included extensive articles each year on tourism in the region that was to host the meeting. "The Wonderland of Washington" introduced teachers who might attend the 1927 meeting in Seattle to Mt. Rainier, the San Juan Islands, and the Olympic peninsula; "The Twin Bread and Butter Cities" presented 1928 meeting host Minneapolis as the home of Minnehaha Falls and Longfellow's Lake Nakomis; and "Going to New York?" pointed out that teachers attending the 1938 meeting would be able to view spectacular architecture, visit science, art, and natural history museums, and perhaps visit other northeastern cities, ending with the question, "Can you afford to miss it?"[11]

In addition to focusing on the NEA meeting location, education journals implicitly encouraged tourism by publishing articles such as "Yellowstone Park Waterfalls" and "A Vacation Trip in Germany," both of which appeared in *The Iowa Normal Monthly* in the 1890s.[12] Increasingly after the turn of the century, journals encouraged tourism more explicitly in travel sections or even entire issues. In *The Intelligence*'s Tour and Travel section in May 1901, Principal Watt advised teachers heading to Europe on what to pack, how much money to take, and how to avoid seasickness on the ship; and *Midland Schools*' April 1936 "Travel Number" stated that teachers were the workers best "fitted personally and professionally to profit from travel."[13] In these sections or sprinkled throughout their winter and spring issues, journals included increasing numbers of advertisements for travel to various regions of the United States and beyond its borders. A 1904 ad for the Santa Fe Railroad promised teachers "rest, recreation, and inspiration for my future work" on a trip to the Grand Canyon, and a 1921 ad for Intercollegiate Tours invited teachers to "add to your cultural capital, to your enthusiasm and your teaching ability the first-hand contact with the great civilizations of Europe."[14] Travel companies' own publications also aimed to recruit teachers. A mid-1910s brochure for travel through Yellowstone with the Shaw & Powell Camping Company included testimonials by the president of Iowa State Teachers College, H. H. Seerley, and schoolteacher J. E. Potzger, who mentioned the "guidance of skilled leaders." Two decades later, a brochure for Morningside Tours of Europe included praise for a tour that was "smooth-running and perfect" from "C. H. Newlin, East High School, Kansas City, Mo.," the signature suggesting that he was a teacher.[15]

Education associations and school boards also facilitated teachers' tourism by providing travel services and a modicum of financial support. From the mid-1880s onward, the NEA negotiated with rail lines to offer reduced fares and long travel windows so that teachers could easily combine tourism with attending the meeting. Before the 1888 gathering in San Francisco, NEA "director" for Texas Percy Pennybacker wrote "To the Teachers of Texas" in the state's school journal, "Special excursion rates will be made from San Francisco to all points of interest in California and to Alaska and the Sandwich Islands." When the state teachers' association in Pennsylvania arranged a special train to the 1899 NEA meeting in Los Angeles, the itinerary included visits to Garden of the Gods, Pike's Peak, Royal Gorge, and "other points of interest" in Colorado, as well as stops in Chicago and Salt Lake City.[16] Shortly after World War I, the Association of Teachers of Spanish established the Committee on Foreign Study and Travel to help teachers arrange travel to Spanish-speaking countries that had not been accessible during the conflict. Around the same time, the Philadelphia Teachers Association established a Travel Service Bureau; its services, the *Pennsylvania School Journal* reported in 1924, were "free to any" teacher "interested in planning vacation trips with a minimum of cost." Three years later, *Midland Schools* mentioned that the Service Bureau of State Teachers' Associations was available to assist teachers, presumably throughout the country, "in planning your summer travel."[17]

Watt stated that the teacher who was "going somewhere" would receive "an increase of salary that at once repays her for the investment" but did not provide details. In at least a couple of cases, the school district did provide some repayment. Elyria, Ohio, decided in 1920 to pay teachers "an additional $50 increase if they have spent at least six weeks of the summer in approved travel in this or foreign country," and during the late 1920s the Evansville, Indiana, Teachers Federation and school superintendent convinced the school board to institute a reward system for summer tourism (and formal study). In 1930, six Evansville teachers each received $200 for travel to Europe, and twenty-eight teachers each received $100 for travel to the East or West Coast of the United States. Federation member Maybelle Hargrave reported, "Teachers . . . by broadened experience reflected in their teaching are proving that this plan is well worthwhile."[18] The state of Maryland did not provide a direct financial reward for tourism but did count "taking a long trip" toward continuing education requirements for teachers, a policy that the NEA *Journal* editor said recognized "the value of travel for teachers."[19] A town in Iowa recognized the value of travel by providing especially generous support for one teacher: Monticello, *The Iowa Normal Monthly* reported in 1910, showed "its appreciation of a faithful, earnest and conscientious teacher by presenting her with sufficient funds for an European trip, and telling her to go abroad during the coming summer vacation."[20]

Although the *Monthly* added, "There are other teachers in other towns who have worked long and hard . . . who would no doubt welcome the same kind of treatment," gestures like Monticello's were extremely rare. Lack of resources simply prohibited travel for some teachers, including Sophie Heckert in Moline, Illinois. Around the turn of the century, she wrote to her friend Sarah Hannah Butler, who taught in Chicago and often traveled during the summer, "I do not know what I am going to do next Summer. . . . Would like, oh so much, to accompany you to California but can I do it, when all I will save this winter at the outside will be $140? . . . Tears are in my eyes, when I think of how inferior I am to my friends."[21] A 1913 NEA study of teacher salaries quoted women teachers in Cincinnati who observed, "A teacher is seldom able to travel befitting her station because of lack of funds," and "One cannot take the proper recreation or travel during the summer months upon the present salaries." In Denver, a woman elementary school teacher stated, "I can live decently and comfortably on my salary but can have very few luxuries and *no* trips," and a woman high school teacher commented that her salary was "a fair one, but doesn't allow enough for spending time in a foreign country—so essential to a teacher of foreign language."[22]

When teachers were able to take touring trips during the summer, it was often because they had made sacrifices during the school year. Like Henry James's Miss Spencer, they prioritized saving money and economizing. Another woman high school teacher in Denver quoted in the NEA study explained that many teachers there were "so situated that they must board [and] live in a way that makes it very inconvenient, if not practically impossible, to receive and entertain their friends . . . a hardship . . . I have always endured for the purpose of saving something for study and travel during the summer vacation." In order to afford a trip west with her mother in August 1928, Wisconsin teacher Irene Lindahl (later Krumpelmann) was "penurious with impunity" while she lived in the "teacherage" during the school year, and then worked in a pea-canning factory through the day before their departure.[23] In her 1938 book on the American "schoolma'am," Frances Donovan noted, "Those who live at home with parents during the working year are more likely to tour during vacation," likely because living at home allowed them to economize; "schoolma'ams," Donovon continued, would "make almost any sacrifice" for a trip to Europe. To facilitate teachers' saving, one bank in Iowa cooperated with the state's teachers association to offer a "Save to Travel" plan. A September 1925 advertisement for the plan promised 4 percent interest on monthly deposits throughout the school year to "finance travel trips" the following summer and stated, "Travel advice and literature furnished free on request."[24]

Lucy Jones (later Townley), a high school teacher in Columbus, Kansas, was concerned about finances during her trip to Europe in 1910, writing in July to her teacher friend Ethel Lowry, "You can imagine the state of my pocket book. . . . Things are not cheap here in Germany." Jones apparently had not saved enough to cover the entire trip, as she wrote from Venice in August, "I'm going deeper and deeper into debt, but when I hear the water lapping and the Italians singing—I just can't be a bit sorry."[25] Jones did not mention from where she borrowed the money, but—in keeping with the rise of consumer credit in the U.S. economy in the 1920s—ads for vacation-travel bank loans soon abounded in education journals. A May 1926 ad depicting a train traversing mountains declared, "Finance Your Vacation Needs with a Dignified Loan," and a May 1929 ad depicting an ocean liner promised, "Take as many as twenty months to repay us. . . . Simply call our office with your teacher's contract and we will hand you the money without delay." Removing the bank from the process, one steamship company began offering consumer credit in the 1930s. "Cunard Will Sell Trips to Europe on Deferred Payments," announced the *Pennsylvania School Journal*, and an ad for Cunard in the NEA *Journal* explained, "A special payment plan for teachers sailing after June 15th defers the first payment until October 1st." When retired Seattle teacher Gladys Charles looked back after six decades on her 1938 trip with another teacher to Europe, she remembered, "I had borrowed from the credit union . . . fifteen hundred dollars for the summer trip."[26]

Teachers also found ways to economize while traveling, sometimes with help from transportation companies. From the early 1880s into the twentieth century, many teachers who visited Yellowstone toured "the Wylie Way" in frugal group tours that provided lodging in a series of camps rather than the more expensive park hotels. The "very pleasant people, mostly schoolteachers" with whom a traveler "spent a happy evening" were Wylie tourists. Another attested in a Wylie Company brochure that his trip could "not have been made nearly so economically in any other way. As a large portion of our party were school teachers and persons of moderate means, this matter was of importance." A 1927 ad for the Rock Island Railroad began, "Teachers! Plan Your Vacation Now!" and explained, "Cost of a vacation in the scenic West is surprisingly low—a trip for every purse."[27] For transatlantic voyages, economically minded passengers could sail on older, slower ships or travel second-class. As historian Robert Gough explains, after the demand for steerage-class tickets evaporated in the wake of U.S. immigration restrictions in the early 1920s, steamship companies created "Tourist Third Class"—also known as "cabin class"—and "marketed it especially to teachers." A 1922 ad for the White Star Line boasted, "Our cabin class passenger ships are making Europe possible for ambitious teachers."[28] Charles and her friend economized on their 1938 European trip by staying in youth hostels and often traveling by bicycle; sixty years later, she marveled that they "had a wonderful time... *on fifteen hundred dollars*!" Also during the Depression, one especially frugal teacher-tourist from California "rode to New York in a chicken car and scrubbed decks on a[n ocean] liner. He toured five countries on $100," according to the NEA *Journal* editor, who added, "He has never eaten eggs since that ride in the chicken car."[29] With encouragement—and limited support—from school leaders, teachers were willing to tolerate less-than-ideal arrangements for school year room and board, indebtedness to the bank or steamship company, staying in tents or hostels, and even riding in a chicken car in order to expand their horizons through tourism. Although historians of tourism state that only wealthy Americans were able to travel in the West and in Europe before the twentieth century,[30] patently nonwealthy teachers found ways from the 1880s onward to travel as tourists throughout the United States and overseas.

Tourism in the United States

When Charles Payne wrote that travel "makes good teachers into better ones," he added, "No travel can be more inspiring and enlarging to American teachers than travel in America!" "National tourism," historian Marguerite Shaffer argues, emerged by the 1880s "as a form of geographical consumption that centered on the sights and scenes of the American nation" and, according to Baranowksi and Furlough, created and provided a new form of cultural capital.[31] In this vein, Principal Jeanette Mills referred to the "joy" of returning from a trip "and talking your friends to death over all of the wonders you have seen," and P. H. Elwood promoted travel for fostering "an interesting and colorful personality," in a 1926 issue of *Midland Schools*.[32] While geographical consumption resulted in personal enrichment, historians of tourism also argue that the consecration of national sights fostered pride in the country. "Tourists," Shaffer continues, "in consuming the nation, also participated in and shaped [the] search for national identity." "Tourism," according to John Sears, "played a powerful role in America's invention of itself as a culture," beginning earlier in the nineteenth century when sights "assumed some of the functions of sacred places." By the 1880s, Sears explains, attractions' sacredness was less explicitly religious and more nationalistic; in the eyes of American tourists, the country's natural formations surpassed the great architecture of Europe. Shaffer adds that in the 1910s and 1920s, the National Parks Service worked to define tourism as "a kind of virtuous consumption" aimed at "generating patriotism" and, no doubt, supporting settler-colonialist ideology.[33] As shapers of citizens during the nonsummer months, teachers would have been ideal participants in sightseeing to generate patriotism, yet their approach to tourism was generally not nationalistic.

Elwood's larger concern in his 1926 article was travel's effects on "spiritual understanding" and its "cultural and refining influences upon character." Similarly, Payne's explanation of how travel would improve teaching—"The really traveled person," he wrote, "has a broader outlook, a greater knowledge of human nature, a deeper understanding of beauty," and the "truly fine teacher must be a truly fine person"—embodied historians' description of the middle class's cultural or heritage conception of tourism for self-improvement.[34] As tourists between the 1880s and the 1930s, schoolteachers engaged deeply with the consumption and consecration of natural features and historical and metropolitan sites through a cultural approach to tourism. Patriotic sentiment was indeed a thread in education journals' treatment of tourism, but nationalism and settler-colonialist sentiment were largely absent in teachers' own accounts of their travels, which expressed wonderment and described their new knowledge. Rather than patriotic consecration, teacher tourism resulted in informed appreciation, or *measured* consecration, of the country's heritage. Teacher-tourists' encounters with natural features mainly in the western half of the country, with historical and metropolitan sites mainly in the eastern half of the country, and with culture more broadly at world's fairs and expositions, supported their approach to professionalization by expanding their stock of cultural capital and enriching their souls and intellects, strengthening their place in the middle class—and making "good teachers into better ones" on their own terms. But first, encountering the country's natural wonders and historical heritage required tourists to travel to new places, and the journey was often an adventure that was especially meaningful for women teachers.

Assertions of Women's Independence

A spirit of excited anticipation infused the announcement in an Iowa education journal of plans for a "teachers' special train" to the Nashville NEA meeting in 1889. The "entire journey" was to be "like a 'jolly picnic on wheels,'" with "a songbook . . . published especially for the occasion" and side trips for sightseeing. A sense of adventure pervaded F. E. Stratton's diary of his visit to Yellowstone National Park in 1895. Not only did the teacher at a Minnesota academy write playful poetry as he toured the park—penning verses such as, "The Yellowstone Party / Are hale and hearty / The further we go / The more we know—Stratton's enthusiasm for having an adventure extended throughout the rail journey across the plains, as he marveled at the South Dakota Badlands and partook in "stories, conundrums, games, [etc.] on the train.[35] For women during this time period, having a travel adventure, especially without a male escort, was an assertion of "the right to broaden their horizons," in the words of Virginia Scharff in her history of women as automobile drivers. Before the 1920s, Scharff argues, only affluent women were able to take the wheel, and in doing so they "made a conspicuous cultural statement about female assertiveness."[36] In seizing opportunities for adventure as tourists, women teachers who traveled by rail, stagecoach, or horse similarly claimed their right to broader horizons. When they began in the 1920s to travel by bus and to drive cross-country in cars, women teacher-tourists further asserted their independence.

Margaret Cruikshank, a single fifty-eight-year-old teacher in Minneapolis, was already an experienced traveler when she rode the Northern Pacific Railroad to Yellowstone National Park in August 1883, just as the rail connection was completed and tourism was emerging in the park. For Cruikshank and her companion, "Miss A.," the real adventure began when they set off to tour the park as stagecoach passengers. As the coach traversed a mountain, Cruikshank explained, "At the steepest places we got out and walked—and then began our sufferings. The dirt was almost ankle deep and the heat and clarity of the air made it a serious business"—and a challenge to Victorian-era gender ideology. In the park, she found, "wherever you go there are streams to ford, corduroy to fall over, sagebrush to crawl along and mountains to cross. The strong can stand it, and enjoy it; but [this] is no place for the delicate." In claiming the right to expand her horizons to include the "uninhabited wilderness" of Yellowstone, Cruikshank demonstrated that she was most certainly not delicate.[37] Travel to and through Yellowstone and other national parks would become easier for the tourists who followed her, and women—many of them teachers—traveling without men became so common that brochures for Wylie and other travel companies by the 1910s boasted of the high number of "ladies traveling in small parties or individually, without male escort," who toured with them, and Yellowstone Superintendent Horace Albright observed in 1928, "During the summer months the school teachers and other feminine vacationists in the parks are so numerous that they far outnumber the men."[38]

While most of the "school teachers and other feminine vacationists" before the 1920s arrived by rail, two women teachers' trips to Yellowstone by horse were conspicuous demonstrations of their self-reliance. Young Nebraska teacher Carrie Belle Spencer rode the train in July 1892 to Gillette, Wyoming, where she embarked with her brother and four others on a six-week, round-trip horse-and-wagon adventure to and through the park. En route, she often rode ahead of the group as a sort of scout, exploring the landscape and occasionally encountering Native Americans. Spencer helped set up camp, bathed in streams, saw coyotes and wolves, and explored mining camps. She further asserted her independence by returning alone on the train to Nebraska for another school year.[39] Nearly three decades later, Montana teacher Mary Lavinia White (later McEwen) embarked on a rugged adventure at Yellowstone in July 1919 with her mother, her sister—also a teacher—and her sister's four daughters. While her sister's family traveled to the park by train, White and her mother made the fifty-four-mile trip by horse and buggy; the ranchers where they camped en route praised "the courage" of their "plucky little outfit." After a ranger "sealed" White's rifle and provided them with instructions on how to handle bears, they spent six weeks exploring and camping in the park, with just one mishap that further demonstrated their pluck. After their horse was spooked on a mountain road and their buggy rolled down the cliff, "strewing camp items," they managed to reassemble their supplies and continue on their way. On the trip home in August, White used her rifle—unsealed by the ranger—to shoot a rabbit for dinner.[40] Anything but delicate Victorian women, White and Spencer, like Cruikshank before them, relished the opportunity for a rigorous travel adventure.

Less rugged but still an assertion of independence was two Detroit schoolteachers' western trip by rail in the summer of 1924. The newspaper "personals" announced, "Miss Cecilia Engel, and Miss Amelia Moeller of Detroit have left on a trip to Yellowstone National Park, and other Western points." Engel's scrapbook of their tour chronicled her broadening horizons with maps of their route—to Saint Paul, Yellowstone, Salt Lake City, Pikes Peak, Colorado Springs, Denver, and Estes Park—as well as ticket stubs, photos, and illustrations cut from brochures or magazines. Hand-written explanations and captions, such as "just a sample of the thrilling rides through Cody," conveyed a spirit of adventure.[41] Railroads continued to promote summer travel for teachers—a 1929 ad for the Canadian Pacific beckoned, "Go West young lady"—but rail travel declined in popularity and was eclipsed by bus and, especially, auto travel by the end of the 1920s.[42]

A 1926 article in *Midland Schools* advocated "sight-seeing, tourist and 'for hire' buses" for "long distance educational trips" during school vacations, and ads for bus companies abounded in education journals during the 1930s. One ad touted a 1939 "Swing Around America" tour from a teacher's "home town to the New York World's Fair, then cross-continent to San Francisco's Golden Gate Exposition (and the N. E. A. Convention)—then back home, all for $69.95!" Unmarried Milwaukee elementary school teacher Margarete Bohle and a friend did not quite make a full swing around the country, but they saw much of the West on a summer bus adventure in 1935. Bohle wrote from Los Angeles to her family that their ride through an Arizona canyon "sure was a thrill" and that they had met "very interesting people" from South Africa and Australia on the bus. From San Francisco, she reported that "a nice girl" from the bus had shown them around Chinatown and that while riding a ferry to Oakland, they had seen "the immense expansion bridge they are building between these two cities." From Portland, she wrote about having "oodles of fun kidding the driver" and explained, "We always try to get front seats so we can ask the driver many questions." From Seattle, Bohle reported that they were heading to Victoria, British Columbia, the next day and would be home a week later—no doubt with broader horizons and a renewed sense of independence.[43]

Even as self-directed bus and auto touring surpassed rail travel, South Dakota school principal Cleata Thorpe—who felt that "a teacher owed it to her profession to broaden her horizon"—embarked on a guided trip for teachers by train and then ship to Alaska in 1934. On the first leg, from Minneapolis to Seattle by rail, she observed, "There was an atmosphere that one misses in independent travel . . . the spirit of a vacation party."[44] But after teachers could afford cars of their own, the opportunity to assert their independence through touring by auto outweighed the attractions of collegial conviviality on the rails. Once Seattle's women teachers were able to purchase cars on credit in the 1920s, historian Doris Hinson Pieroth explains, the number " 'motoring' while on summer vacation increased." Scharff writes, "Amid the multitudes of automobile tourists who took off on cross-country vacations in the 1920s, adventurous American women," including teachers, often "saw themselves as modern pioneers." And in the preface to her social history of U.S. women teachers, Geraldine Clifford reflects that as she was growing up in the 1930s–1940s, her teachers "were the sole independent women my schoolmates and I had ever known. . . . They were the only women who drove their own cars, traveled to distant locales every summer," and "made decisions."[45] The NEA *Journal*'s promotion of the upcoming summer meeting included a road map of the country under the title "All Auto Roads Lead to Atlanta" in 1929, after which maps of "motor routes" to the meeting location were a regular feature in the *Journal*. In anticipation of the 1931 meeting, the caption under a photo of cars parked at a mountain overlook stated, "Hundreds of teachers will drive their own cars to the Los Angeles convention—a matchless trip over forest trails and thru mountain gap—a vacation in itself."[46]

Lillian Compton and Beatrice Cramer were the type of teacher whom the NEA sought to recruit and whom Clifford remembered. The Towson Alumni Association's biography of Compton noted that all of her trips in North and Central America "were taken by automobile." Cramer likewise took many summer trips by car, often with her parents from Gloversville, New York. They "toured part of New England in a Ford" in 1922, "the rest of New England" and eastern Canada in 1923, southern states and the Great Lakes in 1924, and the West in 1925. She left the car at home in 1926, when she toured South and Central America, the U.S. Pacific coast, and Alaska by ship and bus. Auto trips again took Cramer west and south in 1929, 1930, 1931, and 1934. In a car she had named "Polly," she made the latter trip with her mother and her cousin who was also a teacher, grateful that "there was no longer danger of getting stuck in Iowa's 'gumbo',—her roads were all concrete." After having Polly's "valves ground and carbon removed" in Denver, she wrote, they "zigzagged along the very edge of an ugly looking mountain. Summing up all the courage we had, we put Polly in 'low' and crept down along the outside edge of the narrow trail, scarcely

FIGURE 9 "The six school moms just before the take-off," Road Trip Scrapbook, Mildred Van Wyngarden Papers. Courtesy of the Iowa Women's Archives, University of Iowa Libraries, Iowa City, Iowa.

breathing as the wheels moaned around the switch-backs." By the late 1930s, Cramer's continuing summer road adventures were in a car she had named "Susan" in honor of Susan B. Anthony and, no doubt, female assertiveness.[47]

Meanwhile, Margarete Bohle left the bus behind and took extensive auto trips with friends in the summers of 1939 and 1940. In 1939, they drove from Milwaukee to Michigan and, after "a thrilling ride thru the tunnel to Windsor," through Ontario and Quebec and then on to New York—where they visited the World's Fair—and Washington, D.C., before crossing Pennsylvania. On a trip to the West in 1940, they monitored the engine as they drove across the hot desert and then stopped to add water after entering Yosemite National Park. "The rangers get a big kick out of seeing girls drain the radiator and cool the engine," wrote Bohle in her travel journal. Mildred Van Wyngarden and her five friends—"the six school moms" from Iowa (figure 9)—could have crossed paths with Bohle on their summer "motor trip through the western states" in 1940.

Van Wyngarden's scrapbook and account of the trip portrayed a fun adventure that was also an assertion of female independence. Under a photo of one of the "school moms" posing while climbing on boulders in Colorado, she added the caption, "Leona, trying to reach the summit," and when they stayed in a motel cabin in a small Montana town after visiting Yellowstone, Van Wyngarden noted, "Evidently the townspeople were not accustomed to seeing girls attired in shorts, for one of the girls attracted a great many stares when she strolled down the sidewalk thus." Her lighthearted comment about crossing the Columbia River three times "due to a slight mixture of directions" and her somber note that "extra precaution was taken" after they saw the aftermath of a car's fatal plunge off a

California cliff both acknowledged that *they* determined the course of their trip. A high point of the adventure for Van Wyngarden was the "thrill" of a ten-minute sightseeing airplane flight over the mountains in Washington.[48] Although advertisements for airlines began to appear in education journals in the late 1930s,[49] air travel remained out of reach for the vast majority of teachers. Staying on the ground did not inhibit women teacher-tourists, however; those who traveled by car, like their predecessors who traveled by train and horse, asserted their right to broaden their horizons.

Natural Sights in the West

When they reached their destinations in the United States, teacher-tourists engaged in consumption and measured consecration of the country's natural and cultural heritage. Sears explains that Niagara Falls and Mammoth Cave were among the most prominent natural attractions for early tourists in the United States, and their religious significance—the falls brought "pilgrim tourists . . . closer to God" and the Kentucky cave's "enormous halls . . . reminded people of Gothic churches"—did not entirely disappear even as they gained more nationalistic and commercial significance by the late nineteenth century.[50] Education journals and the NEA reified these natural sights as geographical cultural capital by consistently promoting them in conjunction with NEA meetings in the East or South. "No one should go to Nashville without visiting the Mammoth Cave, the great national wonder of this continent," stated an article publicizing the 1889 NEA meeting in Tennessee's capital city. An NEA brochure listing "Some of the Places of Interest" near the 1896 meeting in Buffalo devoted the most space to Niagara Falls, marveling at their "overflowing beauty and glory."[51] While such superlatives had nationalistic undertones, teachers who visited Niagara Falls expressed appreciation for nature and the opportunity to witness it rather than patriotic sentiment. Young California teacher Grace Canan (later Pogue) reflected that her 1909 trip "was a dream come true. I stood on Terrapin Rock, saw the mighty cataract, listened to it roar and wondered if it could really be true that I was there." Three decades later, Margarete Bohle and her friends had a more commercialized experience when they took a tour below the falls in special raincoats and stayed to see the evening illumination, but Bohle still noted simply, "The Falls are grand."[52]

Niagara Falls and Mammoth Cave notwithstanding, the West was the magnet for nature-based tourism in the United States from the late nineteenth century onward. "For America's cultural nationalists," Sears argues, the "natural cathedral" of the Yosemite Valley "rivaled the monuments and mountain scenery of the Old World." Shaffer explains that the main focus of "national tourism" from its origins in the 1880s through the early years of the twentieth century was natural scenery and wonders in the West, and Rothman argues that Western tourism in particular was "an affirmation of American society"—primarily among white upper- and middle-class Americans.[53] Articles and advertisements in education journals cataloged natural sights as cultural capital by repeatedly listing particular stops as essential on any Western trip. High on every list was Yellowstone, the first national park. Virtually any time that the NEA was scheduled to meet in the western half of the country, education journals encouraged teachers to combine attending the meeting with travel to Yellowstone. *The American School Board Journal* suggested that itineraries for trips to the 1899 meeting in Los Angeles include "the world-famed Yellowstone Park," and in a *Midland Schools* ad for the Union Pacific Railroad before the 1927 meeting in Seattle, the headline "To NEA and the Greatest Attraction of the West on One Low Cost Tour" appeared over a drawing of people exploring Yellowstone. *The Intelligence*'s "Summer Outing and Convention Number" in both 1901 and 1902 included photos of Yellowstone's geysers, and a three-page article in the May 1927 issue of the NEA *Journal* described the park's many features in detail. After listing the names of a half-dozen geysers, the author goaded readers to consume these sights: "How many of these have you heard of? Any? They are all important geysers."[54] F. E. Stratton, Margaret Cruikshank, Carrie Belle Spencer, Mary Lavinia White, Cecilia Engel, Margarete Bohle, Lillian Compton, Beatrice Cramer, and Mildred Van Wyngarden all saw the geysers, either as part of a trip exclusively to Yellowstone or on a more wide-ranging adventure.

Engel and Bohle further expanded their geographical cultural capital with visits to Colorado's Pike's Peak and Garden of the Gods, which were also fixtures on lists of Western sights to see. An ad for a "special excursion" for teachers to the NEA 1899 meeting in Los Angeles promised "a free carriage ride through the Garden of the Gods" and "half rate to the top of Pike's Peak." As the country established more national parks, they joined lists of sights to see in the West. When National Park Service director Stephen Mather reported in a 1923 issue of the NEA *Journal* on the country's nineteen parks—such as Yellowstone, Yosemite, Glacier, Mesa Verde, Grand Canyon, Zion, and Mount McKinley—the editors added, "Teachers would do well to visit several of our National Parks in connection with their trip to the Association's next annual meeting in Oakland-San Francisco next July." A dozen years later, a U.S. map in the *Journal* marked the locations of these iconic sights and others—such as Mount Rushmore, Carlsbad Caverns, and the Painted Desert—in anticipation of the upcoming meeting in Denver.[55] Cramer amassed an especially large store of such cultural capital, as her hometown paper reported in 1931, "Mr. and Mrs. Frank Cramer and daughter Beatrice of this city have returned from a motor tour of the Pacific Northwest. Among the points of interest visited were the Black Hills and Wind Cave in South Dakota; Yellowstone and the Grand Teton National Parks in Wyoming; Mount Rainier Park, Washington; Crater Lake, Oregon and Lassen Peak Volcanic Park in California. . . . This trip completes the party's tour of the United States."[56]

In encouraging the consumption of Western natural sights, publications often indulged in nationalistic celebrations of their prestige. Articles declared that the

Rocky Mountains were "far more beautiful and inspiring than those of far-famed Switzerland," that Crater Lake was the "only one great cauldron in all the world," and that Carlsbad Caverns were "the world's greatest caves." Mather claimed in the NEA *Journal* that Yellowstone was "unmatched in its peculiar characteristics anywhere else in the world" and Yosemite's "Mariposa Grove of Big Trees is the largest grove of giant Sequoias in existence," as well as described the Grand Canyon as the "most wonderful piece of earth sculpture." "Nowhere in the world is there such a text book of volcanic history, phenomena and scenic beauty," announced an advertisement for the 1925 Iowa State Teachers Association tour of Yellowstone, Colorado, and Utah. Other travel ads proclaimed that Yellowstone Falls was "Switzerland out-done!"; that to the "canyon region" of Zion, Bryce, and the Grand Canyon there was "nothing at all comparable on our entire planet"; and that "Alaska's scenic grandeur is unparalleled."[57]

Interviewed for the NEA *Journal* in 1923, teacher Minnie B. Addleman of Denver said that on a trip to the Grand Canyon, Yosemite, the Pacific coast, and Yellowstone during the previous summer, she had drunk "in the beauties of our own America." While Addleman did not express the same degree of nationalism as did articles and advertisements in the journal, most teachers were even less overtly patriotic. Another teacher interviewed for the *Journal*, Annie Carleton Woodward of Massachusetts, referred to "the soul's growth that comes from viewing the wonders of nature," which resonated with Elwood's emphasis in his 1926 article on travel's effects on "spiritual understanding." Elwood explained further, "The spirit can never be the same after wide and extensive travel, the soul itself becomes enriched and deeper"; and Payne asked, "And do you imagine for a moment that you can spend a summer seeing such wonderful things as the Grand Canyon of the Yellowstone, for instance, without being a finer person?"[58] Indeed, teachers' own reports and reflections on their tours of Western sights demonstrated that nature tourism touched their souls, as their expressions of consecration were more likely to invoke a higher power than patriotic sentiment. At Yellowstone, Stratton wrote of Mammoth Hot Springs, "I never saw such manifest working of the Almighty," and of the Canyon, "The sunshine and shadow conspire to add sublimity to the scene. . . . What beautiful projections the Almighty has pushed out into this Canyon." Engel's scrapbook (see figure 10) included a poem that began, "God made the world," and the quotation, "God made this wonderful park for you."[59] Teacher Aline Teiche of Butte, Montana, wrote in a letter describing her 1900 trip through Yellowstone that "sulphurous fumes and roaring and boiling suggest the inferno but the presence of their Creator is felt above all," and that no artist could reproduce the Canyon because "it is the touch of the Great-Creator." Finally, regarding her time in Colorado's Rocky Mountains, Cramer wrote, "At times such as these does one feel a closeness to the Divine."[60]

Most teachers' expressions of consecration simply conveyed awe and reverence for the natural sights they saw. Despite her "sufferings" while traveling through

FIGURE 10 Photos of group hike and Old Faithful in Cecilia Engel's scrapbook of her 1924 trip. (Courtesy of the National Park Service, Yellowstone National Park, Cecilia Engel Scrapbook, 1924, YELL 194587.)

Yellowstone, Cruikshank noted seeing "beautiful things, beautiful enough for a poet's dream" and reflected, "mortal language seems entirely inadequate." Spencer wrote that when she arrived at the Yellowstone Falls and Canyon, she "could but stand in awe and wonder. . . . When reaching camp I thought that I had seen more of the beauties of nature than ever before in one day or perhaps that I ever should see." Of the mountains near Yellowstone, Irene Lindahl wrote, "One would have to be callous to remain unmoved by the sight," while White called the same mountains "awe-inspiring" and "breath-taking." Cramer used similar language in her description of a boat trip to the headwaters of the Colorado River: "Words can't describe the reflected beauty of the lake, nor the snow-capped grandeur of the mountains we crossed, nor the feeling of awe which we experienced." Rural California teacher Nila Stevens conveyed awe more prosaically after visiting Glacier National Park on a group trip to the 1937 NEA meeting in Detroit, writing, "We drove around the mountains, 'ohing' and 'ahing' at the waterfalls, glaciers, and other wonderful sights." Van Wyngarden remarked on the "thrill of the first sight of the Pacific Ocean" and noted, "One feels very humble" in the presence of California's redwood trees. And in her essay on the teachers' trip to Alaska, Cleata Thorpe described glaciers, mountains, waterfalls, and wildflowers, reflecting, "The immensity of it all caused us to stand in awed silence before the panorama," and concluding, "It had been an experience of real educational value."[61]

In addition to opening their souls to the nourishing effects of nature's awe-inspiring scenes, many teacher-tourists opened their minds to intellectual nourishment. When not invoking the Almighty, Stratton made scientific notes in his diary about Yellowstone's geological features; next to his description of the "little orifices" emitting "seething, boiling, bubbling, steaming water," he drew a diagram of an opening. He also mentioned "testing" the snow they came upon "in various ways" and concluded that the trip was "one of the most enjoyable, if not the most instructive, summer trips I have ever taken." Teiche noted the effects of volcanic action at Yellowstone, and Lindahl remarked, "My geography book was coming alive."[62] The Wylie tours that guided so many teachers through Yellowstone were not only economical but also more educational than other park tours. William Wylie drew on his own experience as an educator and hired knowledgeable guides—many of whom were teachers during the school year—to present tours full of accurate and engaging information. Alongside the natural features and around the evening campfire, teachers on Wylie tours learned about the park's geology, flora, and fauna. Two women teachers from Iowa who enjoyed a Wylie tour in 1891 reported that "the scientific explanation of the causes of geysers was listened to with delight."[63] The Wylie approach was an inspiration for adding educational programming and the position of ranger naturalist to the Park Service by the 1920s. Cramer learned from "lectures given by the rangers on the floral and animal life of the Grand Tetons" during her 1931 trip, and Bohle explored Yellowstone's geysers with a ranger guide on her 1940 trip.[64] In keeping with the middle-class approach to tourism as well as their own approach to professionalization, teachers nourished their souls and their intellects as they consumed and consecrated nature in the West.

Historical and Metropolitan Sites in the East and South

While natural attractions were the main focus of teachers' tourism in the West, they also visited the region's growing cities and historical sites. Promotion of travel to NEA meetings in the West included the heritage and other highlights of the host city. In anticipation of the 1899 meeting in Los Angeles, an article in *The Intelligence* mentioned "clean well-paved electric-lighted streets" and described the rise of new industries and the historic role of missions, while the program for the meeting listed excursions "To Old Missions." Other journals described 1909 meeting site Denver as "the first city of the Far West . . . a monument to the indomitable spirit of the pioneers" and 1927 host Seattle as having "romance, youth and a personality that is so distinctive that seasoned world travelers almost invariably comment upon it."[65] Beatrice Cramer noted that on her western trips, she visited Seattle, "a delightful city," and "several state capitals, [and] points of historic and literary interest." In Salt Lake City, Mildred Van Wyngarden's group of six teachers took a guided tour of Temple Square, which she remarked was "quite educational," and then went to the Mormon Tabernacle "for the CBS broadcast." Margarete Bohle, on the other hand, was disappointed in the tour of Temple Square "because the guide was too intent on making us Mormons."[66] However, even as the NEA *Journal* encouraged readers heading to the 1936 meeting in Portland to "refresh their minds as to the stirring history of the western half of our nation," when it came to historical tourism, teachers and those who encouraged them to travel focused mainly on the eastern half of the country. "The American West is the logical place to travel for nature study, while the East affords greater opportunity for the student of history, economics and sociology," stated a professor of history and political science in *Midland Schools*, while an ad for House Party Tours listed "Wonderland of the West" and "the Historic East" as its two options in the United States.[67]

When not touring natural features, historian Cindy Aron explains, Americans turned to "places that glorified American achievement, industriousness, ingenuity, perseverance, and heroism." Shaffer adds that the rise of auto travel spurred the promotion of historical tourism and, in the process, "history became heritage." During the Great Depression, the National Parks Service undertook more historical interpretation and conservation, and the passage of the Historic Sites Act in 1935 codified these new duties. Tourists were thus invited to, in Shaffer's words, "comprehend . . . and ultimately possess" sites that revealed "the promise of American civilization."[68] As with natural sights in the West, education journals cataloged historical and metropolitan sites in the eastern half of the country as cultural capital. In the article in which Mills referred to "talking your friends to death over all the wonders you have seen," she listed as the wonders that would most impress them the natural attractions in the West and "the great cities of the East with their historic settings, their museums, art galleries, libraries, parks, public buildings and numerous other places of interest." Journals did not publish as many advertisements for travel to the East and South as to the West, but one for Drake Colonial Tours in 1929 promised that participants would "SEE—the showplaces of the East," such as Washington, D.C., Philadelphia, New York, and Boston, and "PROFIT—from renewed acquaintance with famous sites every American should know."[69] On a group trip in 1908, forty-three teachers, most of whom were from Nebraska and were women, toured cultural and educational institutions in Cleveland, Boston, Albany, Philadelphia, Chicago, and other cities. Bohle acquainted herself with famous eastern sites when her 1939 auto trip took her not only to Niagara Falls but to Detroit, Boston, New York City, Philadelphia, Washington, and the Gettysburg battlefield.[70] For Black teachers such as Charlotte Stephens of Little Rock, this type of geographical cultural capital was more accessible than the natural sights of the West, although they had to contend with restricted access to food, lodging, and fuel due to Jim Crow segregation. In the 1920s, when Stephens was in her sixties and still teaching, she and her daughter—who was also a teacher—took summer trips to New York, Chicago, and Detroit and Niagara Falls.[71]

Echoing the language they used to promote tourism in the West, journals occasionally referred to Eastern sites in nationalistic terms. Hargrave reported that Evansville teachers had received bonuses for summer trips to "the patriotic shrines of the east," and a piece in the NEA *Journal* on touring Washington, D.C., concluded with the statement that "every true American[']s . . . heart will burn, his eyes sparkle, as standing before the Nation's shrines he recalls the wisdom and valor of those who guided the destiny of this land."[72] Aside from the comment that "few buildings in Europe present as imposing a front as the [Capitol] rotunda portico,"[73] however, journals generally did not present nationalistic comparisons of historic or civic sites to those in other countries. Both journals and teacher-tourists consecrated these sites in terms of their cultural and refining influences, often on one's sense of citizenship. Rather than stoke prideful nationalism, educators' cultural approach to tourism in the East and South broadened teachers' horizons in ways that fostered an informed appreciation of the country's heritage in keeping with grassroots teacher professionalization. In each different region of the eastern half of the country, journals' and teachers' cultural tourism focused on a distinct aspect of history or civic heritage.

In New York City, the group of Nebraska teachers visited Ellis Island; Stephens and her daughter enjoyed riding the subway and went to the Statue of Liberty, Battery Park, Columbia University, Grant's Tomb, the Metropolitan Museum of Art, and the Aquarium; and Bohle and her friends visited the Statue of Liberty and Battery Park as well as toured the RCA Building and saw a play. Black teachers Ethel Hilliard of Chicago and Vivian Gonsalves of Gary, Indiana, devoted a week to visiting Harlem on their 1939 trip to the East Coast.[74] Seeing some of the highlights listed in the article promoting the 1938 NEA meeting titled "Going to New York?" which called the city "one of the greatest shows on earth,"[75] these teachers would have reflected on recent urban and immigration history as well as American achievements in architecture and art.

Another article promoting the 1938 NEA meeting described sites in New York that were associated with the longer sweep of U.S. history, including seventeenth-century burial grounds, a church attended by George Washington, and the spot where he took the presidential oath of office.[76] This focus on colonial and Revolutionary history characterized teacher tourism more broadly in the Northeast. Before the 1922 NEA meeting in Boston, the *Journal* published a photo of the Bunker Hill Monument, with a caption noting, "Many teachers now plan to spend a period following the Boston meeting next summer visiting historic places and gathering inspiration for the teaching of history and literature." A few months later, an article profiled sites in Boston associated with literary figures including Longfellow, Emerson, Thoreau, and the Alcotts. And in anticipation of the 1926 NEA meeting in Philadelphia, an article stated that "a visit to its historic sites and shrines is like turning the pages of American history."[77] When the National Association of Teachers in Colored Schools (NATCS) encouraged members to attend its 1920 meeting in Baltimore, it touted the city as the "birthplace of the 'Star Spangled Banner,'" and before the 1932 NEA meeting, "To Atlantic City on Highways of History" encouraged teachers to stop at various historic sites, including many in Pennsylvania and New Jersey that would enable them to "review the stirring events of '75 to '81 and to vitalize their classroom teaching of America's fight for freedom."[78] On her 1939 trip, Bohle and her friends took a historical tour of Boston, noting that Old North Church was in the "Italian district," and stopped at Plymouth Rock as they drove onward. She reported to her family from Philadelphia, "Saw Betsy Ross home, saw Liberty Bell, Independence Hall and many other places."[79]

Soon thereafter, Bohle wrote home that they had "reached Washington OK," but it was the "hardest place in the world to find one's way." She and her friends added to their stock of Revolutionary-era sites with a visit to Mount Vernon and toured the White House, the Smithsonian, the Capitol, and Arlington National Cemetery.[80] It is not surprising that citizenship was the main focus of teacher tourism in the nation's capital. Before the NEA convened there in 1898, the NEA director for New Mexico wrote to the teachers of his state, "This will be a rare opportunity to visit the capital of the nation and to enjoy its many attractions. The daily sessions of Congress and the activity of the executive department in reference to the [Spanish-American] war will make the trip doubly interesting." With the claim, "No teacher can come away from a visit to Washington without being better fitted to prepare young Americans for citizenship in our Republic," *Midland Schools* encouraged teachers to travel on a chartered train to Washington for the 1924 meeting. Before the next NEA meeting in Washington, in the Depression year of 1934, the association's president wrote, "We hope the teachers who come to Washington may cherish that experience in their hearts to let it speak in time of need and doubt."[81] One was Helen Hunt, a rural primary school teacher in Washington state whose trip was sponsored by the NEA Department of Classroom Teachers. In addition to learning a lot at the meeting, she wrote, "The wonders of Washington, about which I had read and heard, became a reality," including "imposing government edifices, the art and scientific buildings, the memorials and other points of historical significance." With a greater appreciation of her nation's seat of government, Hunt reflected, "This has been one of the happiest and most interesting experiences of my life."[82]

In the South, the main focus of teacher tourism was Civil War history. When the NEA was to meet in Nashville in 1889, the *Texas School Journal* promised, "There will be excursions to the scene of the battle above the clouds, and to numerous other battle-fields. To visit these will repay the journey for all teachers; and to talk with the men of the south and the teachers of the south who were engaged in the late unpleasantness, and to witness their devotion to the star-spangled banner, will be a surprise, an inspiration and a delight." *The Iowa Normal Monthly* also recommended visits to the "many famous battle grounds" near Nashville, the Confederate Cemetery, and the National Cemetery for Union soldiers—as well as the homes of former presidents Jackson and Polk, and

Mammoth Cave.[83] In conjunction with the 1900 NEA meeting in Charleston, a Chicago outing club offered a guided trip through the South, with a lecture each morning on the day's "points of interest." Minnesota teacher Mabel Marvin traveled to the meeting on this or a similar tour, which included a stop at Lookout Mountain. She reported, "We saw where Bragg came marching, where the Union men scaled the mountain to fight the Battle above the Clouds.... In the museum are thousands of relics, uniforms, guns, canteens plates, saddles, etc., belonging to both armies." Along a drive through Chickamauga Park, Marvin continued, "The many monuments of Illinois, Indiana, Ohio Cavalry, Kentucky, and Georgia helped us to comprehend somewhat the positions of both armies." Beatrice Cramer drove across the South on the way home from her western swing in 1929, stopping at Lookout Mountain and Antietam. At the end of their trip five years later, Cramer, her mother, and her cousin explored Kentucky, where they visited sites associated with Daniel Boone and the childhood home of Mary Todd Lincoln, and Virginia, where they went to Monticello, the grave of Stonewall Jackson, and Appomattox. "After a little difficulty," Cramer wrote, "we succeeded in locating the grass grown marker where Lee surrendered... and later followed the route used by Lee and the Southern army in its last valiant stand for 'the right' as they saw it."[84]

Cramer, as well as Bohle, also visited an especially popular Civil War historic site that was actually in the North: Gettysburg Battlefield in Pennsylvania. In the NEA *Journal*, "To Atlantic City on Highways of History" and "Going to New York?" both recommended a visit to "historically sacred" Gettysburg. "Heard all about the battle—Saw where Lincoln made his speech and all the monuments," Bohle wrote to her family from her 1939 trip.[85] Black teacher Greene B. Buster likely also visited Gettysburg, as he included several mementos from the historic site in the materials from his long career teaching history and social science at Sumner High School, a segregated Black institution in Kansas City. Among other items, he saved a program from the 1938 celebration of the seventy-fifth anniversary of the battle and *Buohl's Illustrated Map and Guide to Tour the Gettysburg Battlefield*, complete with notes penciled in the margins. Buster also saved postcards from the "Lincoln Farm" and "Lincoln's Cabin" in Kentucky, which he likely acquired on the same or another trip to Civil War sites.[86]

In addition to Civil War history, a lesser focus of teacher tourism in the South was the perseverance and industriousness of its cities following the war. Before the NEA meeting in 1889, *The Iowa Normal Monthly* observed that Nashville's "development during the past decade and a half has been remarkable" and celebrated its "many public buildings" and status as the "Athens of the South." Similarly, "The whole South drives forward toward economic independence. Atlanta is the spearhead of its progress" with "steam, smoke, whistles, and bells" signaling the Gate City's industriousness, reported the NEA *Journal* before the association's 1929 meeting there.[87] Before the 1929 NATCS meeting, its *Bulletin* reported that the host city of Jackson, Mississippi, was adjacent to "many historic spots" and thriving with a 50 percent Black population living "in perfect harmony with all the other people." As she saw some of the South's booming cities in 1900, however, Marvin acknowledged the rise of Jim Crow and the perniciousness of racism. She reported that in rail cars "the white folks always take the front end, but half the time I forget and the conductor reminds me," and that after hearing the story of how one of their guides, who had been enslaved as a child, "was lashed every time he tried to see the white children's speller," she thought, "I am more a Northerner than ever."[88]

Northern cities on the Great Lakes were also thriving, and teacher tourism in this region focused on industriousness and ingenuity as well as culture. The NEA brochure for the 1896 meeting in Buffalo promoted the host city as "the fifth commercial city in the world" and the Ellicott Square Building, which would serve as meeting headquarters, as "the largest and finest office building in the world." Chicago, reported the NEA *Journal* before the 1933 meeting, offered flourishing universities, innovative social settlements, "one of the largest natural history collections" at the Field Museum, a "valuable laboratory" at the Shedd Aquarium, and a unique "device . . . for astronomical study" at the Adler Planetarium.[89] Stephens fulfilled a "great desire" to visit the planetarium when she traveled to Chicago with her daughter, and Iowa teacher Mildred Van Wyngarden visited the Museum of Science and Industry on her way home from a Christian Endeavor convention in 1937.[90] Detroit "is justly proud of its industrial position, but not more than of its schools . . . museums, parks, and art centers," the NEA *Journal* reported in advance of the 1937 meeting. Nearby Greenfield Village included restored historical buildings and the laboratory of Thomas Edison as "a tribute to the past, [and] an inspiration for the future." On her way to Niagara Falls in 1909, California teacher Grace Canan toured Detroit, where she saw Water Works Park's "large clock operated by water power" and "twenty-two automobile shops." Stephens and Van Wyngarden also visited Detroit, and Bohle noted that her stop at Greenfield Village on her auto trip to the East Coast was "very worthwhile."[91] As teacher-tourists like Bohle, Van Wyngarden, Stephens, and Canan focused on industriousness in the Great Lakes region, Civil War history in the South, citizenship in Washington, and Revolutionary-era history in the Northeast, they engaged in measured consecration of sites important to the country's heritage, furthering their own professionalization in the process.

World's Fairs and Expositions

Cities throughout the country also hosted world's fairs and expositions during the decades between the 1880s and 1930s. "A trip to an exposition resembled a touring vacation, except that the former required traveling only to one location . . . to remind vacationers of America's history, achievements, and progress," explains Aron.[92] Once visitors entered the grounds, the fair's location was in many ways irrelevant; whether near or far from home, they could consume a wide range of wonders, however contrived some of them may have been. As with natural attractions in the West and historical sites in the East and South, school leaders advocated, and teachers traveled independently to, world's fairs as destinations for cultural tourism. Teachers and other Texans who were able to attend the 1893 Columbian Exposition in Chicago, wrote T. J. Pattillo of Houston, would return "with much to talk about." The exposition would be especially appealing to the "teacher who . . . wants to make men of his boys, who seeks to elevate his community, and who wishes to become a power among his people and authority in his profession." For California's teachers, the editors of *Pacific Coast Teacher* headlined a trip to the World's Fair as "The Opportunity of a Life-time to see, in the Busiest City on Earth, the Greatest Object Lesson on the Genius of Mankind," while from Chicago, Cook County Normal School Principal Francis W. Parker touted the fair's offerings for all teachers: "Probably never again will be gathered together so many magnificient [*sic*] illustrations of science, art, history, manufacturers, and commerce. It is an object lesson *par excellence*. . . . the greatest educational sxibit [*sic*] on earth. . . . Like Puck, you can put a girdle round the earth in forty minutes and then sit down and choose the country in which you will spend the day."[93] Thus, the Colombian Exposition—and other world's fairs—would enrich teachers' stock of cultural capital and their connection to cultural heritage.

Parker also listed prices for lodging and admission to the 1893 Columbian Exposition and then emphasized, "*Come,*—If you can beg or borrow the money." The *Texas School Journal* provided contact information for a hotel, "rates reasonable," and *The Iowa Normal Monthly* highlighted a special hotel for teachers that would enable "a lady" to "make the trip to and from the World's Fair grounds, unattended, with perfect safety."[94] *The Pacific Coast Teacher* organized "Teachers' Excursions" to Chicago for the exposition, with three special trains leaving San Francisco at one-to-two-week intervals beginning in early June. After visits to Salt Lake City, Denver, and Pike's Peak en route, the California teachers stayed for ten days at Chicago's Hotel Mecca; the journal noted, "The elegant hostelry which is to provide for the comfort of 'Pilgrims to the World's Fair,' is most appropriately named."[95] Some of the California teachers would have been in Chicago during the annual NEA meeting, held in Chicago in 1893 so that attendees could also visit the Columbian Exposition.

One of the first teachers to visit the 1893 World's Fair was a rural teacher who took advantage of a spring "plowing vacation" to scout it out before its formal opening and report back to readers of *The Iowa Normal Monthly*. The Manufactures and Liberal Arts Building, she noted, was "at least one mile long," and the Horticultural Building with its "pyramid of tropical plants under the dome" was "a sight worth the price of admission." Among the buildings representing different states, she saw the "Iowa corn palace," the "beautiful little Idaho house, built of redwood logs," and "Mt. Vernon, the home of Washington," which looked "just as it does in Virginia, except for the unavoidable newness." Finally, "the Esquimaux village" of twelve families was "a sight that every school teacher should see." Aside from praising one Eskimo's talent with his seal skin whip, she did not explain why the village was compelling or how its residents came to be in Chicago, but her account suggested that visiting the exposition had broadened her horizons.[96] Sarah Hannah Butler lived in Chicago's Englewood neighborhood in 1893 and thus did not have to travel far to the World's Fair. After one visit, she wrote to her mother, "The grounds are simply magnificent." Just to see the Art Building would be "a week's work," but she and a friend had enjoyed Norway's exhibit and the statuary. At her Englewood home, Butler ran a rooming house of sorts for fair visitors, including several teachers, who came and went throughout the summer. One of the teachers, Miss Evelyn Bires, later sent Butler a gift of a carved wooden box. In the enclosed note, Bires expressed thanks for "your many kindnesses to me during the summer," and wrote, "Let the box also remind you of our mutual enjoyment of many things at the great Fair."[97]

Before the 1901 Pan-American Exposition in Buffalo, *The Iowa Normal Monthly* advertised a railway's special excursion to the exposition for "teachers and all others," and *The American School Board Journal* announced that the "Teachers' Headquarters" in the Pan American's Johnstown Flood building would offer a place to rest, to send and receive mail, and to connect with other teachers.[98] One teacher who likely stopped by the headquarters multiple times was twenty-three-year-old Buffalo second-grade teacher Mabel Barnes. As historian Margaret Creighton explains in her book on the 1901 exposition, Barnes devoted her summer to the "Pan," regularly riding her bicycle or taking the streetcar there, either alone or with friends. She saw concerts, lectures, pageants, and parades; gathered free samples, guides, and souvenirs; toured state and country exhibits; and took notes throughout the Manufactures and Liberal Arts, Mines, Agriculture, and Electricity exhibit halls. Impressed with the evening "illumination" of the grounds, Barnes said that the glow on the Electric Tower looked "like the first flush which a church spire catches from the dawn." She was fascinated by demonstrations in the "Darkest Africa" exhibit and even made a momentary connection with one of the "natives" when she realized that he spoke English, and noted that he "was of rather an intelligent appearance." In late summer, Barnes and her friend jockeyed to have "first class views" of President McKinley, who would be assassinated the following day.[99] Without leaving town, Barnes was able to witness remarkable innovations, representations of other cultures, and even the chief executive.

The NEA held its 1904 meeting in St. Louis so that educators could make a single trip to the meeting and the Louisiana Purchase Exposition. NEA attendees received reduced-price tickets to the World's Fair, and a circular for Florida teachers explained, "It is extremely desirable that all should spend at least TEN days at the Exposition, as the program—an extremely interesting one—provides for a careful study of many of the exhibits." *The Iowa Normal Monthly* promoted features of the fair including "the Japanese exhibit of diminutive trees," as well as Idaho's "splendid mineral display" and Wyoming's "single piece of soda weighing six thousand pounds" in the Palace of Mines and Metallurgy.[100] The NEA met in Oakland in 1915 so that attendees could also visit San Francisco's Panama-Pacific International Exposition, which the *Pennsylvania School Journal* promised would be "a festival of progress" that would "eclipse all other expositions," and the NEA met in Chicago in 1933 so that educators could also visit the Century of Progress International Exposition. This World's Fair continued through the summer of 1934, when Beatrice Cramer, her mother, and her cousin stopped there on their way west. Cramer wrote, "Exhibits, pageants, displays of various kinds bespoke the part of Science in the world's progress. Especially enjoyed the pageant portraying the advance of transportation. . . . The C.B. and Q's Burlington Zephyr and the Union Pacific's new record breaking 1001 fascinated us."[101]

The New York World's Fair and the Golden Gate International Exposition in San Francisco both spanned the summers of 1939 and 1940. The NEA met in the latter city in 1939, and education journals promoted both fairs. An article that described additions to the Golden Gate for its second summer reported, "Many teachers who visited our nation's exposition last year, either New York or San Francisco, found that they gained considerable store of worthwhile information."[102] Mildred Van Wyngarden and Margarete Bohl both visited the New York World's Fair in 1939 and the Exposition in San Francisco in 1940. Bohl wrote to her family that she and her friends were "a little disappointed" in the New York Fair, in part because the buildings seemed "to be too much alike." The following summer, however, their day at the Golden Gate was "very worthwhile," as they "heard a lovely lecture on the wonders of electricity, sound + light," including "the new black light." Meanwhile, Van Wyngarden noted that she and the five other teachers with whom she went to San Francisco on their western trip saw "many wonders including—the great statue 'Pacifica,' the Tower of the Sun, U.S. Bomber, [and] Coast Guard Demonstration." By 9:00 P.M., she added, they were "nearly exhausted" but "found that the beauty of the fair was much greater after the lights were turned on."[103] For Van Wyngarden, Bohle, and Cramer, world's fairs were brief stops on longer trips to see natural sights in the West or historical sites in the eastern half of the country. In asserting their right to adventure, they, like teachers in earlier decades, engaged in consumption and measured consecration of the country's heritage, bolstering their knowledge and confirming their membership in the middle class. In 1953, Cramer would realize "a dream of long duration" with a trip to Europe,[104] thus joining the long lineage of teachers who partook with the middle and upper classes in international travel.

International Tourism

When Stephen Bush stated in *Midland Schools* that travel "puts more life into the work of teaching," his focus was tourism in Europe, which he claimed possessed a "permanent lure . . . for all intelligent persons." The most well-to-do

Americans, who had been traveling to Europe since early in the nineteenth century, and middle-class Americans, who joined them in increasing numbers during the century's final decades, pursued what historian Harvey Levenstein refers to as "the fabled Grand Tour—the Mother of all Cultural Tourism," established more than two centuries earlier by the English aristocracy. The goal was "to become a cultured person by exposing oneself to the best that Europe had to offer," specifically the cathedrals, museums, historic sites, art performances, promenades, and natural scenery of England, France, and Italy, along with the Alps, the Rhine, and a few high points of Holland and Belgium. The Grand Tour was the epitome of Baranowski and Furlough's notion of "what 'ought' to be seen," and Bush encouraged teachers to obtain this form of cultural capital because "Europe is the source of everything for us, from blood to laws, religion, and ideas."[105] By the end of the nineteenth century, upper-class American tourists in Europe concerned themselves less with seeing the sights and more with consuming the finer things, socializing, and being seen, while middle-class American tourists—especially those on group tours with companies such as Cook's—acquired a reputation for touring so frenetically that they gained only the most superficial understanding of what they saw.[106] Teachers had more in common with the latter than the former group, yet their approach to tourism in Europe generally did allow for thoughtful reflection and cultural uplift both before World War I and afterward, when middle-class Americans shifted their focus to leisure and having fun in Europe.[107]

Reflecting the persistence of the cultural or heritage approach to tourism, Bush instructed teachers who might travel to Europe, "Beautiful things were made to be looked at with joy and not as a duty, not as something to be reported as having been seen." He endorsed the Grand Tour if pursued at a reasonable pace: "It is possible . . . to really see something of Germany, England, France, Italy and Switzerland in a summer" but only with an understanding that "the right kind of trip to Europe . . . enriches life." The value of European travel for cultural uplift, Bush argued, is "inestimable. It makes book knowledge real."[108] As U.S. schoolteachers increased their stock of cultural capital through extensive—and only occasionally frenetic—travels in Europe, they also made connections to their "book knowledge" and enjoyed seeing it and foreign cultures become "real." Before the First World War, the Grand Tour countries dominated teachers' itineraries in Europe. After a pause in tourism during the war, their routes diversified and they took advantage of increasing numbers of more education-oriented tours. Throughout, the transatlantic voyage was an assertion of independence for women teachers and a rite of passage to middle-class status. Teachers also engaged in international tourism beyond Europe, but this travel was often framed as serving similar purposes to European tourism and functioned as a prelude or complement to transatlantic travel. Between the 1880s and the 1930s, teacher-tourists' experiences in non-European countries, on the transatlantic voyage, and in Grand Tour countries and, later, other European nations, broadened their cultural horizons and strengthened their position in the middle class, ultimately putting "more life into the work of teaching."

International Travel to Non-European Countries

When Beatrice Cramer left her car behind in 1926 and sailed aboard the S.S. *Columbia* to the West Indies and Columbia, through the Panama Canal, and on to Central America and Mexico, it was the farthest she had been from her home in New York state and likely whetted her appetite for more international travel, including to Europe. Cramer sailed in the wake of many organized trips for teachers to countries south of the U.S. border, which education journals often billed as more accessible than, and just as historical as, travel to other international destinations. An announcement for an 1897 "summer outing" to Mexico for Texas teachers stated that previous participants testified to "the scenic, climatic and historical interest that a trip to that ancient wonderland affords over any other," and one for a thirty-day "Iowa Educational Excursion" to Mexico in 1906 began by noting that Mexico rivaled Egypt "as a land of the earliest civilization."[109] Later, an advertisement for a water route to California in 1928 stated that passengers would "visit colorful Havana, make the thrilling passage through the Panama Canal and learn the attractions of the Canal Zone" at "low summer rates," and the NEA *Journal* ran ads for a two-week voyage from New York to Los Angeles for the 1931 NEA meeting "thru Panama Canal via gay Havana." A 1938 article encouraging teachers to tour Mexico summarized the draw of international travel close to home, stating, "Mexico is a land of colorful old-world beauty, studded with architectural gems of an age long past," with "more foreign atmosphere for less money."[110]

Also close to home, Canada was the first or only international destination for many teachers, who echoed ads for travel to the United States' northern neighbor in drawing parallels between Canada and Europe. The Canadian Pacific Railway promised California teachers "magic castles in Alpine Fairyland" under the headline, "Going East See Fifty Switzerlands in One" in 1920, and touted Banff to midwestern teachers as "a Swiss mountain village" in 1939.[111] Margarete Bohle and her friends went to Quebec on their 1939 auto trip; "Crossed the border without trouble—must have honest faces," she quipped. They toured Quebec City and saw the changing of the guard, enjoyed driving through "little French towns" near the St. Lawrence River, and found the countryside to be "typical French" with "oxen in field." When Cramer toured the Canadian Parliament buildings in Ottawa with her mother in 1937, she noticed prominent oil paintings of Queen Victoria and other members of the British royal family and remarked that the "courtesy which we encountered . . . was most unusual—at least to persons from 'the states.'" Cramer enjoyed the "natural beauty" of Ontario, but it was her trip to Europe a decade and a half later that was "a dream come true."[112]

While Europe remained the main focus of education journals' advertising for international destinations, in the late 1920s they also began to promise cultural capital through travel to far more distant locales. A trip to "Sunny and Picturesque South Africa" would provide first-hand knowledge of "the Historic Cape, the bourne of many an ancient mariner"; "the mysterious Zimbabwe Ruins;" and "the scenes environing the lives and histories of Cecil John Rhodes . . . and other illustrious characters of whom you have so often read"; as well as the "unspoilt giant Victoria Falls of David Livingstone." Offering "gaiety, adventure and discovery" and "a 'pocket edition of the world,' like many lands yet still unlike all others," travel to Australia and New Zealand, respectively, would broaden one's cultural experiences, while travel to China would open "an ancient door" to "the oldest civilization in the world, a culture that was vigorous before Rome was born."[113] The fifth annual "Dragonland" cruise to Japan, China, and the Philippines was "especially arranged for members and friends of the National Education Association following the close of the Convention in Portland" in 1936; under the guidance of a University of Washington education professor, the trip was sure to be educational. Seattle physical education teacher Sara Luch visited Asia on her own in 1939 and—even though she was not able to visit China's Great Wall due to war—later reported, "I had the time of my life." Luch's tour of Asia was her second of what would be many international trips; it was a trip to Europe the previous summer that hooked her on world travel.[114] While teachers explored other countries in the Americas and ventured as far as Asia, Europe was the pinnacle of cultural tourism for teachers.

Assertions of Independence and Middle-Class Behaviors En Route to Europe

The Pennsylvania superintendent of public instruction, James Wickersham, published a series of letters in the state's education journal describing his 1878 trip to Europe "in order to broaden the views of teachers," whom he seemed to assume would not themselves be able to travel there. His first letter, a description of the actual voyage "over the sea" on the new steamship *Circassia*, listed his male travel companions—a former senator, a doctor, and a lawyer—and painted a picture of middle-class leisure on the "floating palace" with its organ, library, and multicourse meals. In order to pass the time on the ten-day crossing, Wickersham explained, "The passengers read, write, converse, walk on deck. Some of them spend much time in watching the sea, the birds, the fish. . . . Others play shuffleboard, chess, backgammon, checkers, cards, and other games. We have instrumental music, singing and religious exercises." The only downside to this "summer resort" atmosphere was seasickness, which Wickersham presented almost as an initiation ritual: "The afflicted are to be seen everywhere stretched out on settees and chairs, surrounded with wraps, on the decks, and even lying on cabin floors. It is one of the characteristics of this disease that it makes one utterly indifferent to his personal appearance, and fine ladies allow themselves to be exposed."[115] Although Wickersham did not seem to foresee teachers as transatlantic travelers, the voyage for them soon became a rite of passage into the middle class. As his mention of "fine ladies" suggests, it was also becoming increasingly common for wealthy women to make the trip—in family groups and, by the late 1880s, with other women as companions.[116] For the barely-middle-class women teachers who soon joined their ranks, the voyage over the sea was an assertion of independence as well as a route for claiming or affirming middle-class status.

Just a year after Wickersham's transatlantic venture, an advertisement appeared in the *Maryland School Journal* for a summer "Teachers' Excursion" to Europe. In 1880, the ad in the same journal for the "Annual Educational Excursion" to Europe promised "*first-class* travel."[117] The teachers who followed Wickersham across the ocean generally did not state in their letters and travel journals the class of their ticket or whether they were with an organized group, but their burgeoning middle-class identity and sense of independence were clear. Helen Crombie, a forty-two-year-old teacher in Roxbury, Massachusetts, received letters in 1892–1893 from a male friend or relative on a European trip. He wrote, "Remember that you will get to see all this, some day" and added that any "timidity" she might have would "disappear as soon as you have found that you can actually take care of yourself." Soon, Crombie did sail from Boston to Liverpool to spend the summer of 1894 touring Europe.[118] When Mary Elizabeth Pierce, a teacher at the Manual Training School in Boston, made the same steamer crossing in eleven days the following summer, she participated in many of the activities Wickersham had listed. In her travel journal, Pierce mentioned sitting and reading "in a row" of deck chairs with her travel companions, and seeing porpoises, gulls, and other steamers. They were "fortunate enough to be at the first table" for meals, and their "staterooms were very comfortable." Pierce also noted, "Eversomany people are sick" and sympathized with her friend Alice as she endured this initiation ritual: "Poor girl she has suffered, but she has a tremendous amount of pluck." With just a touch of noblesse oblige, she also remarked, "Poor steerage passengers must have suffered so much." When they finally approached land, Pierce observed, "Everyone came on deck and gorgeous clothes appeared," and she and her companions enjoyed the views of Ireland and Wales alongside their fellow middle-class passengers.[119]

When Lillian Herrick went to Europe in 1907 at the end of her fourteenth year of teaching chemistry, physics, and domestic science at the public Elmira Free Academy in New York state, it was her third transatlantic voyage. For her, the trip was a confirmation of class privilege and a somewhat reluctant assertion of independence. She traveled in a small group that included her sister Jessie, whose trip to the Glens Falls Training School in 1887 had stoked a desire for wider horizons. Aboard the White Star Line's S.S. *Canopic*, Herrick wrote in her journal on July 3 with "a <u>seasick</u> sigh," but enjoyed celebrations the following day on the hurricane deck. The "crowd sang 'The Star Spangled Banner,'" she reported, and "the guns fired a salute + with bared heads we pledged allegiance to our flag." In the evening, she listened to speeches by the captain and a politician, after which there was a "dance on deck. We sat on the hurricane deck + sang + sang." After brief stops in the Azores and Gibraltar, she found the Mediterranean "choppy but foam filled with rainbows" and reflected the night before they arrived in Italy, "The journey has a splendid thread of love woven into it." During the return trip from Liverpool in late August, middle-class socializing seemed to come easily to Herrick, as she noted that she "never visited so much in my life" and laughed with others over dinner. She had been reluctant to leave home out of a sense of duty to her mother and now missed her sister Jessie, who had stayed longer in Britain. But as she crossed the North Atlantic, Herrick reflected, "I have my own life to live + must live it alone tho with people. . . . It has been good for me to be away from Dearest these days + to lean upon myself."[120]

Sisters Evangeline and Maude Lewis did not seem to hesitate in asserting independence and claiming membership in the middle class during their transatlantic trip. Instead of their usual practice of spending the summer on the family farm in Indiana, Eva—a forty-five-year-old high school teacher and principal—and Maude—a primary school teacher—sailed from Philadelphia to Antwerp on the SS *Manitou* in June 1910. Choppy seas initiated them into seasickness early in the trip; "When we attempt dinner we retreat ignominiously after the soup course and the dining room knows us no more for several meals," they wrote home. "We try it on the deck alternately leaning over the rail and reclining in our steamer chairs." Within a couple of days, however, they were well enough to socialize with other passengers, establishing connections with socially prominent Indianans on the *Manitou*. The Lewis sisters also enjoyed a concert displaying "very fine talent," a professor's lectures on Turkey, reading, and promenading on deck, although they dined on deck to avoid the six-course dinner in the "stuffy dining room."[121]

Another Midwesterner who went to Europe in 1910 was Kansas teacher Lucy Jones, who sailed with her friend Pearl from New York City, where they saw a parade for former President Theodore Roosevelt and tried "a real cocktail" before departing on a Hamburg Amerika Line steamer. When Jones wrote to her friend and fellow teacher Ethel Lowry about making social connections on the ship, she mentioned "a multi-millionaire" who was "interesting to talk to," a Kansas City banker on his way to visit his mother in Berlin with whom she practiced speaking German, a Viennese millionaire who complimented her German, and violin player Herr Weiner, "the prize package" on whom Pearl had "a copyright." She also explained that a dance on the ship "was rather hard work—as the floor wasn't very smooth—and the ship did such unexpected things."[122] Yet another Midwesterner who made the transatlantic crossing in 1910, Helen Tearse, seemed quite comfortable with the privilege of traveling first class. The Winona, Minnesota, high school teacher and Smith College alumna wrote to her mother on SS *Cymric* stationery, "I'm glad you kept insisting on an outer room. They are so much nicer. . . . The English servants are just perfect—they can't wait on you enough." Tearse would return to Europe under very different circumstances eight years later, after she had left teaching. While tourism to Europe was on hold during the Great War, she traveled with the Smith College "canteen unit" to France, where she provided support for Allied soldiers.[123] Tearse's earlier exercise of independence on her journey to Europe likely helped to steel her for the challenges of this new role.

Following World War I, faster ocean liners shaved a few days off the transatlantic crossing, and advertisements for steamship lines abounded in education journals. A 1922 ad for the White Star Line began, "The war has internationalized the world. . . . Now, as never before, a trip to Europe is for the progressive teacher a necessity, not a luxury." Rather than the benefits to teaching, however, most of these ads touted the ships' onboard amenities, especially in the new tourist third class. A 1925 ad for White Star boasted "Neat comfortable staterooms. Good table and service. Broad decks for games and lounging. Commodious, well-appointed public rooms." The photo in the ad, with the caption "Dancing on deck—A glimmer of moonlight . . . Stars, laughter and music," conveyed middle-class sociability and a hint of romance. A few years later, the Holland America Line emphasized more intellectual aspects of middle-class culture, specifically, "Libraries, Lectures, College Music, Entertainment." "Sailing for Europe is such fun!" exclaimed journalist Margaret Patch in an article reprinted in education journals throughout the country in 1928. Patch did not mention seasickness but otherwise portrayed similar activities to those enjoyed by the teachers on transatlantic trips in earlier decades: "deck tennis," shuffleboard, "lazy afternoons with a book, a friendly chat, [that] slip by as we lie snugly blanketed in our deck chairs," and "gay" evenings "with music, dancing, cards." Meanwhile, the *Pennsylvania School Journal* quoted the observation of the general manager of a travel company in 1928 that "more teachers go to Europe than formerly,"[124] indicating that increasing numbers of teachers were sharing shipboard expressions of middle-class identity.

By the 1930s, the fastest ocean liners made the transatlantic crossing in as few as four or five days, and steamer lines continued to advertise in education journals, albeit less frequently than during the previous decade. Perhaps as an antidote to the effects of the Great Depression, ads emphasized fun and good companionship on the voyage. "Let's play our way to Europe," stated one 1931 ad, while a 1933 ad touted "the charming folk you'll find aboard" as well as "remarkably low rates."[125] Middle-class respectability did not disappear from steamer trips, however; Seattle teacher Sara Luch remembered that when she and her friends sailed to Scotland on the *Athenia* in 1938, the "dear old Scotch ladies [who] were stewardesses . . . couldn't understand young girls traveling without a chaperone." Acknowledging their independence, she added with a laugh, "I was 29 at the time. . . . We had fun." Luch also noted that the *Athenia* would be the first ship to go down in the Second World War.[126] She and other teachers, both during the interwar period and between the 1880s and the First World War, asserted self-determination and engaged in middle-class behaviors while en route to Europe; their experiences there would reinforce these qualities and broaden their personal and professional horizons.

The Grand Tour of Europe, 1880–1914

Guidebooks, tour companies, and the almost exclusively white middle- and upper-class American tourists who patronized them adhered to a very well-defined European itinerary during the decades preceding World War I. Superintendent Wickersham and the 1880 "Annual Educational Excursion" toured the same set of countries: England, Scotland, France, Italy, Switzerland, Austria, Germany, Holland, and Belgium. Wickersham spent the most time in London, Paris, and Rome, and the excursion visited "All the Great Musical, Art and Educational Centres of the Old World." Two decades later, an ad for Ward's Tours listed "France, Switzerland, Germany, the Rhine, Belgium, and England" as its forty-seven-day "Vacation Tour."[127] Whether in a group like Ward's or on their own, teacher-tourists during this period traveled almost entirely in these countries that constituted the Grand Tour. As they pored over their guidebooks and saw "what 'ought' to be seen," teachers avoided joining the ranks of the superficial "Cook's Hordes" by adhering to the cultural approach to tourism. Nearly two decades before Stephen Bush wrote that unhurried travel in Europe "enriches life" and "makes book knowledge real," H. L. Hargrove sounded the same themes in a 1908 issue of the *Texas School Journal*, writing of "the vast culture gained from" such a trip: "Not only is travel" for teachers "a source of pleasure but of profit; not merely selfish, but for the ultimate good of those taught."[128] As they each toured a few, several, or all of the Grand Tour countries in Europe, Helen Crombie, Mary Pierce, Lillian Herrick, Eva and Maude Lewis, Lucy Jones, Helen Tearse, and other teachers focused on gaining "vast culture" by deepening their understanding of literature, architecture, art, music, history, natural scenery, and local customs; in the process, they gained cultural capital and strengthened their position in the middle class.

"England teems with interest for an American," stated Hargrove. London alone was home to the "haunts" of a long list of literary greats, historic architecture, "art galleries . . . filled with the masterpieces of the world," and people exhibiting a range of "manners and customs." After arriving in Liverpool, Crombie thoughtfully soaked in all of these aspects of Britain. She wrote to her mother about Stratford, "Fancy sitting in Shakespeare's chair," and after visiting Holyrood castle in Scotland, "The person in charge was a droll old fellow who reeled off 'Tam o'Shanter as if he loved it—it was great fun to hear him recite Burns in the native dialect." Crombie not only saw the King's College Chapel in Cambridge and the Chester, St. Paul's, Canterbury, and Durham Cathedrals, but she attended two services at York Cathedral and one at the Tower of London's chapel, "where Ann Bolyn [*sic*]—Lady Jane Grey and the rest of the beheaded unfortunates are buried." After her second visit to Westminster Abbey, she wrote, "One never grows tired of this wonderful old abbey with all its famous memorials. I have just received permission from the Dean to visit the Henry V Chapel. We shall go next week some time." Crombie also saw a Becket play at the Lyceum Theatre and visited the National Gallery—"a real treat—There are a great many of the Old Masters"—more than once. She must also have gained a sense of local culture in York, as she wrote home that her landlady there was "true Yorkshire."[129]

Other teacher-tourists similarly deepened their connections to history and literature in England. During their 1895 trip, Pierce and her companions walked along the city wall in Chester and "were fortunate enough to find the janitor" at St. John the Baptist's who "showed us all over the church and ruins in the most charming manner." In London, they made "a B line" for the British Museum, where they had "such a fine time" seeing exhibits including the Elgin Marbles from the Parthenon and the Rosetta Stone. Fifteen years later, Tearse and her friends also saw the Rosetta Stone as well as Egyptian artifacts at the British Museum; their guide "made it so interesting" that she was "sorry to leave." A "strenuous day" for Tearse in London included visits to Westminster Abbey and the National Gallery. At a slower pace, she engaged with literature through visits to Wordsworth's Dove Cottage in the Lake District—where the scenic views were "<u>wonderful</u>"—and Anne Hathaway's cottage in Stratford. Beyond visiting highbrow attractions, Tearse spent half of a day shopping in Chester and went to Madame Tussaud's Wax Works in London. Pierce's group, on the other hand, deepened their understanding of British manufacturing and education by venturing to the London borough of Lambeth to see "one of the finest iron works in England" and visiting schools in Manchester and London, where they talked with teachers and viewed students' iron and lathe work.[130]

Teachers' cultural tourism in the Grand Tour countries on the continent also incorporated the features Hargrove listed. While their letters and journals mentioned local customs, art, architecture, natural scenery, history, music, and literature in most of the countries, teachers' accounts tended to focus mainly on particular aspects of each nation's culture. In France, Crombie, Herrick, and Tearse enjoyed Paris's beautiful parks and spent a lot of time at the Louvre but wrote more about the customs and manners of the people they observed. Tearse was fascinated by the behavior of the "crowds [who] were out riding or walking in the Bois de Bologne" and observed of French fashion, "They are wearing the skirts <u>so very</u> tight from the knees down that it won't stay in style very long." Crombie gladly adapted to haggling over prices at the Palace Royale arcade of shops: "It's great fun beating down the trades men—they will take off a Franc or two—if you refuse to purchase—and will come after you to tell you [that you] may have things for less." Overall, however, she found Frenchmen's manners to be "dreadful." "I would like to mention the politeness of the French," she wrote to her mother. "They are pigs." In the same vein, Tearse commented later in her trip, "The Italians all seem so much happier than the French—and so much more polite. Of all the people we have seen the French were rudest."[131]

In Italy, teacher-tourists focused primarily on art and architecture, touring at a pace that bordered on frenetic at times but usually allowed them to absorb and appreciate centuries' worth of culture. The Italian segment of Eva and Maude Lewis's trip began in Milan, where they saw Da Vinci's *Last Supper* and were awed by the cathedral—and where their landlady told them "with great relish of atrocities committed by Americans abroad." From there, they went to Certosa di Pavia, about which Maude wrote, "You may imagine beautiful things but, when you see them! Wonderful altars of different marbles inlaid with precious stones . . . loveliest of paintings, the choir stalls with pictures of saints and prophets all made with inlaid wood." After more than a week in Florence, Eva wrote home, "We cannot begin to tell you of the art treasures we have seen."[132] Lucy Jones and her friend Pearl spent much less time there; Jones wrote, "Florence we did up in one day, Sunday. Wouldn't that shock the art critics?" Still, they took it seriously: "But really we did see the most famous things and enjoyed them. We had a guide." After describing a few of the works they saw by Michelangelo, Jones reflected, "All of his work is so simple and strong." Tearse educated herself about the art in Florence through a lecture and touring with an art teacher friend of one of her companions, saying, "It was interesting to hear her comments." She found it hardest to leave Venice, "the most beautiful" city, and Jones called Venice "lovely and fascinating. . . . Just imagine the streets being water!"[133]

From Rome, Eva Lewis wrote home, "As we approached the city we saw St. Peters dome rising in the distance and experienced some of the thrills we came to Europe to get." In the Italian capital, the Lewises visited the Colosseum twice, laughed with "the jolly old" priest at the catacombs who teased them about being Protestant, and gained a new appreciation for Raphael, whom Eva said they "learned to love . . . especially here where most of his work seems to be." At the Vatican, they spent an hour "studying" the ceiling and walls in the Sistine Chapel. Maude remarked, "So much sightseeing runs us down" but added that they continued to review their "guide books at a fearful rate" in order to learn all that they could. Meanwhile, Jones visited the Colosseum and the Pantheon, which she noted was "the best preserved of the old Roman buildings—built long B.C." She also remarked on the importance of Raphael's *Coronation of the Virgin* and *The Transfiguration*. She and Pearl climbed to the top of St. Peter's dome, which she said was "beautiful—entirely made of mosaics of gold and other colors." They even had an audience with the Pope Pius X, "a very simple old man." After the Pope departed, they appreciated the Vatican meeting rooms; "They are all very simple but magnificent," Jones wrote, with "marble floors and priceless tapestries on the walls."[134]

After immersing themselves in Italy's art and architecture, Jones and Pearl took a day trip organized by Cook's from Naples to Mount Vesuvius. A carriage ride and two-and-a-half hours of "fierce" climbing and stepping in "lava over our shoe tops" took them to the "bubbling and boiling" of an active volcano.[135] Awe-inspiring natural sights were the main focus of teacher tourism in Switzerland, where teachers also strengthened their understanding of folk history. Herrick marveled over the sight of the Jungfrau and Eiger Mountains from Interlaken and spent a "glorious day" walking near Lauterbrunnen, where she enjoyed "the green of the meadows, the blue of the sky, the rushing foaming stream along the roadside, the snow on the mountain + God's glory all of it." The Lewises also enjoyed views of the Jungfrau and "a lovely walk along a mountainside," where they were "never more impressed with the wonderful forces of nature." Herrick, the Lewises, and Tearse all took a boat trip on Lake Lucerne to a monument dedicated to William Tell. The Lewises' account of their visit to Tell's Platz summarized what they learned about his story: "We walked down to a tiny chapel erected on the exact spot where Tell leaped from the boat onto this rock giving the boat a push as he did so. He thus escaped from Gessler and his men. Four mural paintings tell us much of Tell history."[136]

In Germany, Pierce, the Lewises, and Tearse all took the obligatory boat tour on the Rhine River past castles and vineyards. The main foci of teacher tourism in Germany, however, were art and music, specifically paintings and opera. Pierce and Jones were especially moved by paintings they saw in Dresden. Pierce wrote of "the Gallery" there, "of all the beautiful collections this has to be the most." She and her companions returned twice to the gallery, and she marveled, "To see the originals of the pictures we have known always from photographs, or engravings, and have the richness of color added is more than joyous." Jones similarly wrote of Raphael's *Sistine Madonna*, "I never cared greatly for the prints I have seen of it—but it is grand. The expressions on the faces, the coloring, it is all indescribable." Pierce saw her first opera in Dresden, a culturally enriching experience: "The orchestra was simply perfect, the stage setting was indescribable. The voices all good and such choruses. . . . I do not believe there was ever anything that at all compares with it in Boston." Jones saw two operas in Berlin—where she also saw soldiers march along Unter den Linden and rated the monuments and fountains as superior to those in other cities. She watched *Meistersingers* in the standing-room section, where a man who spoke English summarized the plot for her between acts, and thought *Rhine Gold* was "beautiful." Jones and Tearse went to Oberammergau for the renowned Passion Play. Jones noted in her travel diary that the costumes were "gorgeously rich and beautiful," the scenery looked "like paintings by the old masters," and the audience was "deeply affected" by the eight-hour performance, while Tearse wrote to her father that the play was "wonderful" and the area surrounding the village was "beautiful."[137]

In addition to art and music, another important component of Jones's cultural tourism in Germany as well as Austria was learning the German language while experiencing local social customs. Jones—who taught German and English in Kansas—and her friend Pearl stayed with local families, first in Leipzig and then in Vienna, as Jones studied German with an instructor and Pearl took music lessons. On the train to Leipzig, Jones took notes on German words related to rail travel. From Leipzig, she wrote to her friend Ethel, "Dear Liebe, ... The German lessons go pretty well.... I have just finished writing the story of Othello for part of my Monday's lesson. I'm wondering how much she will cut it up. The hardest thing is to pronounce to suit her." Early in their stay in Leipzig, Jones and Pearl laughed over their informal lesson on the custom of women wearing hats: "After supper—dusk—we started to walk around the block without our hats—and the old [land]lady most had a spell, said they would stare at us. So we went to our room and privately had convulsions—then as we passed out[side] with our hats on we heard them having convulsions in the dining room. On the streets we saw plenty of women bareheaded—but on close inspection I guess it must be only the serving girls who go without hats." In Vienna, their host mother spoke only German and their host sister, who spoke a little English, guided them around the city. "Things and people are not so very different over here," Jones observed. At another point in the trip, they joined in the German custom of beer drinking at the Lowenbraukeller, a beer garden in Munich. "I tried a stein of beer for the first time," Jones wrote in her travel diary. While "the men around laughed at the graceful way" she "handled the big thing," she "managed to dispose of 1/2 of it." Jones relished the opportunity to imbibe German culture on multiple levels.[138]

Teachers' accounts of their experiences in Belgium and Holland focused on the various elements of cultural tourism without emphasizing any in particular. Literature came to life for Eva and Maude Lewis in Ghent when they repeated Longfellow's line "I am Roland, I am Roland" to the sound of the chimes in his poem. In Bruges, their hotel was across from "the Belfry of Bruges," and their landlady told them that Longfellow had written the poem from a room one floor below theirs. The architecture of Brussels's Palace of Justice impressed Herrick; she noted that it was the "largest building in the world." Maude Lewis reported from Belgium, "We are learning much about the architecture of cathedrals and the wonderful paintings shown on walls and stained glass windows." The art collection at Antwerp's Royal Museum compelled Maude to reflect, "We may hate King Leopold but we must admire his love for art and what he has done for it." The Belgian folk art of lace drew Herrick and the Lewises to the souvenir shops. The Lewises also paid special attention to local customs related to agriculture, which they reported to their family on the farm in Indiana. From the train en route to Bruges, they noticed fields of grain and potatoes. And after they traversed Holland on an "electric tram," Eve reported, "Everywhere it is so irrigated by canals, and ditches that everything is growing luxuriantly.... Such haycrops! The yield is wonderful. Except for one little mower and one simple hay-rake all the work is done in the old fashioned way.... And dotting the country everywhere we see windmills."[139] While the Lewises enhanced their knowledge in the highbrow areas of literature, architecture, and art, they remained connected to their roots on the farm.

Pierce and her companions also traveled in Belgium on their 1895 trip through Europe, yet their itinerary was ahead of its time in two important respects. First, their trip included visits to educational institutions including those in Manchester and London as well as in Weimar and Leipzig, Germany. Second, their tour extended beyond the Grand Tour countries when they ventured to Copenhagen, Denmark, and Gothenburg, Sweden. In Copenhagen, they went to the Thorvaldsen Museum, where Pierce found the sculptor's works "wonderfully beautiful"; sailed up the Kattegat River to see "the ghosts at Elsinore," the castle in which Shakespeare's *Hamlet* was set; and visited a school and exhibit on art industries. In Gothenburg, they watched from their hotel balcony as local citizens saluted the crown prince, princess, and their children; but the main purpose of their stay was to visit a special normal school that prepared teachers in sloyd, a system of handcraft education. At the institution, they observed classes and met with famous sloyd educator Otto Solomon. "The spirit of the place is beautiful," Pierce wrote in her travel journal.[140] Teachers' tourism would expand in the 1920s to incorporate more attention to education in Europe as well as to include countries beyond those on the Grand Tour. In the meantime, tourism paused after war gripped Europe in 1914.

When war broke out in August 1914, American tourists found themselves stranded throughout Europe. Among them was a group on a tour organized by H. G. Campbell, a philosophy professor at Morningside College in Iowa. Campbell organized the Morningside Travel Club after sabbatical study at universities in Berlin and Heidelberg in 1910–1911 stoked his deep interest in international relations and travel. The club was to offer summer tours especially for teachers, but its first trip, in 1914, came to an abrupt halt in Paris when the French government froze transactions in foreign currency upon the outbreak of fighting. Campbell and his charges scrambled to cash checks, book tickets, and navigate through mobilizing soldiers in order to escape the war and return home.[141] After this inauspicious beginning, the Morningside Travel Club, and teacher tourism in general, would evolve and expand as teachers continued to deepen their cultural understanding as well as strengthen their standing in the middle class during the interwar period.

The Evolving and Expanding European Tour, 1920s–1930s

Tour companies and publishers of guidebooks wasted little time in resuming activities in Europe after the end of the First World War in November 1918. By the early 1920s, transatlantic travel attracted increasing numbers of middle-class Americans, including African Americans who found Europe to be refreshingly free of racial segregation. As white teachers continued, and some Black teachers began, to travel to Europe, they were more visible because growing school systems were hiring more of them; *The New York Times* reported in 1926 that one reason for the rise in American tourism in Europe was "the numerical increase in the class of population from which a high percentage of summer tourists is

FIGURE 11 Advertisement for Intercollegiate Tours: "See Europe This Summer," *Midland Schools* 35, no. 6 (1921): 196. (Courtesy of HathiTrust.)

drawn—namely, the American school teacher."[142] These teacher-tourists deepened their knowledge of literature, art, and other prestigious subjects through a cultural approach to tourism that matured during the interwar period. In his 1925 article on "the Use of Going to Europe," Stephen Bush stated, "Foreign tours are now pretty well standardized in accord with the enormous experience of organizers as to what people like best."[143] The Grand Tour that had been the standard for middle-class tourists, including teachers, throughout the decades preceding the war indeed continued to dominate itineraries during the 1920s and 1930s. But teachers' tours of Europe evolved in some respects, as reflected in the advertisement for Intercollegiate Tours that appeared in several spring 1921 issues of *Midland Schools* (figure 11). "See Europe This Summer," the ad beckoned, "before the battlefields are cleaned up. Add to your cultural capital, to your enthusiasm and your teaching ability. . . . Our tours are different. We stress the intellectual values of travel. Special lecturers in each of the countries visited."[144] As the ad's reference to battlefields indicated, the Grand Tour incorporated new sites. And, belying Intercollegiate Tours' claim to be "different," many organized tours patronized by teachers during this period adopted an intellectual focus, which institutionalized the cultural approach to tourism even as American tourists in general took a more recreational approach. At the same time, teachers began to pursue cultural tourism in a greater variety of European countries. As their travels in Europe evolved and expanded in the 1920s and the 1930s, thoughtful reflection and cultural uplift remained at the heart of teacher tourism.

The advertisements for European tours that abounded in education journals in the 1920s and persisted in the 1930s listed Grand Tour countries far more than any others. A 1924 ad for "A Tour of Quality and Character at Moderate Price" invited teachers to "Visit points of chief interest in France, Italy, Switzerland, Belgium, Holland and England"; Mentor Tours' "Standard Tour" in 1928 covered "England, Holland, Belgium, Rhine, Switzerland, Italy, Riviera and France" in 60 days; and travel guide Mrs. R. S. Ridgeway's two tours in 1930 both went to England, Holland, Belgium, and France, while Tour A added Switzerland

and Germany—including the Oberammergau *Passion Play* for an extra fee—and Tour B also went to Wales and Scotland."[145] When the Morningside College newspaper reported on professor Campbell's revived Travel Club in the 1920s, it listed itineraries comprising Grand Tour countries. "School-teachers especially have taken advantage of the opportunity offered by the Morningside Tours," reported the college paper in 1924. When the Morningside Travel Club expanded its offerings in the 1930s, the Grand Tour countries remained the center of most tours; the 1937 "Short Tour" went to Scotland, England, Holland, Belgium, and France, with "many miles by motor."[146]

Journalist Margaret Patch's syndicated account of what she saw on her trip to Europe in the mid-1920s was a catalog of Grand Tour attractions, including the Tower of London, scenes from Dickens, and "Shakespeare country" in England; Brussels pastry in Belgium; the Hague's Peace Palace, windmills, and tulips in Holland; Cologne Cathedral and a "trip down the castle-flanked Rhine" in Germany; the Eiffel Tower, Notre Dame, and the Louvre in France; the Sistine Chapel and Venice's Grand Canal in Italy; and the Jungfrau and Byron's Chillon Castle in Switzerland.[147] Education journals published Patch's account on the assumption that it would resonate with teachers who had taken or would soon take similar trips to Grand Tour countries. One such teacher was twenty-six-year-old Jan Gelb of New York City, for whom visiting Paris for the first time in 1929 was about far more than simply acquiring cultural capital. Seeing Notre Dame, she wrote in her diary, "affected me like the most profound and noble symphony." After a full day in the Louvre, she "staggered out, cleansed of soul," and at the opera she was awed not only by the building but by the "exquisite" performance of her first ballet. Adolph Hodge, a Black physical education teacher in New York City, organized a group trip to Grand Tour countries in 1933 in which he was pleased with the lack of racial issues in general and one German hostel owner's especially welcoming attitude.[148] California teacher Anabel Read Scott, whose "itching foot" took her all over the world, stuck mainly to the Grand Tour on a 1934 trip with friends, "our objective being Oberammergau." They explored Ireland, walked along Unter den Linden in Berlin, and stopped in other German cities and Salzburg before reaching their objective and enjoying "peace secure from modern unrest" during their stay in the home of one of the *Passion Play* actors. From Oberammergau, their travels took them to Italy and France.[149] Gelb, Hodge, and Scott had meaningful European experiences through a cultural approach to tourism.

Teachers on the Grand Tour in the 1920s and the 1930s also saw new sites along with the longtime standards. Foremost among the new types of geographical European cultural capital were the Great War battlefields mentioned in the Intercollegiate Tours advertisement. In 1922, an ad for the Morningside Travel Club similarly listed "the Battlefields" alongside "the *Passion Play*" as trip highlights. From Paris, Patch visited the nearby battlefield of Meaux. She explained, "Army trucks once used to transport American troops through the war sectors have been rebuilt as charabancs and now carry loads of American tourists over the same roads. . . . Here and there, where a blackened tree thrusts its gaunt and crooked arms heavenward, we can for a moment picture war-torn France."[150] Another new attraction was Fontainebleau, a French castle-turned-luxurious-palace that had become a national museum in 1927. Ads for Temple Tours began in the late 1920s to highlight the palace museum; summarizing tours in cultural-capital shorthand, a 1929 ad listed, "Motoring to Italian Hill Towns, Shakespeare Country, Fontainebleau" and a 1930 ad listed "Oberammergau, Bavarian Castles, Fontainebleau, Shakespeare Country."[151]

Teachers were increasingly able to see both new and classic attractions on the Grand Tour through organized tours that explicitly adopted an intellectual focus and thus institutionalized the cultural approach to travel. Temple emphasized that its leaders were "cultured" and began offering tours specializing in architecture, art, music, English literature, or history, listing such offerings in 1928 as the "Intercollegiate Series." Guild Travel Bureau advertised "Cultural Tours . . . for teachers, art lovers, writers and others"; the opportunity to "Study European History, Art, Music, Literature"; and "Collegiate" tours with "experienced guides."[152] Ella Preston, an art educator in Davenport, Iowa, toured ten countries in 1934 as part of an "Art Pilgrimage" that ended with the meeting of the International Art Congress in Prague. In addition to standard Grand Tour sites, Preston reported, the "Pilgrimage" included "the exquisite exhibits of Turner's watercolors" at London's Tate Gallery; the "exquisite murals of Puvis de Chavannes" at the Pantheon and "the rare tapestries and rich handicraft housed in Cluny Museum" in Paris; Rembrandt's home and "rich collections of the works of the 'Little Dutchman'" in Amsterdam; and the Kaiser Friedrich Museum, "a marvelous storehouse of the past which no student of art or archeology should miss," in Berlin.[153]

The University Travel Bureau had offered "something more than accelerated sight-seeing" since before the First World War, and company names in interwar-period ads, like Students Travel Club and The College Travel Club, suggested an academic focus. The 1921 ad for Intercollegiate Tours that promised cultural capital also listed tours focusing on particular academic subjects, and a 1928 ad for Intercollegiate Tours boasted of "authoritative leaders in . . . Art, Music, Literature, French, History."[154] Despite their names, these companies' tours did not necessarily offer college credit, and they were intended for more than just students—although college students and their parents who sought to enhance their social class standing were a growing market.[155] Tours led by college professors, including not only Campbell of Morningside but also Stephen Bush of the University of Iowa, also had an intellectual air. Mae Irene Ludeman, a twenty-nine-year-old history teacher in Burlington, Iowa, toured the Grand Tour countries under Bush's guidance in 1929. Her travel diary described cultural and historic sites from London to Rome as well as "great fun punting on Cam River" in Cambridge with Professor Bush guiding the boat, and dancing with German university students in Frankfort.[156]

On the Morningside Travel Club's 1924 tour, Campbell and the group visited a new high school in Amsterdam. Some other intellectually oriented tours focused on European education. Also in 1924, Des Moines Director of Elementary Education Bessie Bacon Goodrich organized an "educational adventure" for Iowa teachers to join a tour of "Contemporary European Education" conducted by a Northwestern University professor. In England, France, Germany, Belgium, and Switzerland, participants toured schools, heard lectures by leading educators, and visited "London, Paris, Munich, Brussels, Zurich, and many intervening points." Among the "cultural" tours of Europe listed in a 1932 ad for the Intercollegiate Travel Extension Service was an "Education Study Tour" led by a professor at Columbia University's Teachers College; Teachers College also offered educational tours of England, France, and Germany, with an option to earn university credit.[157] European educators likewise offered programs for American teachers and other travelers during the interwar period. Beginning in 1922, the City of London Vacation Course in Education included morning lectures by leading scholars on English schools and other education-related topics. Isaac App, a Pennsylvania school superintendent who attended the course in 1927, reported that afternoons were usually devoted to "visiting many places of historic interest," and that they received an "official welcome extended by the Lord Mayor of London" and "services were held for members of the Course at Westminster Abbey and St. Paul's Cathedral." "Altogether for an American teacher," stated the *Pennsylvania School Journal* in 1929, "this is one of the most attractive courses in the world."[158]

One of the many ads in *Midland Schools* for European travel beckoned, "Visit Europe—1931—with the Universities of Belgium." H. F. Blank, a teacher in Council Bluffs, Iowa, and a World War I veteran, returned to Europe in the early 1930s for one of these tours, which, he explained in an article in the same journal, was "planned by well-informed educators, [and] included the study of the history of art, history of the countries in which we visited, and a meager study of French." Those countries were Holland, where he found "Amsterdam a modern cosmopolitan city"; Belgium, where, Blank reported, "our professor guides were anxious to show us with what speed their kinsmen had rebuilt since the great war"; France, where their afternoon at Versailles "completed a full day of French history"; and "Switzerland, Oberammergau's Passion Play, and Italy," where they "found that the cathedral in Milan was a Gothic architectural triumph." Happy to return home with "an intimate knowledge of Europe and its customs," Blank apparently did not earn academic credit for his trip. European universities were slower than those in the United States to offer studies for credit in the summertime, but the French government did work with the American Association of High School Teachers of French in 1921 to provide a summer school in France, as well as a sight-seeing tour. By 1934, the French Line steamship company's ad encouraged teachers to travel to "attend courses in one of the summer schools conducted by French universities," saying, "You owe it to yourself, for your professional advancement, to go this year."[159]

While Grand Tour countries remained the main focus of teacher tourism in Europe throughout the interwar period, teachers also ventured to a widening array of other countries, both on organized cultural tours and on their own. Like the French government, the Spanish Bureau of the Institute of International Education organized programs for summer study in Madrid with weekend trips to other areas of Spain as well as France and Switzerland. By the mid-1920s, Stratford Tours offered "French and Spanish Study Tours" and Boyd Tours advertised "A Student Tour That Is Different: Eight Countries with Spain."[160] Eastern Europe and Scandinavia joined the Grand Tour on many itineraries by the late 1920s. Among the many options offered by Guild Travel Bureau were trips that included Hungary, Czechoslovakia, Norway, and Sweden, as well as Spain. While Anabel Scott and her friends traveled mainly in Grand Tour countries in 1934, they also visited Budapest and Prague, while Morningside Tours—led by Mrs. Campbell after Professor Campbell's death in 1934—began to include these cities in its "Standard Tour." A 1928 ad for James Boring's Cruises touted visits to "Iceland, Norway's Fjords, Land of Midnight Sun, Scandinavia's Capitals," and Mrs. Campbell wrote after taking a group to Denmark, Sweden, and Norway in 1936 that they were "quite thrilled with Scandinavia, whether more for the wonderful scenery or the wonderful meals, I can not say."[161]

Some groups ventured farther east in the 1930s. Open Road's advertisement in 1934 stated that many teachers and others would "spend this summer in Soviet Russia," both because "American Russian relations are influencing the world" and because it was relatively affordable. Four years later, Open Road offered a trip focusing on "the psychology of social change" in the Soviet Union and three other countries, and a trip exclusively to the Soviet Union with visits to "Leningrad, Moscow, Volga, the Caucuses, Soviet Armenia, Crimea, Kiev, etc." With the 1933 trip to Grand Tour countries under his belt, New York City Black teacher Adolph Hodge led a group trip to the Soviet Union in 1936. Two years later, Seattle teacher Sara Luch and her friends continued on from Scotland to the continent, including Scandinavia. She enjoyed dancing with a young Norwegian sailor in Oslo, noticed anti-Semitic posters in Vienna, and was subject to "a long song and dance about the wonders of Hitler" by a waiter in Berlin.[162] These ominous signs of impending conflict gave her insight into events to come, just as other teachers' travel in Grand Tour countries before World War I and throughout Europe during the interwar period deepened their understanding of cultural subjects. As they asserted their independence and affirmed their membership in the middle class through summer travels in Europe, teachers also enhanced their work in classrooms at home.

Making "Good Teachers into Better Ones"

When Charles Payne and Stephen Bush advocated that teachers travel in the United States and Europe, respectively, they argued that cultural tourism would augment instructors' professional skills. Teachers did not reflect much, if at all, about teaching in their travel journals and the letters they sent home, perhaps because the connections between their tourist experiences and their teaching were obvious to them. Surely, F. E. Stratton's exploration of Yellowstone and his scientific notes on and diagrams of its thermal features enhanced his instruction in geology. Margarete Bohle's historical tours of Boston and Philadelphia would have enriched her classes on the Revolutionary War, while Bohle's, Beatrice Cramer's, and Greene Buster's visits to Gettysburg Battlefield would have breathed life into their lessons on the Civil War. Sitting in Shakespeare's chair and hearing Burns in his native Scottish dialect undoubtedly invigorated Helen Crombie's literature classes, just as walking in Longfellow's footsteps in Belgium helped Eva and Maude Lewis bring the poet to life for their students. And Mary Peirce's observations of sloyd instruction in Sweden would have greatly influenced her work at the Manual Training School in Boston. Even though these teachers did not articulate the professional impact of tourism in their journals and letters, teachers' actions in the classroom and their published testimonials, backed by school leaders' comments, demonstrated how tourism supported grassroots professionalization by making "good teachers into better ones" and putting "more life into the work of teaching."[163]

Eminent adventurer and travel writer Emma Shaw (later Colcleugh) began her professional life as a teacher in Providence, Rhode Island, in the 1880s. After traveling through the West, she published a "class exercise" that outlined a group recitation of geographical, historical, and descriptive points about Yellowstone National Park. The lesson plan suggested that the teacher post a map and included a range of statistics as well as poetry about nature and the park.[164] Although they did not write them up as published lessons, other teachers' actions in the classroom similarly infused their summer experiences as tourists into their work with students. In Buffalo, Mabel Barnes used souvenirs from the Pan-American Exposition, including a vial in which bees were preserved in alcohol, in her second-grade class. After California teacher Grace Canon Pogue traveled with her son to the southern part of the state in 1933, she reported, "The glass bottomed boat at Catalina furnished material for many stories when I returned to my pupils in September. The trip to Tia Juana and the souvenirs collected provided the basis for a social studies unit." Seattle teachers similarly used artifacts and souvenirs from their wide-ranging travels in the classroom, while Mildred Van Wyngarden's school in Iowa announced in a short article, "The fourth grade Geography class is making scrapbooks about their imaginary trip across the U.S. on the Lincoln Highway," the lesson undoubtedly inspired by Van Wyngarden's own scrapbooks of her trips.[165]

Lucy Jones's German lessons and exposure to culture and customs in Germany and Austria in the summer of 1910 surely enriched the German classes that she taught when not teaching English in Columbus, Kansas. In order to share her new knowledge more extensively, in 1911 she moved to Everett, Washington, to teach German exclusively in the high school.[166] In Battle Creek, Michigan, in the early 1920s, Eleanor Glass enlivened her high school history classes with first-hand knowledge of England based on her summer stay in Oxford. Inspired by her teacher, Merze Tate visited England in the summer of 1931 while studying in Geneva, Switzerland, and from 1932 through 1935 was the first African American woman to attend Oxford University.[167] Jones and Glass acted to improve their high school teaching based on their experiences in Europe, just as Shaw, Barnes, Pogue, and Van Wyngarden used souvenirs and new knowledge from U.S. travel to enliven their elementary classes.

A 1933 survey found that 95 percent of teachers who had taken a group tour said that it was more valuable to their career than attending summer school, and a 1940 survey on job satisfaction revealed that teachers in Michigan placed a high value on improving "instruction as a result of travel."[168] Teachers and commentators agreed that travel improved instruction, especially in particular subjects such as geography. Travel, explained Des Moines "training teacher" Elizabeth Matthews in *The Iowa Normal Monthly* in 1896, makes the teacher's "work in the school room more real, more telling, and gives her a broader culture. . . . In the study of geography, will the pupils not be more interested in the White Mountains, Niagara Falls, Yellowstone Park, if the teacher describes as she actually saw?" After a 1924 Iowa State Teachers Association tour of the West offered "first hand investigation of strange earth forms and interesting scientific studies," two teachers testified that it had enhanced their instruction. Edith Hogle said, "The trip has influenced my work decidedly this year," and Flossie Brown stated, "Many times during the year I have found my experience of last summer of benefit in my class work."[169]

An article written for education journals in the 1930s about a tour for teachers in Alaska listed more specific benefits to instruction in geography: "As an immediate result of the teachers' trip, [to] pupils in schoolrooms in many localities . . . Alaska is now where immense forests grow, where hordes of fish flash through swfit [*sic*] clear water . . . and where mountains yield up fortunes in shining metals." Hawaii teacher Mary Blanchard emphasized in the NEA *Journal* that in order to teach geography well, teachers should head east as well as west: "The Western teacher should become an eye witness of the industrial wonder of the East and the teacher born and bred on the Atlantic Coast should cross the Appalachians and rhapsodize over the Scenic West. We teach what we are and travel makes us mentally wealthy." Similarly, university dean John Foster stated in a commentary on "Why Teachers Should Travel" that "the teacher of physiography should, of course, be familiar with physiographic features in the immediate neighborhood, but he should also be able to say: 'I have journeyed from El

Portal up the Yosemite Valley, past El Capitan, the Happy Isles and other marvelous rock and water effects. . . . I have gone over the Little Scheidegg Pass from Lauterbrunnen to Grindelwald. I have watched Old Faithful and have seen the Rhine and the Nile.'"[170]

History and literature were also prominent subjects in teachers' and school leaders' testimonials to the beneficial effects of tourism on instruction. Wisconsin teacher Charlotte Kohn reflected that "a summer trip through the East—visiting the cities, buildings, and places that have played such a part in the making of our Nation, visiting the ports of entry for our European brothers, our battlefields, the homes and halls of our patriots" had provided her with "a rich background," and that "to be able to vitalize teaching with personal experience and travel is a great asset." The brochure for Morningside Tours' 1937 trips to Europe included Lilyan Duden's endorsement, "My experiences last summer have given me a wealth of material for my history classes." And Des Moines history teacher Iola Quigley touted the benefits of "European Travel for the Teacher" based on her own trip to Europe in the early 1930s. For the history teacher, she asserted, travel in Europe "is rich beyond measure," offering opportunities to explore, to lodge in century-old dwellings, and to see artifacts like the Magna Carta and the Domesday Book. Quigley continued, "Every day in your classroom some such memory will add its gleam to make real and vital the characters of history. Go to the museums of Berlin, see the remains of the Pergamum and of Babylon; go to the British museum to study, the Elgin marbles and the Greek statuettes; and return with a profound respect for the minds which created them." For the English teacher, Quigley argued, "it does mean something to wander in Anne Hathaway's garden; to walk the streets of old Stratford; to make a pilgrimage to Canterbury; to gather daisies in Ayr; to sit where Wordsworth sat."[171]

After serving as a judge for an essay contest on course units based on teachers' travel experiences, NEA *Journal* editor William Boutwell wrote that he was "deeply impressed with what travel meant to the teachers who wrote the units and to the children taught by these traveled teachers." He described one teacher's comprehensive tour of Plymouth, Massachusetts, during which she visited historic buildings and graveyards and took notes in the museum. "I feel sure that every time Thanksgiving rolls around," he reflected, "this teacher turns with particular pleasure to the story of the Pilgrims. And I am sure that the pupils in her class take part more eagerly in the Pilgrim unit because of the familiarity of their teacher with Plymouth." In Boutwell's article, photo captions presented as quotations of students emphasized the positive impact of teachers' travels on instruction; captions included, "Say, wouldn't I have liked to help my teacher explore those prehistoric ruins in southwestern Colorado," and "Honestly, Miss Brown? Did you *really* see Whittier's home in Danvers, Massachusetts?" Foster underscored Boutwell's and teachers' testimonials on the importance of tourism for teaching history and English: "Youngsters studying history should have a teacher who has been to Independence Hall, covered Boston and its vicinity, wandered through the palace of Versailles and the Forum in Rome. . . . The teacher of literature must not fail to linger in Westminster Abbey, Washington Irving's essay in hand; he must not fail to stop at Stratford-on-Avon." Principal Jeanette Mills summarized, "How alive is the situation in the classroom where the teacher can supplement the text with her own personal [tourist] experiences in the literature, geography, art or history classes."[172]

Foster and Quigley also mentioned the benefits of tourism for art teachers, and Ella Preston's "Art Pilgrimage" to Europe in 1934 certainly would have enhanced her teaching of art. Preston framed the article on her trip, however, in terms of the importance of tourism in teachers' efforts to inculcate a sense of citizenship—not flag-waving, nationalistic U.S. citizenship, but world citizenship. "Now, more than ever before," she began, "we who are teachers, realize that our pupils are potential citizens of the world, and that we need every help we can get in making vivid to them this world in which they must achieve worthy citizenship. We need to give them some idea of the cultures, past and present, of the lands beyond the sea. . . . It is for this reason that travel is so valuable a part of the equipment of teachers." In the same vein, Quigley reported that on her return voyage when a fellow passenger asked what had "most profoundly impressed" her on the trip, she replied, "The necessity for France and the United States to get each other's point of view." Similarly, Detroit teacher Lila Fyan testified, "My summer abroad helped me to appreciate other ways of living, other points of view, other standards, as nothing else had done. Not only did this vacation result in a more intimate feeling for literature and history, but also in warmer sympathy with different nationalities and races with whom I come in contact at home."[173]

School leaders and other commentators also stressed that tourism would better enable teachers to guide students toward good citizenship. *The Iowa Normal Monthly* stated in 1907 that the NEA, by holding its meetings alternately on the East Coast, the West Coast, and the Great Lakes, "has enabled the teachers of the nation to learn something of the real extent of our country, of its diversity of resources and of its fertility, wealth and beauty . . . an experience that is not only helpful to" the teacher "but particularly helpful to the young people who come under his care." In keeping with the cultural approach to tourism—which Payne argued created "a broader outlook, a greater knowledge of human nature" and Bush said "enriches life"—better understanding "the real extent" of the United States and other countries would help teachers provide their students with a sense of others' points of view and shared humanity. Bush explained further that, after touring Europe, "we are better able to pierce through the shell of living and get at what is fundamental beneath. Our prejudices weaken a little and we see realities better." Foster added that "better teaching" would result from "more emphasis on the teacher's outlook, his realization" through traveling, "of what is in the universe, and his appreciation of the ideas and ideals of millions of human beings very different from himself."[174] Commentators such as Foster, Bush, and Payne thus echoed teachers' actions in the classroom and testimonials as to how their experiences as tourists enlivened their work with students and enriched their teaching of academic subjects and world citizenship.

Cultural tourism between the 1880s and the 1930s was ideally suited to enhance teachers' work in the classroom. In the United States, they enriched their souls and intellects through measured consecration of natural features in the West and historical sites in the East and South, as well as through visiting world's fairs. Abroad, mainly in the Grand Tour countries of Europe, they deepened their understanding of history, literature, art, and other subjects. Touring natural and historic sites in the United States and Europe also increased teachers' stock of cultural capital, fortifying their position in the middle class. School leaders encouraged and provided limited support for teachers to travel, as enhanced professional skills and higher class status for teachers were beneficial to the schools. But tourism was also a means for teachers, especially women teachers, to assert their independence through adventures on the rails, the roads, and the ocean. Historian Robert Gough captures tourism's role in grassroots professionalization: "Since tourism was a legitimate, even necessary part of the occupation of teaching, teachers could quietly use it in individualistic ways to temper the bureaucratic norms imposed on them" by school leaders.[175] Thus, like other summer activities, tourism imparted professional benefits while also planting seeds for teachers to exercise autonomy within their occupation. In addition, historians of tourism explain that, along with cultural tourism, the middle class during this period engaged in recreational tourism for rest and regeneration.[176] Teachers' activities in the interest of resting from the demands of the school year similarly satisfied the wishes of school leaders while also providing a means for them to evade restrictions.

5

Rest

Putting "New Blood into My Veins"

In late June 1878, twenty-four-year-old Anna Mills (later Johnston) headed to Dillon's Mill in the Sierra Nevada Mountains, where, she later wrote, "two weeks peering into Nature's beauties, enjoying the invigorating mountain air and the breath of the pines . . . seemed to put new blood into my veins." The "new blood" restored Mills's energy after her first year of teaching in Porterville, California. A graduate of Oswego State Normal School in New York and a well-regarded teacher, Mills had moved to California in search of new challenges in the classroom and new adventures in her personal life. From Dillon's Mill, she set off with a group of men and women from Porterville for five weeks of hiking, camping, and summiting mountain peaks. On August 3, they ascended "Devil's Ladder" and climbed over angular rocks to reach the peak of Mount Whitney. Mills felt "supreme joy" to be "at last standing on the summit." She wrote, "For the time being I forgot that I ever was tired; one glance was enough to compensate for all the trials of the trip. The day was perfect, and so were the surroundings. How strange it seemed to be standing on the highest point in the United States." Perhaps it seemed strange because Mills and others in her party were the first women to summit Mount Whitney. After they descended "on foot down the mountain, over rocks, through brush, and up cliffs, which seemed impassable for an animal (or an Anna Mills) to travel over," they journeyed through canyons and past springs, reaching Porterville in mid-August. Mills returned to the classroom in the fall with robust health and, undoubtedly, greater confidence and a heightened sense of independence. During future summers "off" from her lengthy teaching career, she would hike up mountains throughout the United States and Europe.[1]

While Kathleen Weiler acknowledges Mills's accomplishments as a summer mountaineer in her account of California's "country schoolwomen," most historians of women teachers in the late nineteenth and early twentieth centuries tell a story primarily of restrictions and corporeal control during the school year. Indeed, administrative rules regarding teaching methods and teachers' appearance, leisure activities, ingestion, and even procreation constrained not only their professional and personal lives but also their bodies. Jane Addams observed after she became a member of the Chicago Board of Education in 1905, "Teachers were so restricted 'that they had no space in which to move about freely and the more adventurous of them fairly panted for light and air.'" Historians explain that inadequate and dilapidated school facilities had adverse health effects, and illness and injuries further enervated teachers' bodies.[2] Kate Rousmaniere and Kristen Chmielewski also outline how constructions of ability versus disability have shaped the occupation of teaching throughout its history, limiting it to women and men who exhibited "good health" even as teaching conditions often caused health problems. In addition, Jonna Perrillo illustrates how administrators during the interwar years escalated corporeal regulation. Linking student success to teacher health, they worked to "refigure" women teachers by enforcing weight limits and instructing them to wear "smart" fashion and makeup. Perrillo also mentions briefly that education journals praised teachers "who returned to school after summer vacation with 'pliant muscles and good resistance.'"[3]

As Perrillo suggests, corporeal oversight of teachers extended into the summer months through directives on how they should rest to recover from the previous school year and prepare for the next. In his history of summer school in the United States, Kenneth Gold explains that one motivation for the adoption of the nine-month school year in the 1850s–1880s was concern for pupils' and teachers' health. In arguments for setting aside a period for recuperation, education leaders cited medical literature on the physical harm to children from "overstudy" and on the dangers that teaching posed to mental and physical health, especially for women. As school districts in both rural and urban areas began to adopt a nine-month calendar, leaders advised teachers to devote their summers to rest, or "quietude." Such advice corresponded to the rise during the same period of vacations of "quiet idleness" for the white middle class to counter the perceived health threats posed by increasing urbanization and industrialization.[4] *American Educational Monthly* in the 1860s, Gold explains, "consistently told teachers to 'welcome, then, the summer vacation, in which both the mind and the body may have recreation, relaxation, and more especially, repose, *rest*.'" The journal also warned that failure to rest "led to unfortunate health conditions because 'excess of oxygen burns up the blood [and] too much excitement paralyzes the brain.'"[5] Through such instructions, administrators sought to extend their control over teachers' bodies to include a period essentially of enforced convalescence.

Advice for teachers on how to spend the summer months, as Gold also notes and as the previous chapters explain, began to shift after the long vacation became standard in the 1880s. As the types of recommended activities expanded, leaders continued to prescribe rest for teachers; Illinois Superintendent of Education F. G. Blair stated in 1914 that "a considerable number of teachers should give up their entire vacation to quiet and rest that 'knits the raveled sleeve of care.'" The meaning of "rest," however, evolved along with the ideal of the middle-class vacation. By the 1880s, "rest" for the white middle class primarily meant reinvigoration through breathing fresh air and engaging in temperate recreation.[6] Administrators' directives for resting during the summer months correspondingly focused on spending time in nature and, increasingly, participating in moderate physical activity—often in combination with studies and travel. Full of vitality, white teachers' own accounts of their summer activities demonstrated how they adapted administrative directives to meet their own needs. (Teachers of color rarely had the means to pursue any version of rest.) Rural white teachers expanded their physical capacities by engaging in agricultural work and participating in other outdoor activities, and urban white teachers reinvigorated themselves by communing with nature and exercising in the open air. As they did so, women teachers like Anna Mills challenged gender boundaries by demonstrating a lack of frailty and the robustness of a "new woman" or Gibson girl, and men teachers reinforced gender boundaries—and thus challenged images of male educators—by demonstrating rugged masculinity.[7] Summer rest not only rejuvenated teachers' bodies and minds but also strengthened the sense of autonomy and independence that was essential to their view of professionalism.

Administrators' Evolving Prescriptions for Summer "Rest"

The education journal *Iowa Normal Monthly* declared in 1890 that for schoolteachers, "a period of relaxation is actually necessary, because the physical nature, sympathfzing [*sic*] with the mental, becomes debilitated, and the wasted tissues demand that relief from active toil that promises them a restoration to their normal condition of health and vitality." As rest remained a recommended summer activity through the 1930s, administrators' views on how best to rest shifted quickly away from convalescence and toward the middle-class ideal of fresh air and moderately robust pursuits. For the white middle class, spending time in the wilderness had become essential to shoring up one's health in the new industrial age. As early as 1878, the *Monthly* not only declared summer "the season for *rest*, both physical and intellectual" but added that rest should include a "little *roughing it*," which for male teachers meant hunting and fishing in "God's free sun and air" and for female teachers meant "a prolonged picnicking and camping-out excursion."[8] In the decades that followed, journals continued to advocate communing with nature—usually without distinguishing between activities for men and for women—and began to recommend gender-appropriate exercise as the best form of rest for teachers, both in and of itself and as a component of summer studies and travel.

In a summer advice article published in 1886, high school "professor" W. B. Harlow invoked Henry David Thoreau, "the philosopher of the woods," in urging teachers to spend time in the forest. "None of us are too poor to worship with Thoreau at the shrine of nature," he concluded. An 1888 letter in *Century* magazine similarly declared that, as the "vacation and how it may be profitably spent are matters of importance to teachers . . . much to be desired is the cool retreat by lake or wood . . . where bracing breezes are laden with life-giving oxygen, and where the fresh, plain, savory fare of the farm and garden and orchard put new color into the cheek and new blood into the veins." In August, teachers should "go off into the woods. Commune with nature . . . and prepare for the best year's work in your life—the next," recommended the editors of the *Texas School Journal* in 1894. Two years later in *The Iowa Normal Monthly*, a Des Moines "training teacher" painted a pastoral picture of rest—likely intended for urban teachers more than for rural teachers—when she described the teacher hastening "herself away to the quiet farm life for a few weeks, taking with her, light airy gowns, hammock, and some choice treasures in the way of books," and unconsciously studying "birds, flowers, trees, insects, and all living things." She concluded, "The teacher will return to her school room full of vigor, enthusiasm and healthful helpfulness from this close contact with nature." A teacher's end-of-the-year ruminations in the June 1926 issue of *The Journal of the National Education Association* echoed the rejuvenating power of the outdoors. The teacher described her "annual feeling" at the end of the school year that she wanted to leave teaching and explained that after spending time in the park, swinging her "heels in careless abandon against the stone wall along the lake," and feeling "the soft, clover-scented wind," she would be ready to return "joyously" in the fall.[9]

Journals also profiled efforts to establish summer communities for teachers in restful natural settings. The *Texas School Journal* reported in 1897 that the International Teachers' Home Association aimed to "establish and maintain Homes or Retreats in different parts of the United States and Canada for the active teachers during the vacation season" and had acquired land in six locations, from Goodrich, Ontario, to Denver, Colorado; and *The Iowa Normal Monthly* reported in 1898 that Chicago teachers were organizing a cooperative "Teachers' Country Club, where rest and healthy [*sic*] may be obtained and out-of-door sports may be indulged in." The group sold shares and set out to purchase land near a lake in rural Wisconsin on which to build summer cottages, a "model farm," and tennis courts. Two years later, *The American School Board Journal* reported that the Teachers' Rest Association (TRA) had acquired land on

Spooner Lake in Wisconsin, "covered with an abundance of trees, flowers, birds, [and] wild berries." The article promised, "Boating, hunting and fishing are good." The Texas and Iowa journals both reported in 1908 on efforts to establish a "summer farm" or "rest farm" for NEA members in the shadow of Colorado's mountains, explaining that former Denver Superintendent L. C. Greenlee would present the plan to the NEA and that the farm "would be a delightful change for the teachers who spend the winter months in the school rooms." Finally, the Massachusetts Teachers Association in 1925 acquired Riverbank Lodge, a sprawling farm property with views of the Charles River Valley, and planned to turn it into "a fine home for teachers." Aside from a score of TRA members building, or planning, cottages on Spooner Lake in the mid-1910s, few of these ventures were successful. Still, the articles on them encouraged teachers to retreat to the farm, the lake, or the mountains and engage in outdoor activities.[10]

The summer communities' inclusion of "out-of-door sports" reflected another element of the new middle-class vacation ideal: physical activity or even manual labor in natural settings, especially for men.[11] Education leaders often folded physical activity and exercise into their instructions for resting in nature in a further effort to reinvigorate—and oversee—teachers' bodies, which also implicitly invited the women among them to embrace the Gibson-girl lifestyle. A publication of the Chautauqua Institution stated in a 1907 article titled "Chautauqua and the Teachers," "Most people are tired when vacation time comes, but by no means tired out. They need rest and exercise, and if they spend their vacations wisely the result of both the exercise and rest is that they go back to work with renewed vigor and fresh enthusiasm." *The Iowa Normal Monthly* in 1911 instructed teachers to "refuse to recognize any illness. Live in pure air and sunshine" and, most of all, be active because "you cannot rest by being idle." More than two decades later, the NEA *Journal* acknowledged teaching's tendency "to deplete the teacher's physical resources" and recommended, "The teacher who spends the summer [out of doors], in sun and air, near the sea or mountains—with plenty of hiking, swimming, tennis, gardening, or other exercise—will approach the new school year with added zest and vitality."[12]

Some leaders explicitly encouraged women teachers to engage in rigorous exercise. In the preface to his 1918 book titled *Recreation for Teachers*, Henry Curtis acknowledged, "Some one may say that the recreation recommended is unduly strenuous and adventurous for women, and better suited to men" but countered, "we are on the eve of a new era." He went on to summarize recent studies that found teachers to be in poor health, which he said was "caused mostly by worry and a sedentary life." "To overcome the tendency to tuberculosis," he wrote, "the teacher should be out of doors as much as possible and develop her lungs by proper exercise." In a chapter recommending summer activities, Curtis specified, "Every teacher should cultivate an enthusiasm for some occupation which will take her out of doors every day." His foremost recommendation was walking: "No teacher is in condition to teach school, or to be married, unless she can walk ten miles a day without undue weariness." He also suggested tennis, horseback riding, canoeing, swimming, and camping to make women teachers "healthier and handsomer." The "pliant muscles and good resistance" to which historian Perrillo referred resulted from "creative resting," described in a publication for New York City teachers in 1932. Administrator Blanche Howell stated in the article, "Resting during the vacation does not necessarily imply the cessation of all activity. Many of us need physical activity or the chance to do something creative with our hands to get ourselves into physical trim for the year's work." She presented the example of two women teachers who spent a summer shingling, painting, and plastering a dilapidated farmhouse. The result was not only a lovely residence but also "two well-browned women with plaint muscles and good resistance" who returned, rejuvenated, to teaching in the fall.[13]

Rest through communing with nature and engaging in physical activity was also woven into advice and advertisements for professional development and travel in the summer. New England educator William Mowry was president for many years of the Martha's Vineyard Summer Institute, the founders of which, he explained, "believed that some work with more rest was advantageous." The institute they created provided teachers with "a few weeks stay by the seaside, resting a larger part of the time, but spending a few hours each day in the consideration of questions relating to the best methods of teaching." Many of the other early summer schools for teachers were also in appealing natural locations. *The Intelligence* pointed out in 1901 that the institution on the "quiet shores" of Chautauqua Lake was both "an ideal place with ideal environments as a resting place for teachers" and the largest summer school in the country.[14]

Perhaps in an effort to compete with the likes of the Chautauqua Institution, advertisements for growing university and teachers college summer sessions often highlighted their natural settings and available activities. On the same page as an ad that described Martha's Vineyard as "Out in the Atlantic" and "Cool and Healthful," an ad for the University of Michigan touted its "Picturesque and healthful location." The University of Wisconsin boasted, "On account of the beautiful lakes and drives the opportunity for recreation and pleasure are exceptional. Boating, swimming, cool nights, balmy air, pure drinking water, beautiful surroundings, etc., make Madison an ideal spot." Meanwhile, the University of Wyoming billed itself as "The Coolest Summer School in America" where one could "combine recreation and serious study," and Colorado State Teachers College promised that teachers would find its summer school "beneficial to their health" and "go back to their schools refreshed." In the NEA *Journal*'s state-by-state list of summer schools for 1928, many entries mentioned sports facilities or opportunities for outdoor exercise; Oklahoma's Central State Teachers College had "New gymnasium with swimming pool" and at the State Teachers College in East Stroudsburg, Pennsylvania, the "scenery of Delaware Water Gap [was] romantic and beautiful; conducive to outdoor sports and recreation." Articles aimed at teachers attending summer school instructed in 1896, "Work about three hours and the rest, 'Loaf and invite your soul,' as Walt Whitman advises"; and, in 1925, "Play": "Learn to swim, or renew your pleasure in tennis, etc."; attend "receptions, outings, and parties"; and, finally, "Work hard but have a good time; store up life enthusiasms."[15]

Journals' promotion of host cities and travel routes to summer meetings of state teachers' associations and the NEA often included descriptions of opportunities for outdoor rest and activities. Before the Maryland State Teachers' Association's 1880 meeting in Ocean City, *The Maryland School Journal* reported, "The hotel is on the beach, on the verge of the Atlantic Ocean. The bathing is unsurpassed. Teachers cannot select a better place to recuperate in after the fatigue of a year's work." Before the 1888 NEA meeting, *The Iowa Normal Monthly* published a "Greeting from Colorado to Iowa Teachers," which observed, "It was wise in the National Association to select San Francisco as a meeting place, for then the teacher-pilgrim must needs pass through Colorado and learn a little of the gospel of rest." In Colorado, the article explained, "We offer you such rest as *rests*, such scenery as delights, such air and sunshine as invigorates, such mountain heights as lift one above the relentless grind of every-day occupations." Before the 1902 NEA meeting in Minneapolis, the *Texas School Journal* promoted Minnesota's "great number of shimmering lakes . . . whose cool waters and wooded shores are inviting and restful." Similarly, the NEA *Journal* highlighted opportunities for the teacher to "wander along the waterfront, and fill her lungs with salt air" as well as to enjoy "cool breezes and nature's unsullied loveliness" in conjunction with the 1927 meeting in Seattle; to hike in California's Sierra Nevada Mountains—"an ideal rest for the teacher who has just closed a busy school year"—in conjunction with the 1931 meeting in Los Angeles; and to vacation on the beach in conjunction with the 1932 meeting in Atlantic City. Regarding the latter destination, the NEA *Journal* echoed the Maryland *Journal* five decades earlier in explaining, "No tonic is so wholesome and invigorating as the tang of the salt air, no prescription more potent than the healing rays of the seaside sun."[16]

Advertisements and articles that looked beyond meeting locations to promote summer travel destinations throughout the country and around the world also touted opportunities to breathe fresh air and improve one's physical stamina. Ads aimed at teachers claimed that the air at Lake Superior was "a fine tonic for the overworked," that "the tired brain-worker builds up faster" in Nova Scotia "than in any other land," and that California's Harbin Hot Springs provided "the needed change and the finest natural hot baths in the state." An ad for a cruise to Hawaii beckoned, "See what the tonic ozone of cool southern trade-winds will do for tired nerves. Find yourself eager for new action—for surf-boarding and outrigger-canoeing at Waikiki . . . for a trudge across the frozen lava and through the giant tree-fern jungle of Kilauea Volcano." The *Pennsylvania School Journal* cautioned that summer excursions were "excellent only so far as they give enlargement of knowledge, and better furnishing of the mind and body for future needs," and, in *The Intelligence*'s Tour and Travel section, a school principal advised educators traveling to Europe, "Get all the exercise you possibly can while on the ship," and then be "willing to walk and climb" in order to see "all the delightful things that can be seen."[17]

For the teacher who would state, "I want rest, recreation and inspiration for my future work," a Texas railroad company recommended "above all else Nature's Magnificent Masterpiece 'The Grand Canyon of Arizona.'" For outdoor rest and rejuvenation, though, education journals promoted Yellowstone National Park more than any other location. Typical was a short article in *The Iowa Normal Monthly* which referred to the "pleasure and health" to be derived from finding the park's many waterfalls. A longer article in the NEA *Journal* detailed a tour through Yellowstone's "wonders of nature," advising, "Stay a few days in each place to imbibe the 'atmosphere'; at the same time you will get a wonderful rest." The *Journal* also published a lengthy article by National Park Service director Stephen T. Mather on all of the national parks, which he called "great outdoor breathing spaces for the nation."[18] Between the 1880s and the 1930s, education leaders sought to extend their oversight of teachers' bodies beyond the school year. Although controlling, administrators' expectations that teachers rest during the summertime were more revitalizing than debilitating, as they prescribed breathing fresh air and engaging in physical activities in natural settings, rarely differentiating between advice for female versus male teachers. Many teachers were able to fulfill these expectations in ways that satisfied their desire for rejuvenation while furthering grassroots professionalization.

Teachers' Approaches to Summer "Rest"

As the end of the school year approached in 1886, rural Kansas teacher Nora Stewart received caring advice. "You only have two weeks" remaining, wrote her friend. "Nora dear, you must take more rest [as] you have been extending your self too much, body + mind will give away some time if they do not have rest." A quarter century later, the NEA report on teachers' salaries acknowledged the detrimental health effects of teaching and teachers' arguments for salary increases to allow "for a vacation to recuperate their exhausted strength." The report quoted one teacher's observation, "There is no line of work which so drains vitality," and another's plea, "Summer vacations are a necessity and failure to take them increases the size of the doctors' bills."[19] Such comments might suggest that summer was a time of convalescence, but accounts of women and a few men teachers in rural and urban areas between the 1880s and 1930s evince otherwise. While they acknowledged being tired at the end of the school year, teachers' summers were full of vitality. They did not refer directly to education leaders' prescriptions and generally did not call their pursuits "rest," but they did breathe plenty of fresh air and engage in various forms of physical activity—in addition to or in conjunction with attending teachers' institutes or summer school, touring, and sometimes working for wages. One piece of advice that teachers did *not* follow was the directive to head to a quiet farm with books, a hammock, and airy gowns. Rural teachers who spent the summer on a farm had little time to lounge in hammocks as they busied themselves with agricultural work, and town/city teachers took part in recreational activities and, if they were able to travel, went to the mountains or the shore. In both rural and urban areas, women teachers transgressed gender boundaries as they challenged themselves physically and exercised robust independence, while men teachers reinforced gender boundaries through physical exhibits of masculinity. By revitalizing bodies enervated by the constraints of teaching and asserting agency over gender norms, teachers used summer "rest" to pursue their own version of professionalism.

In rural schools, women teachers welcomed the end of the term. Fellow teacher Libbie Burbank wrote to Nora's sister Amanda Stewart in spring 1891, "I am awfully tired. . . . I shall be so glad when school closes"; and Elizabeth "Bachelor Bess" Corey wrote to her mother in spring 1911, "My school closed last Saturday. We had a fine time tho it rained a little. None of us shed many tears at parting—I would have, only I forgot to put an onion in my pocket." Corey, like many other rural teachers, would recuperate in the fresh air and strengthen her muscles through the physical labor of farm work. As explained in chapter 3, it was very common during this period for female one-room-school teachers to board during the session and return home for the summer to help on the farm of their family of origin. When Gertrude Black (later La Due) in northern Minnesota and Ruby Dresselhouse in southern Michigan followed this pattern, they benefitted physically. Both picked large quantities of berries. Black noted in her diary that on one day in June 1901, "I was in the berry patch near five hours. A good place to talk to the Lord and meditate." Dresselhouse kept track of her haul: On seven different days in August 1928, she picked a total of 159 quarts of strawberries and 12 quarts of raspberries. Both women did various other chores—Black, for example, hoed, stacked hay, and milked cows—but also enjoyed outdoor activities off the farm. Black rode a bicycle, or "wheeled" like a Gibson girl, for miles during a long visit with church friends; and Dresselhouse went with friends to a lake cottage and a riverbank park. These teachers' summer activities were not only a far cry from convalescence but physically challenging.[20]

Other women rural teachers engaged robustly in farm work away from their families of origin. After Corey left her family's Iowa farm in 1909 to teach in rural schools and homestead in South Dakota, she taught and spent the summers establishing and tending her claim, challenging gender ideology as she built muscle and stamina. She broke sod, grew vegetables, raised livestock, built fences, and shot many rattlesnakes. Corey also attended teachers' institutes and occasionally stayed in town to work at short-term indoor jobs in order to make ends meet. Viewing her farm work as a respite from these other obligations, she wrote to her mother in July 1912 that she regretted accepting a job in town, "for I did so want to go out to the claim after institute and rest up." After several weeks of working in the fresh air and sunshine on her land in 1918, Corey exhibited physical independence and self-reliance when she wrote, "This has surely been a great summer. . . . Wouldn't you like to see me on the water wagon? Or riding a plow?"[21]

Black also eventually secured her own homestead, which was near her family's farm. A few weeks after moving to her claim early in the summer of 1904, she noted in her diary, "Kept very quiet. My nerves are very weak as is my whole body. Pain is hard to bear." Black did not clarify the cause of her pain, but being in her own home seemed to ease it. After a couple of weeks, she noted, "Planted radishes, lettuce and peas. Rested + read. . . . These are restful days to my nerves." The aches and exhaustion that other rural teachers noted during the summer arose from physical undertakings that strengthened their muscles. Dresselhouse wrote at one point, "My legs have been stiff for 2½ days from picking strawberries. . . . I lay down for part of the PM." She picked berries again the following day, and two days later spent the afternoon lying on the porch swing and "went to bed quite early." Corey told her mother that after working in town as household help for much of one summer, she had to leave the position because "I was going to drop in my tracks." She later wrote that moving five loads of manure on her claim during another summer had made her tired, then achy, and, finally, numb. Their sore muscles attest that these women teachers exercised their bodies quite vigorously—likely beyond what education leaders had in mind. The fresh air and activity most certainly liberated them from the grind of teaching and strengthened their self-reliance.[22]

Rural teachers who were men also balanced teaching with the fresh air and physical exertion of farm work as well as outdoor recreation during the summer months. B. H. Meyer's activities were similar to those of women teachers. As noted in chapter 3, Meyer helped his family's Wisconsin farm weather the drought of 1886. He assisted with an early harvest but also was able to relax at picnics and on a boat ride. Meanwhile, in Illinois, Walker wielded his masculinity by helping with hay and corn crops as well as fishing and camping—but also allowed himself an occasional day at home, "sleepy at times relieved by a nap." The farm labor that future NEA executive secretary Willard Givens performed during summers off from teaching in a one-room Indiana school was especially grueling. He worked on his family's farm, dug ditches for neighbors, and, with a friend in 1909, hitched rides on freight trains to Nebraska, where they hauled manure and cut wheat from sunup to sundown. Although the summer studies Givens pursued in subsequent years must have seemed appealing after his experience in Nebraska, such rigorous farm labor both strengthened his muscles and testified to his masculinity, restoring both his vitality and the gender boundaries threatened by his work as a teacher. The NEA committee on teachers' salaries discouraged work during school breaks, with the exception of "manual labor in the open air" because it fit the ideal of pastoral rest. Men as well as women rural-school teachers got plenty of this type of rest, although the committee likely intended it more as a benefit for urban teachers.[23]

The teachers who shared their health concerns with the NEA committee were from Cincinnati. Town and city women teachers like them also welcomed the arrival of summer. On May 31, 1894, Barbara Schatte wrote to her beau John Nolen in anticipation of the end of her second year of teaching at James Forten Elementary, a manual training school for Black students in Philadelphia, "I am so glad that June is hurrying on—and then, July is not far beyond and then rest!" As the end of the term drew closer in mid-June, she described the Forten faculty as "worn out." In extensive correspondence during Schatte's four years as a teacher—she would leave the profession when they married in 1896—Nolan praised her work and emphasized that she needed to rest during the summer. He often called her work "noble," adding at one point, "You are doing much good I am sure, but it is trying work." After they were engaged, he wrote in late May 1895 that his mother had inquired "anxiously" about Barbara's health. "I had to tell her, dearie," he explained, "that you were a little pale, but" would soon have "a good two months rest, which will make me so happy." From his summer position as superintendent at a club in the Catskill Mountains, he wrote to Schatte about the beauties of the mountains and nature, and implored, "You must take care of yourself, for you know you have a very hard task before you for the winter, which you perform most faithfully."[24]

Schatte enjoyed the privilege of free time during her summers off from teaching. Orphaned when young, she had been taken in by a couple with the means to own two homes and employ household staff. She remained with them until she married, spending the colder months at their home in Philadelphia and the warmer months at their large home outside the city in Ardmore, Pennsylvania. At the latter residence, she spent the summers relaxing, sewing, dabbling in the garden, playing tennis, and receiving many visitors. In mid-July 1894, she wrote to Nolen, "I think I grow more rested—I know I look rested—and like a different person." In early August, she went to Binghamton, New York, to stay with a friend's family. From there, she wrote, "Since I came I have done nothing but rest which I find I need very sorely. It is indeed, good, for a time, to have nothing to do." Rather than actually doing nothing, or convalescing, however, she engaged in outdoor recreational activities in Binghamton, writing to Nolen that she had played tennis and had set out "without any hat as I love to do. . . . I walked, ran down hill, up again—back and forth . . . having had a glorious time and a feeling that it was good to be alive." She added that she had gained weight, and he responded, "I am glad to hear of your gain of two pounds. Go right ahead and store up energy." Later in the summer, Schatte reported that at nearby Quaker Lake, she "rowed, played tennis, went in bathing + out fishing + then on the lake in the evening" and that on a trip to Rhode Island, she swam and went sailing. Schatte's activities not only conformed to administrators' expectations for teachers on summer break but demonstrated the robustness of a new woman.[25]

While Lillian Herrick taught science at Elmira Free Academy from 1894 until she married in 1908, she spent most of her summers at her family's home in nearby

Horseheads, New York. At the end of the term in 1899, she noted in her diary that she was "saving all strength possible for needed work." Five days later, she wrote that she was "very weak from operation of yesterday." She continued for several weeks to refer to being unwell, until finally reporting on July 25, "I am certainly stronger." Herrick never stated the cause or nature of her medical issue and rarely mentioned being tired for the remainder of that summer or in other years. Like Schatte's, her summers were generally full of visits and outdoor recreation—as well as attending to her family (as discussed in chapter 3). Herrick "wheeled" to nearby Ithaca and climbed with a male friend in Watkins Glen. She also took short trips to the Finger Lakes, where she stayed in cottages or at resort hotels. Soon after her recovery in 1899, she enjoyed rowing, a "tramp in the glen," and a "moonlight walk" at Seneca Lake; and in 1901, she relished rowing, a "shooting party," and another "tramp" at Canandaigua Lake.[26]

Herrick expressed an especially strong sense of both physical independence and rejuvenation through communing with nature during the summer. At Cornell University's geology field camp in 1900 (described in chapter 2), Herrick—one of only a few women in the program—camped in the woods and spent her days studying natural phenomena. Early in July, she noted that she was "lying in a hammock with the blue sky visible between the trees" and exclaimed, "What a wonderful world this is! What a wonderful life I am living!" A couple of weeks later, she wrote about a group walk "along a beautiful wooded road" with "nothing to break the silence except . . . the songs of the birds in the branches overhead." Afterward, she left the group to roam "thru the meadows + cornfield[,] leaping the board fences + rolling under the wire ones—to what is geologically known as a Kettle Moraine." She called another day "such a beautiful day here in the woods" and noted soon after returning home, "I have felt so at rest." In 1901, seeing Niagara Falls prompted Herrick to write, "Nature is lovely," and the excursion to Watkins Glen inspired her to feel "childish enjoyment—free with only loving nature . . . very happy." Herrick found the natural world to be particularly inspiring during a trip to the Adirondack Mountains the following summer. She hiked, rowed, climbed, fished, shot a rifle, and wrote in her journal about the beautiful scenery. On a rainy day, she described the "dense mist" clinging to peaks and added, "This is rest." Toward the end of her stay in the mountains, she observed that she was "happy + free—away from all—a privilege given to so few." During a summer trip to Europe several years later (discussed in chapter 4), Herrick would marvel at the beauty of Switzerland's mountains.[27]

Like Herrick, women teachers in Western towns and cities experienced nature's revitalizing effects and enjoyed physical independence in the natural world. As she met the challenges of teaching a wide variety of subjects at East Denver High School in the 1880s, young teacher Alice Eastwood "craved to spend time in the mountains," according to her biographer. As soon as each school year ended, she headed to the Rockies, where she spent her summers exploring and collecting botanical specimens. Undaunted—indeed, strengthened—by the physical challenges of her avocation, Eastwood's summers were "filled with wonder and adventure." Before she left teaching for a career in botany (as discussed in chapter 3), "the serenity and happiness of deep religious fervor" that Eastwood felt during her alpine summers rejuvenated her for each new school year. Farther west, the seasonality of teaching allowed California teacher Grace Canon Pogue not only to further her education, to work on her family's ranch, and to travel (as explained in chapters 2, 3, and 4, respectively), but to recover from serious illness. After she became very sick with the flu at the end of her first year as an "Americanization" teacher in Woodlake, Pogue spent the first month of the summer of 1927 in a remote cabin, where the woods and fresh air rehabilitated her.[28]

Many women teachers in Seattle also immersed themselves in nature to restore their health or energy. Fourth-grade teacher Lulie Nettleton offered recommendations in a 1920 issue of *Grade Club Magazine*. She wrote that Puget Sound had "pastimes and resorts to suit all tastes, and pocketbooks" and that Hood Canal offered "fine camping sites and several delightful boarding places." Some of Seattle's women teachers acquired summer cottages on Orcas and Whidbey Islands, where they could relax in the sea air of Puget Sound. Nettleton also recommended a spot in the mountains for its "lovely" woods, and Lake Chelan, where one could "take a splendid trip up to Horseshoe Basin into the real wilderness." Beginning in the mid-1920s, the Stillaguamish Country Club made it possible for single women to build rustic cabins in the Washington woods. Historian Doris Pieroth explains that many of Seattle's women teachers, especially faculty members at conservation-oriented John Muir Elementary, bought lots, built cabins, and then spent their vacations at Stillaguamish. With her father's help, sixth-grade teacher Nina Bonnell cleared a patch of "fallen logs and undergrowth" to build a Stillaguamish summer home that she would enjoy for decades. In addition, Nettleton and many of her colleagues were active in the Seattle Mountaineers' summer outings. Nettleton hiked up Mount Si on a group trip in 1907, and physical education teacher Mabel Flurry took part in summer outings throughout the 1910s–1940s. For these teachers, "the wildwood, the flowery mead and the mountain fastness afford[ed] a rest, a solace, and an inspiration," as expressed in a Mountaineer publication.[29]

Other women urban teachers traveled west to immerse themselves in nature. An early adventurer was Minneapolis teacher Margaret Andrews Cruikshank, whose 1883 trip to Yellowstone National Park is discussed in chapter 4. The mountain air and challenges of traversing Yellowstone in its early years as a park bolstered Cruikshank's stamina, while the awe-inspiring views of geysers and waterfalls vitalized her for the next school year. Western travel had improved significantly by the time of Irene Lindahl's journey from Wisconsin four decades later. In Washington, she found a hike on Mount Rainier to be especially invigorating: "How lucky we were that it was a clear day!" she wrote. "We could see Mt. Hood in Oregon 200 miles away, and Mt. St. Helen's and Mt. Adams in

Washington. Not even a fringe of clouds obscured our view of the peaks. I had never seen such a breath-taking sight!" A dip in Puget Sound was not only refreshing but an assertion of independence for Lindahl: "There, for the first time in my life, I dared to let myself go and actually swim. I threw away my water wings." From a long bus trip through the West in 1935, Milwaukee teacher Margarete Bohle wrote to her family about "wonderful scenery" and reflected that the sunrise on Pike's Peak "sure was beautiful. . . . The air is very rare."[30]

Beatrice Cramer, who taught in Gloversville, New York, breathed the rare air of the West during many of her summers off in the 1920s and the 1930s. Her numerous driving trips throughout the United States (described in chapter 4) often included invigorating sojourns in natural settings. She wrote that at Mount Rainier National Park in 1931, their "camp site was located at the foot of Nisqually Glacier . . . a view never to be forgotten." The mountains' rejuvenating effects on Cramer were particularly clear in her account of "a few glorious weeks" camping in Rocky Mountain National Park in 1934. Her group camped "8,500 feet above sea level where the days were cool and refreshing and the nights drew everyone close around a balsamy fire." She was physically active, enjoying several trail rides on horses, including one on "switch-back after switch-back," past the timberline. The reward was a view of "an emerald lake reflecting glacier, falls, rocky ledges, in its cool depths," which inspired her to exclaim, "At times such as these does one feel a closeness to the Divine!"[31] Like other women teachers in cities and towns, Cramer revitalized herself through fresh air and outdoor activity during the summertime.

Urban teachers who were men also engaged in physical activities in nature. Some of their undertakings, like those of rural male teachers, were demonstrations of rugged masculinity. Future dean of the Harvard Graduate School of Education Paul Hanus's account of an "extensive" summer "camping trip" celebrated both nature and physical endurance. After teaching at Denver High School in 1878–1879, Hanus set out with six others on an ambitious five-hundred-mile trek through largely uninhabited country in the Rocky Mountains. For six weeks, they hiked up and down steep grades, hunted and fished for sustenance, and battled mosquitoes. Hanus reflected that it "had been a strenuous and rough outing" but that all had "thoroughly enjoyed" the experience. He wrote, "I had gained closer and more intimate acquaintance with the grandeur and picturesqueness of the Colorado mountains, and my memory was permanently enriched by what I had seen. Strengthened muscles and a heavy coat of tan were incidental advantages." Hanus's experience both liberated his body from the restraints of teaching and asserted his male gender identity.[32]

Three decades after Hanus's adventure in the Rockies, Norman Clyde embarked at age twenty-five on an eighteen-year career as a teacher of history, science, and Latin in various schools in the West, including Lowell High School in San Francisco. The seasonality of this work enabled Clyde to devote most of his summers to climbing mountains in the Sierra Nevada and Rocky Mountains, where he earned a reputation for his many ascents. During the summer of 1919, he climbed Mt. Whitney twice, as well as five other peaks in the Sierras. In early July 1923, he ascended Mount Shasta in record time and then broke that record two days later. From Mount Shasta, Clyde headed to Glacier National Park, where his achievements led the National Park Service to announce in a press release, "He Climbs a Mountain a Day During 36 Days of Hiking, Establishing a World Record." The last of the thirty-six peaks was Mount Wilber, which most people had assumed to be unclimbable. Three years later, Clyde traveled with the Sierra Club to Yellowstone and Jackson Hole, Wyoming, where he led two different groups up Grand Teton, the highest peak in the Teton Range. In between, he completed a solo climb of Mount Moran and, afterward, he ascended several other peaks in Montana and Idaho before returning to California for the new school year.[33] During his months off from a female-dominated profession, Clyde's achievements, confidence, and independence as a climber demonstrated his manhood, which he would affirm by leaving teaching to write about and pursue mountaineering year-round.

Almost half of the climbers whom Clyde guided up Grand Teton in 1926 were women. He was supportive of women in mountaineering, perhaps due to his experiences of working with female teachers. But the women of Clyde's generation also had role models in the urban and rural women teachers in the West who had used the summer break to literally reach new heights, bending gender boundaries and stoking their sense of autonomy in the process. After Anna Mills climbed Mount Whitney in 1878, rural Washington schoolteacher Fay Fuller in 1890 was the first woman to ascend Mount Rainier (figure 12). With her climbing party, she rode on horseback "through the wilderness, alone with nature and her wonders," forded a river, camped at high elevations, traversed a glacier where "one wrong step or several loose rocks giving way would land one in the unknown world," climbed "hand over hand" up an "almost perpendicular cliff," and finally reached the summit, "a heavenly moment." Summiting mountains, she reflected, allowed one to "fall in love with the world again. The beauty and grandeur and inspiration you will find there will add new life." Helen Gompertz (later Le Conte), who taught in Berkeley, California, was one of the first women to climb Yosemite's Mount Lyell. "At noon, on the glorious summer day, July 9th, 1892," she wrote, "we flung ourselves, exhausted, but triumphant, upon the top-most rock of the slender peak which we had so longed to reach. We basked in the sunshine, not daring to mar by speech the sublimity of the moment." Following Mills's, Fuller's, and Gompertz's achievements, Lulie Nettleton and fellow women teachers who were also Seattle Mountaineers climbed Mount Adams in Washington and Mount Hood in Oregon in 1911. Nettleton went on with the Sierra Club to summit Mount Whitney and four other Sierra peaks higher than ten thousand feet in 1922. Winona Bailey, who taught at Seattle's Queen Anne High School and completed the 1911 Mount Adams climb, in 1922 was the first

FIGURE 12 Fay Fuller with climbing party. (Courtesy of Mount Rainier National Park Archives.)

woman to ascend Mount Olympus in Greece, a feat that required an extension of her summer break through a short leave of absence.[34]

The bodies of the Western women teachers who climbed mountains were most certainly not frail. They and other women as well as men teachers in rural areas and towns and cities throughout the country revitalized bodies worn down by the enervating effects of teaching through engaging in life in the mountains, in the woods, on the lake, or on the farm. These women defied gender ideology, while their male counterparts reinforced it, through robust activity in the open air. In doing so, they adapted administrators' efforts to control their bodies during their time off as well as through the academic year, using summer "rest" to further grassroots professionalization by building stamina and exercising independence. In the following decades, regulation of teachers' personal lives and bodies would shift as leaders would encourage women teachers to marry and have children. While such changes were liberating, it is an open question whether they would enhance or restrict the physical independence that some teachers experienced during the summertime between the 1880s and the 1930s.

Epilogue

In his profile of a high school English teacher named Horace Smith in the early 1980s, Theodore Sizer outlined a summer dilemma that was a century old: "Teachers do have summer 'vacation' times, so they can supplement their salary somewhat then. Often, however, the months of July and August are needed for study; almost always, some portion is needed for rest."[1] While Horace was a man, the majority of his colleagues would have been women, as had been the case since the mid-nineteenth century. Their circumstances, however, changed after the Second World War. School districts finally eliminated remaining marriage bars, and, perceiving the seasonality of teaching to be compatible with raising a family, married women became the majority of teachers. Gone also were other behavioral restraints on teachers such as prohibitions of dancing and drinking. But rather than disappear, efforts to control teachers' personal and professional lives simply changed course. Rising homophobia and Cold War anticommunism brought unprecedented scrutiny of teachers' sexual identity, gender expression, and political views both in and outside of school, and then the accountability movement and corporate school reform cast teachers not as independent professionals but—in the words of historian Diana D'Amico Pawlewicz—"as problems to be managed."[2]

Contrary to school leaders' ongoing conceptualization of teacher professionalism as rigid obedience to administrators' directives, historian Kate Rousmaniere explains, teachers from the mid-twentieth century onward needed more than ever to be "ready to adapt, accommodate, and improvise at the drop of a hat."[3] While parental responsibilities dictated more teachers' summer pursuits and other developments reshaped their now-traditional summer activities, many still used professional development, academic studies, tourism, rest (if possible), and various forms of work as means of grassroots professionalization.

Indeed, from the postwar period into the twenty-first century, teachers' summer activities continued to enhance their classroom methods, subject-matter knowledge, middle-class identity, professional independence, and, especially in the case of women and teachers of color, personal agency—to the ultimate benefit of their students and the education system.

The National Education Association (NEA) and the American Teachers Association (ATA, the former National Association of Teachers in Colored Schools), which merged in 1966, continued to provide summer professional development opportunities for teachers even as the NEA gradually recast itself as a trade union and shifted its main focus to improving teachers' material interests. Founded as a union in the early twentieth century, the American Federation of Teachers (AFT) likewise mixed professional development with instruction in blue-collar organizing in the interest of securing middle-class salaries and benefits. Although the leaders of the NEA, ATA, and AFT often spoke *for* teachers rather than championing their power as individuals, the three groups offered summer programs throughout the post–World War II decades that enabled individual teachers to advance their classroom work and strengthen their professional confidence.[4]

As the large summer NEA convention became a representative assembly of local unions, the organization sponsored various smaller gatherings for teachers. Beginning in the early 1940s, its Department of Classroom Teachers held a conference each summer at which attendees learned both new classroom methods and organizational tactics. In 1948, two hundred teachers from thirty-three different states came together at Miami University in Oxford, Ohio, for two weeks of morning lectures, afternoon small-group discussions, evening social activities, and shared meals. A teacher from Washington reported that they discussed teacher evaluation more than any other topic, and a teacher from Wyoming reflected, "A conference of this kind, in addition to making teachers better leaders in their organizations, should also help them to become better teachers of our boys and girls back home." Beginning in the mid-1950s, the NEA also sponsored a six-week summer "Washington Seminar" during which teachers studied the roles of political parties and the courts; met with senators and representatives; and visited the Supreme Court, various national bureaus, the U.S. State Department, and the offices of other officials. Teachers could earn academic credit for the seminar, which enhanced their lessons on government as well as empowered them as citizens. Participant Virginia Lee Mabey, a high school teacher in California, reflected, "Here life is breathed into issues which only a few weeks ago were of academic interest only," while the "cosmopolitan character of the group . . . affords a priceless opportunity to share teaching experiences, to grab a new idea or technique."[5] Like the NEA's "Oxford Conference," ATA summer conventions in the mid-twentieth century focused on improving both Black teachers' work and the conditions in which they worked. Meeting themes included "Current Challenges to the Teaching Profession" in 1950 and

"Conserving All Our Human Resources through Adequate-Equitable-Effective Education" in 1957, when group discussion topics ranged from "Improved Techniques of Instruction in the Elementary School" to "Teacher Welfare and Teacher Security." At the 1962 ATA meeting, Kenneth Clark addressed "The Negro Teacher in America Today," and Horace Mann Bond delivered a speech on testing.[6]

Separate from its annual conventions, AFT summer "workshops" emphasized unionization and labor rights while also immersing teachers in broader democratic and historical topics. For two weeks at the University of Wisconsin in August 1947, teachers took courses such as "Professional and Organizational Problems of Union Teachers," "The World Scene in 1947," and "Current Federal and State Legislation." For New Jersey teacher Celia Rohrberg, the workshop provided "a much broader view of what is really taking place in the educational world throughout our country," and Connecticut teacher Ione Proctor found the experience to be "just what I needed as a high school teacher of modern and American history, and as a citizen." Prominent labor historian Selig Perlman headed the workshop in 1949 and 1950, when *The American Teacher* promised that it would "afford the student an unusual opportunity to enrich his knowledge of national and world labor, economic and political affairs."[7] Through such modernized teacher institutes, the AFT, ATA, and NEA helped teachers empower themselves for contract negotiations and day-to-day work in the classroom.

Later in the twentieth century, other new types of teacher institutes provided further opportunities for professional development. For example, the National Endowment for the Humanities (NEH) organized fifteen different six-week immersive academic seminars for high school teachers during the summer of 1983. The NEH offered financial compensation but not college credit, and the program was so popular that, according to *Time* magazine, it could accommodate only 10 percent of the teachers who applied. University of Texas classics professor Karl Galinksy, who taught a course on Homer and Vergil, said of his students, "I'm constantly amazed by their motivation and the amount of initiative displayed in class every day"; the group even read from the *Aeneid*, in Latin, at a party marking one teacher's birthday. University of Iowa English professor Miriam Gilbert complimented the teachers' "commitment" to her seminar on Shakespeare, and a teacher-student from Oklahoma observed, "In this program, high school teachers are recognized as having scholarly interests." With support from the Mellon Foundation, the NEH expanded the initiative the following summer, and NEH institutes for teachers at all levels continued into the twenty-first century, when high school history teacher Coleen Curry "had the best time"—and earned professional development credit—attending the 2019 "Rethinking the Gilded Age & Progressivisms" institute at Loyola University.[8]

Had he lived to see the NEH institutes, education statesman James Bryant Conant would have been pleased. In the early 1960s, he visited several university summer schools and thought it was a "pity" that the teachers he observed studied education administration more than the liberal arts and sciences, although he was impressed with the level of instruction, teachers' devotion to their studies, and the value of "out-of-class discussions with other teachers." By this time, college graduation was a universal requirement for new teachers, and most senior teachers had earned a bachelor's degree, often through summer study.[9] As more teachers held college degrees, universities offered more graduate-level summer courses. In advance of 1958 summer sessions, for example, the University of Maryland advertised greater "variety and the extent of offerings, especially at the graduate level," while Baltimore's Johns Hopkins University and Towson State Teachers College both publicized their master of education degrees. Hopkins emphasized that MEd electives could include the arts and sciences, and Wesleyan University in Connecticut advertised that in its Graduate Summer School for Teachers, educators could earn a "unique" master of arts in liberal studies degree with a major in art, behavioral science, literature, math, natural science, social science, or "an inter-field."[10] Conant must not have visited Hopkins or Wesleyan.

Entering the field with a bachelor's degree did not excuse teachers from attending summer classes; Sizer discussed Horace's need to "upgrade" his skills and replenish his "academic capital." While Horace's and others' experiences on campus were somewhat different than those of teachers before World War II, summer sessions still played an important role in grassroots professionalization. At the University of Arkansas, Black teacher-students in the early 1950s were among the first to integrate the campus. When they enrolled in summer school to complete their master's degrees, they made themselves at home in the dormitories, dining halls, the student union, and social activities, no doubt stoking their sense of agency. Throughout the country, year-round students dominated summer enrollments, and programming no longer catered mainly to teachers; "There was little to differentiate this term from the regular academic year," wrote a University of Iowa dean.[11] Iowa teacher Mary Johnston Elson, who had earned a two-year certificate in the 1930s, pursued summer studies to complete her bachelor's degree at Coe College in 1966. Unfazed by the campus's focus on traditional students, Elson treated it with a sense of humor: When graduates were invited to return for their fiftieth reunion, she wrote, "I remarked to the young man sitting by me that I would be 102 years old by that time (I was 52). He had a hard time containing himself and kept suppressing a laugh." Black teacher Beatrice Morton—who had enrolled in summer courses throughout the 1930s while teaching in Cincinnati and had since become a professor at Southern University—was finally able in 1959 to fulfill her life goal of spending a summer at Harvard University. The experience, she later wrote, was "glorious," as the younger students treated her with respect and she was able to immerse herself in "essential tangible and intangible values that renew and sustain one's faith in . . . learning."[12] Along with faith in learning, intangible benefits of summer studies also included middle-class identity and intellectual independence.

Attending summer school at Harvard also provided Morton with the opportunity to tour Cambridge and Boston. As jet travel, even to Europe, became more affordable and the family vacation became more entrenched in middle-class identity, tourism remained an important summer activity for teachers, who were more likely than their predecessors to travel with a spouse and children. A 1949 Greyhound advertisement in a teacher journal noted, "Travel credits for the renewal of teachers' certificates are authorized in 40 of the 48 states by State Board of Education," and organized tours for teachers proliferated in the postwar era. Groups of teachers "and their friends" from South Carolina, West Virginia, and Michigan stopped at Yellowstone National Park on western bus tours or "field trips" organized in 1950 by teachers' associations or higher-education institutions, and teachers from North Carolina and Tennessee toured Yellowstone in conjunction with attending the 1951 NEA meeting in San Francisco. Established soon after the war, the NEA Division of Travel Service in 1947 offered organized tours of Mexico, Cuba and the West Indies, and New England and Canada In addition to "a full sight-seeing schedule of the scenic, historic, and other points of interest," the trips included social programs with local teachers, school visits, and "talks given by local authorities." Eleven NEA tours in 1950 covered several regions of the United States, Canada, and Mexico, and participants could earn college credit by completing academic assignments related to their trip.[13]

One-quarter of the one thousand teachers from forty-six different states who traveled with NEA groups during the summer of 1953 earned academic credit for their experiences. Director of the Division of Travel Service Paul Kinsel wrote that all of the traveling teachers were able to "get to know and understand" the other countries and regions of the United States they visited by getting "off the beaten tourist paths" and visiting "the homes and schools of their colleagues," and that most returned with "luggage straining at the seams" from the large volume of material they gathered for use in the classroom. Kinsel quoted the statement of a participating teacher from Illinois that NEA tours place teachers "in a higher position socially," and a California teacher's reflection that "travel gives the teacher a complete change and many times a new outlook on life. Visiting new places and meeting new people, she returns to the classroom in better physical condition and usually better psychologically adjusted."[14] NEA tour destinations and opportunities to earn academic and/or professional development credit expanded in the following decades. Tours specifically for art educators in 1971 went to the Soviet Union and to Scandinavia and Central Europe; the Soviet Union trip included visits to the Kremlin and medieval cathedrals in Moscow, a worker's rest home in Sochi, a monastery in Kyiv, and the Hermitage Museum in Leningrad, as well as an excursion on the Volga-Don Canal. An "Orient Holiday" in 1974 took teachers to Tokyo, Bangkok, and Hong Kong; and a trip to Peru in 1977 allowed teachers to explore archeological sites, Machu-Picchu, and Lima, where, the NEA travel manager said, they would witness "the opulence of a bygone colonialism" as they widened their geographical and cultural horizons.[15]

Other teachers set off on their own, as they had before World War II. Two women social studies teachers from Maryland devoted two months in the summer of 1947 to touring twenty-five states in the continental United States, the territory of Alaska, five provinces in Canada, and Mexico, mainly by rail and steamship. They wrote in an article about the trip that they "gasped in admiration" at the grandeur of the Canadian Rockies; felt like they could reach out and touch the indigenous villages they saw from the ship on Alaska's inland passage; marveled at Seattle's growth, San Francisco's bridges, and Hollywood; enjoyed traveling by burro in Mexico; and resolved that teachers should see more of the country "to appreciate its wonders."[16] Six decades later, married Georgia high school teachers Bonnie and Grant Sinclair devoted every summer for more than a decade to traveling both abroad and in the United States, especially by recreational vehicle to national parks. "Though they briefly leave the classroom behind," an article on their adventures explained, "they take their passion for learning and teaching with them." Not only did Grant enjoy "seeing firsthand how history influenced the books he reads with his American literature students," but he incorporated his travel experiences, complete with photos, into his courses.[17] Less tangible benefits of the Sinclairs' and countless other teachers' trips include broader horizons and empowerment through seizing the right to have an adventure.

The Sinclairs' travels also enabled them to return to school "in better physical condition and usually better psychologically adjusted," as the California teacher explained after an NEA trip in the early 1950s. Teachers continued to engage in vigorous forms of rest during the postwar years. Denver teacher Janet Johnson, for example, was by her thirtieth birthday in 1966 among the first twenty women to climb to the summit of each of the more than fifty Colorado mountain peaks higher than 14,000 feet. But rest in general was increasingly elusive. Sizer acknowledged Horace's need for rest but suggested that he found little time for it, and historian Kenneth Gold noted the prevalence of reports of "fatigue and burnout" at the turn of the twenty-first century. Finally, the spring 2021 headline "Summer School Is More Important Than Ever. But Teachers Are 'Fried' and Need a Break" captured teachers' dire need for rest even as they were increasingly likely to spend that summer teaching as the country began to emerge from the coronavirus pandemic.[18]

Even before the pandemic, another headline captured the reality for many teachers: "'I Do Not Have 2–3 Months Off': Teachers on Summer Break Are Working, a Lot." Based on the outpouring of #NoSummersOff tweets in 2019, the article mentioned summer studies but focused mainly on "grinding at side jobs."[19] Increasingly unusual in the second half of the twentieth century and the opening decades of the twenty-first were teachers who were able to indulge their passions and sense of adventure and/or refine their progressive teaching techniques through summer work. Among them were Wisconsin teacher Herbert Lystrup and Minnesota teacher Mildred Ericson, who worked as seasonal naturalists at Yellowstone well into the 1960s. Lystrup's published reflections on the summer of 1952 demonstrated his continuing enthusiasm for learning about the park and teaching visitors about nature there: He was excited when a visitor's question prompted him to discover that snails rarely live in streams near geyser basins due to a lack of calcium carbonate, and he never tired of surprising visitors by showing them the flowers on pine trees. In the early 1960s, Ericson enjoyed giving "cone talks" to large crowds in front of Old Faithful and leading three-hour hikes to Observation Point above the geyser area. She reflected, "My greatest thrill in being a ranger-naturalist in Yellowstone Park is this feeling of sharing with others my life-long love of the outdoors."[20] Iowa special education teacher Sarah Pratt pursued a very different passion when she began in the mid-2000s to devote her summers to creating butter sculptures at state fairs throughout the Midwest. Known especially for life-sized "butter cows," she is also passionate about teaching others about butter sculpting through hands-on demonstrations.[21] But opportunities for jobs like these declined over time; seasonal service positions at Yellowstone were increasingly filled by college students as more young people went to college and more teachers' childcare responsibilities anchored them at home—and butter-carving jobs are few and far between.

As summer work more commonly took the form of "grinding at side jobs" in the postwar era, even a 1951 ad recruiting teachers to sell encyclopedias during the summer focused on how much they could earn rather than the change of scenery or adventures that the job might bring: "It's a grand feeling to be *money ahead* when school reopens," the ad promised. Sizer's Horace worked at a liquor store of which he was a part owner, and upwards of four in ten teachers in the early 2000s either worked in a nonteaching job or taught summer school. Because the summer school curriculum mainly replicated academic year work, it offered teachers little opportunity to experiment or branch out, while nonteaching jobs were often in service industries. Philadelphia high school teacher John Adelman reported that during the 1970s and 1980s, he worked "all kinds of jobs" in the summertime, including "as a restaurant manager in Atlantic City," where, he explained, restaurants "needed a lot of people, but they were anxious to get rid of people once the summer ended. So a teacher is perfect. That summer job was murder. Some of those jobs I had as restaurant manager were fourteen, sixteen hours a day." Adelman would have been "money ahead" but hardly rested or brimming with new ideas for his classes when he returned to school in the fall.[22]

By assisting teachers like Adelman in achieving a middle-class standard of living, even "grinding" summer jobs have contributed to grassroots professionalization. Other teachers' summer travels and experiences in university summer sessions and union- and NEH-sponsored institutes have affirmed their middle-class identity and stoked their intellectual and professional independence, helping prepare them to "adapt, accommodate, and improvise at the drop of a hat" in the classroom. Like teachers between the 1880s and the 1930s, teachers in recent decades have utilized professional development programs, teachers college and university summer sessions, various types of work, tourism, and middle-class approaches to rest to shape their own versions of professionalism; however, they have also had to contend with what a 2015 headline in *The Atlantic* termed "The Myth of a Teacher's 'Summer Vacation.'"[23] Not only does this myth fail to acknowledge the valuable role that summer activities have played in shaping an effective teaching force, but it has also contributed to the occupation's reputation as less than fully professional. As Dan Lortie and John Goodlad note in their classic studies, teachers' short official work year is a factor in their "special but shadowed social standing" and "not quite" professional status, respectively.[24] Since the nine-month school year took shape a century and a half ago, school leaders have issued directives and imposed requirements for teachers' "off" months, and teachers have shaped their activities to support grassroots professionalization. Instead of dismissing the summer months as vacation time for teachers, legislators, policymakers, and communities should recognize and better support teachers' activities during these crucial months.

Acknowledgments

This book would not be possible without the scholarship and mentorship of Jurgen Herbst (1928–2013) and Geraldine Clifford (1931–2024). As my doctoral advisor, Jurgen modeled innovative thinking about the history of higher education and teacher preparation. He also directed me to Geraldine, whose pioneering research and occasional in-person chats laid the foundation for my investigations of women teachers' education and lives outside the classroom. While Jurgen and Geraldine paved the way, Karen Graves sparked the project; when I mentioned that I had enjoyed the Ken Burns documentary on the national parks, she suggested, "You should write a book on the history of teachers during the summertime." Little did either of us know at the time that she had inspired a decade-plus journey that would take me to countless published and online sources, six state or municipal archives, collections at eight different universities, and specialized archives in splendid locations from Chautauqua, New York, to Yellowstone. Thanks so much, Karen, for proffering such an interesting and creative line of research!

A multitude of archivists and librarians throughout the country facilitated my inquiry. They include William Eigelsbach of Special Collections at the University of Tennessee, Chautauqua Institution archivist Jon Schmitz, Wade Myers at the National Park Service's Harpers Ferry Center, Debbie Miller at the Minnesota Historical Society, Lois Ho O.P. at the Sinsinawa Dominican Archives, and Lincoln University archivist Mark Schleer. Wholehearted thanks also to the dedicated personnel at the state archives of Arkansas, Massachusetts, and Wisconsin; the Yellowstone Heritage and Research Center; the Schlesinger Library of Radcliffe Institute; Harvard's Monroe C. Gutman Library; the Iowa Women's Archives; the Kenneth Spencer Research Library at the University of Kansas; the Abraham Lincoln Presidential Library; the Newberry Library; the Chicago Historical Society; the Municipal Archives of the City of New York; the

New York Public Library; Special Collections at George Washington University; and the archives of Harvard University, the University of Iowa, Morningside College, Emporia State University, and Towson University. I am grateful to the latter two institutions for inviting me to speak at anniversary celebrations and to stay on for archival research. At the University of Iowa, the efforts of the interlibrary loan staff were invaluable.

The feedback and suggestions I received when I presented threads of this project at meetings of the History of Education Society, the International Standing Conference for the History of Education, the Social Science History Association, the Southern History of Education Society, the American Educational Research Association, and the Association for the Study of Higher Education, were tremendously helpful. Special thanks to Andrew Abbott, Nancy Beadie, Barbara Beatty, Sonia Birocheau, Jackie Blount, Tim Cain, Victoria Cain, Pete Clancy, Diana D'Amico Pawlewicz, Linda Eisenmann, Jim Fraser, Jarvis Givens, Bob Gough, Karen Graves, Bob Hampel, Michael Hevel, Benjamin Jacobs, Polly Kaufman, Karen Leroux, Emil Marklund, Michelle Morgan, Maggie Nash, Steve Ostrach, Bill Reese, Rebecca Rogers, Rachel Rosenberg, Kate Rousmaniere, John Rury, Campbell Scribner, Sevan Terzian, Marc VanOvebeke, Johannes Westberg, and Christine Woyshner. I am delighted that this book will be part of the New Directions in the History of Education series at Rutgers University Press, where series editor Ben Justice offered insightful comments and senior editor Peggy Solic was unfailingly supportive and patient. Thanks also to Lisa Banning and the rest of the Rutgers editorial team, as well as the anonymous reviewers of the manuscript.

Research for the book was made possible by grants from the College of Education Research Fund at the University of Iowa, the UI Internal Funding Initiative, and the Spencer Foundation (#201700104). The views expressed are my own and do not necessarily reflect those of the Spencer Foundation or UI. Thanks also to research assistants Tania Lefevre and Kristen Chmielewski; I especially appreciated Kristen's sharp eye, enthusiasm for the project, and good humor. I would also like to acknowledge the support of a UI Career Development Award and the UI department of Educational Policy and Leadership Studies.

Thanks to the following publishers for permission to use content from the following pieces: Cambridge University Press for Christine A. Ogren, "Out-of-Class Project: American Teachers' Summertime Activities, 1880s–1930s," *History of Education Quarterly* 56, no. 1 (2016): 8–35; Taylor & Francis Ltd., www.tandfonline.com, on behalf of Stichting Paedagogica Historica, for Christine A. Ogren, "Revitalizing Teachers' Bodies: Prescriptions for Rest and Teachers' Summer Activities in the United States, 1880s–1930s," *Paedagogica Historica* 54, no. 1–2 (2018): 154–168 (copyright 2017); and Teachers College Press, Columbia University, for Christine A. Ogren, "The Myth that Teachers Take the Summer Off," in Sherman Dorn and David A. Gamson, eds., *23 Myths About the History of American Schools: What the Truth Can Tell Us and Why It Matters* (New York:

Teachers College Press, copyright 2024). For providing photos and permission to reprint them, thanks to the Chautauqua Institution Archives; the Rare Book Collection at the University of North Carolina's Wilson Library; the Harvard University Archives; Gottesman Libraries at Teachers College, Columbia University; Special Collections at the University of Tennessee; the South Dakota Historical Society; the Yellowstone Heritage and Research Center; the Iowa Women's Archives at the University of Iowa; Mount Rainier National Park Archives; and HathiTrust.

Finally, I would like to thank my friends and family for their encouragement and support. Shana Crosson and Jenny Staben listened attentively to my ideas and encouraged my progress; Shana even used her extensive online search skills to track down sources. Throughout this project, my husband Bruce Hostager cheerfully drove me to and from the airport, celebrated my grants, listened as I reported my research successes and vented my frustrations, helped me to formulate the title, and patiently started cooking dinner while I finished one more paragraph. I'm just sorry that I wasn't able to find examples of teachers who pursued particular summer activities that he dryly suggested. Bruce's airplane-building project coincided with my book project; the completion of both means that we'll be able to enjoy many summertime adventures in N211CB!

Abbreviations

ALPL	Abraham Lincoln Presidential Library, Springfield, Illinois
ASA	Arkansas State Archives, Little Rock, Arkansas
CIA	Chautauqua Institution Archives, Oliver Archives Center, Chautauqua, New York
ESUSC	Special Collections and Archives, Emporia State University, Emporia, Kansas
HFP	Herrick Family Papers, MC 728, Schlesinger Library, Radcliffe Institute, Harvard University, Cambridge, Massachusetts
HGSESC	Special Collections, Monroe C. Gutman Library, Harvard Graduate School of Education, Cambridge, Massachusetts
HUSS	Harvard University, Summer School of the Arts and Sciences and Education, Administrative Files, 1923–1980, Harvard University Archives, Cambridge, Massachusetts
INM	*The Iowa Normal Monthly*
IWA	Iowa Women's Archives, The University of Iowa Libraries, Iowa City, Iowa
JNEA	*The Journal of the National Education Association*
KSRL	Kenneth Spencer Research Library, University of Kansas, Lawrence, Kansas
LFP	Lewis Family Papers, 1775–1977, bulk 1850–1950, Special Collections, Newberry Library, Chicago, Illinois
LUA	Lincoln University Archives and Ethnic Studies Center, Inman E. Page Library, Lincoln University, Jefferson City, Missouri

MHS	Minnesota Historical Society, St. Paul, Minnesota
NPSHC	National Park Service History Collection, Harpers Ferry Center, Harpers Ferry, West Virginia
PPCUT	Philander P. Claxton Papers, Special Collections, University of Tennessee Libraries, Knoxville, Tennessee
PSJ	*Pennsylvania School Journal*
RNEA	Records of the National Education Association, Special Collections Research Center, Gelman Library, The George Washington University, Washington, DC
SLFP	Stewart-Lockwood Family Papers, RH MS 114, Kenneth Spencer Research Library, University of Kansas, Lawrence, Kansas
SSSUT	Summer School of the South Collection, Special Collections, University of Tennessee Libraries, Knoxville, Tennessee
TCDC	Teachers College Digital Collection, Columbia University, https://teacherscollege.primo.exlibrisgroup.com/discovery/collectionDiscovery?vid=01TCCU_INST:01TCCU&inst=01TCCU_INST (registration and fee required for access)
TSJ	*Texas School Journal*
TUSC	Special Collections, Albert S. Cook Library, Towson University, Towson, Maryland
UISCA	Special Collections and Archives, University of Iowa Libraries, Iowa City, Iowa
UISSR	Summer Session Records, Special Collections and Archives, University of Iowa Libraries Iowa City, Iowa
WHSA	Wisconsin Historical Society Archives, Madison, Wisconsin
YNPA	Yellowstone National Park Archives, Gardiner, Montana

Notes

Introduction

1 Max Cohen, "'I Do Not Have 2–3 Months Off': Teachers on Summer Break Are Working, a Lot," *USA Today*, July 11, 2019, www.usatoday.com/story/news/education/2019/07/11/teachers-summer-break-jobs-work-living-wage/1524677001/.
2 Kevin M. Cline (@TheKevinMCline), "Excited to start . . . ," Twitter, July 8, 2019; Carrie Lillard (@hokieattheview), "Conquered @Mount Vernon . . . ," Twitter, July 9, 2019; Coleen Curry (@mscurry), "4 weeks and 68.5 PD hours later . . . ," Twitter, July 25, 2019; NEA (@NEAToday), "Professional development . . . ," Twitter, July 19, 2019; instagram.com/explore/tags/nosummersoff/.
3 David Tyack and Elisabeth Hansot, *Learning Together: A History of Coeducation in American Public Schools* (New Haven, CT: Yale University Press, 1990), chap. 3–4; Kenneth M. Gold, *School's In: The History of Summer Education in American Public Schools* (New York: Peter Lang, 2002), chap. 1–3.
4 Jackie M. Blount, *Fit to Teach: Same-Sex Desire, Gender, and School Work in the Twentieth Century* (Albany: State University of New York Press, 2005), 52. Clifford emphasizes that marriage bars were not universal and that prior to 1945 "far more American wives (including mothers) taught school . . . than generally recognized." She also notes that Black women were more likely than white women to teach after marriage, and Fairclough elaborates, "In the rural South, it was normal for black women teachers to carry on working after they married, and to return to teaching after bearing children," although "most black city teachers were unmarried." Nevertheless, Clifford also explains, as late as 1930, 80 percent of women teachers in the United States were single. Geraldine J. Clifford, *Those Good Gertrudes: A Social History of Women Teachers in America* (Baltimore, MD: Johns Hopkins University Press, 2014), 124, 126; Adam Fairclough, *A Class of Their Own: Black Teachers in the Segregated South* (Cambridge, MA: Harvard University Press, 2007), 276. On marriage bars, see Clifford, *Those Good Gertrudes*, 128–132; and Blount, *Fit to Teach*, 15–16, 74–75.
5 Gold, *School's In*, 74.
6 "School Sessions in Summer," *PSJ* 63, no. 1 (July 1914): 28; Charles Judd et al., "Educational News and Notes," *Elementary School Teacher* 14, no. 9 (1914): 410.

7 SLFP; Philip Gerber, ed., *Bachelor Bess: The Homesteading Letters of Elizabeth Corey, 1909–1919* (Iowa City: University of Iowa Press, 1990); Beatrice E. Cramer memoir and diary, Box 1, HGSESC.

8 David Tyack, *The One Best System: A History of American Urban Education* (Cambridge, MA: Harvard University Press, 1974); David Tyack and Elisabeth Hansot, *Managers of Virtue: Public School Leadership in America, 1820–1980* (New York: Basic Books, 1982); Kathleen Weiler, *Country Schoolwomen: Teaching in Rural California, 1850–1950* (Stanford, CA: Stanford University Press, 1998); Margaret K. Nelson, "Female Schoolteachers as Community Builders," in *The Teacher's Voice: A Social History of Teaching in Twentieth Century America*, ed. Richard J. Altenbaugh (London: The Falmer Press, 1992), 78–89; Nancy Hoffman, *Woman's "True" Profession: Voices from the History of Teaching*, 2nd ed. (Cambridge, MA: Harvard Education Press, 2003), 16; Kate Rousmaniere, *City Teachers: Teaching and School Reform in Historical Perspective* (New York: Teachers College Press, 1997); Blount, *Fit to Teach*; Clifford, *Those Good Gertrudes*; Victoria-Maria MacDonald, "The Paradox of Bureaucratization: New Views on Progressive Era Teachers and the Development of a Woman's Profession," *History of Education Quarterly* 39, no. 4 (1999): 427–453; Shaun Johnson, "The Woman Peril and Male Teachers in the Early Twentieth Century," *American Educational History Journal* 35, no. 1 (2008): 163. On male teachers, see also Geraldine Joncich Clifford, "Man/Woman/Teacher: Gender, Family, and Career in American Educational History," in *American Teachers: Histories of a Profession at Work*, ed. Donald Warren (New York: Macmillan, 1989), 293–343.

9 Howard K. Beale, *Are American Teachers Free?* (New York: Charles Scribner's Sons, 1936), 641; Jurgen Herbst, *And Sadly Teach: Teacher Education and Professionalization in American Culture* (Madison: University of Wisconsin Press, 1989), chap. 7; Diana D'Amico Pawlewicz, *Blaming Teachers: Professionalization Policies and the Failure of Reform in American History* (New Brunswick, NJ: Rutgers University Press, 2020), 14, 45. See also Rousmaniere, *City Teachers*. On the history of teachers' unions, see Wayne J. Urban, *Why Teachers Organized* (Detroit: Wayne State University Press, 1982); Marjorie Murphy, *Blackboard Unions: The AFT and the NEA, 1900–1980* (Ithaca, NY: Cornell University Press, 1990); and Kate Rousmaniere, *Citizen Teacher: The Life and Leadership of Margaret Haley* (Albany: State University of New York Press, 2005).

10 Carl F. Kaestle, *Pillars of the Republic: Common Schools and American Society, 1780–1860* (New York: Hill and Wang, 1983), 123–127; John L. Rury, "Who Became Teachers? The Social Characteristics of Teachers in American History," in *American Teachers: Histories of a Profession at Work*, ed. Donald Warren (New York: Macmillan, 1989), 17, 25; Linda M. Perkins, "The History of Blacks in Teaching: Growth and Decline Within the Profession," in *American Teachers: Histories of a Profession at Work*, ed. Donald Warren (New York: Macmillan, 1989), 359; Fairclough, *Class of Their Own*, 223; Clifford, *Those Good Gertrudes*, 126.

11 Tyack, *One Best System*, 255–257; Rousmaniere, *City Teachers*, 48; Kathleen Weiler, "Women's History and the History of Women Teachers," *Journal of Education* 171, no. 3 (1989): 9–30; Weiler, *Country Schoolwomen*, 16–21; Fairclough, *Class of Their Own*, 226.

12 Rousmaniere, *City Teachers*, 36; Burton J. Bledstein, *The Culture of Professionalism: The Middle Class and the Development of Higher Education in America* (New York: W. W. Norton, 1976), 30; Daniel T. Rogers, *The Work Ethic in Industrial America, 1850–1920* (Chicago: University of Chicago Press, [1974] 1978), chap. 4; Cindy S.

Aron, *Working at Play: A History of Vacations in the United States* (New York: Oxford University Press, 1999). On the formation of middle-class culture, see also Lawrence W. Levine, *Highbrow/Lowbrow: The Emergence of Cultural Hierarchy in America* (Cambridge, MA: Harvard University Press, 1988). On women workers and middle-class status, see Daniel J. Walkowitz, *Working With Class: Social Workers and the Politics of Middle-Class Identity* (Chapel Hill: University of North Carolina Press, 1999), preface and prologue.

13 National Education Association (NEA), *Report of the Committee on Teachers' Salaries and Cost of Living* (Ann Arbor, MI: NEA, 1913), 240; Beale, *Are American Teachers Free?*, 393; Fairclough, *Class of Their Own*, 4; Robert S. Lynd and Helen Merrell Lynd, *Middletown: A Study in Contemporary American Culture* (New York: Harcourt, Brace and Company, 1929), 209; Marguerite Clark, "What the Teacher Contributes to the Social and Cultural Life of America," *High School Teacher* 8 (June 1932): 214. On teacher education and cultural capital acquisition, see Christine A. Ogren, *The American State Normal School: "An Instrument of Great Good"* (New York: Palgrave Macmillan, 2005), chap. 3, 5.

14 Rousmaniere, *City Teachers*, 36; Linda Van Ingen, "'One Can't Live on Air': Sarah McComb and the Problem of Old-Age Income for Single Women Teachers, 1870s–1930s," *History of Education Quarterly* 54, no. 2 (2014): 184; D'Amico Pawlewicz, *Blaming Teachers*, 15, 44–45; Perkins, "The History of Blacks," 351–352; Fairclough, *Class of Their Own*, 16–17, 286. On the role of whiteness in women's professional identity, see Walkowitz, *Working with Class*, prologue.

15 "School Sessions," 28; Judd et al., "Educational News," 410. A New York appellate court ruled in 1938 that "no teacher has an inherent or statutory right to a vacation of two months or more." *Juddson v. Board of Education of City of New York* 255 a.d. 1024 (December 31, 1938).

16 Gold, *School's In*, chap. 3.

17 William A. Mowry, *Recollections of a New England Educator, 1838–1908* (New York: Silver, Burdett and Company, 1908), 237; "The National Educational Association," *INM* 13, no. 11 (1890): 445; "What Shall We Do with the Long Vacation?," *INM* 1, no. 12 (1878): 360; "Making the Most of the Summer," *JNEA* 24, no. 5 (1935): 135. Most U.S. states and territories published education journals such as *The Iowa Normal Monthly* and the *Texas School Journal* during this period, mainly as a tool for state- and county-level administrators to communicate with teachers and school districts as "an essential step in the professionalization of teachers." Mindy Spearman, "'Everything to Help, Nothing to Hinder': The Story of the *Texas School Journal*," *Southwestern Historical Quarterly* 111, no. 3 (2008): 282–302.

18 "How Shall I Spend the Summer?" *TSJ*, no. 6 (June 1889): 170; W. F. Barr, "The Summer School," *INM* 20, no. 10 (1897): 421; James Lawrey, "The Summer School," *INM* 20, no. 11–12 (1897): 450; "The Vacation," *PSJ* 62, no. 12 (1914): 564–565; *Journal of Proceedings and Addresses of the National Education Association* (NEA, 1907–1922); *JNEA* 12–23 (1923–1934); "The Summer Vacation," *JNEA* 10, no. 6 (1921): 108.

19 *Intelligence* 21, no. 5 (1901); 21, no. 9 (1901); 21, no. 10 (1901); 22, no. 9 (1902); 22, no. 10 (1902); 23, no. 8 (1903); quotations from 20, no. 13 (1900): 493, and 23, no. 10 (1903): 369.

20 Suggestions for Summer Touring and Educational Recreation Travel sections, *Midland Schools* 45, no. 8 (1931): 309–313; W. C. Ruediger, "Baiting Teachers," *School and Society* 17 (March 24, 1923): 331. See also Lucy N. Brickhouse, "Leaves of Absence for Study and Travel," *The Fourth Yearbook of the Department of Classroom Teachers* (Washington, DC: NEA, 1923), 140.

21 *American School Board Journal* 31, no. 1 (July 1905): cover.
22 Beale, *Are American Teachers Free?*, 640; Karen L. Graves, *And They Were Wonderful Teachers: Florida's Purge of Gay and Lesbian Teachers* (Urbana: University of Illinois Press, 2009), 134–137; Rousmaniere, *City Teachers*, 2; Margaret K. Nelson, "Using Oral Histories to Reconstruct the Experiences of Women Teachers in Vermont, 1900–50," in *Studying Teachers' Lives*, ed. Ivor F. Goodson (London: Routledge, 1992), 167, 184; Fairclough, *Class of Their Own*, 15; Jarvis R. Givens, *Fugitive Pedagogy: Carter G. Woodson and the Art of Black Teaching* (Cambridge, MA: Harvard University Press, 2021).
23 D'Amico Pawlewicz, *Blaming Teachers*, 6, 7.
24 Virginia Scharff, *Taking the Wheel: Women and the Coming of the Motor Age* (Albuquerque: University of New Mexico Press, 1991), 33; Blount, *Fit to Teach*, chap. 1; Weiler, *Country Schoolwomen*, 143; Clifford, *Those Good Gertrudes*, ix, 314.
25 Givens, *Fugitive Pedagogy*.

Chapter 1 Professional Development in Institutes and Association Meetings

1 Huftalen quoted in Suzanne L. Bunkers, *"All Will Yet Be Well": The Diary of Sarah Gillespie Huftalen, 1873–1952* (Iowa City: University of Iowa Press, 1993), 275, note 12; "One Way," *Chautauqua Assembly Herald* 10, no. 9 (1885): 1; Jessie L. Herrick Diary, August 2, 1887, HFP; Nettie Rae Rankin, "World Understanding Given Prominence at Minneapolis Meeting," *News Bulletin of the Department of Classroom Teachers of the National Education Association* 2, no. 1 (1928): 1, NEA1005.RG, Series 8, Box 1546, RNEA.
2 Historians have incorporated local teachers' institutes in their accounts of teachers' preparation and experiences, but they have not examined institutes held during the summer per se, or considered the ramifications of training during months when teachers were not officially employed. While Elsbree's early work mentions Glens Falls and other nationally known independent summer programs, Fraser's recent overview history of teacher preparation does not discuss the role of summer education. And histories of teacher preparation rarely mention the meetings of state teachers' associations and the National Education Association. See Willard S. Elsbree, *The American Teacher: Evolution of a Profession in a Democracy* (Westport, CT: Greenwood Press, [1939] 1970); Mary Hurlbut Cordier, *Schoolwomen of the Prairies and Plains: Personal Narratives from Iowa, Kansas, and Nebraska* (Albuquerque: University of New Mexico Press, 1992); James W. Fraser, *Preparing America's Teachers: A History* (New York: Teachers College Press, 2007); Adam Fairclough, *A Class of Their Own: Black Teachers in the Segregated South* (Cambridge, MA: Belknap Press of Harvard University Press, 2007). Wesley's history of the National Education Association provides copious information on summer gatherings but does not consider their role in teacher education. Edgar B. Wesley, *NEA: The First Hundred Years; The Building of the Teaching Profession* (New York: Harper & Brothers, 1957).
3 Fraser, *Preparing America's Teachers*, 3.
4 Diana D'Amico Pawlewicz, *Blaming Teachers: Professionalization Policies and the Failure of Reform in American History* (New Brunswick, NJ: Rutgers University Press, 2020), introduction.
5 Jarvis R. Givens, *Fugitive Pedagogy: Carter G. Woodson and the Art of Black Teaching* (Cambridge, MA: Harvard University Press, 2021); Geraldine G. Clifford, *Those Good Gertrudes: A Social History of Women Teachers in America* (Baltimore:

Johns Hopkins University Press, 2014), ix; Virginia Scharff, *Taking the Wheel: Women and the Coming of the Motor Age* (Albuquerque: University of New Mexico Press, 1991), 33.

6 W. C. Rote, "Summer Normal Institutes," *TSJ* 2, no. 1 (1884): 18.

7 Elsbree, *The American Teacher*, chap. 13; Fraser, *Preparing America's Teachers*, chap. 4; Melinda Jo Spearman, "'The Peripatetic Normal School': Teachers' Institutes in Five Southwestern Cities (1880–1920)" (PhD diss., University of Texas at Austin, 2006). On the heyday of the state normal school, see Christine A. Ogren, *The American State Normal School: "An Instrument of Great Good"* (New York: Palgrave Macmillan, 2005).

8 William Carl Ruediger, *Agencies for the Improvement of Teachers in Service, United States Bureau of Education Bulletin* 3, no. 449 (Washington, DC: Government Printing Office, 1911): 42, 26; Kate V. Wofford, *An History of the Status and Training of Elementary Rural School Teachers of the United States, 1880–1930* (Pittsburgh: Thomas Siviter and Company, 1935), 72.

9 Ruediger, *Agencies*, 34–41, 46–48; "State of New York Education Department: Announcement of Summer Institutes for 1905," Chautauqua Institution Circulars, CIA; "New York State Teachers' Institute," *Chautauqua Assembly Herald* 22, no. 7 (1897): 1; "Review of the Season," *Chautauquan Daily* 31, no. 45 (1906): 3; "Gain in Summer Schools," *Chautauquan Daily* 32, no. 44 (1907): 6.

10 Spearman, "'Peripatetic Normal School,'" 84–86, 90–91, 165; Ruediger, *Agencies*, 44–45, 34–35.

11 John T. Thompson, "County Institutes," *Twenty-Fourth Annual Report of the State Board of Education . . . Maryland . . . 1890* (Baltimore, 1891), xlv; *Thirty-Fifth Annual Report of the State Board of Education . . . Maryland . . . 1901*, lvi, TUSC.

12 Aaron D. Purcell, "'The Greatest Event Since the Civil War': Progressivism and the Summer School of the South at the University of Tennessee," *Journal of East Tennessee History* 76 (2004): 2–3; Clinton B. Allison, "Training Dixie's Teachers: The University of Tennessee's Summer Normal Institutes," *Journal of Thought* 18, no. 3 (1983): 27–36.

13 Ruediger, *Agencies*, 34–41, 44–48, quotation on 48.

14 "Summer Normal Schools," *TSJ* 2, no. 5 (1884): 142–143, 147; "Editorial Department," *TSJ* 2, no. 8 (1884): 241; "Summer Normal Institute," *TSJ* 3, no. 2 (1885): 38; "Editorial Department," *TSJ* 6, no. 11 (1888): 321; "Sup't Carlisle's Address," *TSJ* 9, no. 10 (1891): 322; "The Summer Normals," *TSJ* 11, no. 9 (1893): 284; V. M. Fulton, "The Proper Mission of Summer Normal Institutes," *TSJ* 20, no. 9 (1903): 444; "Editorial Department," *TSJ* 21, no. 2 (1903): 596; Ruediger, *Agencies*, 48. See also Spearman, "'Peripatetic Normal School,'" chap. 2.

15 Cordier, *Schoolwomen*, 56; Edwards quoted in Thompson, "County Institutes," xlix; Clarence Ray Aurner, *History of Education in Iowa*, vol. 2 (Iowa City: State Historical Society of Iowa, 1914), 180–181; Ruediger, *Agencies*, 34–41, quotations on 44, 46; Andrea Radke, "'I Am Very Aspiring': Muirl Dorrough and the Alliance Junior Normal School," *Nebraska History* 81, no. 1 (2000): 5–9; R. McLaran Sawyer, "No Teacher for the School: The Nebraska Junior Normal Movement," *Nebraska History* 52, no. 2 (1971): 191–203.

16 "The Institute," *TSJ* 8, no. 3 (1890): 60; "How Shall I Spend Vacation?" *TSJ* 8, no. 5 (1890): 117.

17 Paul H. Hanus, *Adventuring in Education* (Cambridge, MA: Harvard University Press, 1937), 62–63.

18 Quoted in Cordier, *Schoolwomen*, 57.

19 "The Summer Normals," *TSJ* 2, no. 8 (1884): 247; "News and Notes," *TSJ* 10, no. 9 (1892): 681.
20 P. C. Petherbridge to Amanda Stewart, June 21, 1885, and July 26, 1885, Box 6, SLFP. On the Stewarts' teaching careers, see Clifford, *Those Good Gertrudes*.
21 May Stewart to family, July 1, 1906, Box 47, SLFP.
22 Gillespie quoted in Bunkers, *"All Will Yet Be Well,"* 70, 95; Cordier, *Schoolwomen*, 59–60.
23 "Editorial Department," *TSJ* 3, no. 4 (1885): 117; "Examination Papers for Summer Normal Certificates," *TSJ* 2, no. 8 (1884): 233–235; "Questions for Summer Normal Certificates, 1890," *TSJ* 8, no. 8 (1890): 204–206; "Examinations for Teachers' Certificates," *TSJ* 24, no. 1 (1906): 29.
24 "Certificates Granted and Enrollment," *TSJ* 3, no. 9 (1885): 281; "Final Report of Summer Normal Board of Examiners," *TSJ* 24, no. 1 (1906): 27.
25 Spence quoted in Michael Fultz, "Determination and Persistence: Building the African American Teacher Corps through Summer and Intermittent Teaching, 1860s–1890s," *History of Education Quarterly* 61, no. 1 (2021): 18; "Institutes and Reading Circles," *TSJ* 7, no. 9 (1889): 254; Liberty Summer Normal advertisement, *TSJ* 20, no. 1 (1902): 31.
26 "Summer Normal Editorial Notes," *TSJ* 11, no. 8 (1893): 275.
27 "Our Last Institutes," *Midland Schools* 15, no. 2 (1900): 64.
28 G. P. Randle to Edgar Strain, August 18, 1887, Strain, Edgar W. Papers, Folder 1, ALPL.
29 Miranda Cather to Nellie Covert, June 25, 1885, and Vallie P. Williams to Nellie Covert, July 12, 1885, Nellie Penelope Covert Papers, ESUSC.
30 Mary [no last name] to Nora Stewart, July 7, 1887, Box 9, SLFP; May Stewart to family, July 1, 1906.
31 "The Institute," *TSJ* 8, no. 3 (1890): 60; Anna J. H. Pennybacker, "Letters to a Young Lady No. III," *TSJ* 8, no. 4 (1890): 82. On Pennybacker, see Kelley Ann King, *Call Her a Citizen: Progressive-Era Activist and Educator Anna Pennybacker* (College Station: Texas A & M University Press, 2010).
32 Pennybacker, "Letters . . . No. III," 82; Lille Shaver, "Hunt County Normal" in "Institute and Reading Circle," *TSJ* 6, no. 9 (1888): 251.
33 "State of New York . . . Summer Institutes for 1905," 2.
34 "Our Last Institutes," 64; Gillespie quoted in Bunkers, *"All Will Yet Be Well,"* 146; Liberty Summer Normal ad, 31; "The Summer Normals," *TSJ* 2, no. 8 (1884): 246–248.
35 Allison, "Training Dixie's Teachers," 31–33.
36 Allison, "Training Dixie's Teachers," 32–33; Clinton B. Allison, *Teachers for the South: Pedagogy and Educationists at the University of Tennessee, 1844–1995* (New York: Peter Lang, 1998), 6–14; "State of New York . . . Summer Institutes for 1905," 2.
37 "The Summer Normals," *TSJ* 2, no. 8 (1884): 246–248; "The Summer Normals," *TSJ* 4, no. 8 (1886): 267; "Institute and Reading Circle," *TSJ* 6, no. 8 (1888): 222.
38 Emma Wormwood Diaries, August 5, 1898, Folder 3, Special Collections, Newberry Library, Chicago.
39 Pennybacker, "Letters . . . No. III," 82–83.
40 "How Shall I Spend," 118; "Institute and Reading Circle," *TSJ* 6, no. 11 (1888): 316; G. P. Randle to Edgar Strain, August 3, and August 9, 1887, Strain, Edgar W. Papers, Folder 1.
41 Gillespie quoted in Cordier, *Schoolwomen*, 59; Bunkers, *"All Will Yet Be Well,"* 141.

42 "Institute and Reading Circle," *TSJ* 6, no. 11 (1888): 315; "Teachers' Reception," *Chautauqua Assembly Herald* 28, no. 5 (1903): 1.

43 Mr. Walker Diary, July 22–August 8, 1886, ALPL; G. P. Randle to Edgar Strain, August 3, August 9, and August 18, 1887, Strain, Edgar W. Papers, Folder 1.

44 "Our Last Institutes," *Midland Schools* 15, no. 2 (1900): 64.

45 A. W. Eddins in "What Should the Summer Normal Do for the Teacher?," *TSJ* 21, no. 8 (1904): 909; "Summer Normals," *TSJ* 2, no. 8 (1884): 247; "Institute and Reading Circle," *TSJ* 6, no. 11 (1888): 315; Liberty Summer Normal ad, 31.

46 Allison, "Training Dixie's Teachers," 29; "Teachers' Reception," 1; Vallie P. Williams to Nellie Covert, July 12, 1995, Nellie Penelope Covert Papers.

47 "Institute and Reading Circle," *TSJ* 6, no. 11 (1888): 315; P. C. Petherbridge to Amanda Stewart, July 26, 1885, Box 6, SLFP.

48 "Institute Souvenir Edition," *Peabody News* 2, no. 16 (1901): 3, Nellie Penelope Covert Papers; "News and Notes" (1892), 681.

49 Armstrong to Edgar Strain, July 16, 1887, Strain, Edgar W. Papers, Folder 1; A Village School Ma'am, "The Institute or Sumer Vacation, Which?" *INM* 16, no. 2 (1892): 72.

50 J. Lawrey, "The Summer School," *INM* 20, no. 9 (1897): 361; Editorial, *Midland Schools* 20, no. 10 (1906): 366.

51 "Regulations for Summer Normal Institutes," *TSJ* 21, no. 7 (1904): 900; "News and Notes," *TSJ* 23, no. 8 (1906): 36; Ruediger, *Agencies*, 9, 47.

52 Aurner, *History of Education in Iowa*, 184–185; Elsbree, *The American Teacher*, 365–366; Wofford, *History of the Status*, 73–75.

53 Spearman, "'Peripatetic Normal School,'" 110–117.

54 "Summer County Normal Schools," *PSJ* 65, no.9 (1917): 390.

55 Aula Thompkins to Vivian Bullock, June 19, 1921, Scarlett-Bullock Family Papers, Box 2, Folder 2, ASA.

56 Radke, "'I Am Very Aspiring,'" 10. The junior normal schools ended in 1914, by which time Nebraska had opened additional state normal schools.

57 Philip Gerber, ed., *Bachelor Bess: The Homesteading Letters of Elizabeth Corey, 1909–1919* (Iowa City: University of Iowa Press, 1990), 146, 192, 338, 353.

58 Gerber, *Bachelor Bess*, 193–194, 197, 261, 312.

59 Gerber, *Bachelor Bess*, 88, 90, 193.

60 Fairclough, *Class of Their Own*, 248, 319–320.

61 W. W. Willoughby, "The History of Summer Schools in the United States," *Report of the Commissioner of Education for the Year 1891–91*, vol. 2 (Washington, DC: Government Printing Office, 1894), 893–959, quotations on 894, 895.

62 Elsbree, *American Teacher*, 370.

63 Jeffrey Simpson, *Chautauqua: An American Utopia* (New York: Harry N. Abrams, 1999), chap. 1, 2, and 4; Cindy S. Aron, *Working at Play: A History of Vacations in the United States* (New York: Oxford University Press, 1999), chap. 4, quotation on 111; Gwyneth King Roe, Autobiography, 2–3, Gwyneth King Roe Papers, Box 4, Folder 9, WHSA. See also Theodore Morrison, *Chautauqua: A Center for Education, Religion, and the Arts in America* (Chicago: University of Chicago Press, 1974), 49–50, 76–78. These histories mention only in passing the large presence of teachers at the Chautauqua summer assembly.

64 Alfreda L. Irwin, *Three Taps of the Gavel: Pledge to the Future: The Chautauqua Story*, revised ed. (Chautauqua, NY: Chautauqua Institution, 1987), 48; "Two Boys at Chautauqua," *Chautauqua Assembly Herald* 5, no. 17 (1880): 1; Anna J. H.

Pennybacker, "Letter on Chautauqua," *TSJ* 9, no. 10 (1891): 319. Pennybacker had a deep relationship with Chautauqua; see King, *Call Her a Citizen*.

65 "Chautauqua Assembly, 1901," *Intelligence* 21, no. 5 (1901): 197.

66 "Chautauqua and the Teachers," *Chautauquan Weekly* 1, no. 43 (1907): 1; "Registrar's Report of Summer Schools," *Chautauquan Weekly* 23, no. 5 (1923): 1; "The Teachers' Retreat," *Chautauqua Assembly Herald* 19, no. 11 (1894): 4.

67 *Chautauqua Assembly Herald* 27, no. 40 (1902): 1; Typed manuscript, 1951, and unsigned letter, Jewett House, Folder 16i, Historical Research Boxes, CIA; Frank Chapin Bray, *A Reading Journey Through Chautauqua* (Chautauqua, NY, 1905), 31, CIA.

68 *Chautauqua Institution: A System of Popular Education: President's Reports, 1924 and 1925*, 11, 24, CIA; "Opening Summer Schools Commons," *Chautauquan Weekly* 4, no. 47 (1910): 1. Bestor's son and namesake, who grew up at Chautauqua, became a well-known critic of U.S. education in the mid-twentieth century.

69 "Dining Room Force," *Chautauquan Weekly* 3, no. 52 (1909): 3.

70 "Kentucky Teachers for Chautauqua," *Chautauquan Weekly* 1, no. 40 (1907): 1; "Pittsburg [*sic*] Teachers' Vacation," *Chautauquan Weekly* 4, no. 44 (1910): 2; "Pittsburg [*sic*] Scholarships," *Chautauquan Weekly* 5, no. 45 (1911): 5.

71 "Half Scholarships Awarded," *Chautauquan Weekly* 4, no. 42 (1910): 1; "Full Scholarship Holders," *Chautauquan Weekly* 4, no. 41 (1910): 1; "Scholarships Awarded," *Chautauquan Weekly* 4, no. 38 (1910): 1; "Full Scholarships Awarded," *Chautauquan Weekly* 6, no. 40 (1912): 1; "Scholarships Awarded," *Chautauquan Weekly* 12, no. 44 (1919): 1; Charles E. Peirce to Miss Marian Amy, May 18, 1931, Historical Research Boxes, Box, 2, Folder 2e, CIA; *Chautauquan Daily* 51, no. 27 (1926): 10, CIA.

72 "Teachers' Retreat," 4.

73 Morrison, *Chautauqua*, 49–50, 76–78; Simpson, *Chautauqua*, 21, 51–54.

74 Diary of Eva Moll, November 18, 1884, and March 27, 1887, Diaries Related to Chautauqua, CIA; "The Twelfth Chautauqua Assembly," *Chautauquan* 6, no. 1 (1885): 43, CIA; "One Way," 1. On Dickinson, see Robert T. Brown, *The Rise and Fall of the People's Colleges: The Westfield State Normal School, 1839 to 1914* (Westfield, MA: Institute for Massachusetts Studies, 1988), 48.

75 "Teachers' Retreat," *Chautauqua Assembly Herald* 15, no. 4 (1890): 1; "Chautauqua Teachers' Retreat," *Chautauqua Assembly Herald* 16: advance issue (June 1891): 14; Pennybacker, "Letter on Chautauqua," 319.

76 *Chautauqua Year-Book for 1895*, Box 123, CIA. On Hervey, see Lawrence A. Cremin, David A. Shannon, and Mary Evelyn Townsend, *A History of Teachers College Columbia University* (New York: Columbia University Press, 1954).

77 "Nature Study and Agriculture," *Chautauquan Weekly* 2, no. 39 (1908): 1; "National Education Association and Chautauqua Institution," *Chautauquan Weekly* 2, no. 44 (1908): 3.

78 "The Summer Schools," *Chautauquan Weekly* 6, no. 1 (1911): 8; "Chautauqua Summer Schools," *Chautauquan Weekly* 5, no. 44 (1911): 2; "Opportunities for Teachers," *Chautauquan Weekly* 7, no. 32 (1913): 24; Simpson, *Chautauqua*, 94.

79 "The Oldest Summer Schools in the United States," *Chautauquan Weekly* 23, no. 37 (1924): 43–45; Irwin, *Three Taps*, 47–49.

80 "Numbered Among Devoted Chautauquans," *Chautauquan Daily* 58, no. 31 (1934): 3.

81 Henry James, ed., *The Letters of William James* vol. 2 (Boston: Atlantic Monthly Press, 1920), 40–42.

82 *Chautauqua Year-Book for 1895*, 41; [no title], *Chautauquan Weekly* 1, no. 46 (1907): 8.

83 "Educational Conference," *Chautauquan Daily* 39, no. 16 (1914): 4; *Chautauqua Institution: A System of Popular Education; President's Report, 1919*, n.p., Box 123, CIA.
84 Otis M. Shackelford, *Seeking the Best* (Kansas City, MO: Burton Publishing Co., 1911), 76–77.
85 "Teachers' Retreat," 4.
86 King Roe, Autobiography, 7–8.
87 *Chautauqua Year-Book for 1895*, 32–33; Hollingsworth quoted in *Chautauqua Assembly Herald* 23, no. 4 (1898): 1.
88 Diary of Eva Moll, November 27, 1884; Shackelford, *Seeking the Best*, 76; King, *Call Her a Citizen*, 25, 66–67. It was common for teachers to study the curriculum of the Chautauqua Literary and Scientific Circle throughout the year. Chautauqua Institution cofounder John H. Vincent established the four-year course of independent study called the CLSC in 1878, and it was extremely popular throughout the country in the late nineteenth century. Morrison, *Chautauqua*, chap. 5; Simpson, *Chautauqua*, chap. 3.
89 "One Opinion," *Chautauqua Assembly Herald* 11, no. 5 (1886): 5; Shackelford, *Seeking the Best*, 76.
90 Simpson, *Chautauqua*, 91.
91 Diary of Eva Moll, November 18, 1884, and March 27, 1887; King Roe, Autobiography, 6; "One Way," 1.
92 *The Chautauqua Program: Season of 1908*, Chautauqua Institution Circulars, CIA; "The Coburn Players," *Chautauquan Weekly* 6, no. 49 (1912): 6; Morrison, *Chautauqua*, 127; Dorothy Osborne, "Off the Plaza," *Chautauquan Daily* 60, no. 38 (1936): 3.
93 Pennybacker, "Letter on Chautauqua," 319–320.
94 King Roe, Autobiography, 7–15.
95 "Personal," *Chautauqua Assembly Herald* 25, no. 4 (1900): 2.
96 "Flights Finished," *Chautauquan Daily* 38, no. 39 (1913): 4.
97 Morrison, *Chautauqua*, chap. 10; Anita C. Danker, "'Redeeming the Time': Learning Vacations at the New England Chautauqua Assembly," *Massachusetts Historical Review* 17 (2015): 67–97; Willoughby, *The History of Summer Schools*, 939; Bay View ad, *Intelligence* 21, no. 10 (1901): 366; Aron, *Working at Play*, 116; Editorial, *TSJ* 24, no. 10 (1907), 52; "News and Notes," *TSJ* 24, no. 9 (1907): 31; Colorado Chautauqua ad, *TSJ* 25, no. 8 (1908): 43.
98 Willoughby, *History of Summer Schools*, 895, 945.
99 Willoughby, *History of Summer Schools*, 946–948. See also Ellsbree, *American Teacher*, 372–373.
100 Willoughby, *History of Summer Schools*, 948.
101 William A. Mowry, *Recollections of a New England Educator, 1838–1908* (New York: Silver, Burdett and Company, 1908), 237–244, quotation on 239; Willoughby, *History of Summer Schools*, 949–952.
102 Marthas Vineyard Summer Institute ad, *Intelligence* 23, no. 8 (1903): 315.
103 Willoughby, *History of Summer Schools*, 955–956; Herrick Diary, August 2, 1887.
104 Herrick Diary, August 1–August 19, 1887, quotations from August 2, 3, 4, 12, and 16.
105 Herrick Diary, August 1–August 19, 1887, quotations from August 6, 8, 10, 12, and 18.
106 Herrick Diary, August 1–August 19, 1887, quotations from August 4, 6, 8, 9, 11, 13, 15, 16, and 19.
107 Herrick Diary, August 1–August 19, 1887, quotations from opening page, August 2 and 8.
108 Willoughby, *History of Summer Schools*, 956–957. See also Elsbree, *American Teacher*, 373.

109 Spearman, "'Peripatetic Normal School,'" 65–73; Editorial Department, *TSJ* 6, no. 4 (1888): 106; Summer School of Methods ad, *TSJ* 6, no. 5 (1888): n.p.; "Official Department," *Texas SSJ* 14, no. 6 (1896): 217–218; School of Methods ad, *TSJ* 22, no. 1 (1904): n.p.

110 Allison, *Teachers for the South*, 69–82; P. P. Claxton, "Summer School of the South," *Teacher-Education Journal* 3 (December 1941): 137.

111 Sister Mary Salome, "The American Hierarchy and Education: Studies in Catholic Education History of the United States (1492–1920)" (PhD diss., Marquette University, 1934), 356, 453; Mary Synon, *Mother Emily of Sinsinawa: American Pioneer* (Milwaukee: Bruce Publishing Company, 1955), 178; St. Clara Convent, 1847–1855 Annals, Vols. 1–7, Boxes 1–4, Sinsinawa Dominican Archives, Sinsinawa, WI; "Summer School at Sinsinwa," *Young Eagle* 23 (September 1897): 10, Sinsinawa Dominican Archives.

112 Robert D. Cross, *The Emergence of Liberal Catholicism in America* (Cambridge, MA: Harvard University Press, 1958), 160; Kate Rousmaniere, *Citizen Teacher: The Life and Leadership of Margaret Haley* (Albany: State University of New York Press, 2005), 40; Robert L. Reid, ed., *Battleground: The Autobiography of Margaret A. Haley* (Urbana: University of Illinois Press, 1982), 28; Margaret Haley's Unpublished Autobiography, 1935 Version, 312, Chicago Teachers' Federation records, Box 34, Folder 2, Chicago History Museum Archives, Chicago.

113 Kate E. Sartori, "Columbian Catholic Summer School," clipping from Le Mars, Iowa, newspaper, Scrapbook 1 (unprocessed), Sinsinawa Dominican Archives; Synon, *Mother Emily*, 180–181.

114 Justine Ward, *Thomas Edward Shields: Biologist, Psychologist, Educator* (New York: Charles Scribner's Sons, 1947), 108–121; Synon, *Mother Emily*, 181–182; Haley's Unpublished Autobiography, 310; Rousmaniere, *Citizen Teacher*, 41; Reid, *Battleground*, 28.

115 Joseph Emory Avent, *The Summer Sessions in State Teachers' Colleges* (Washington, DC: National Education Association, 1925), 26; Mowry, *Recollections*, 243–244; *Chautauqua Institution: Proceedings of the Mid-Winter Meeting of the Trustees*, 1910, 6, CIA; *Chautauqua Institution: President's Reports, 1922 and 1923*, 1923, 6, CIA.

116 Ruediger, *Agencies*, 90.

117 See Wayne J. Urban, *Gender, Race, and the National Education Association: Professionalism and Its Limitations* (New York: RoutledgeFalmer, 2000); and Fraser, *Preparing America's Teachers*.

118 Elsbree, *American Teacher*, 515–519; David Tyack and Elisabeth Hansot, *Managers of Virtue: Public School Leadership in America, 1820–1980* (New York: Basic Books, 1982), 64, 138–140, 192–193; Fairclough, *Class of Their Own*, 314. NATCS changed its name from National Colored Teachers Association in 1907 to make room for white teachers who taught in Black schools, renamed itself the American Teachers Association in 1937, and merged with the NEA in 1966. Thelma D. Perry, *History of the American Teachers Association* (Washington, DC; National Education Association, 1975). On segregation in the NEA, see Linda M. Perkins, "The History of Blacks in Teaching: Growth and Decline within the Profession," in *American Teachers: Histories of a Profession at Work*, ed. Donald Warren (New York: Macmillan, 1989), 352; and Urban, *Gender, Race*.

119 *Maryland School Journal* 6, no. 10 (1880): 394; "Pennsylvania State Teachers' Association," *PSJ* 31, no. 12 (1883): 488.

120 "State Teachers' Association, Waco," *TSJ* 15, no. 6 (1897): 227–228; "Change of Place of Meeting," *TSJ* 15, no. 5 (1897): 204; John Collier, "State Teachers' Association," *TSJ* 2, no. 5 (1884): 146.

121 "State Association at Washington," *PSJ* 30, no. 3 (1881): 79–80; "Members in Attendance," *PSJ* 31, no. 3 (1882): 129–130; "Members in Attendance," *PSJ* 35, no. 3 (1886): 133–134; "Members in Attendance," *PSJ* 40, no. 3 (1891): 147–148.

122 "Texas State Teachers' Association," *TSJ* 2, no. 7 (1884): 211.

123 Editorial Department, *TSJ* 4, no. 7 (1886): 232–233; "Texas Teachers—Tenth Annual Convention," *TSJ* 7, no. 11 (1889): 282; "The Colored Teachers' Association," *TSJ* 4, no. 8 (1886): 274; "Third Annual Session of the Colored Teachers' State Association," *TSJ* 5, no. 8 (1887): 230.

124 "News and Notes," *TSJ* 5, no. 5 (1887): 147; "Meeting of the State Association at York," *PSJ* 29, no. 3 (1880): 97, 119; "Meeting of the State Association at Allentown," *PSJ* 35, no. 3 (1886): 121, 123.

125 "Programme of State Teachers Association," *TSJ* 3, no. 6 (1885): 186; "Texas Teachers—Tenth Annual Convention," 289–290; "Texas State Teachers' Association," *TSJ* 11, no. 2 (1893): 58–63.

126 "Colored Teachers' Association," 274–275; "Institutes and Reading Circles," *TSJ* 7, no. 5 (1889): 150.

127 "Institutes and Reading Circles," 152; Givens, *Fugitive Pedagogy*, 6; Fairclough, *Class of Their Own*, 321.

128 "Pennsylvania State Teachers' Association," *PSJ* 31, no. 3 (1882): 81, 84; Editorial, *TSJ* 7, no. 7 (1889): 183–184.

129 "State Association at Washington," 96; "Meeting State Association Allentown," 92; "Third Annual Session," 230; "Institutes and Reading Circles," *TSJ* 6, no. 6 (1888): 168; "Texas Teachers—Tenth Annual Convention," 285.

130 "Meeting State Association York," 101; "State Association at Washington," 122; "The Pennsylvania State Teachers' Association: Bedford Meeting," *PSJ* 40, no. 3 (1891): 98.

131 "Colored Teachers' Association," 274; "Institutes and Reading Circles," 150; "Texas Teachers—Tenth Annual Convention," 287.

132 "Meeting State Association York," 97, 101, 119, 135; "State Association at Washington," 81, 88, 102.

133 "Third Annual Session," 230–231; "News and Notes," *TSJ* 10, no. 8 (1892): 655; "Texas Teachers," 283, 285, 288, 289; "Editorial: The Austin Meeting," *TSJ* 14, no. 7 (1896): 256–257; "Texas State Teachers' Association," *TSJ* 20, no. 7 (1903): 364.

134 Wesley, *NEA*, 255–261; "N. E. A.: The Madison Meeting, July, 1884: An Historical Address by Hon. Thomas W. Bicknell" (1912), NEA1001.RG Governance Records, Box 1312, RNEA.

135 "Teachers Are Being Advised" (newspaper clipping, n.d.), NEA 1001.RG Governance Records, Box 550, RNEA.

136 *National Educational Association, Buffalo, N. Y.* (flyer); *'On to Washington': National Educational Association* (brochure); and *National Educational Association Fortieth Annual Convention* (brochure), NEA1001.RG, Box 550 (Shepard Papers), RNEA.

137 "Our National Association: Its Representative Assembly," *JNEA* 13, no. 5 (1924): 153–154; "Our National Association: What Its Meetings Mean to Education," *JNEA* 13, no. 4 (1924): 116; Maybelle Hargrave, "Evansville Gives Teachers Bonus for Travel and Study," *News Bulletin of the Department of Classroom Teachers* 4, no. 1 (1930): 3, NEA1005.RG, Series 8, Box 1546, RNEA.

138 "Columbus Convention, N. E. A.," *PSJ* 78, no. 10 (1930): 607.
139 *TSJ* 3, no. 5 (1885): 151–152; "To the Teachers and Friends of Education of Iowa," *INM* 12, no. 10 (1889): 575.
140 E. L. Briggs in *Transactions of the Michigan State Teachers' Association . . . 1889* (1889), 48; *Intelligence* 19, no. 10 (1899): 375.
141 "The N. E. A. Meeting at Los Angeles," *INM* 30, no. 10 (1907): 551; "National Educational Association," *TSJ* 25, no. 9 (1908): 13; "National Educational Association," *Midland Schools* 35, no. 9 (1921): 304.
142 "Oakland, California" and "Annual Meeting—Program," *JNEA* 12, no. 6 (1923): 221–223, 249; "Classroom Teachers at Summer Meeting," *JNEA* 12, no. 7 (1923): 293; "Our National Association: What Its Meetings Mean" (1924): 115–116; "Classroom Teachers at Washington," *JNEA* 13, no. 9 (1924): 303–304; "The Denver Convention" and "Come to Denver," *JNEA* 24, no. 5 (1935): 161–163.
143 G. L. Gorton in *Transactions of the Michigan State Teachers' Association . . . 1889*, 50; "Review of the National Association," *INM* 15, no. 1 (1891): 24; "The National Educational Association," *INM* 20, no. 1 (1896): 9; "National Educational Association," *INM* 25, no. 9 (1902): 451; "National Educational Association," *TSJ* 25, no. 9 (1908): 13.
144 "Oakland-San Francisco Convention," *PSJ* 72, no. 1 (1923): 16; "Washington Convention of the N.E.A.," *PSJ* 73, no. 1 (1924): 18–20; "Atlanta Convention of the National Education Association," *PSJ* 87, no. 1 (1929): 16; "The Columbus Convention of the National Education Association," *PSJ* 79, no. 1 (1930): 20–21.
145 Wesley, *NEA*, 131–132; "N. E. A.: The Madison Meeting"; "Getting Ready for Columbus," *JNEA* 19, no. 6 (June 1930): 203; Anna E. M. Dwyer, "Convention Impressions," *News Bulletin of the Department of Classroom Teachers* 10, no. 1 (1936): 1, 8.
146 Wesley, *NEA*, chap. 24; "Getting Ready for Columbus," 203; Rankin, "World Understanding," 1.
147 Dwyer, "Convention Impressions," 1; Wesley, *NEA*, 258–260; Briggs in *Transactions . . . 1889*, 49. Booker T. Washington also addressed the NEA in 1896, 1904, and 1908; his conservative views on Black education were palatable to association leadership. Perkins, "History of Blacks," 355.
148 Conrad G. Selvig, *A Tale of Two Valleys* (Los Angeles: Grover Jones Press, 1951), 48; Clement E. Foust in "The Minneapolis Convention of the National Education Association," *PSJ* 77, no. 1 (1928): 12.
149 Briggs in *Transactions . . . 1889*, 48; L. E. Wolfe, "The Los Angeles Meeting," *TSJ* 25, no. 1 (1907): 48; F. Theodore Struck in "The Indianapolis Convention," *PSJ* 74, no. 1 (1925): 9; Calvin Hogg in "The Columbus Convention," 17–18; R. W. Robinson in "The Los Angeles Convention," *PSJ* 80, no. 1 (1931): 20–21.
150 "National Educational Association," *PSJ* 65, no. 1 (1916): 38; "Oakland-San Francisco Convention," 11–12; Fred W. Diehl in "The Philadelphia Convention," *PSJ* 75, no. 1 (1926): 15–16; Walter Douthett in "Los Angeles Convention," 19–20; Margaret J. Lowman and D. A. Kline in "Indianapolis Convention," 10–12.
151 Belmont Farley, "The Washington Convention," *JNEA* 23, no. 6 (1934): 166; Dwyer, "Convention Impressions," 1.
152 Wesley, *NEA*, 47; "National Educational Association," *PSJ* 65, no. 1 (1916): 38–39.
153 Rankin, "World Understanding," 3; "Washington Convention of the N.E.A.," 12; Dwyer, "Convention Impressions," 1, 8; Mildred D. Babcock, "Eastern Delegate Relates Impressions of Detroit Meeting," *News Bulletin of the Department of Classroom Teachers* 11, no. 1 (1937): 1.

154 Dwyer, "Convention Impressions," 1; Mildred D. Babcock, "Eastern Delegate," 1; "National Educational Association," *PSJ* 65, no. 1 (1916): 38; "Atlanta Convention," 9; "Classroom Teachers at Indianapolis," *JNEA* 14, no. 8 (1925): 254; Lillian Fuller, "A Thousand Teachers Attend Annual Dinner on Biltmore Terrace," *News Bulletin of the Department of Classroom Teachers* 3, no. 1 (1929): 4; "Helen Hunt, Western Teacher, Attends Convention," *News Bulletin of the Department of Classroom Teachers* 8, no. 1 (1934): 1.

155 "Washington Convention," 13; Fred D. Cram, "With the N.E.A.," *Midland Schools* 51, no. 1 (1936): 13; "Our National Association: What Its Meetings Mean," 116; Euphemia M. Mann in "Indianapolis Convention," 13; Mary B. McAndrew in "Philadelphia Convention," 17.

156 Cram, "With the N.E.A.," 13; "Classroom Teachers at Indianapolis," 254; "Our National Association: Its Representative Assembly," 154; "Our National Association: What Its Meetings Mean," 115; McAndrew in "Philadelphia Convention," 17.

157 Rousmaniere, *Citizen Teacher*, 106–114; 179–182; Wesley, *NEA*, 280–281, 324–327.

158 "Oakland-San Francisco Convention," 12; Babcock, "Eastern Delegate," 1; Lotta Fowler, "Teacher Is Impressed at Denver Meeting," *News Bulletin of the Department of Classroom Teachers* 9, no. 1 (1935): 2.

159 Perry, *American Teachers Association*, 48; "National Notes," *National Note-Book Quarterly: Official Bulletin of the National Association of Teachers in Colored Schools* 2, no. 2 (1920): 8–9, NEA1007.RG, Box 3044, RNEA.

160 "The Baltimore Meeting," *National Note-Book Quarterly* 2, no. 3 (1920): 4–7; "Attention: Delegates," *Bulletin: Official Organ NATCS*. 1, no. 2 (1922): 4–5; "Our Annual Meeting," *Bulletin* 2, no. 2 (1923): 16; "Editor's Page," *Bulletin* 11, no. 1 (1930): 10; and "Proceedings," *Bulletin* 3, no. 4 (1923): 6, NEA1007.RG, Box 3044, RNEA; W. J. Hale, "Purpose and Program of the National Association of Teachers in Colored Schools," *Bulletin* 9, no. 1 (1928): 7, https://curiosity.lib.harvard.edu /black-teacher-archive; photo of "Twenty-Seventh Annual Session," *Bulletin* 11, no. 1 (1930): cover, NEA1007.RG, Box 3044, RNEA.

161 Digest of the Sixteenth Annual Meeting," *National Note-Book Quarterly* 1, no. 4 (1919): 1, 3, 5; and "Digest of Proceedings of the Seventeenth Annual Meeting," *National Note-Book Quarterly* 2, no. 4 (1920): 3, https://curiosity.lib.harvard.edu /black-teacher-archive.

162 "Program: Nineteenth Annual Meeting," *Bulletin* 1, no. 2 (May 1922): 26; "Proceedings," 8–9; and "Next Annual Meeting," *Bulletin* 3, no. 4 (1923): 21, NEA1007.RG, Box 3044, RNEA.

163 Givens, *Fugitive Pedagogy*, 194; Perkins, "History of Blacks," 352–353; "Proceedings," 6; Fred McCuistion, "Comparative Costs of Public Education White and Colored," *Bulletin* 11, no. 1 (1930): 14, NEA1007.RG, Box 3044, RNEA; "Proceedings of the Seventeenth," 1; "The Exhibit," *Bulletin* 2, no. 2 (1923): 16, NEA1007.RG, Box 3044, RNEA; "The National Association of Teachers in Colored Schools' Twenty-Fifth Birthday," *Bulletin* 9, no. 1 (1928): 8, https://curiosity.lib.harvard.edu /black-teacher-archive.

164 "National Notes," 10; "Proceedings of the Seventeenth," 3; "Program: Nineteenth Annual Meeting," 25; "Proceedings," 6; "What Happened at the Atlantic City Meeting," *Bulletin* 17, no. 1 (1940): 4, https://curiosity.lib.harvard.edu/black -teacher-archive; "The Editor's Page," *Bulletin* 9, no. 7 (1929): 10, NEA1007.RG, Box 3044, RNEA.

165 Givens, *Fugitive Pedagogy*, 172; "A Good Word," *National Note-Book Series* 1 (October 1918): n.p.; "Proceedings of the Seventeenth," 5–6; "Report of Findings

Committee," *Bulletin* 6, no. 1 (1926): 7; and "Louisville Meeting of the N. A. T. C. S.," *Bulletin* 12, no. 4 (1933): 11–12, https://curiosity.lib.harvard.edu/black-teacher-archive.

166 "National Notes," 10; "Baltimore Meeting," 7; "Proceedings," 6, 8; "Program of the Twenty-First Annual Meeting," *Bulletin* 4, no. 4 (1924): 6–7, https://curiosity.lib.harvard.edu/black-teacher-archive; "Editor's Page," *Bulletin* 11, no. 1 (1930): 10, NEA1007.RG, Box 3044, RNEA; "The Forthcoming Convention," *Bulletin* 11, no. 9 (1931): 6, https://curiosity.lib.harvard.edu/black-teacher-archive.

167 "Educational Notes and Announcements," *Bulletin of High Points in the Work of the High Schools of New York City* 1, no. 7 (1919): 28; "Second Annual Conference on Elementary Education," *JNEA* 27, no. 5 (1938): 157; "Plans for the Summer Meeting," *JNEA* 11, no. 5 (1923): 205; "Our Coming Conventions," *JNEA* 14, no. 5 (May 1925): 141; "World Federation at Toronto," *JNEA* 16, no. 3 (1927): 85; "Getting Ready for Geneva," *JNEA* 18, no. 4 (1929): 113; "World Federation of Education Associations," *JNEA* 20, no. 3 (1931): 84; "The World Federation in Tokyo," *JNEA* 26, no. 5 (1937): 272.

168 Editorial, *Intelligence* 19, no. 13 (1899): 493.

Chapter 2 Studies at Normal School, College, and University Summer Sessions

1 Clipping in Newspaper Publicity folder, Box 3, HUSS.

2 Raymond Walters, "America's Summer School Army," *JNEA* 12, no. 5 (1923): 197; Raymond Walters, "On the Summer-School Campus," *Scribner's Magazine*, July 1926, 60.

3 Frank F. Foster, "Summer Sessions for Teachers," *National Survey of the Education of Teachers* 3, no. 10 (1933): 403. See also Ivan A. Booker, "Trends in Summer School Attendance," *School and Society* 37, no. 947 (1933): 230–232.

4 Fraser's recent overview history of teacher preparation does not mention summer programs, but many works on the history of teacher education do discuss university summer sessions. This scholarship generally focuses on individual programs' internal organizational structures and contributions to teacher preparation rather than the experiences of the teachers who attended. See James W. Fraser, *Preparing America's Teachers: A History* (New York: Teachers College Press, 2007); Willard S. Elsbree, *The American Teacher: Evolution of a Profession in a Democracy* (Westport, CT: Greenwood Press, [1939] 1970); Geraldine Jonçich Clifford and James W. Guthrie, *Ed School: A Brief for Professional Education* (Chicago: University of Chicago Press, 1988); Lawrence A. Cremin, David A. Shannon, and Mary Evelyn Townsend, *A History of Teachers College Columbia University* (New York: Columbia University Press, 1954); Arthur G. Powell, *The Uncertain Profession: Harvard and the Search for Educational Authority* (Cambridge, MA: Harvard University Press, 1980); Linda Eisenmann, "The Influence of Bureaucracy and Markets: Teacher Education in Pennsylvania," in *American Teachers: Histories of a Profession at Work*, ed. Donald Warren (New York: Macmillan, 1989), 287–329; and Clinton B. Allison, *Teachers for the South: Pedagogy and Educationists in the University of Tennessee, 1844–1995* (New York: Peter Lang, 1998), chap. 3.

The historiography of higher education pays little attention to summer sessions or to teacher education in general. See Frederick Rudolph, *The American College and University: A History* (Athens: University of Georgia Press, [1962] 1990); John R. Thelin, *A History of American Higher Education* (Baltimore: Johns

Hopkins University Press, 2004); and Charles Dorn, *For the Common Good: A New History of Higher Education in America* (Ithaca, NY: Cornell University Press, 2017). In his history of higher education prior to World War II, Geiger mentions that teachers "were especially numerous among summer students" during the University of Chicago's summer quarter beginning in the 1890s. And in his history of research universities, Geiger acknowledges that "actual and future teachers," including those who attended summer sessions, "accounted for much of the absolute growth of American higher education in the 1920s," but he turns away from this line of analysis with the observation that "their precise share cannot be accurately determined." Roger L. Geiger, *The History of American Higher Education: Learning and Culture from the Founding to World War II* (Princeton, NJ: Princeton University Press, 2015), 347; Roger L. Geiger, *To Advance Knowledge: The Growth of American Research Universities, 1900–1940* (New Brunswick, NJ: Transaction Publishers, [1986] 2004), 110.

5 National Educational Association, *Report of the Committee on Secondary School Studies* (Washington, DC: Government Printing Office, 1893), 54.

6 Linda Eisenmann, "The Influence," 298; Walter Jessup to Thomas H. Macbride, July 17, 1914, Box 5, UISSR; "Getting the Summer School Habit," *PSJ* 70, no. 1 (September 1921): 23; Walters, "America's Summer School Army," 197.

7 Fraser, *Preparing America's Teachers*, 190; Foster, "Summer Sessions," 436; E. C. Denny, "Why Go to Summer School?" *Midland Schools* 49, no. 8 (1935): 256.

8 "Summer Session," ad, *Sierra Educational News* 16, no. 4 (1920): 241; "To the Ambitious Teacher," ad, *Bulletin: Official Organ of the NATCS* 9, no. 7 (1929): 28, NEA1007.RG, Box 3044, RNEA.

9 "Summer Schools," ad, *Intelligence* 22, no. 8 (1902): 312; Brief Announcement, Harvard University, HUSS; University of Denver ad, *JNEA* 25, no. 3 (1936): A-48; Adele Humphrey, "Opportunities in Summer Schools—1928," *JNEA* 17, no. 5 (1928): 155–159; Adele Humphrey, "Opportunities in Summer Schools—1929," *JNEA* 18, no. 4 (1929): 123–130; *Summer Session Report 1931*, Box 6, and *Summer Session Report 1934*, Box 8, UISSR; Frederick J. Moffit, "Summer School," *Midland Schools* 53, no. 8 (1939): 239.

10 Clifford and Guthrie, *Ed School*, 134; Stephen P. Duggan, "Summer Sessions, Here and Abroad," *News Bulletin of the Institute of International Education* 5, no. 7 (1930): 1, Box 1, HUSS; Foster, "Summer Sessions," 437; William Carl Ruediger, *Agencies for the Improvement of Teachers in Service, United States Bureau of Education Bulletin* 3, no. 449 (Washington, DC: Government Printing Office, 1911): 114–115. See also Geraldine Jonçich Clifford, *"Equally in View": The University of California, Its Women, and the Schools* (Berkeley, CA: Center for Studies in Higher Education and Institute of Governmental Studies, 1995).

11 A. J. McK., "The Summer School of the South," *Outlook*, August 2, 1902, 896; Raymond Walters, "The Growth of the Summer School," *JNEA* 11, no. 1 (1922): 12; Walters, "Summer-School Campus," 63, 64.

12 Clara G. Langvick, "Teacher Growth in Service," *JNEA* 11, no. 6 (1922): 218; W. E. Maddock, "How Public Schools Reward Teachers for Summer Study," *Nation's Schools* 10, no. 5 (1932): 36–38; "Summer Schools," *JNEA* 11, no. 5 (1922): 196; Booker, "Trends in Summer School," 230.

13 Margaret M. Alltucker, "Adding Refreshment to Our Pails," *JNEA* 14, no. 3 (1925): 79; E. M. Sipple, "Professional Growth Through Summer School," *Midland Schools* 38, no. 8 (1924): 291; "I Went to Summer School," *Midland Schools* 53, no. 8 (1939): 258–260.

14 Kate Rousmaniere, *Citizen Teacher: The Life and Leadership of Margaret Haley* (Albany: State University of New York Press, 2005), 16–17.

15 "California School of Methods," *Pacific Coast Teacher* 1, no. 7 (1892): 270–271; California School of Methods ad, *Pacific Coast Teacher* 1, no. 8 (1892): 339.

16 Charles A. Harper, *Development of the Teachers College in the United States, with Special Reference to the Illinois State Normal University* (Bloomington, IL: McKnight & McKnight, 1935), 353; "The Summer School at the State Normal," *State Normal Monthly* 13, no. 1 (1900): 15, ESU002, Box 59, ESUSC; David Sands Wright, *Fifty Years at the Teachers College* (Cedar Falls: Iowa State Teachers College, 1926), 205–206; Editorial Department, *TSJ* 21, no. 10 (1904): 1023; Kate V. Wofford, *An History of the Status and Training of Elementary Rural Teachers of the United States, 1860–1930* (Pittsburgh: Thomas Siviter & Company, 1935), 74; Ruediger, *Agencies*, 49; Joseph Emory Avent, *The Summer Sessions in State Teachers' Colleges* (Washington, DC: National Education Association, 1925), 213.

17 Avent, *Summer Sessions*, 167, 170–173, 189. On the characteristics of normal school students, see Christine A. Ogren, *The American State Normal School: "An Instrument of Great Good"* (New York: Palgrave Macmillan, 2005), chap. 2.

18 "Summer Term Opens," *College Eye* (Cedar Falls, IA) 14, no. 12 (1922): 1; "Summer Students Older; Experienced," *College Eye* 21, no. 22 (1930): 3.

19 Daniel W. Lewis Collection, Kansas Collection, RH MS 427, KSRL.

20 Editorial, *Normal Eyte* (Cedar Falls, IA) 10, no. 2 (1900): 29; "First Summer Session Started Here in 1896," *College Eye* 26, no. 6 (1934): 1; Harper, *Development*, 354; "Summer School State Normal," 15; *Annual Catalogue of the Officers and Students of the State Normal School, Emporia, Kansas, Thirty-Seventh Year—1900–1901*, 34, ESU003.008.006, Box 1, ESUSC.

21 "Report by Dr. W. S. Hertzog," *PSJ* 65, no. 9 (1917): 390–393; "The Pennsylvania State Normal Schools," ad, *PSJ* 73, no. 10 (1925): 590; *Maryland State Normal School Bulletin, Towson, Maryland: Summer School Number 1923*, TUSC; "Summer Session," ad, 241.

22 *Annual Catalogue—1900–1901*, 34; "The Summer Term Bulletin," *Normal Eyte* 12, no. 33 (1902): 515; "Unsurpassed Opportunities," ad, *Midland Schools* 35, no. 7 (1921): 246; "Pennsylvania State Normal Schools," ad, 590; *Maryland State Normal 1923*, 4; "Summer School Catalogue," *Kansas State Teachers College of Emporia Bulletin of Information* 14, no. 1 (1934): 2, and *Education and Recreation*, flyer (1937), ESU003.008.006, Box 14, ESUSC.

23 Avent, *Summer Sessions*, 196. At Maryland State Normal School in 1923, for example, half of the summer faculty were MSNS faculty members, and the others were area teachers or administrators, officers of the Maryland Public Athletic League, a supervising teacher from Detroit, Michigan, and an assistant superintendent from Providence, Rhode Island. *Maryland State Normal 1923*, 3.

24 "Program, Summer School, 1905," *Kansas State Normal School, Emporia* 4, no. 5 (1905): 186, ESU003.008.006, Box 13, ESUSC; "What Happened During the Summer," *College Eye* 1, no. 1 (1911): 3; "The Summer Term," *College Eye* 3, no. 18 (1914): 302; "Summer Session," ad, 241.

25 "Summer Session," ad, 241; *The Maryland State Normal School at Towson, Maryland: Summer Session Announcement 1927*, 9, TUSC; "Preliminary Announcement: 1930 Summer Session," *Kansas State Teachers College of Emporia Bulletin of Information*, no. 79 (March 15, 1930): n.p., ESU003.008.006, Box 14, ESUSC; "Summer Sessions in State Teachers Colleges," *PSJ* 80, no. 10 (1932): 714; "Slippery Rock's Nature Study and Health Education Camp," *PSJ* 76, no. 2 (1927): 77–78.

26 Pennsylvania Retired Public School Employees Association (PRPSEA), *Bicentennial Pennsylvania 1976: So Your Children Can Tell Their Children* (Pittsburgh: Geyer Printing Company, 1976), 332–333, 343–344, 8–9.
27 Grace Canan Pogue, *The Swift Seasons* (Hollywood, CA: Cloister Press, 1957), 61, 65–66, 71, 75, 81–82, 92, 122–123; Beatrice Cramer memoir and diary, Box 1, HGSESC.
28 "We desire . . . ," *Normal Eyte* 6, no. 31 (1897): 36; "Program, Summer School, 1905," 186; "Summer Session," ad, 241; "Summer School Directory," *Sierra Educational News* 19, no. 5 (1923): 283; "Preliminary Announcement: 1930," n.p.; "1932 Summer School Announcement," *Kansas State Teachers College Emporia Kansas Bulletin of Information* 106 (March 1932): 5, ESU003.008.006, Box 14, ESUSC.
29 Ruby M. Dresselhouse Diary, 1928, July 3, July 9, July 18, and July 19, HGSESC.
30 Cramer, memoir and diary; Pogue, *Swift Seasons*, 122–123, 104.
31 Editorial, *Normal Eyte* 7, no. 2 (1897): 14; "Summer Term," *Normal Eyte* 8, no. 2 (1898): 22; "It Was Some Summer Term," *College Eye* 12, no. 2 (1920): 2; "Some Summer Term," *College Eye* 13, no. 2 (1921): 2; "Summer School Students Are More Studious," *College Eye* 25, no. 9 (1933): 1; "In Summer School, Life Is Just a Bowl Of 'A' Students," *College Eye* 27, no. 53 (1935): 2; "Several Say They're Better Students," *College Eye* 28, no. 0 (1937): 1; "Students Differ in Summer," *College Eye* 30, no. 38 (1939): 1.
32 "The Summer School," *INM* 24, no. 2 (1900): 73; "What Happened During the Summer," *College Eye* 1, no. 1 (1911): 3; "Summer Term," *Normal Eyte* 8, no. 2 (1898): 22; "News," *Normal Eyte* 8, no. 14 (1898): 193; Dresselhouse Diary, 1928, July 26, June 26, and July 10.
33 "Summer School," 73; "Summer Term Program Ready," *College Eye* 2, no. 32 (1912): 1; *Maryland State Normal School 1927*, 4–5; "Preliminary Announcement: 1930," n.p.; "1932 Summer School Announcement," 4; "Summer Sessions State Teachers Colleges," *PSJ* 79, no. 10 (1931): 690.
34 "The Summer Term," *Normal Eyte* 7, no. 33 (1898): 8; *Maryland State Normal School 1927*, 4–5.
35 "Summer Term Program Ready," 1; "Wesley M. Gewehr to Give Address," *College Eye* 17, no. 11 (1925): 1; "Noted Astronomer to Give Lecture," *College Eye* 17, no. 8 (1925): 1; "Big Sioux Chief Redfox Will Appear," *College Eye* 17, no. 6 (1925): 1.
36 Avent, *Summer Sessions*, 105; "Class Schedules for Summer Session 1926," 5–6.
37 "School Play Will Be Repeated," *College Eye* 1, no. 12 (1911): 4; "Preliminary Announcement: 1930," n.p.; "Summer Term Program Ready," 1; "1932 Summer School Announcement," 4; Avent, *Summer Sessions*, 104; "Devereux Players Here Next Week," *College Eye* 17, no. 2 (1925): 1; "Will Present Skits on June 22, 23," *College Eye* 29, no. 35 (1938): 1.
38 "In Concert Friday," *College Eye* 17, no. 1 (1925): 2; "E. Harold Geer, Organist at Vassar," *College Eye* 17, no. 4 (1925): 1; "Singers Have Fine Personalities," *College Eye* 17, no. 7 (1925): 1; "Cedar Falls Concert Band to Play Friday," *College Eye* 17, no. 2 (1925): 1; "Preliminary Announcement: 1930," n.p.; "1932 Summer School Announcement," 4.
39 Dresselhouse Diary, 1928, July 10, 12, and 25.
40 "Summer Term," 22; Avent, *Summer Sessions*, 104; *Maryland State Normal School 1927*, 4; "Members of Musical Organizations Selected," *College and Campus: Iowa State Teachers College* 1, no. 3 (1926): 1; "Class Schedules for Summer Session 1926," 6; *The Maryland State Normal School at Towson, Maryland: Summer Session Announcement 1928*, 5–6, TUSC.

41 "Summer Session," *State Normal Monthly* (Emporia, KS) 11, no. 7 (1899): 7; Avent, *Summer Sessions*, 104; "Ball Fans Will Soon See League," *College Eye* 17, no. 3 (1925): 1; "Track and Field Men," *College Eye* 16, no. 6 (1925): 1; "Tennis Tournament," *College Eye* 17, no. 3 (1925): 1; "Summer Session Activity," *College Eye* 26, no. 1 (1934): 1; "Y. W. Hikes on Saturday Morning," *College Eye* 17, no. 4 (1925): 1; Dresselhouse Diary, 1928, June 28, July 30.

42 Avent, *Summer Sessions*, 73, 72.

43 Dresselhouse Diary, 1928; Pogue, *Swift Seasons*, 82; Cramer, memoir and diary.

44 W. E. B. Du Bois, *The Souls of Black Folk* (Boston: Bedford Books, 1997), 73, 75–76, 95; Michael Fultz, "Determination and Persistence: Building the African American Teacher Corps Through Summer and Intermittent Teaching, 1860s–1890s," *History of Education Quarterly* 61, no. 1 (2021): 4–7. As late as 1905, the Fisk catalog stated, "Students who are sufficiently advanced in scholarship earn money by teaching public schools during vacation, and at other times, thus doing good to others while benefiting themselves." *Catalogue of the Officers and Students of Fisk University, 1904–1905* (Nashville, 1905), 20.

45 Bobby L. Lovett, *America's Historically Black Colleges & Universities: A Narrative History* (Macon, GA: Mercer University Press, 2015), 22; Joe M. Richardson, *A History of Fisk University, 1865–1946* (Tuscaloosa: University of Alabama Press, 1980), 13; Michael Fultz, "Teacher Training and African American Education in the South, 1900–1940," *Journal of Negro Education* 64, no. 2 (1995): 201–202.

46 Joseph D. Caver, *From Marion to Montgomery: The Early Years of Alabama State University, 1867–1925* (Montgomery, AL: New South Books, 2020), 95, 116, 146.

47 "The Summer School of Methods," *Southern Workman* 38, no. 8 (1899): 283–285; Kathleen Weiler, *Maria Baldwin's World: A Story of Black New England and the Fight for Racial Justice* (Amherst: University of Massachusetts Press, 2019), 2, 5, 48, 79–80, 135–136.

48 *Thirty-Second Annual Catalogue of Lincoln Institute, Jefferson City, Mo., 1903–1904*, 26, LUA; William Sherman Savage, *The History of Lincoln University* (Jefferson City, MO: Lincoln University, 1939), 29, 35, 61, 97; Lincoln Institute/University catalogs and bulletins, LUA.

49 Caver, *From Marion to Montgomery*, 164, 217, 222, 196; Tuskegee Institute ad, *Bulletin* 6, no. 1 (1926): 31, NEA1007.RG, Box 3044, RNEA; Fisk University ad, *National Note-Book Quarterly: Official Organ of the National Association of Teachers in Colored Schools* 2, no. 2 (1920): n.p., NEA1007.RG, Box 3044, RNEA; Ambrose Caliver, *Education of Negro Teachers, U.S. Office of Education Bulletin*, no. 10 (Washington, DC: U.S. Government Printing Office, 1933), 92.

50 Jarvis R. Givens, *Fugitive Pedagogy: Carter G. Woodson and the Art of Black Teaching* (Cambridge, MA: Harvard University Press, 2021).

51 Lovett, *America's Historically Black Colleges*, 67; Fultz, "Teacher Training," 202, 204.

52 Caver, *From Marion to Montgomery*, 205; Savage, *History of Lincoln*, 120, 174; *Thirty-Third Annual Catalogue of Lincoln Institute, Jefferson City, Mo., 1904–1905*, 66, LUA; *Lincoln University Summer School Bulletin, June 15 to August 6, 1925*, 2, LUA; Morehouse-Spelman ad, *Bulletin* 9, no. 7 (1929): 29, NEA1007.RG, Box 3044, RNEA.

53 Fultz, "Teacher Training," 202; Aaron D. Purcell, "'The Greatest Event Since the Civil War': Progressivism and the Summer School of the South at the University of Tennessee," *Journal of East Tennessee History* 76 (2004): 20; *Thirty-Second 1903–1904*, 27; *Thirty-Fourth Annual Catalog of Lincoln Institute, Jefferson City, MO, 1905–1906*, 19, LUA; *Lincoln University 1925*, 2–5; *Lincoln University Bulletin:*

Summer Session, June 8 to August 12, 1932, 11–16, LUA; *Bulletin of Lincoln Institute Department of Education, March, 1921*, 17, LUA.

54 Fisk University ad (1920); Tuskegee Institute ad, *Bulletin* 2, no. 2 (1923): n.p., NEA1007.RG, Box 3044, RNEA.

55 *Lincoln University 1925*, 1, 3; *Lincoln University 1932*, 4; *Bulletin of Lincoln University: Summer School Bulletin, June 9 to August 4, 1926*, 3–4, LUA; *Lincoln University Bulletin: Summer Session, June 6 to August 10, 1934*, 26, LUA; *Bulletin of Lincoln University: Summer School Bulletin, June 7 to August 3, 1927*, 3, LUA; *Lincoln University Bulletin: General Announcements for Summer Session June 15 to August 7, 1936*, 8, LUA.

56 *Lincoln University Bulletin 1936*, 7–8; Fisk University ad, *Bulletin* 9, no. 7 (1929): 29, NEA1007.RG, Box 3044, RNEA.

57 Septima Poinsette Clark and LeGette Blythe, *Echo in My Soul* (New York: E. P. Dutton & Co., 1962), 26–27, 83–84, 86, 90; Katherine Mellen Charron, *Freedom's Teacher: The Life of Septima Clark* (Chapel Hill: University of North Carolina Press, 2009), 137.

58 John C. Wright, "Summer Schools and Professional Development," *Bulletin* 9, no. 6 (1929): 5, https://curiosity.lib.harvard.edu/black-teacher-archive; Savage, *History of Lincoln*, 109; *Thirty-Third 1904–1905*, 17; *Thirty-Eighth Annual Catalog of Lincoln Institute, Jefferson City, MO, 1909–1910*, 29, LUA; *Forty-Seventh Annual Catalog of Lincoln Institute, Jefferson City, MO, 1918–1919*, 18, LUA; Fisk University ad (1920).

59 *Bulletin of Lincoln University 1926*, 4–5; Fisk University ad (1929); *Lincoln University Bulletin 1936*, 14–20.

60 Wright, "Summer Schools," 6, 18; *Lincoln University Bulletin 1936*, 20, 17; *Bulletin of Lincoln University 1926*, 4; *Lincoln University 1932*, 14, LUA; *Lincoln University 1934*, 28; *The Lincoln University Bulletin: The Summer Session, June 12 to August 4, 1939*, 19, LUA; Givens, *Fugitive Pedagogy*, 90–91, 186.

61 *Thirty-Second 1903–1904*, 27; *Lincoln University 1925*, 2; *Lincoln University 1934*, 10.

62 Purcell, "'Greatest Event,'" 20; Caver, *From Marion to Montgomery*, 190, 192, 217; Arthur A. Schomburg, "Excerpt from 'Racial Integrity: A Plea,'" in *The Afro-Latin@ Reader: History and Culture in the United States*, ed. Román, Miriam Jiménez, and Juan Flores (Durham, NC: Duke University Press, 2010), 68; Givens, *Fugitive Pedagogy*, 64.

63 Savage, *History of Lincoln*, 113; *Thirty-Fourth 1905–1906*, 19; *Lincoln University 1925*, 2; *Lincoln University 1932*, 5; Wright, "Summer Schools," 5.

64 Adam Fairclough, *A Class of Their Own: Black Teachers in the Segregated South* (Cambridge, MA: Belknap Press of Harvard University Press, 2007), 321; Givens, *Fugitive Pedagogy*, 161.

65 *Thirty-Second 1903–1904*, 26; *Bulletin of Lincoln University 1927*, 6; *Lincoln University 1925*, 2; *Lincoln University Bulletin 1936*, 10.

66 Margaret Haley's Unpublished Autobiography, 1935 Version, Chicago Teachers' Federation Papers, Box 33, Folder 4, Chicago History Museum, Chicago; Robert Reid, ed., *Battleground: The Autobiography of Margaret A. Haley* (Urbana: University of Illinois Press, 1982), 27; Rousmaniere, *Citizen Teacher*, 40.

67 N. Henry Black, "The Harvard Summer School," *Harvard Alumni Bulletin* 35, no. 30 (1933): 835; Walters, "On the Summer-School Campus," 62; Elsbree, *American Teacher*, 367–370; *Annual Reports of the President and Treasurer of Harvard College, 1875–76* (Cambridge, MA, 1877), 32; Merle Curti and Vernon Carstensen, *The University of Wisconsin: A History, 1848–1925* (Madison: University of Wisconsin Press, 1949), Vol. 1, 547, 735.

68 Paul H. Hanus, *Adventuring in Education* (Cambridge, MA: Harvard University Press, 1937), 108, 132.

69 Forest Chester Ensign, *The First Century of Teacher Training in the State University of Iowa* (Iowa City: State University of Iowa Centennial Study, 1947), 65–68; *Calendar of the State University of Iowa, 1899–1900* (Iowa City: University of Iowa, 1900), 123, UISCA.

70 Elsbree, *American Teacher*, 373; Clifford and Guthrie, *Ed School*, 134; Cremin et al., *History of Teachers College*, 67–68; Henry C. Johnson and Erwin V. Johanningmeier, *Teachers for the Prairie: The University of Illinois and the Schools, 1868–1945* (Urbana: University of Illinois Press, 1972), 77, 103; Curti and Carstensen, *University of Wisconsin*, Vol. 2, 758; W. H. Pool, "Summer Schools in Texas," *TSJ* 15, no. 4 (1897): 153–154; "University Summer School and State School of Methods," *TSJ* 16, no. 2 (1898): 44; J. A. Burns and Bernard J. Kohlbrenner, *A History of Catholic Education in the United States* (New York: Benziger Brothers, 1937), 223–224.

71 Morningside College ad, *Midland Schools* 35, no. 6 (1921): 194; Coe College ad, *Midland Schools* 35, no. 7 (1921): 245; Iowa Wesleyan ad, *Midland Schools* 36, no. 8 (1922): 292; Walters, "On the Summer-School Campus," 61.

72 "Constitution of the Association of Summer School Directors" (1925) and "Summer Session Directors—1930," in *Summary of Reports of the Association of Summer School Directors, 1930*," Box 11, HUSS; Walters, "America's Summer School Army," 197; Ellen Condliffe Lagemann, *The Elusive Science: The Troubling History of Education Research* (Chicago: University of Chicago Press, 2000), 31.

73 Cremin et al., *History of Teachers College*, 70; Curti and Carstensen, *University of Wisconsin*, Vol. 1, 731; Hanus, *Adventuring*, 132. Eisenmann writes that at Penn State "involvement with teacher education had been mild before 1910," when summer sessions began and attracted large numbers of students. Eisenmann, "Influence," 300. See also Allison, *Teachers for the South*; and Powell, *Uncertain Profession*.

74 Levine explains that, especially by the 1920s and 1930s, "major state universities attempted to emulate the elite institutions of the private sector," and "both types of institutions catered generally to young people from the middle and upper classes." David O. Levine, *The American College and the Culture of Aspiration, 1915–1940* (Ithaca, NY: Cornell University Press, 1986), 162.

75 "Pittsburg [*sic*] Teachers Vacation," *Chautauquan Weekly* 4, no. 44 (1910): 2–3, CIA; "Pittsburg [*sic*] Scholarships," *Chautauquan Weekly* 5, no. 45 (1911): 5. Twelve of the 1911 scholarship winners who had attended Harvard Summer School expressed their gratitude by forming a club to raise money for community organizations and college scholarships. Over six decades, the Phoebe Brashear Club provided more than four hundred scholarships for graduates of Pittsburgh high schools. PRPSEA, *Bicentennial Pennsylvania*, 277.

76 "Large Summer School," *PSJ* 62, no. 3 (1913): 133–134; *Minutes of the Thirteenth Annual Meeting of the Association of Deans and Directors of Summer Sessions . . . 1930*, 99, Box 11, HUSS.

77 P. P. Claxton to Knoxville Board of Trade, September 23, 1907, Reports of the Superintendent, Box 1, Series 1, Folder 6, SSSUT; P. P. Claxton to J. W. Brister, May 11, 1911, Superintendent Correspondence, Box 8, Series 2, Folder 6, SSSUT; P. P. Claxton to Board of Trustees of SSS, May 2, 1911, Reports of the Superintendent, Box 1, Series 1, Folder 6, SSSUT; "Summer School of the South, 1912," *University of Tennessee Record* 15, no. 2 (1912): 7, Box 17, PPCUT; Philip P. Chase to W. C. Saeger, July 8, 1929, Box 1, Folder: "Remission of Tuition Fees, 1929," HUSS.

78 *Summer School of the South*, booklet (1908), Box 13, Series 5, Folder 1, SSSUT; Philander Claxton to Wallace Buttrick, October 11, 1905, Superintendent Correspondence, Box 8, Series 2, Folder 1, SSSUT; Allison, *Teachers for the South*, 81; Philander Claxton to Houghton Mifflin Company and Philander Claxton to Macmillan Company, May 5, 1911, Superintendent Correspondence, Box 8, Series 2, Folder 6, SSSUT; E. P. Lane, "Reveries of an Idler," *Summer School Spectator* 1, no. 3 (1909), Box 1, Series 1, Folder 2, SSSUT.

79 University of Texas ad, *TSJ* 24, no. 7 (1907): n.p.; *Catalogue of the State University of Iowa, 1900–01* (1900), 125, UISCA; "Report by Dr. W. S. Herzog," *PSJ* 65, no. 9 (1917): 391; Ruediger, *Agencies*, 48; *Summary of Reports of the Association of Summer School Directors 1928*, Box 1, UISSR; *Minutes of the Fourteenth Annual Meeting of the Association of Deans and Directors of Summer Sessions . . . 1931*, 39, 44, Box 11, HUSS.

80 University of Chicago ad, *TSJ* 21 (1903–1904), n.p.; Slosson quoted in John W. Boyer, *The University of Chicago: A History* (Chicago: University of Chicago Press, 2015), 93; "Notes from the State University," *TSJ* 21, no. 8 (1904): 926; "The Summer School of Arts and Sciences: Brief Announcement" (1905), HUSS.

81 Emily L. Morley to Prof. Chas. Ferris, March 14, 1903; Hattie R. Kent to Prof. Ferris, April 13, 1903; Hattie R. Kent to Chas. E. Ferris, May 12, 1903; Hattie R. Kent to Prof. Chas. Ferris, May 14, 1903; SSS to Hattie R. Kent, May 21, 1903; H.R.K. to Prof. Chas. Ferris, May 22, 1903; C. V. Neuffer to Prof. Chas. Ferris, June?, 1903; and SSS to C. V. Neuffer, June 5, 1903, Student Employment Materials and Correspondence, Box 1, Series 2, Folders 19–23, SSSUT.

82 "Dean Places 15 Women," *Daily Iowan* 30, no. 206 (1922): 1; *Summer Session Catalogue Number 1939* (Iowa City: University of Iowa, 1939), 17, UISCA; "Around the Yard," *Harvard Summer School News* 2, no. 6 (1938): 2, HUSS.

83 Purcell, "Greatest Event,'" 13–14; *Calendar 1899–1900*, 125; "Summer Session, 1914," *Bulletin of the State University of Iowa* 74 (April 18, 1914): 8–9, UISCA; "Summer Session, 1928," *Bulletin of the State University of Iowa* 444 (March 3, 1928): 8, UISCA; Black, "Harvard Summer School," 837; "Summer Session Announcement, 1921," *Columbia University Bulletin of Information* (New York: Columbia University, 1921): 16–18, TCDC.

84 Tim Brady, "Paradise on Mendota," *On Wisconsin* 121, no. 2 (2020): 46–51; E. David Cronin and John W. Jenkins, *The University of Wisconsin: A History, 1925–1945* (Madison: University of Wisconsin Press, 1994), 759–760; *University of Iowa Summer Camp, 1928* (brochure) in *Summer Session Report 1928*, *University of Iowa Summer Camp, 1929* (brochure) in *Summer Session Report 1929*, and *Summer Session Report 1930*, 78–96, Box 6, UISSR.

85 Allison, *Teachers for the South*, 40, 78; Purcell, "'Greatest Event,'" 16; "The Pennsylvania State College Summer Session of 1922," *PSJ* 71, no. 6 (1923): 268. On the backlash against women students, see Barbara Miller Solomon, *In the Company of Educated Women* (New Haven, CT: Yale University Press, 1985), 58–60; and Lynn D. Gordon, *Gender and Higher Education in the Progressive Era* (New Haven, CT: Yale University Press, 1990), 43–44.

86 Allison, *Teachers for the South*, 79; Purcell, "'Greatest Event,'" 16; "List of Topics Suggested for Discussion," 1929, NASSD documents, Box 11, HUSS.

87 Clifford and Guthrie, *Ed School*, 134; *Directory of Summer Session Students, 1913* (New York: Columbia University, August 1, 1913), 120, TCDC; Sarah Manekin, "Gender, Markets, and the Expansion of Women's Education at the University of Pennsylvania, 1913–1940," *History of Education Quarterly* 50, no. 3 (2010);

University of Pennsylvania ad, *PSJ* 73, no. 10 (1925): 585; Press releases, March 21, 1931, and July 1–2, 1933, Box 1, Folder: "Newspaper Publicity," HUSS; Powell, *Uncertain Profession*, 137.

88 "News and Notes," *TSJ* 22, no. 12 (1905): 604; *Minutes of the Thirteenth Annual Meeting 1930*, 39; Clark, *Echo*, 84; "Patricia M. Ewell," *Bulletin* 11, no. 9 (1931): 1, https://curiosity.lib.harvard.edu/black-teacher-archive; Amato Nocera, "'May We Not Write Our Own Fairy Tales and Make Black Beautiful?': African American Teachers, Children's Literature, and the Construction of Race in the Curriculum, 1920–1945," *History of Education Quarterly* 63, no. 1 (2023): 49–50.

89 Linda M. Perkins, "The History of Women Black Graduate Students, 1921–1948," in *The SAGE Handbook of African American Education*, ed. Linda C. Tillman (SAGE Publications, 2009), 52–65; *Minutes of the Thirteenth Annual Meeting 1930*, 39; Edgar W. Knight, "It's the People We Meet," *Outlook and Independent* 152 (May 1–August 28, 1929): 373.

90 Walters, "On the Summer-School Campus," 64, 60; Knight, "It's the People," 372–373; *Report of the Resolutions Committee* in *Summer Session Report 1930*.

91 Knight, "It's the People," 372; Walters, "On the Summer-School Campus," 64; "News and Notes," *TSJ* 23, no. 8 (1906): 36.

92 "Summer School of the South," *University of Tennessee Record* 4–19 (1903–1916), Box 17, PPCUT; *Summer School of the South* (booklet, 1908), Box 13, Series 5, Folder 1, SSSUT; P. P. Claxton, "Summer School of the South (In Retrospect)," *Teacher-Education Journal* 3, no. 3 (1941): 137.

93 "Notice," *INM* 25, no. 10 (1902): 495; "English for Teachers," *Daily Iowan* 2, no. 62 (1903): 1; "Summer Session Prospects," *Daily Iowan* 7, no. 171 (1908): 3; *1905 Summer School of Arts and Sciences* (flyer), HUSS; "News and Notes," *TSJ* 22, no. 9 (1905): 451.

94 "Prominent Men to Lecture," *Summer School News* 1, no. 1 (1914): 8, Box 13, Series 5, Folder 6, SSSUT; G. Stanley Hall to SSS, March 12, 1908, Box 20, PPCUT; Secretary to Josephine I. Kendall, May 29, 1912, Box 1, Series 2, Folder 25, SSSUT; "Psychology II—Dr. Thorndike," Box 19, PPCUT; Scrapbook of newspaper clippings, 1904, Box 12, Series 5, SSSUT; B. C. Gregory to P. P. Claxton, March 13, 1908, Box 20, PPCUT.

95 "Summer Session Courses in Teachers College, 1910"; "Summer Session Announcement, 1912," *Columbia University Bulletin of Information*; "Teachers College Preliminary Announcement, Summer Session," 1914, 1915, 1916, and 1920; and Ellwood P. Cubberley to James E. Russell, October 7, 1914, TCDC.

96 "School Registers 1,977 Students," *Harvard Summer School News* 3, no. 2 (1939): 2, HUSS; "News and Notes," *TSJ* 22, no. 1 (1904): 22; "Summer School of the South, 1906," *University of Tennessee Record* 9, no. 1 (1906): 4, Box 17, PPCUT; "Summer Session, 1914," 2; Ensign, *First Century*, 170, 241; "Large Summer School," 134; *Proceedings of the Meeting of the Association of Summer School Directors 1927*, 10, Box 10, HUSS; "Summer Session Announcement, 1912," 24; "The Demonstration School—Summer Session, 1916," TCDC.

97 Septima Clark, *Ready from Within: Septima Clark and the Civil Rights Movement* (Navarro, CA: Wild Trees Press, 1986), 115; Cramer, memoir and diary.

98 Boyer, *University of Chicago*, 93–94; "Summer Session Announcement, 1912"; *Minutes of the Thirteenth Annual Meeting 1930*, 81–84.

99 Obituary and grade report, Margarete Bohle Papers, Box 1, WHSA.

100 Curti and Carstensen, *University of Wisconsin*, Vol. 1, 642; "Summer School of Arts and Sciences: Brief Announcement"; "New Summer School Work," *Boston*

Transcript, April 6, 1917 (clipping), Box 3, Folder: Advertising, HUSS; "School Registers 1,977 Students," 2; "Summer School of the South, 1906," 11, 29; "Summer School of the South, 1910," *University of Tennessee Record* 13, no. 1 (1910): 17, 35–36, Box 17, PPCUT; "An Institute for English Education at Penn State," *PSJ* 74, no. 8 (1926): 523; Lena Beatrice Morton, *My First Sixty Years: Passion for Wisdom* (New York: Philosophical Library, 1965), 38, 102.

101 "Summer Session, 1917," *Bulletin of the State University of Iowa* 126 (March 1, 1917): 3, UISCA; "The Lehigh University," *PSJ* 73, no. 8 (1925): 485; University of Minnesota ad, *Midland Schools* 35, no. 8 (1921): 276; New York University ad, *JNEA* 14, no. 5 (1925): A-135; *Calendar 1899–1900*, 128; *The State University of Iowa Calendar, 1901–1902* (1902), 253, UISCA; "The Summer Session of 1918," *Bulletin of the State University of Iowa* 144 (April 1, 1918): 28–29, UISCA; *Summer Session News* (1920), 4, Box 5, UISSR; "Summer Session 1923," *Bulletin of the State University of Iowa* 242 (February 15, 1923): 28, UISCA.

102 Cornell University ad, *Intelligence* 20, no. 6 (1900): 234; Conrad G. Selvig, *A Tale of Two Valleys* (Los Angeles: Grover Jones Press, 1951), 39–40, 49; J. H. Voris to Eva Lewis, July 10, 1900, Box 4, Folder 80, LFP; "Summer School of Arts and Sciences: Brief Announcement"; *Calendar 1899–1900*, 130–132, 124.

103 McK., "Summer School of the South"; "Summer School of the South, 1903," *University of Tennessee Record* 6, no. 4 (1903): 710, 24, Box 17, PPCUT; A. H. Patterson to P. P. Claxton, March 9, 1908, Box 20, PPCUT.

104 Wythe went on to complete medical school and return to serve as a doctor in the Oakland schools. Margaret Wythe, "Personal Experiences in Education," in *Yes, I'm a Pioneer Teacher: The Fifth Historical Year Book of the California Retired Teachers' Association*, ed. Laura Esta Settle (California Retired Teachers Association, 1938), 45–52; Clark, *Ready from Within*, 115.

105 *Intercollegiate Field Course* (flyer), HUSS; "Educational News and Notes," *School and Society* 5, no. 122 (1917): 496; "Excursions to Coal Mines Tomorrow," *Summer School Spectator* 1, no. 6 (1909): 4, Box 1, Series 1, Folder 2, SSSUT; "Dr. Holdsworth's Classes," *Summer School Spectator* 2, no. 8 (1910): 2, Box 13, Series 5, Folder 5, SSSUT; *Summer School News* 1, no. 8 (1914): 8; University of Wyoming ad, *Midland Schools* 38, no. 7 (1924): 270.

106 Lillian Herrick, letters to family, June 28–August 22, 1900, Box 12, HFP.

107 Thomas H. Macbride, "The Okoboji Lakeside Laboratory," *Proceedings of Iowa Academy of Science* 16 1909), 132–133; and "Iowa Lakeside Laboratory (Twenty-Fifth Year)," Iowa Lakeside Laboratory Papers, Box 10, UISCA; Frederick J. Lazeld, "Impressions of Lakeside Laboratories," *Iowa Alumnus* 9, no. 2 (1911): 34; Maude Brown, "Iowa Lakeside Laboratory as a Student Sees It," *Okoboji Protective Association Bulletin* 5 (1910): 11–13. See also Debby Zieglowsky, "Thomas Macbride's Dream: Iowa Lakeside Laboratory," *Palimpsest* 66, no. 2 (1985): 42–56, 61–65; and Michael J. Lannoo, *Iowa Lakeside Laboratory: A Century of Discovering the Nature of Nature* (Iowa City: University of Iowa Press, 2012).

108 "Summer School of Arts and Sciences: Brief Announcement"; "Summer School of the South, 1906," 26–27; *Iowa Calendar, 1901–1902*, 250; A. U. Crull to Eva Lewis, July 28, 1899, and August 9, 1900, Box 4, Folder 78, LFP.

109 Alexander Fite letter, July 24, 1918, Box 66, and Mary Lockwood to Aunts, August 22, 1922, Box 69, SLFP; Samuel N. Baker, "Some Impressions of the Middlebury Summer School of Spanish," *Bulletin of High Points in the Work of the High Schools of New York City* 4, no. 3 (1922): 35–36; 'Teachers Learn to Speak French," *Summer Session News* (1920), 1.

110 University of Chicago ad, *TSJ* 21 (1903–1904), n.p.; "The University of Texas Summer Schools for 1903," *TSJ* 20, no. 8 (1903): 422; "University Notes," *TSJ* 21, no. 10 (1904): 1028; "Summer School of the South, 1914," *University of Tennessee Record* 17, no. 1 (1914): 9–10, Box 17, PPCUT; Weekly calendars, 1924, Box 5, UISSR; *Summer Session Report 1939*, Box 9, UISSR; *Campus Forums, 1937* (brochure) in *Summer Session Report 1937*, Box 8, UISSR; *Campus Forums, 1938* (brochure) in *Summer Session Report 1938*, Box 9, UISSR; "Thought and Action in Platform Balance," *Harvard Summer School News* 2, no. 4 (1938): 1; "Harvard Astronomers to Hold 'Open House,'" *Harvard Summer School News* 2, no. 1 (1938): 6.

111 Claxton, "Summer School of the South," 137–138; "Summer Session Announcement, 1917," *Columbia University Bulletin of Information* (March 3, 1917), 12–13, TCDC; *Summer Session Report 1928*, Box 6, UISSR; "Puccini Opera First Federal Music Project," *Harvard Summer School News* 1, no. 2 (1937): 1; "Coolidge Quartet, Symphony Concert," *Harvard Summer School News* 2, no. 2 (1938): 4; "Music This Week," *Harvard Summer School News* 1, no. 6 (1937): 1.

112 Editorial page, *Summer School Spectator* 2, no. 9 (1910): 2, Box 13, Series 5, Folder 5, SSSUT; "Summer Session Announcement, 1917," 13; *Summer Session Report 1933*, Box 7, UISSR; *Summer Session Report 1936*, Box 8, UISSR; "Social Union," *Harvard Summer School News* 1, no. 1 (1937): 1; "Three Major Social Events This Week," *Harvard Summer School News* 1, no. 3 (1937): 1; "Moliere's 'Le Medecin' Tuesday Movie," *Harvard Summer School News* 2, no. 1 (1938): 6.

113 "Harvard Summer School," *INM* 20, no. 10 (1897), 423; "News and Notes," *TSJ* 23, no. 1 (1905): 33; *Summer Session Report 1930*, 69–71; *Summer Session Report 1934*, 64–66, Box 8, UISSR; Frederick Hicks to P. P. Claxton, March 12, 1908, Box 20, PPCUT; *Report of the Summer School of the South, 1904*, Reports of the Superintendent, Box 1, Series 1, Folder 6, SSSUT; "A Sane and Salutary Fourth," *Summer School Spectator* 3, no. 1 (1911): 4, Box 13, Series 5, Folder 5, SSSUT; "Summer Session Announcement, 1923," *Columbia University Bulletin of Information*, 20–23, TCDC; Southern Club programs, Personal Papers of Dr. Earle T. Hawkins, Box 4, TUSC.

114 Cremin et al., *History of Teachers College*, 118–119; "Summer Session Announcement, 1912," 14–15, 27–29; "Summer Session Announcement, 1917," 14–16; "Summer Session Announcement, 1923," 18–20; Nocera, "'May We Not Write,'" 50–51.

115 "Harvard Summer School," 423; Louise Mackierman to Florence Abbott, June 28, 1933, and George Miller to Newton Black, August 2, 1932, Box 7, Folder: "Extracurricular, 1929–1933," HUSS; "The Asheville Trip," *Summer School Spectator* 1, no. 4 (1909): 2; and "Mammoth Cave Excursion," *Summer School Spectator* 1, no. 6 (1909): 1, Box 1, Series 1, Folder 2, SSSUT; "Society and Personals," *Summer School News* 1, no. 5 (1914): 5; "The Amana Colonies" and "60 Students Go to Amana," *Daily Iowan* 11, no. 206 (1922): 2, 4; *Summer Session Report 1927*, 6–7, Box 6, UISSR; *Summer Session Report 1934*, 93.

116 "Col. C. H. French," *Summer School Spectator* 1, no. 2 (1909): 2, Box 1, Series 1, Folder 2, SSSUT; "Paris," *Summer School Spectator* 2, no. 8 (1910): 1, Box 13, Series 5, Folder 5, SSSUT; "To Give Speech," *Daily Iowan* 12, no. 9 (1930): 1; Weekly calendars, 1924; "What Is Happening in Spain" and "Soviet Russia Today," *Harvard Summer School News* 1, no. 3 (July 1937): 1; "Problems of Central Europe," *Harvard Summer School News* 1, no. 4 (1937): 1; "Talks on China," *Harvard Summer School News* 3, no. 5 (1939): 4.

117 "Dr. Hall Concludes His Work," scrapbook of newspaper clippings, 1904; "Declaration of Principles, 1907," Box 1, Series 1, Folder 1, SSSUT; "Southern Branch of the American School Peace League Organized" and "Peace League," *Summer School*

Spectator 1, no. 5 (1909): 1, 2, Box 1, Series 1, Folder 2, SSSUT; "The Woman of the Twentieth Century," Box 19, PPCUT; "Interracial Meeting—Summer Session 1929," TCDC; Knight, "It's the People," 373.

118 *Summer School of the South, 1903*, 8; *Proceedings of the Meeting of the Association of Summer School Directors . . . 1928*, 21, Box 10, HUSS; Hanus, *Adventuring*, 149.

119 "The University of Texas Summer Schools for 1903," *TSJ* 20, no. 8 (1903): 422; "University Notes," *TSJ* 21, no. 10 (1904): 1028–1029; *Iowa Calendar, 1901–1902*, 246; "Round Table on Friday Night," *Summer School News* 1, no. 3 (1914): 2; "Campus Forums, 1937"; *Summer School of the South, 1904*, 1; "Summer School Down to Work," scrapbook of newspaper clippings, 1904; "New Features of School This Year," *Summer School News* 1, no. 4 (1914): 2; *Summer Session 1912* (University of Iowa, 1912), 5–6, UISCA; *Summer Session Report 1937*; "Wellesley President First Lecture Speaker," *Harvard Summer School News* 1, no. 1 (1937): 1; "Six Men at Harvard," *Harvard Summer School News* 1, no. 2 (1937): 1; "American School Teachers Timid," *Harvard Summer School News* 1, no. 4 (1937): 1; "How to Save Democracy," *Harvard Summer School News* 3, no. 5 (1930): 4; "Dr. Jones Lectures," *Summer School Spectator* 2, no. 6 (1910): 3, Box 13, Series 5, Folder 3, SSSUT; "Sane and Salutary Fourth," 4.

120 "Declaration of Principles," 1902, Box 1, Series 1, Folder 1, SSSUT; "State Delegations Outrival Celebrations of Previous Years," *Summer School News* 1, no. 5 (1914): 2–3.

121 *Proceedings of the Meeting 1927*, 16; "Basketball Played at Men's Gymnasium" and "Manaugh Is Champion in Tennis Tournament," *Daily Iowan* 4, no. 182 (1920): 4; "Lawn tennis . . . ," scrapbook of newspaper clippings, 1904; "Tennis Tournament," *Summer School News* 1, no. 7 (1914): 7; "Annual Regatta," *Harvard Summer School News* 1, no. 5 (1937): 4.

122 "Three Major Social Events," *Harvard Summer School News* 1, no. 3 (1937): 1, 4; "Boat Ride: Outing on the Tennessee River," *Summer School Spectator* 2, no. 1 (1910): 2, Box 13, Series 5, Folder 3, SSSUT; "Summer Students Have Good Times Outside Classes," *Summer Session News* (1920), 1; Cramer, memoir and diary; Invitation (1905), HUSS; "Dr. Dewey Completes His Course," scrapbook of newspaper clippings, 1904; *Summer Session Report 1930*, 121–122; *Summer Session Report 1939*, 96; "Reception Tonight," *Harvard Summer School News* 1, no. 2 (1937): 1.

123 Lane, "Reveries of an Idler," 1.

124 Walters, "On the Summer-School Campus," 63; Cronin and Jenkins, *University of Wisconsin*, 758–759; Ensign, *First Century*, 283.

125 *Proceedings of the Meeting 1927*, 16; Southern Club programs; "Tea for Teachers," *Harvard Summer School News* 1, no. 6 (1937): 4; *Summer Session Report 1930*, 122; Knight, "It's the People," 372.

126 Daniel W. Lewis Collection; "1928 Summer Session Enrollments," *PSJ* 77, no. 1 (1928): 50; "Smith Family Sets Attendance Record," *College Eye* 27, no. 53 (1935): 1; Turpin, Clarence Lillard, Alumni Vertical Files, LUA; Lucile H. Bluford, "The Lloyd Gaines Story," *Journal of Educational Sociology* 32, no. 6 (1959): 243; Alice Duffy Rinehart, *Mortals in the Immortal Profession: An Oral History of Teaching* (New York: Irvington Publishers, 1983), 84–85; Powell, *Uncertain Profession*, 137.

Chapter 3 Work for Family, for Supplemental Income, and for an Exit Strategy

1 Gertrude Black La Due Diaries, July 6–July 23, 1901, Gertrude Black La Due and Family Papers, Box, 1, MHS.

2 National Education Association (NEA), *Report of the Committee on Teachers' Salaries and Cost of Living* (Ann Arbor, MI: NEA, 1913), 233; Merle Janice Schroeder Papers, Boxes 1–2, Manuscript Collections, YNPA; Herbert T. Lystrop, "In Retrospect—1949," *Yellowstone Nature Notes* 23, no. 6 (1949): 62–64, NPSHC; Carol Green Wilson, *Alice Eastwood's Wonderland: The Adventures of a Botanist* (San Francisco: California Academy of Sciences, 1955), 15–29.

3 On professionalization, see Diana D'Amico Pawlewicz, *Blaming Teachers: Professionalization Policies and the Failure of Reform in American History* (New Brunswick, NJ: Rutgers University Press, 2020).

4 NEA, *Report*, 240; "How Shall I Spend Vacation?," *TSJ* 8, no. 5 (1890): 117.

5 "What Shall We Do with the Long Vacation?," *INM* 1, no. 12 (1878): 361; Doris Hinson Pieroth, *Seattle's Women Teachers of the Interwar Years: Shapers of a Livable City* (Seattle: University of Washington Press, 2004), 161–163.

6 "Teachers' Vacations," *Midland Schools* 25, no. 10 (1911): 291; "The Vacation," *PSJ* 62, no. 12 (1914): 564; Joy Elmer Morgan, "Making the Most of the Summer," *JNEA* 24, no. 5 (1935): 135.

7 NEA, *Report*, 93–94.

8 Geraldine J. Clifford, *Those Good Gertrudes: A Social History of Women Teachers in America* (Baltimore: Johns Hopkins University Press, 2014), chap. 3 and 6; Jackie M. Blount, *Fit to Teach: Same-Sex Desire, Gender, and School Work in the Twentieth Century* (Albany; State University of New York Press, 2005), chap. 4; Adam Fairclough, *A Class of Their Own: Black Teachers in the Segregated South* (Cambridge, MA: Harvard University Press, 2007), 276.

9 Jas. W. Turner, *Half a Century in the School Room, or Personal Memories of Jas. W. Turner* (Carrier Mills, IL: Turner Publishing Company, 1920), 43, 60; B. H. Meyer Papers, June 5, 1886, August 24, 1886, WHSA.

10 Black La Due Diaries, July 5–October 1, 1901, June 2–August 29, 1902, June 27–September 20, 1903.

11 Philip Gerber, ed., *Bachelor Bess: The Homesteading Letters of Elizabeth Corey, 1909–1919* (Iowa City: University of Iowa Press, 1990), xvii–xix, xli–xlii, 130–131.

12 Amanda Stewart to "My dear Sister," June 4, 1885, Box 6; Maude Stewart to May Stewart, June 9, 1887, Box 8; May Stewart to "girls," June 7, 1892, Box 16; and J. C. Petherbridge to Amanda Stewart, June 13, 1894, Box 19, SLFP.

13 Grace Canan Pogue, *The Swift Seasons* (Hollywood, CA: Cloister Press, 1957), 31–31, 59–61, 75–83, 85–87, 153. See also Kathleen Weiler, *Country Schoolwomen: Teaching in Rural California, 1850–1950* (Stanford, CA: Stanford University Press, 1998), chap. 4.

14 Suzanne L. Bunkers, *"All Will Yet Be Well": The Diary of Sarah Gillespie Huftalen, 1873–1952* (Iowa City: University of Iowa Press, 1993), 76–77, 79, 94–95, 102–103, 107, 120, 123–124.

15 Bunkers, *"All Will Yet Be Well,"* 155, 157, 168, 171.

16 NEA, *Report*, 226–227; Lillian Herrick: diary, 1902–1905, June 14, 1904, July 28, 1904, September 12, 1904, April 11, 1906, May 4, 1906, and September 23, 1906, Box 14, HFP.

17 Lillian Herrick: diary, 1901–1902, September 1, 1901, Box 13, HFP.

18 Pieroth, *Seattle's Women Teachers*, 21; Morgan, "Making the Most," 135.

19 Herrick: diary, 1901–1902, September 11, 1901; A. J. Covert to Nellie Covert, June 26, 1895, March 30, 1900, July 4, 1900, and July 20, 1903; and Andrew Jackson Covert obituary, Nellie Penelope Covert Papers, ESUSC.

20 Fairclough, *Class of Their Own*, 4, 274.

21 NEA, *Report*, 94, 232.
22 Walker, Mr., diary, June 29–September 24, 1886, ALPL; Willard E. Givens, biographical data and transcript of interview with Paul Hopper, 1968, Office of the Executive Secretary, Box 614, RNEA.
23 "State News," *Minneapolis Tribune*, August 19, 1878, 3.
24 Black La Due Diaries, April 13, 1904, May 17, 1904, August 13, 1904.
25 Paula M. Bauman, "Single Women Homesteaders in Wyoming, 1880–1930," *Annals of Wyoming* 58, no. 1 (1986): 40–41, 44–45, 48; Cynthia Yost Andrews, "The Life of a Homesteader," in Yost, Cynthia (Andrews), Alumni Files, TUSC. On homesteading, see also Blount, *Fit to Teach*, 49.
26 Gerber, *Bachelor Bess*, 25, 87, 311–313, 355–356.
27 Gerber, *Bachelor Bess*, 195, 145–147, 189–191.
28 "What Shall We Do?," 261; Miranda Cather to Nellie Covert, June 25, 1885, Nellie Penelope Covert Papers; NEA, *Report*, 233; Septima Clark, *Ready from Within: Septima Clark and the Civil Rights Movement* (Navarro, CA: Wild Tree Press, 1986), 110; J. C. Petherbridge to Amanda Stewart, June 14, 1888, Box 10, SLFP; Herbert Evison, Oral History Interview of Lemuel A. Garrison, March 25, 1973, Oral History Materials, NPSHC.
29 Irene Krumpelmann, "1924–1926 As I Saw It," 18, and "1926–1928: School Days and Dates Anew," 9, 13, Irene Krumpelmann Papers, Box 1, MHS; Weiler, *Country Schoolwomen*, 153, 298, note 83.
30 Ruth Jacknow Markowitz, *My Daughter, the Teacher: Jewish Teachers in the New York City Schools* (New Brunswick, NJ: Rutgers University Press, 1993), 127; NEA, *Report*, 233.
31 "Teacher Attention!" ad, *TSJ* 7, no. 7 (1889): n.p.; "100 Teachers," ad, *Intelligence* 22, no. 8 (1902): 312; "Vacation Made Profitable," ad, *TSJ* 24, no. 8 (1907): 45; "Vacation This Summer," ad, *Midland Schools* 41, no. 8 (1927): 317; "How to Spend," ad, *TSJ* 22, no. 11 (1905): 556.
32 "Agents Wanted," ad, *TSJ* 14, no. 7 (1896): n.p.; "School Men Wanted," ad, *Midland Schools* 25, no. 8 (1911): 251; "Make Big Income," ad, *Midland Schools* 39, no. 5 (1925): 149; "Teachers Make More Money," ad, *TSJ* 8, no. 7 (1890): n.p.; "Make $500," ad, *PSJ* 70, no. 10 (1922): 387; "Spend a Delightful Vacation," ad, *Midland Schools* 35, no. 10 (1921): 356; Givens, biographical data and transcript.
33 "The World Book," ad, *Midland Schools* 35, no. 7 (1921): 260; "Summer Work," ad, *JNEA* 23, no. 4 (1934): A-40; "Summer Employment," ad, *JNEA* 28, no. 4 (1939): A-84; "Wanted: Women," ad, *Sierra Educational News* 19, no. 4 (1923): 228; "To Women Teachers," ad, *JNEA* 21, no. 3 (1932): A-61; "The Facts," ad, *PSJ* 78, no. 8 (1930): 513; "Pleasure and Profit in the Long Vacation," ad, *Midland Schools* 35, no. 6 (1921): 202.
34 "Spend a Profitable Summer Traveling," ad, *Midland Schools* 36, no. 6 (1922): 188.
35 Lesley Poling-Kempes, *The Harvey Girls: Women Who Opened the West* (New York: Paragon House, 1989), 40–43, 55, 75.
36 "What Are You Going to Do This Summer?," ad, *PSJ* 76, no. 11 (1928): 557; Cindy S. Aron, *Working at Play: A History of Vacations in the United States* (New York: Oxford University Press, 1999), 233.
37 Irene Krumpelmann, "More Yesterdays," 1, 8–9, Irene Krumpelmann Papers.
38 William Wallace Wylie autobiography, 1926, Merrill G. Burlingame Special Collections, Montana State University Libraries, Bozeman, MT; Elizabeth Ann Watry, "More than Mere Camps and Coaches: The Wylie Camping Company and the Development of a Middle-Class Leisure Ethic in Yellowstone National Park,

1883–1916," (master's thesis, Montana State University, 2010), guest quoted on 47–48; Jane Galloway Demaray, *Yellowstone Summers: Touring with the Wylie Camping Company in America's First National Park* (Pullman: Washington State University Press, 2015), 107; *Wylie Permanent Camping Co., Yellowstone National Park*, brochure (1910), YPNA; Aubrey L. Haines, *The Yellowstone Story: A History of Our First National Park*, Vol. 2 (Yellowstone Library and Museum Association and Colorado Associated University Press, 1977), 134–137.

39 Polly Welts Kaufman, *National Parks and the Woman's Voice: A History* (Albuquerque: University of New Mexico Press, 1996), 8; Shirley Sargent, *Pioneers in Petticoats: Yosemite's Early Women, 1856–1900* (Los Angeles: Trans-Anglo Books, 1966), 73–75.

40 Kaufman, *National Parks*, 91–92.

41 Kaufman, *National Parks*, 92; Elizabeth A. Watry, *Women in Wonderland: Lives, Legends, and Legacies of Yellowstone National Park* (Helena, MT: Riverbend Publishing, 2012), 111–116; Herbert Evison, Oral History Interview of Mrs. H. S. Sanborn, n.d., Oral History Materials, NPSHC.

42 Watry, *Women in Wonderland*, 203–209.

43 Yellowstone Park Company instructions and 1936–1939 Albums, Merle Janice Schroeder Papers, Boxes 1–2, Manuscript Collections, YNPA.

44 Kenneth Gold, *School's In: The History of Summer Education in American Public Schools* (New York: Peter Lang, 2002). Fultz explains that rural Black schools in the South met in the summer in lieu of the spring and fall through the end of the nineteenth century and that college students commonly taught in the summer sessions. See Michael Fultz, "Determination and Persistence: Building the African American Teacher Corps through Summer and Intermittent Teaching, 1860s–1890s," *History of Education Quarterly* 61, no. 1 (2021): 4–34.

45 Larry Cuban, *How Teachers Taught: Constancy and Change in American Classrooms, 1890–1990*, 2nd ed. (New York: Teachers College Press, 1993); Gold, *School's In*, 133.

46 Markowitz, *My Daughter*, 127.

47 Adolphine Fletcher Terry, *Charlotte Stephens: Little Rock's First Black Teacher* (Little Rock: Academic Press of Arkansas, 1973), 103–104.

48 Gold, *School's In*, chap. 4, 141–142, 148; Mrs. I. S. Blackwelder, "Extracts from the Last Report of the Superintendent of the Chicago Vacation Schools," *Elementary School Teacher* 5, no. 7 (1905): 433; *Third Annual Report of the City Superintendent of Schools for the Year Ending July 31, 1901* (Department of Education, City of New York, 1901), 52; "Report of Evangeline E. Whitney," *Fourth Annual Report of the City Superintendent of Schools for the Year Ending July 31, 1902* (Department of Education, City of New York, 1902), 172. See also William J. Reese, *Power and the Promise of School Reform: Grassroots Movements During the Progressive Era*, rev. ed. (New York: Teachers College Press, 2002), 131–144. On the racial and gender composition of the teaching force in New York, see D'Amico Pawlewicz, *Blaming Teachers*, 8–9.

49 Reese, *Power*, 134; *First Annual Report of the City Superintendent of Schools for the Year Ending July 31, 1899* (Department of Education, City of New York, 1899), 140; Gold, *School's In*, 126, 130–133; *Fourth Annual Report*, 65; Blackwelder, "Extracts," 432; Buffalo pledge quoted in Gold, *School's In*, 122; *Ninth Annual Report of the City Superintendent of Schools for the Year Ending July 31, 1907* (Department of Education, City of New York, 1907), 520.

50 E. E. Whitney, "Vacation Schools, Vacation Playgrounds, and Recreation Centres," *Tenth Annual Report of the City Superintendent of Schools for the Year Ending*

July 31, 1908 (New York, 1908), 517; *Eleventh Annual Report of William H. Maxwell, City Superintendent of Schools, the City of New York, Year Ending July 31, 1909* (Department of Education, City of New York, 1909), 109; E. E. Whitney, "Vacation Schools, Vacation Playgrounds, and Recreation Centres," *Eleventh Annual Report*, 554, 556–558; *Tenth Annual Report*, 94.

51 Gold, *School's In*, 171, 156, 149, 202; Reese *Power*, 142, 144.

52 Gold, *School's In*, 136; Dominick Cavallo, *Muscles and Morals: Organized Playgrounds and Urban Reform, 1880–1920* (Philadelphia: University of Pennsylvania Press, 1981), 3, 44–46; Elizabeth A. Gagen, "Playing the Part: Performing Gender in America's Playgrounds," in *Children's Geographies: Playing, Living, Learning*, ed. Sarah L. Holloway and Gill Valentine (London: Routledge, 2000), 213–229; Whitney, "Vacation Schools," *Eleventh Annual Report*, 559; NEA, *Report*, 95; E. E. Whitney, "Vacation Schools, Vacation Playgrounds, and Recreation Centres," *Ninth Annual Report*, 521. See also Reese *Power*, 144–157.

53 Abigail A. Van Slyck, *A Manufactured Wilderness: Summer Camps and the Shaping of American Youth, 1890–1960* (Minneapolis: University of Minnesota Press, 2006), xx, xxiv, xxvii–xxix, 42, 71, 77, 110; Markowitz, *My Daughter*, 127; Leslie Paris, *Children's Nature: The Rise of the American Summer Camp* (New York: New York University Press, 2008), 86–87, 208, 236–238.

54 Paris, *Children's Nature*, 46–49, 97; Van Slyck, *A Manufactured Wilderness*, 89.

55 Kaufman, *National Parks*, 65–67; Newell F. Joyner, "An Outline of the History of Educational Activities in Yellowstone Park," in *Ranger Naturalists Manual of Yellowstone National Park* (National Park Service, Department of the Interior, June 1, 1929), 172, NPSHC; Albright quoted in Memorandum of the History of Women in Uniform (NPS) in Yellowstone National Park by Aubrey L. Haines, October 1961, Employees, Vertical File Collection, YNPA; Watry, *Women in Wonderland*, 203.

56 Correspondence between J. M. Johnson and Horace Albright, 1923, Interpretation and Education Records, Series 2: Communications, Box 1, YNPA; Park Naturalist Bauer, "The 1934 Naturalist Staff," *Yellowstone Nature Notes* 11, nos. 5–6 (1934): 20–22, NPSHC; "Who's Who Among the Ranger Naturalists and the Permanent Staff of Yellowstone Park, 1939," *Yellowstone Nature Notes* 16, nos. 5–6 (1930): 34–37, NPSHC; Lystrup, Herbert (file), NPSHC.

57 "Plan of Administration and Manual of Instruction for Educational Department, Yellowstone Nat'l Park, 1930," Interpretation and Education Records, 1900s–Present, Series 3, Box 2, YNPA; Watry, *Women in Wonderland*, 220–221; Willis Smith, "Beavers Prefer Pond Lily," *Yellowstone Nature Notes* 11, nos. 7–8 (1934): 31–32, NPSHC; W. Smith, "Picket Pins Hibernate Early," *Yellowstone Nature Notes* 11, nos. 9–10 (1934): 34–35, NPSHC; Herbert T. Lystrup, "Observation—Speculation—Meditation," *Yellowstone Nature Notes* 27, no. 1 (1953): 2, NPSHC.

58 Herbert Evison, Oral History Interview of Mildred J. Ericson, 1962?, Oral History Materials, NPSHC; Junior Nature Explorers Book I, July 9, July 13, July 26, and August 20, Mildred Ericson, "Junior Explorer Nature Program," 1947, YNPA.

59 Clifford, *Those Good Gertrudes*, 319–328, 121–134.

60 Wylie, autobiography, 18–19, 94–95.

61 Sargent, *Pioneers in Petticoats*, 75; Kaufman, *National Parks*, 91–92; Evison Interview of Garrison.

62 Evison Interview of Sanborn; Rufus Steele, "Summer Savages," *Outlook* May 12, 1926, 57; Watry, *Women in Wonderland*, 119, 127–129, 131–137.

63 Wilson, *Alice Eastwood's Wonderland*, 17, 20.

64 Black La Due Diaries, June 28, 1901, July 2, 1901, July 7, 1901, July 9, 1901, July 24, 1901, August 21, 1901, June 22, 1902, June 30, 1902, August 16, 1903, August 23, 1903, August 13, 1904, December 19, 1904, May 7, 1905, September 1–30, 1906.
65 J. C. Petherbridge to Amanda Stewart, June 14, 1888, Box 10, August 30, 1889, Box 13, and June 13, 1894, Box 19, SLFP; Libbie Burbank to Amanda Stewart, June 22, 1887, Box 8, SLFP; Libbie Burbank to May and Amanda Stewart quoted in Clifford, *Those Good Gertrudes*, 243; "Business Education," ad, *TSJ* 22, no. 12 (1905): n.p.
66 Conrad G. Selvig, *A Tale of Two Valleys* (Los Angeles: Grover Jones Press, 1951), 31, 24–40; Conrad Selvig to Christopher Oftedal, September 7, 1896, Conrad George Selvig Papers, Box 1, MHS.
67 "Use Your Vacation," ad, *Midland Schools* 35, no. 19 (1921): 358; "Attractive Vacation Position," ad, *Midland Schools* 38, no. 7 (1924): 274; "Teachers: Earn Money," ad, *JNEA* 17, no. 2 (1928): A-58; "Summer Work," A-40; "The Facts," 513; "To Women Teachers," A-61; "A Message from a Few of the Many Teachers," ad, *Sierra Educational News*19, no. 5 (1923): 234.
68 Autobiographical Statement, n.d., Herma Albertson Baggley Papers, 1927–1957, Box 1, Manuscript Collections, YNPA; Watry, *Women in Wonderland*, 218–231.
69 Clifford, *Those Good Gertrudes*, 122–132; Markowitz, *My Daughter*, 14.
70 A. P. Marble, "N. E. A. at Nashville, 1889," *TSJ* 7, no. 1 (1889): 23; "Sweethearting by Moonlight," *TSJ* 9, no. 8 (1891): 219–220.
71 Clifford, *Those Good Gertrudes*, 229.
72 Libbie Burbank to Amanda Stewart, May 13, 1881, Box 2, and Eva to Amanda Stewart, March 10, 1884, Box 4, SLFP; Nelle to Vivian Bullock, June 9, 1920, Joanne to Vivian Bullock, June 7, 1921, Bess to Vivian Bullock, Ju?? [June or July] 1921, and Mary Faust to Vivian Bullock, July 25, 1921, Box 2, Scarlett-Bullock Family Papers, ASA; "Cupid Takes No Vacation," *Midland Schools* 42, no. 2 (1927): 73.
73 Correspondence between Charles Brown and Nellie Williams, September 1881–November 1883, Boxes 5–7, Williams to Brown, July 11, 1882, Box 5, Williams to Brown, June 2, 1883, Box 6, and Brown to Williams, June 6, 1883, Box 6, WHSA.
74 Herrick: diary, 1901–1902, July 8, July 17, July 25, August 15, 1901, Box 13; Herrick: diary, 1902–1905, July 28, 1905, Box 14, HFP. Lillian Herrick Chapman later became a minister in the Presbyterian Church.
75 William Scarlett to Vivian Bullock, March 8, 1923, and August 2, 1923, Box 2, Scarlett-Bullock Family Papers.
76 Irene Krumpelmann, "1926–1928: School Days," 6, and "More Yesterdays," 1, 2, 7–11, 14, 17, 20, Irene Krumpelmann Papers. Louis died in 1947. After a remarriage and divorce, Irene Krumpelmann returned to teaching in the mid-1960s, when she was in her late fifties. She taught with the peace corps in Liberia and in St. Paul elementary schools.
77 "The Hamilton Saga," 1–33, Ruth Hamilton Papers, Box 1, IWA.
78 Johannes Westberg, "How Did Teachers Make a Living? The Teacher Occupation, Livelihood Diversification and the Rise of Mass Schooling in Nineteenth-Century Sweden," *History of Education* 48, no. 1 (2019): 19–40.

Chapter 4 Tourism

1 Alumni Association Officers, 1951–, 1–2, Alumni Relations, A05020, TUSC.
2 Gary Kriss, "Miss Cramer Honored at Reception," *Reporter Dispatch*, June 13, 1967, in Beatrice E. Cramer memoir and diary, Box 1, HGSESC.

3 W. E. Watt, "Teachers as Travelers," *Intelligence* 21, no. 10 (1901): 371; Robert Gough, "What I Did on My Summer Vacation: The Significance of Tourism for American Teachers, 1919–1940," *Journal of Tourism History* 3, no. 3 (2011): 270.

4 H. Z. Osborne, "A Midsummer Ramble: Being a Descriptive Sketch of the Yellowstone National Park," in *Ho! For Wonderland: Travelers' Accounts of Yellowstone, 1872–1914*, ed. Lee H. Wittlesey and Elizabeth A. Watry (Albuquerque: University of New Mexico Press, 2009), 127; N. E. Corthell, "A Family Trek to Yellowstone—1903" quoted in M. Mark Miller, *Adventures in Yellowstone: Early Travelers Tell Their Tales* (Helena, MT: Twodot, 2009), 236.

5 Henry James, *Four Meetings* (New York, 1909), 267, 274, 279.

6 John F. Sears, *Sacred Places: American Tourist Attractions in the Nineteenth Century* (New York: Oxford University Press, 1989), 10–11; Hugh De Santis, "The Democratization of Travel: The Travel Agent in American History," *Journal of American Culture* 1 (Spring 1978): 1–17; Cindy S. Aron, *Working at Play: A History of Vacations in the United States* (New York: Oxford University Press, 1999), 5, chap. 4, 138–140; Shelly Baranowski and Ellen Furlough, "Introduction," in *Being Elsewhere: Tourism, Consumer Culture, and Identity in Modern Europe and North America*, ed. Shelly Baranowski and Ellen Furlough (Ann Arbor: University of Michigan Press, 2001), 9.

7 Hal K. Rothman, *Devil's Bargains: Tourism in the Twentieth-Century American West* (Lawrence: University Press of Kansas, 1998), 23–24; Harvey Levenstein, *Seductive Journey: American Tourists in France from Jefferson to the Jazz Age* (Chicago: University of Chicago Press, 1998), xiii, 139–182.

8 Watt, "Teachers as Travelers," 371–372; Charles A. Payne, "Travel—A Higher Education," *Midland Schools* 39, no. 8 (1925): 231; Stephen H. Bush, "What Is the Use of Going to Europe?" *Midland Schools* 39, no. 8 (1925): 236; "The Teacher and Travel," *Midland Schools* 44, no. 6 (1930): 228; "Our Modern Crusaders," *Midland Schools* 51, no. 8 (1937): 272. On the expansion of tourism during the Great Depression, see Michael Berkowitz, "A 'New Deal' for Leisure: Making Mass Tourism during the Great Depression," in *Being Elsewhere: Tourism, Consumer Culture, and Identity in Modern Europe and North America*, ed. Shelly Baranowski and Ellen Furlough (Ann Arbor: University of Michigan Press, 2001), 185–212.

9 Edgar B. Wesley, *NEA: The First Hundred Years: The Building of the Teaching Profession* (New York: Harper & Brothers, 1957), 256; "The National Educational Association," *INM* 14, no. 11–12 (1891): 483–484. On segregation in the NEA, see chap. 1.

10 Chas. S. Fee, "A Talk to Teachers," *Intelligence* 19, no. 8 (1899): 312; Martha Ingersoll Robinson, "Southern California Points of Interest to N. E. A. Visitors," *Intelligence* 19, no. 10 (1899): 377–384; "California," *Intelligence* 19, no. 11 (1899): 426–429.

11 Julia A. Shourek, "The Wonderland of Washington," *JNEA* 16, no. 6 (1927): 183–184; "The Twin Bread and Butter Cities," *JNEA* 17, no. 4 (1928): 109; Lyle W. Ashby, "Going to New York?" *JNEA* 27, no. 3 (1938): 72–73.

12 "Yellowstone Park Waterfalls," *INM* 20, no. 3 (1896): 116; Richard Jones, "A Vacation Trip in Germany," *INM* 16, no. 4 (1892): 147–150.

13 W. E. Watt, "Touring in Europe," *Intelligence* 21, no. 9 (1901): 353–354; "Some Glimpses of Grandeur," *Midland Schools* 50, no. 8 (1936): 248.

14 Santa Fe Railroad ad, *TSJ* 21 (1904), n.p.; Intercollegiate Tours ad, *Midland Schools* 35, no. 6 (1921): 196.

15 "Yellowstone Park by Camp," Yellowstone Park Company Records, Series 9, Box 178, YNPA; *Europe 1937: The Morningside Tours* (brochure), William and Garnett

(Williams) Kirchner Collection, Morningside College Archives, Hickman-Johnson-Furrow Learning Center, Sioux City, IA

16 Percy V. Pennybacker, "National Educational Association," *TSJ* 6, no. 4 (1888): 110; *The National Educational Association, Los Angles, California, July 11–14, 1899* (flyer), NEA1001.RG, Series 4, Box 550, RNEA.

17 "Educational Notes and Announcements: Opportunities for Study and Travel Abroad," *Bulletin of High Points In the Work of the High Schools of New York City* 2, no. 1 (1920): 23; "Travel Service Bureau," *PSJ* 72, no. 7 (1924): 429; "Service Bureau Helps Tours," *Midland Schools* 41, no. 7 (1927): 219.

18 Watt, "Teachers as Travelers," 371; Elyria, Ohio, newspaper quoted in Gough, "What I Did," 276; Maybelle Hargrave, "Evansville Gives Teachers Bonus for Travel and Study," *News Bulletin of the Department of Classroom Teachers of the National Education Association* 4, no. 1 (1930): 3, NEA1005.RG, Series 8, Box 1546, RNEA.

19 William Dow Boutwell "Going Places," *JNEA* 23, no. 3 (1934): 79. A few other districts also counted summer travel as continuing education or toward merit pay or licensure renewal. See Gough, "What I Did," 275–277.

20 "State News and Notes," *INM* 33, no. 6 (1910): 293.

21 "State News and Notes," 293; Sophie Heckert to Sarah Butler, n.d., Horace Butler Papers, Box 5, Folder: Sarah Hannah Butler, 1896–1904, ALPL.

22 National Education Association (NEA), *Report of the Committee on Teachers' Salaries and Cost of Living* (Ann Arbor: NEA, 1913), 225–227.

23 NEA, *Report*, 226; Irene Krumpelmann, "1926–1928: School Days and Dates Anew," 13, and "Gifts of Music—A Simple View," 9, Irene Krumpelmann Papers, Box 1, MHS.

24 Frances R. Donovan, *The Schoolma'am* (New York: Frederick A. Stokes Company, 1938), 244, 246; Iowa Loan & Trust ad, *Midland Schools* 40, no. 1 (1925): 17.

25 Lucy Jones to Ethel Lowry, July 13, 1910, and August 10, 1910, Lucy Jones Townley Collection, Kansas Collection, RH MS 1270, KSRL.

26 State Loan Company ad, *Midland Schools* 40, no. 9 (1926): 334; Household Finance Corporation ad, *Midland Schools* 43, no. 9 (1929): 353; "Cunard Will Sell Trips to Europe on Deferred Payments," *PSJ* 80, no. 8 (1932): 592; Cunard Line ad, *JNEA* 23, no. 5 (1943), A-61; Charles quoted in Doris Hinson Pieroth, *Seattle's Women Teachers of the Interwar Years: Shapers of a Livable City* (Seattle: University of Washington Press, 2004), 196.

27 Jane Galloway Demaray, *Yellowstone Summers: Touring with the Wiley Camping Company* (Pullman: Washington State University Press, 2015), 3, 106–107; Corthell, "A Family Trek," 236; Traveler quoted in W. W. Wylie, *Yellowstone National Park* (brochure), YNPA; Rock Island ad, *PSJ* 75, no. 12 (1927): 661.

28 Foster Rhea Dulles, *Americans Abroad: Two Centuries of European Travel* (Ann Arbor: University of Michigan Press, 1964), 108; Gough, "What I Did," 272; White Star Line ad, *Midland Schools* 36, no. 9 (1922): 338.

29 Charles quoted in Pieroth, *Seattle's Women Teachers*, 196; Boutwell "Going Places," 79–82.

30 Rothman, *Devil's Bargains*, 23, 47, chap. 3–4; Aron, *Working at Play*, 10, 142, 149. Baranowski and Furlough point out that some historians have recently challenged the "'class to mass' trajectory that earlier studies have suggested." Baranowski and Furlough, "Introduction," 7.

31 Payne, "Travel," 231; Marguerite A. Shaffer, *See America First: Tourism and National Identity, 1880–1940* (Washington, DC: Smithsonian Institution Press, 2001), 3; Baranowski and Furlough, "Introduction," 9.

32 Jeanette Mills, "Travel," *Midland Schools* 40, no. 8 (1926): 284; P. H. Elwood, "Travel—Man's Greatest Educator," *Midland Schools* 40, no. 8 (1926): 281.

33 Payne, "Travel," 231; Shaffer, *See America First*, 5, 94; Sears, *Sacred Places*, 4, 5, chap. 1–2. On settler colonialism, see Adam Dahl, *Empire of the People: Settler Colonialism and the Foundations of Modern Democratic Thought* (Lawrence: University Press of Kansas, 2018). Löfgren explains that tourism as a "quest for a national identity" was not confined to the United States. The "nationalization of the landscape," he writes, "is most evident in countries that saw themselves as marginal to the grand narrative of Western civilization—the Scandinavian countries, the United States, and, later, Canada." Ovar Löfgren, *On Holiday: A History of Vacationing* (Berkeley: University of California Press, 1999), 35.

34 Elwood, "Travel," 284; Payne, "Travel," 231; Rothman, *Devil's Bargains*, 23–24, 44; Aron, *Working at Play*, chap. 5.

35 "The Route to Nashville," *INM* 12, no. 10 (1889): 592–593; Diary: F. E. Stratton, 1895, 2, 5–6, 40, F. E. Stratton Family Papers, Manuscript Collections, YNPA.

36 Virginia Scharff, *Taking the Wheel: Women and the Coming of the Motor Age* (Albuquerque: University of New Mexico Press, 1991), 33, 68.

37 Margaret Ann Cruikshank, "Notes on Yellowstone Park" (1883), Visitors, Vertical File Collection, YNPA; Margaret Andrews Cruikshank, ed. Lee H. Whittlesey, "A Lady's Trip to Yellowstone, 1883" *Montana: The Magazine of Western History* 39 (Winter 1989): 4–15.

38 Wylie Permanent Camping Co., *Yellowstone National Park* (brochure, 1910), 13, YNPA; Horace M. Albright and Frank J. Taylor, *"Oh, Ranger!" A Book About the National Parks* (Stanford, CA: Stanford University Press, 1928), 31.

39 Carrie Belle Spencer, "Journal of a Trip to Yellowstone National Park, 1892," https://sites.rootsweb.com/~nekeyapa/Carrie%20Belle%20Spencer.html.

40 Mary Lavinia White McEwen, 1919 Account of a Visit to Yellowstone, Visitors, Vertical File Collection, YNPA.

41 Cecilia Engel Scrapbook 1924, Manuscript Collections, YNPA.

42 Canadian Pacific ad, *PSJ* 77, no. 10 (1929): n.p.; Rothman, *Devil's Bargains*, chap. 6.

43 Jesse T. Hiller, "Educational and Sight-seeing Tours," *Midland Schools* 40, no. 8 (1926): 279; *JNEA* 28, no. 5 (1939): A-109; Margarete Bohle to family, May 30, 1935, June 1, 1935, June 8, 1935, June 12, 1935, June 14, 1935, Margarete Bohle Papers, Box 1, Folder 1, WHSA.

44 Cleata Thorpe, "Adventuring to Alaska," 1, essay included in letter from W. D. Conklin to M. M. Goodsill, April 12, 1935, Northern Pacific Railway Company, Advertising and Publicity Department: William A. McKenzie: Historical Subject Files, 1875–1966, 135.I.19.2F, Box 1, MHS.

45 Pieroth, *Seattle's Women Teachers*, 76; Scharff, *Taking the Wheel*, 137; Geraldine J. Clifford, *Those Good Gertrudes: A Social History of Women Teachers in America* (Baltimore: Johns Hopkins University Press, 2014), x.

46 "All Auto Roads Lead to Atlanta," *JNEA* 18, no. 1 (1929): 11; Map of "Motor Routes to Los Angeles," *JNEA* 19, no. 9 (1930): 296; "Special Convention Features," *JNEA* 20, no. 6 (1931): 231.

47 Alumni Association Officers, 1951–, 2; Cramer memoir and diary.

48 Margarete Bohle, Travel Journal (1939–1953), quotations from August 5, 1939, and August 11, 1940, Bohle Papers, Box 1, Folder 6; Scrapbook, Mildred Van Wyngarden Papers, Box 1, IWA.

49 United Air Lines ad, *JNEA* 27, no. 5 (1938): A-99.

50 Sears, *Sacred Places*, chaps.1, 2, 8, quotations on 14, 38, 13.

51 "Tennessee's Capital City," *INM* 12, no. 10 (1889): 584; *National Educational Association, Buffalo, N. Y., June 2, 1896* (flyer), NEA1001.RG, Series 4, Box 550, RNEA.

52 Grace Canan Pogue, *The Swift Seasons* (Hollywood, CA: Cloister Press, 1957), 40; Bohle, Travel Journal, August 6, 1939.

53 Sears, *Sacred Places*, 122, 133; Shaffer, *See America First*, 6, chap. 1; Rothman, *Devil's Bargains*, 49. See also Mark Daniel Barringer, *Selling Yellowstone: Capitalism and the Construction of Nature* (Lawrence: University Press of Kansas, 2002). On African Americans' lack of access to tourism before the 1920s, see Aron, *Working at Play*, chap. 7. In his article on Blacks at Yellowstone, Whittlesey does not discuss tourism and mentions only a few people who were employed at the park. Lee Whittlesey, "A Brief History of Black Americans in the Yellowstone National Park Area, 1872–1907," *Annals of Wyoming* 69 (Fall 1997): 13–20.

54 "Teachers to Yellowstone Park," *American School Board Journal* 18, no. 2 (1899): 9; Union Pacific ad, *Midland Schools* 41, no. 8 (1927): 301; *Intelligence* 21, no. 10 (1901), cover; *Intelligence* 22, no 10 (1902), cover; James D. Landsdowne, "Yellowstone National Park," *JNEA* 16, no. 5 (1927): 145–147.

55 Engel Scrapbook 1924; Bohle, Travel Journal (1939–1953), August 25–26, 1940; Audubon Publishing Company ad, *American School Board Journal* 18, no. 5 (1899): n.p.; Stephen T. Mather, "Glimpses of the National Parks," *JNEA* 12, no. 3 (1923): 85–89; "Teachers Turn to the West for Seventy-Third Meeting," *JNEA* 24, no. 3 (1935): 88–89.

56 "Return from Extended Trip" (clipping), Cramer memoir and diary.

57 A. R. Sale, "National Educational Association," *INM* 28, no. 11–12 (1895): 471; Harold B. Say, "Beauties of the Oregon Country," *Midland Schools* 50, no. 9 (1936): 291; "Drake University Motor-Bus Tours," *Midland Schools* 45, no. 8 (1931): 312; Mather, "Glimpses," 86–87; Iowa State Teachers Association Tour ad, *Midland Schools* 39, no. 6 (1925): 172; Milwaukee [Rail]Road ad, *PSJ* 76, no. 8 (1928): 330; Union Pacific ad, *Midland Schools* 43, no. 8 (1929): 315; Canadian National ad, *JNEA* 17, no. 2 (1928): A-59.

58 "Investing a Vacation," *JNEA* 12, no. 6 (1923): 219; Elwood, "Travel," 281, 284; Payne, "Travel," 231.

59 Diary: F. E. Stratton, 1895, 15, 64, 66, 67; Engel Scrapbook 1924, 1, 57.

60 Aline E. Teiche to "Friends," September 3, 1900, Visitors, Vertical File Collection, YNPA; Cramer memoir and diary.

61 Cruikshank, "A Lady's Trip," 11; Cruikshank, "Notes on the Yellowstone Park," 13; Spencer, "Journal of a Trip," August 10, 1892; Krumpelmann, "1926–1928," 14; McEwen, 1919 Account, 3; Cramer memoir and diary; "Rural Teacher from West Gives Story of Convention Trip," *News Bulletin of the Department of Classroom Teachers* 11, no. 1 (1937): 3, NEA1005.RG, Series 8, Box 1546, RNEA; Scrapbook, Van Wyngarden Papers; Thorpe, "Adventuring to Alaska," 7, 8.

62 Diary: F. E. Stratton, 1895, 13, 19, 81; Aline E. Teiche to "Friends," September 3, 1900; Krumpelmann, "1926–1928," 13.

63 Jane Galloway Demaray, *Yellowstone Summers: Touring with the Wylie Camping Company in America's First National Park* (Pullman: Washington State University Press, 2015), 107; *Logansport Reporter*, July 27, 1891, quoted in Elizabeth Ann Watry, "More Than Mere Camps and Coaches: The Wylie Camping Company and the Development of a Middle-Class Leisure Ethic in Yellowstone National Park, 1883–1916" (master's thesis, Montana State University, 2010), 34–35.

64 Horace M. Albright as told to Robert Cahn, *The Birth of the National Park Service: The Founding Years, 1913–33* (Salt Lake City: Howe Brothers, 1985), 119–120; Cramer memoir and diary; Bohle, Travel Journal, August 6, 1940.

65 Jane A. Stewart, "Life in the Sunshine City," *Intelligence* 19, no. 10 (1899): 376–377; "National Educational Association, Los Angeles, Cal., July 11–14, 1899" (program), NEA1001.RG, Series 4, Box 550, Folder 1, RNEA; "Facts About Colorado," *INM* 32, no. 11–12 (1909): 598; "Seattle and the N. E. A. Convention," *PSJ* 75, no. 11 (1927): 616.

66 Cramer memoir and diary; Scrapbook, Van Wyngarden Papers; Bohle, Travel Journal (1939–1953), August 9, 1940.

67 "Pioneer Trails Lead to Portland," *JNEA* 25, no. 3 (1936): 87; S. P. Fogdall, "Travel and Education," *Midland Schools* 38, no. 8 (1924): 290; House Party Tours ad, *PSJ* 77, no. 10 (1929): n.p.

68 Aron, *Working at Play*, 143; Shaffer, *See America First*, chap. 4, 218, 180; Rothman, *Devil's Bargains*, 154–157; Douglas Brinkley, *Rightful Heritage: Franklin D. Roosevelt and the Land of America* (New York: Harper Collins, 2016), 190.

69 Mills, "Travel," 284; C. C. Drake Company ad, *Midland Schools* 43, no. 9 (1929): 345.

70 "Notes and Comment," *INM* 32, no. 1 (1908): 1; Margarete Bohle to family, August 19, 1939, August 25, 1939, August 26, 1939, Bohle Papers, Box 1, Folder 1; Bohle, Travel Journal, August 4–August 28, 1939.

71 Adolphine Fletcher Terry, *Charlotte Stephens: Little Rock's First Black Teacher* (Little Rock: Academic Press of Arkansas, 1973), 125–126; Mark S. Foster, "In the Face of 'Jim Crow': Prosperous Blacks and Vacations, Travel and Outdoor Leisure, 1890–1945," *Journal of Negro History* 84, no. 2 (1999): 130–149.

72 Hargrave, "Evansville Gives," 3; J. M. R., "Washington: The Nation's Capital," *JNEA* 13, no. 1 (1924): 30.

73 "Washington: The Workshops of Democracy," *JNEA* 13, no. 3 (1924): 79.

74 "Notes and Comment," 1; Terry, *Charlotte Stephens*, 125; Margarete Bohle to family, August 19, 1939, Bohle Papers, Box 1, Folder 1; Bohle, Travel Journal, August 19–22, 1939; Gough "What I Did," 283.

75 Ashby, "Going to New York?" 72.

76 Frederick Houk Law, "Memories of History in New York City," *JNEA* 27, no. 4 (1938): 114–115.

77 Bunker Hill Monument photo and caption, *JNEA* 11, no. 2 (1922): 67; "Literary Pilgrimages," *JNEA* 11, no. 5 (1922): 175–176; J. M. R., "Historic Philadelphia," *JNEA* 15, no. 5 (1926): 153.

78 "The Baltimore Meeting," *National Note-Book Quarterly: Official Bulletin of the Teachers in Colored Schools* 11, no. 3 (1920): 4–5, NEA1007.RG, Series 1, Box 3044, Folder 1, RNEA; "To Atlantic City on Highways of History," *JNEA* 20, no. 9 (1931): 325–326.

79 Bohle, Travel Journal, August 14, 1939, August 16, 1939; Margarete Bohle to family, August 25, 1939, Bohle Papers, Box 1, Folder 1.

80 Margarete Bohle to family, August 19, 1939, Bohle Papers, Box 1, Folder 1; Bohle, Travel Journal, August 26, 1939.

81 C. M. Light to Fellow Teachers of New Mexico, April 28, 1898, NEA1001.RG, Series 4, Box 550, RNEA; "N. E. A. Goes to Washington—Special Train," *Midland Schools* 38, no. 7 (1924): 275; Jessie Gray, "Our Coming Convention in Washington," *JNEA* 22, no. 8 (1933): 270.

82 "Helen Hunt, Western Teacher, Attends Convention as Department Guest," *News Bulletin of the Department of Classroom Teachers* 8, no. 1 (1934), NEA1005.RG, Series 8, Box 1546, RNEA.

83 A. P. Marble, "N. E. A. at Nashville, 1889," *TSJ* 7, no. 1 (1889): 23; "Tennessee's Capital City," 584.

84 J. M. Turner, "A Summer Outing Trip for Teachers and Their Friends," *Intelligence* 20, no. 9 (1900): 357; "Trip Through the South," *Winona Daily Republican*, July 12, 1900; Cramer memoir and diary.

85 "To Atlantic City," 325; "Going to New York," 73; Margarete Bohle to family, August 26, 1939, Bohle Papers, Box 1, Folder 1.

86 Greene B. Buster Collection, Box 2, Kansas Collection, RH MS 512, KSRL. On Buster's career, see Kim Cary Warren, *The Quest for Citizenship: African American and Native American Education in Kansas, 1880–1935* (Chapel Hill: University of North Carolina Press, 2010), chap. 5.

87 "Tennessee's Capital City," 580; "Two Gates of Atlanta," *JNEA* 18, no. 3 (1920): 81.

88 "Jackson and Mississippi Awaits the Coming of the National Association," *Bulletin* 9, no. 7 (1929): 3, NEA1007.RG, Series 1, Box 3044, Folder 1, RNEA; "Trip Through the South."

89 *National Educational Association, Buffalo* (flyer); B. F., "Chicago, a Center of Culture," *JNEA* 22, no. 3 (1933): 96; Edmund Wilson, "Hull House in 1932," *JNEA* 22, no. 4 (1933): 126.

90 Terry, *Charlotte Stephens*, 125; Van Wyngarden Papers, Box 2, IWA.

91 "Detroit Invites the Nation's Teachers," *JNEA* 25, no. 9 (1936): 301; Belmont Farley, "Past and Present in Detroit," *JNEA* 26, no. 4 (1937): 122–123; Pogue, *Swift Seasons*, 40; Terry, *Charlotte Stephens*, 125; Van Wyngarden Papers, Box 2; Bohle, Travel Journal, August 5, 1939.

92 Aron also notes that world's fairs reinforced notions of white racial superiority, and "African Americans participated in the touring experience that world's fairs offered, but often faced discriminatory treatment." Aron, *Working at Play*, 150, 153.

93 T. J. Pattillo, "Texas Schools at the World's Fair," *TSJ* 11, no. 6 (1893): 199–200; "To the World's Columbian Exposition," *Pacific Coast Teacher* 2, no. 3 (1892): 55; Francis W. Parker, "Teachers of America, Come to the World's Columbian Exposition," *INM* 17, no. 2 (1893): 72–73.

94 Parker, "Teachers of America," 73; "Editorial Mention," *TSJ* 11, no. 3 (1893): 123; "A World's Fair Hotel for Teachers," *INM* 16, no. 5 (1892): 237.

95 "Teachers' Excursions to the World's Fair," *Pacific Coast Teacher* 11, no. 8 (1893): 183–189.

96 "The Village School Ma'am Sees the Fair," *INM* 16, no. 10 (1893): 433–435.

97 Sarah Hannah Butler to mother, n.d., and Evelyn Bires to Sarah Hannah Butler, n.d., Horace Butler Papers, Box 4, Folder: Sarah Hannah Butler, 1871–1894.

98 "Personally Conducted Teachers' Excursion to Pan-American Exposition, Buffalo, N. Y.," *INM* 24, no. 8 (1901): 344; Teachers' Headquarters ad, *American School Board Journal* 22, no. 6 (1901): n.p.

99 Margaret Creighton, *The Electrifying Fall of Rainbow City: Spectacle and Assassination at the 1901 World's Fair* (New York: W. W. Norton & Company, 2016), 21–22, 25–26, 81, 123.

100 "To State Directors—Circular Letter No. 1," March 31, 1904, and *National Educational Association at St. Louis, June 27–July 1* (flyer), May 28, 1904, NEA1001.RG, Series 4, Box 551, RNEA; "World's Fair News Notes," *INM* 28, no. 1 (1904): 38–39.

101 "Great World's Fair at San Francisco," *PSJ* 63, no. 9 (1915): 426–428; Cramer memoir and diary.
102 Fred G. Tredway, "Fun in San Francisco," *Midland Schools* 54, no. 8 (1940): 252.
103 Margarete Bohle to family, August 19, 1939, Bohle Papers, Box 1, Folder 1; Bohle, Travel Journal, August 11, 1940; Scrapbook, Van Wyngarden Papers.
104 "Mile Stones: A Five Year Diary," Beatrice E. Cramer, Box 2, HGSESC.
105 Bush, "What Is the Use?" 233; Levenstein, *Seductive Journey*, 4, 44; Baranowski and Furlough, "Introduction," 9. See also Dulles, *Americans Abroad*, chap. 1, 4–6, 8; Christopher Hibbert, *The Grand Tour* (New York: G. P. Putnam's Sons, 1969).
106 Levenstein, *Seductive Journey*, 140–182. See also Dulles, *Americans Abroad*, chap. 10.
107 Dulles, *Americans Abroad*, chap. 12; Levenstein, *Seductive Journey*, 235, 246.
108 Bush, "What Is the Use?" 233, 236.
109 Cramer memoir and diary; Geo. A. Hill, Letter, Personal Department, *TSJ* 15, no. 3 (1897): 116; "Iowa Educational Excursion," *Midland Schools* 20, no. 10 (1906): 379.
110 Panama Pacific Line ad, *Midland Schools* 42, no. 8 (1928): 327; Panama Pacific Line ad, *JNEA* 20, no. 2 (1931): A-50; Fred Tredway, "Let's Have a Fiesta," *Midland Schools* 52, no. 8 (1938): 254.
111 Canadian Pacific ad, *Sierra Educational News* 16, no. 4 (1920): 196; Canadian Pacific ad, *Midland Schools* 53, no. 8 (1939): 251.
112 Bohle, Travel Journal, August 10–12, 1939; Cramer memoir and diary.
113 South African Tourist Bureau ad, *Midland Schools* 43, no. 2 (1928): 71; South African Bureau ad, *JNEA* 16, no. 6 (1927): A-181; Australia and New Zealand ads, *JNEA* 26, no. 2 (1937): A-33–34; Travel Guild ad, *Midland Schools* 44, no. 8 (1930): 329.
114 Dragonland Cruise ad, *JNEA* 25, no. 3 (1936): A-47; Pieroth, *Seattle's Women Teachers*, 197.
115 J. P. Wickersham, "Over the Sea: Letters from the Editor," *PSJ* 27, no. 2 (1878): 57–61.
116 Levenstein, *Seductive Journey*, 184.
117 "A Summer Vacation in Europe," ad, *Maryland School Journal* 5, no. 6 (1879): 241; "Europe and the Holyland," ad, *Maryland School Journal* 6, no. 6 (1880): 236.
118 Jim L. T. to Helen Crombie, November 7, 1892, and May 18, 1893; Helen Crombie to Mother, July 6, 1894, Crombie family papers, 1809–1937, Massachusetts Historical Society archives, Massachusetts Historical Society, Boston.
119 Mary Elizabeth Pierce, Journal of trip to Europe, June 15–26, 1895, Henry Pierce family papers, 1771–1921, Box 1, Massachusetts Historical Society archives.
120 Lillian Herrick: diary, 1905–1908, July 3–9 and August 26–27, 1907, HFP. On Jessie Herrick's trip to Glens Falls, see chapter 1.
121 Eva and Maude Lewis to "Dear Ones," n.d., LFP.
122 Jones to Lowry, June 21, 1910, Townley Collection.
123 Helen Tearse to Mother, June 21, 1910, and photocopy of newspaper clipping, n.d., Helen H. Tearse Papers, 1910–1919, MHS.
124 Margaret Patch, "Europe . . . Dreams Come True," *PSJ* 76, no. 10 (1928): 474; and *Midland Schools* 42, no. 6 (1928): 203; "More Teachers Now Go to Europe," *PSJ* 76, no. 8 (1928): 357.
125 White Star, Red Star Atlantic Transport ad, *PSJ* 79, no. 10 (1931): 652; White Star Line ad, *JNEA* 22, no. 4 (1933): A-54. Transatlantic airline service began in 1939, but it was prohibitively expensive for teachers until after the Second World War. Dulles, *Americans Abroad*, 164–165.
126 Luch quoted in Pieroth, *Seattle's Women Teachers*, 196–197.
127 Wickersham also visited Ireland and Wales, and the educational excursion included "Grand Supplementary Excursions to *Egypt and Palestine*." J. P. Wickersham,

"European Tour," *PSJ* 27, no. 7 (1879): 246; "Europe and the Holyland" ad; Ward's Tours ad, *Intelligence* 22, no. 9 (1902): 358. On the "striking whiteness of tourism" during this period, see Löfgren, *On Holiday*, 106. On the standard itinerary of countries, see Dulles, *Americans Abroad*, chap. 6; and Hibbert, *Grand Tour*.

128 Bush, "What Is the Use?" 236; H. L. Hargrove, "Culture Resulting From Travel," *TSJ* 25, no. 10 (1908): 27. On guidebooks and "Cook's Hordes," see Levenstein, *Seductive Journey*, 158–161, 182; and Dulles, *Americans Abroad*, chap. 8.

129 Hargrove, "Culture Resulting," 27; Helen Crombie to Mother, July 6, 1894, July 7, 1894, July 14, 1894, July 20, 1894, August 9, 1894, Crombie family papers.

130 Pierce, Journal of trip to Europe, June 27–28, July 6–14, 1895; Helen Tearse to Mother, July?, 1910, Tearse Papers.

131 Helen Crombie to Mother, July 27, 1894, August 2, 1894, Crombie family papers; Herrick: diary, 1905–1908, August 11, 1907; Helen Tearse to Mother, July 12 and July 31, 1910, Tearse Papers.

132 Eva Lewis to Dear Ones, August 6, 1910; Eva Lewis to Dear Ones, August 15, 1910; and Maude Lewis to Dear Ones, August 5, 1910, Box 3, Folder 65, LFP.

133 Jones to Lowry, August 23, 1910, August 10, 1910, Townley Collection; Helen Tearse to Mother, July 31, 1910, Tearse Papers.

134 Eva and Maude Lewis to Dear Ones, August 21, 1910, Box 11, Folder 194, LFP; Eva Lewis to Dear Ones, August 27, 1910, Box 3, Folder 65, LFP; Jones to Lowry, August 23, 1910, Townley Collection; Lucy Jones, Diary—to Europe, August 26, 1910, August 25, 1910, Townley Collection.

135 Jones, Diary—to Europe, August 29, 1910.

136 Herrick: diary, 1905–1908, July n.d. and July 30, 1907; Eva and Maude Lewis to Dear Ones, July 23, 1910, Box 5, Folder 95, LFP; Helen Tearse to Father, July 19, 1910, Tearse Papers.

137 Pierce, Journal of trip to Europe, July 26–30, 1895; Eva Lewis to Dear Ones, July?, 1910, Box 3, Folder 65, LFP; Helen Tearse to Father, July 19, 1910, Tearse Papers; Jones to Lowry, July 13, 1910, Townley Collection; Jones, Diary—to Europe, July 1–2 and July 9, 1910, Townley Collection.

138 Jones to Lowry, July 17, and July 26, 1910, Townley Collection; Jones, Diary—to Europe, July 11–12, 1910, Townley Collection.

139 Maude Lewis to Dear Ones, July 2, 1910, Box 5, Folder 95, LFP; Herrick: diary, 1905–1908, July n.d.; Eva Lewis to Dear Ones, Box 3, Folder 65, LFP.

140 Pierce, Journal of trip to Europe, August 2–4, 1895.

141 Levenstein, *Seductive Journey*, 217; H. G. Campbell obituary, Campbell, Herbert G., Faculty/Administration/Staff—Pamphlets/clippings, Morningside College Archives; "Chapel Notes," *Collegian Reporter*, September 30, 1914, 5, https://morningside.historyarchives.online/.

142 Levenstein, *Seductive Journey*, 224–225; *New York Times* quoted in Gough, "What I Did," 269. On African American travel in Europe, see Levenstein, *Seductive Journey*, 229–232; Harvey Levenstein, *We'll Always Have Paris: American Tourists in France Since 1930* (Chicago: University of Chicago Press, 2004), 49–53; and Gough, "What I Did," 283.

143 Bush, "What Is the Use?" 233.

144 Intercollegiate Tours ad, 196.

145 "A Tour of Quality and Character," ad, *Midland Schools* 38, no. 6 (1924): 204; Mentor Tours ad, *Midland Schools* 42, no. 9 (1928): 367; Mrs. R. S. Ridgeway ad, *JNEA* 19, no. 1 (1930): A-279.

146 Hugh Fouke, "Morningsiders to Tour European Lands," *Collegian Reporter*, April 30, 1920, 2, https://morningside.historyarchives.online/; "Morningside Tours Attract Many," *Collegian Reporter*, May 24, 1924, 2, https://morningside.historyarchives.online/; *Europe 1937: The Morningside Tours* (brochure), Kirchner Collection.

147 Patch, "Europe," 203; Margaret Patch, "Europe . . . Dreams Come True! (Part 2)," *Midland Schools* 42, no. 7 (1928): 234; Margaret Patch, "Europe . . . Dreams Come True! (Part 3)," *Midland Schools* 42, no. 8 (1928): 320.

148 Gelb quoted in Levenstein, *We'll Always Have Paris*, 5; Gough, "What I Did," 283.

149 Anabel Read Scott quoted in Mabel E. O'Farrell, "She Has an Itching Foot," in *Reminiscences of Some Early California Teachers: The Fourth Historical Year Book of the California Retired Teachers' Association*, compiler Laura Esta Settle (California Retired Teachers Association, 1937), 115–116.

150 Morningside Travel Club ad, *Midland Schools* 36, no. 7 (1922): 267; Patch, "Europe (Part 2)," 234.

151 Temple Tours ad, *Midland Schools* 43, no. 6 (1929): 212; Temple Tours ad, *Midland Schools* 44, no. 8 (1930): 328.

152 Temple Tours ad, *Midland Schools* 39, no. 8 (1925): 254; Temple Tours ad, *JNEA* 19, no. 1 (1930): A-279; Temple Tours ad, *Midland Schools* 42, no. 8 (1928): 321; Guild Travel Bureau ad, *PSJ* 77, no. 10 (1929): n.p.; Travel Guild ad, *Midland Schools* 45, no. 7 (1931): 265; Guild Travel Bureau ad, *JNEA* 17, no. 2 (1928): A-56.

153 Ella E. Preston, "Fruits of a European Tour," *Midland Schools* 48, no. 8 (1934): 242.

154 University Travel Bureau quoted in Dulles, *Americans Abroad*, 141; Students Travel Club and the College Travel Club ads, *Midland Schools* 45, no. 8 (1931): 310; Intercollegiate Tours ad (1921), 196; Intercollegiate Tours ad, *Midland Schools* 42, no. 7 (1928): 287.

155 Levenstein, *Seductive Journey*, 252–253.

156 European trip: Travel diary, 1929, n.p., Mae Irene Ludeman Papers, Box 1, IWA.

157 "Prof. Campbell at Head of Tourists," *Collegian Reporter*, September 20, 1924, https://morningside.historyarchives.online/; "Something New in European Travel," *Midland Schools* 38, no. 7 (1924): 275; Intercollegiate Travel Extension Service ad, *JNEA* 21, no. 3 (1932): A-55; "Educational Tours," *PSJ* 80, no. 9 (1932): 643.

158 Isaac D. App, "Visiting European Schools," *PSJ* 76, no. 3 (1927): 154; "City of London Vacation Course in Education," *PSJ* 77, no. 10 (1920): 610.

159 H. F. Blank, "Historic Travels Through Europe," *Midland Schools* 48, no. 7 (1934): 212–213; "Educational Notes and Announcements: American Association of High School Teachers of French," *Bulletin of High Points* 3, no. 3 (1921): 21; French Line ad, *JNEA* 23, no. 5 (1934): A-63.

160 "Educational Notes and Announcements: Study and Travel in Spain," *Bulletin of High Points* 3, no. 3 (1921): 23; Stratford Tours ad, *Midland Schools* 39, no. 5 (1925): 149; Boyd Tours ad, *Midland Schools* 42, no. 8 (1928): 321.

161 Guild Travel Bureau ad, *JNEA* 17, no. 2 (1928): A-56; O'Farrell, "She Has an Itching Foot," 116; *Ireland and Standard Tour 1937* (brochure), Kirchner Collection; James Boring's Cruises ad, *Midland Schools* 42, no. 7 (1928): 287; Mrs. H. G. Campbell to Travel Friends, December 25, 1936, Kirchner Collection.

162 Open Road ad, *JNEA* 23, no. 3 (1934): A-30; Open Road ad, *JNEA* 27, no. 3 (1938): A-58; Gough, "What I Did," 273; Luch quoted in Pieroth, *Seattle's Women Teachers*, 197.

163 Payne, "Travel," 231; Bush, "What Is the Use?" 236.

164 Emma Shaw, "The Yellowstone Park: A Class Exercise" (clipping), Emma Shaw Colcleugh file, Polly Welts Kaufman Collection, NPSHC.

165 Creighton, *Electrifying Fall*, 22; Pogue, *Swift Seasons*, 82; Pieroth, *Seattle's Women Teachers*, 174; "Des Moines No. 6" (clipping), Van Wyngarden Papers, Box 2.

166 Isabel Townley Voss, "Memories of a Kansas Childhood," 1980, 5, Townley Collection.

167 Joseph E. Harris, "Professor Merze Tate (1905–1996): A Profile," *Negro History Bulletin* 61, no. 3–4 (1998): 78–81. Thanks to Dellyssa Edinboro for teaching me about Merze Tate.

168 Surveys cited in Gough, "What I Did," 283.

169 Elizabeth K. Matthews, "Vacation," *INM* 20, no. 1 (1896): 14–15; Iowa State Teachers Association Second Annual Tour ad, *Midland Schools* 39, no. 9 (1925): 282; Hogle and Brown quoted in "The Yellowstone Trip," *Midland Schools* 39, no. 8 (1925): 238.

170 Rachel Murrow, "Alaska Vacation—Study Plan Realized by Cruise," n.p., Northern Pacific Railway Company, Advertising and Publicity Department: William A. McKenzie: Historical Subject Files, 1875–1966, 135.I.19.2F, Box 1; Blanchard quoted in "Investing a Vacation," 219; John E. Foster, "Why Teachers Should Travel," *Midland Schools* 42, no. 9 (1928): 342.

171 Kohn quoted in "Investing a Vacation," 219; *Europe 1937: The Morningside Tours* (brochure); Iola B. Quigley, "European Travel for the Teacher," *Midland Schools* 49, no. 7 (1935): 212.

172 Boutwell, "Going Places," 79–80, 82; Foster, "Why Teachers Should Travel," 342; Mills, "Travel," 284.

173 Preston, "Fruits," 242; Quigley, "European Travel," 212; Fyan quoted in "Investing a Vacation," 219.

174 "The N. E. A. Meeting at Los Angeles," *INM* 30, no. 10 (1907): 551–552; Payne, "Travel," 231; Bush, "What Is the Use?" 236; Foster, "Why Teachers Should Travel," 342.

175 Gough, "What I Did," 282.

176 Aron, *Working at Play*, 3–5, chap. 1; Rothman, *Devil's Bargains*, 23–24, 146–150; Shaffer, *See America First*, 246–249.

Chapter 5 Rest

1 Anna Mills Johnston, "A Trip to Mt. Whitney in 1878," *Mt. Whitney Club Journal* 1, no. 1 (1902): 18–28; Leonard Daughenbaugh, "On Top of Her World: Anna Mills' Ascent of Mt. Whitney," *California History* 64, no. 1 (1985): 46–51; Kathleen Weiler, *Country Schoolwomen: Teaching in Rural California, 1850–1950* (Stanford, CA: Stanford University Press, 1998), 126–129, 132–133.

2 Weiler, *Country Schoolwomen*, 132–133; Addams quoted in David Tyack, *The One Best System: A History of American Urban Education* (Cambridge, MA: Harvard University Press, 1974), 259. See, for example, Kate Rousmaniere, *City Teachers: Teaching and School Reform in Historical Perspective* (New York: Teachers College Press, 1997), chap. 4; Ruth Jacknow Markowitz, *My Daughter, the Teacher: Jewish Teachers in the New York City Schools* (New Brunswick, NJ: Rutgers University Press, 1993), chap. 6

3 Kate Rousmaniere, "Those Who Can't, Teach: The Disabling History of American Educators," *History of Education Quarterly* 53, no. 1 (2013): 90–103; Kristen Chmielewski, "'Hopelessly Insane, Some Almost Maniacs': New York City's War on 'Unfit' Teachers," *Paedagogica Historica* 54, no. 1–2 (2018): 169–183; Jonna

Perrillo, "Beyond 'Progressive' Reform: Bodies, Discipline, and the Construction of the Professional Teacher in Interwar America," *History of Education Quarterly* 44, no. 3 (2004): 337–363, quotation on 342.

4 Kenneth M. Gold, *School's In: The History of Summer Education in American Public Schools* (New York: Peter Lang, 2002), chap. 3; Daniel T. Rogers, *The Work Ethic in Industrial America, 1850–1920* (Chicago: University of Chicago Press, [1974] 1978), chap. 4; Cindy S. Aron, *Working at Play: A History of Vacations in the United States* (New York: Oxford University Press, 1999), 33–40; David Strauss, "Toward a Consumer Culture: 'Adirondack Murray' and the Wilderness Vacation," *American Quarterly* 39, no. 2 (1987): 277. On health concerns, see also Martha H. Verburgge, *Able-Bodied Womanhood: Personal Health and Social Change in Nineteenth-Century Boston* (New York: Oxford University Press, 1988).

5 Gold, *School's In*, 97, 98.

6 "The Vacation," *PSJ* 62, no. 12 (1914): 565; Strauss, "Toward a Consumer Culture," 270–272, 278.

7 On conceptions of women's frailty and the rise of outdoor exercise in the interest of health, see Verburgge, *Able-Bodied Womanhood*. On the new woman and the Gibson girl, see Sara M. Evans, *Born for Liberty: A History of Women in America* (New York; Simon and Schuster, [1989] 1997), 147. On masculinity, see Michael S. Kimmel, *Manhood in America: A Cultural History*, 2nd ed. (New York: Oxford University Press, 2006), part 2.

8 "The National Educational Association," *INM* 13, no. 11 (1890): 445; "What Shall We Do with the Long Vacation?" *INM* 1, no. 12 (1878): 360–361. On the middle class and vacationing, see Rogers, *Work Ethic*, chap. 4; and Aron, *Working at Play*.

9 W. B. Harlow, "Summer Schools," *Academy: A Journal of Secondary Education* 1, no. 4 (1886): 151–153; H. W. Compton, "Open Letters: The Teacher's Vacation," *Century: A Popular Quarterly* 36, no. 4 (1888): 636; "Editorial," *TSJ* 12, no. 8 (1894): 279; Elizabeth K. Matthews, "Vacation," *INM* 20, no. 1 (1896): 14; Mae Traller, "Spring Fever," *JNEA* 15, no. 6 (1926): 168. On the role of the wilderness in middle-class vacationing, see Strauss, "Toward a Consumer Culture," 272, 275; and Aron, *Working at Play*, 156.

10 "Facts About the International Teachers' Home Association," *TSJ* 15, no. 1 (1897): 26; "Country Retreat for Teachers," *INM* 22, no. 5 (1898): 190–193, quotation on 190; "Recreation for Teachers," *American School Board Journal* 21, no. 2 (August 1900): last page; "Rest Farm for Teachers," *INM* 31, no. 11–12 (1908): 597–598; "News and Notes," *TSJ* 25, no. 9 (1908): 20; "Riverbank Lodge," *JNEA* 15, no. 1 (1926): 21; *The Historical Collections of Washburn County and the Surrounding Area* (1916?), 399, Washburn County Historical Society, Shell Lake, WI.

11 Strauss, "Toward a Consumer Culture," 277–278; Aron, *Working at Play*, 177.

12 "Chautauqua and the Teachers," *Chautauquan Weekly* 1, no. 43 (1907): 1, CIA; "A Happy Vacation," *INM* 34, no. 11–12 (1911): 482–483; "Making the Most of the Summer," *JNEA* 24, no. 5 (1935): 135.

13 Henry S. Curtis, *Recreation for Teachers; or the Teacher's Leisure Time* (New York: Macmillan, 1918), ix, 4, 55, 184–186; Blanche Howell, "Creative Resting," *High Points in the Work of the High Schools of New York City* 14, no. 7 (1932): 42–43.

14 William A. Mowry, *Recollections of a New England Educator, 1838–1908* (New York; Silver, Burdett and Company, 1908), 238, 237; "The Chautauqua Institution," *Intelligence* 21, no. 5 (1901): 197.

15 University of Michigan ad, *Intelligence* 23, no. 8 (1903): 315; University of Wisconsin ad, *Midland Schools* 20, no. 4 (1905): 157; University of Wyoming ad, *Midland*

Schools 36, no. 9 (1922): 324; Colorado State Teachers College ad, *Midland Schools* 41, no. 7 (1927): 263; "Opportunities in Summer Schools—1928," *JNEA* 17, no. 5 (1928): 155–159; Henry G. Schneider, "The Summer School and the Teacher," *Education* 17 (December 1896): 230; Margaret M. Alltucker, "Adding Refreshment to Our Pails," *JNEA* 14, no. 3 (1925): 79.

16 Editorial, *Maryland School Journal* 6, no. 10 (1880): 394; F. B. Gault, "Greeting from Colorado to Iowa Teachers," *INM* 12, no. 10 (1888): 403; "Minnesota Lakes," *TSJ* 20, no. 1 (1902): 25; Julia A. Shourek, "The Wonderland of Washington," *JNEA* 16, no. 6 (1927): 183–184; "Trails of the High Sierras," *JNEA* 20, no. 5 (1931): 157; "The Joys of the Open Road," *JNEA* 21, no. 5 (1932): 168.

17 Lake Superior ad, *Intelligence* 22, no. 9 (1902): 356; Nova Scotia ad, *Midland Schools* 10, no. 7 (1896): 247; Skaggs Hot Springs ad, *Sierra Educational News* 14, no. 6 (1918): 375; Hawaii cruise ad, *JNEA* 17, no. 1 (1928): A-21; "Summer Excursions," *PSJ* 35, no. 2 (1886): 64; W. E. Watt, "Touring in Europe," *Intelligence* 21, no. 9 (1901): 353–354.

18 Santa Fe Railroad ad, *TSJ* 21 (1903–1904): n.p.; "Yellowstone Park Waterfalls," *INM* 20, no. 3 (1896): 116; James D. Landsdowne, "Yellowstone National Park," *JNEA* 16, no. 5 (1927): 145; Stephen T. Mather, "Glimpses of the National Parks," *JNEA* 12, no. 3 (1923): 85–89, quotation on 89.

19 Mary Hull? to Nora Stewart, June 3, 1886, Box 7, SLFP; National Education Association (NEA), *Report of the Committee on Teachers' Salaries and Cost of Living* (Ann Arbor, MI: NEA, 1913), 240.

20 Libbie Burbank to Amanda Stewart, March 6, 1881, Box 2, SLFP; Philip Gerber, ed., *Bachelor Bess: The Homesteading Letters of Elizabeth Corey, 1909–1919* (Iowa City: University of Iowa Press, 1990), 134–135; Ruby M. Dresselhouse Diary, August 7–13, 1928, HGSESC; Gertrude Black La Due Diaries, June 22–July 31, 1901, June 3–August 29, 1902, June 2–July 23, 1903, Gertrude Black La Due and Family Papers, MHS.

21 Gerber, *Bachelor Bess*, 193, 358.

22 Black La Due Diaries, May 2 and May 17, 1904; Dresselhouse Diary, August 9, August 10, and August 13, 1928; Gerber, *Bachelor Bess*, 147, 356.

23 B. H. Meyer Papers, June 5, July 4, and August 24, 1886, WHSA; Walker, Mr., diary, June 1–September 22, ALPL; Willard E. Givens, biographical data and transcript of interview with Paul Hopper, 1968, Office of the Executive Secretary, Box 614, RNEA; NEA, *Report*, 94.

24 NEA, *Report*, 240; Barbara Schatte to John Nolen, May 31 and June 12, 1894, John Nolen to Barbara Schatte, August 20 and September 20, 1894, May 30, 1895, July 20, 1894, Nolen Family Papers, Schlesinger Library, Radcliffe Institute, Harvard University, Cambridge, MA. John Nolen would go to become a distinguished and well-known landscape architect and city planner.

25 Schatte to Nolen, July 9–18 and August 4, 1894, Nolen to Schatte, August 6, 1894, and Schatte to Nolen, August 12 and August 26, 1894, Nolen Family Papers.

26 Lillian Herrick Chapman Diaries, 1898–1904, quotations from June 20, July 25, August 6, and August 17, 1899, August 15, 1901, HFP.

27 Herrick Chapman Diaries, 1898–1904, quotations from July 4, July 20, July 29, and August 27, 1900, July 5 and July 23, 1901, July 3 and July 25, 1902.

28 Carol Green Wilson, *Alice Eastwood's Wonderland: The Adventures of a Botanist* (San Francisco: California Academy of Sciences, 1955), 17, 21; Grace Canan Pogue, *The Swift Seasons* (Hollywood, CA: Cloister Press, 1957), 68.

29 Doris Hinson Pieroth, *Seattle's Women Techers of the Interwar Years: Shapers of a Livable City* (Seattle: University of Washington Press, 2004), 188–189, 184–185, 19–20.

30 Margaret Ann Cruikshank, "Notes on the Yellowstone Park" (1883), Visitors, Vertical File Collection, YNPA; Irene Krumpelmann, "1926–1928: School Days and Dates Anew," 12, 9, Irene Krumpelmann Papers, Box 1, MHS; Margarete Bohle to family, May 30, 1935, June 20, 1935, Box 1, Margarete Bohle Papers, WHSA.
31 Beatrice E. Cramer memoir and diary, Box 1, HGSESC.
32 Paul H. Hanus, *Adventuring in Education* (Cambridge, MA: Harvard University Press, 1937), 71–77, quotations on 71, 77.
33 Robert C. Pavlik, *Norman Clyde: Legendary Mountaineer of California's Sierra Nevada* (Berkeley, CA: Heyday Books, 2008), 7–8, 12–15, 24–28.
34 Pavlik, *Norman Clyde*, 25, 27, 62; Johnston, "Trip to Mt. Whitney in 1878," 18–28; Fay Fuller, "A Trip to the Summit," *Every Sunday*, August 23, 1890, reprinted in *Island in the Sky: Pioneering Accounts of Mount Rainier, 1833–1894* (Seattle: Mountaineers, 1987), 128–131, 133, 135, 140; Helen M. Gompertz, "A Tramp to Mt. Lyell," *Sierra Club Bulletin* 1 (May 1894): 140; Pieroth, *Seattle's Women Teachers*, 184–185, 187. See also Polly Welts Kaufman, *National Parks and the Woman's Voice: A History* (Albuquerque: University of New Mexico Press), 15, 20–22.

Epilogue

1 Theodore R. Sizer, *Horace's Compromise: The Dilemmas of the American High School* (Boston: Houghton Mifflin, 1984), 185.
2 Dan C. Lortie, *Schoolteacher: A Sociological Study* (Chicago: University of Chicago Press, 1975), 16–17, 31–32; Jackie M. Blount, *Fit to Teach: Same-Sex Desire, Gender, and School Work in the Twentieth Century* (Albany: State University of New York Press, 2005), chap. 4–5; Karen L. Graves, *And They Were Wonderful Teachers: Florida's Purge of Gay and Lesbian Teachers* (Chicago: University of Illinois Press, 2009); Diana D'Amico Pawlewicz, *Blaming Teachers: Professionalization Policies and the Failure of Reform in American History* (New Brunswick, NJ: Rutgers University Press, 2020), chap. 4–5, epilogue (quotation on 181); Dana Goldstein, *The Teacher Wars: A History of America's Most Embattled Profession* (New York: Doubleday, 2014), chap. 5–10.
3 Kate Rousmaniere, *City Teachers: Teaching and School Reform in Historical Perspective* (New York: Teachers College Press, 1997), 135.
4 On the post–World War II history of the NEA, ATA, and AFT, see Wayne J. Urban, *Gender, Race, and the National Education Association: Professionalism and Its Limitations* (New York: RoutledgeFalmer, 2000); Marjorie Murphy, *Blackboard Unions: The AFT & the NEA, 1900–1980* (Ithaca, NY: Cornell University Press, 1990); D'Amico Pawlewicz, *Blaming Teachers*, chap. 4–5, epilogue.
5 *Miami Conference: Classroom Teachers* (booklet); Kenneth McPhaden, "Evaluation of Discussion Groups"; and "Report on the Oxford Conference—1948," NEA1005. RG, Series 8, Box 1540, RNEA; "Washington Seminar to Be Sponsored by Units of NEA," *Maryland Teacher* 15, no. 8 (1958): 21; *Washington-United Nations Seminar* (brochure), NEA Collection, Special Services, Box 2599, RNEA.
6 "The 47th Convention," *Bulletin* 26, no. 1 (1950): 1; "The 54th ATA Convention to Meet at Durham," *Bulletin* 31, no. 1 (1957): 1; and "The First General Assembly," *Bulletin* 35, no. 5 (1962): 14, https://curiosity.lib.harvard.edu/black-teacher-archive.
7 "Fourth Annual AFT Vacation Workshop," *American Teacher* 31, no. 8 (1947): 12; "They Liked the AFT Workshop—So Would You," *American Teacher* 32, no. 7 (1948): 4; "The 1949 A.F.T. Workshop," *American Teacher* 33, no. 7 (1949): 10–11;

Vidkunn Ulriksson, "Seventh Annual AFT Vacation Workshop," *American Teacher* 34, no. 8 (1950): 16–18.

8 Kenneth M. Pierce, "Summer with Homer and Vergil," *Time* 122, no. 7 (1983): 39; Coleen Curry (@mscurry_feehan), "I had the best time . . . ," X (formerly Twitter), December 1, 2022.

9 James Bryant Conant, *The Education of American Teachers* (New York: McGraw-Hill, 1963), 192–193; James W. Fraser, *Preparing America's Teachers: A History* (New York: Teachers College Press, 2007), 193.

10 "Special Summer Courses Offered at Maryland," Johns Hopkins advertisement; Earle T. Hawkins, "A New Program of Graduate Studies"; and Wesleyan University ad, *Maryland Teacher* 15, no. 8 (1958): 2, back cover, 31–33, 27.

11 Sizer, *Horace's Compromise*, 20; Robert A. Leflar, *The First 100 Years: Centennial History of the University of Arkansas* (Fayetteville: University of Arkansas Foundation, 1972), 285–286; Forest Chester Ensign, *The First Century of Teacher Training in the State University of Iowa* (Iowa City: State University of Iowa Centennial Study, 1947), 283.

12 Mary Johnston Elson papers, Box 1, Folder: Biographical Materials, IWA; Lena Beatrice Morton, *My First Sixty Years: Passion for Wisdom* (New York: Philosophical Library, 1965), 57, 59.

13 Morton, *My First Sixty*, 57; Greyhound ad, *Maryland Teacher* 6, no. 7 (1949): 5; Letters, Management and Accountability Records, Series 4, Box 21, YNPA; "NEA Travel Program," *News Bulletin for Classroom Teachers* 20, no. 3 (1947): 5; and "NEA Tours, 1950," *News Bulletin for Classroom Teachers* 23, no. 3 (1950): 4, NEA1005.RG, Series 8, Box 1546, RNEA. On travel after World War II, see Foster Rhea Dulles, *Americans Abroad: Two Centuries of European Travel* (Ann Arbor: University of Michigan Press, 1964), chap. 13.

14 Paul H. Kinsel, "Teachers Bring the World to the Classroom," *Virginia Journal of Education* 47, no. 2 (1953): 16–17.

15 *Two Travel Projects for Art Educators in 1971* and *Announcing the NEA 17-Day Orient Holiday* (brochures), Special Services, Box 2598, Folder 5, RNEA; Letter to NEA members, March 1977, Special Services, Box 2599, RNEA.

16 Ida Belle Thomas and Susan Q. Griffith, "Seeing America First," *Maryland Teacher* 4, no. 1 (1947): 23, 30.

17 "Their Wander-Filled Life," *AAA Living* 42, no. 3 (2020): 30–31.

18 Kinsel, "Teachers Bring," 17; John Branch, "Ghosts on the Glacier," *New York Times*, December 9, 2023, www.nytimes.com/interactive/2023/12/09/world/americas/aconcagua-mountain-expedition-photos.html; Sizer, *Horace's Compromise*, 185; Kenneth M. Gold, *School's In: The History of Summer Education in American Public Schools* (New York: Peter Lang, 2002), 220; Madeline Will, "Summer School Is More Important Than Ever. But Teachers Are 'Fried' and Need a Break," *Education Week*, April 26, 2012, www.edweek.org/leadership/summer-schools-is-more-important-than-ever-but-teachers-are-fried-and-need-a-break/2021/04#.

19 Max Cohen, "'I Do Not Have 2–3 Months Off': Teachers on Summer Break Are Working, a Lot," *USA Today*, July 11, 2019, www.usatoday.com/story/news/education/2019/07/11/teachers-summer-break-jobs-work-living-wage/1524677001/.

20 Herbert T. Lystrup, "Observation—Speculation—Meditation," *Yellowstone Nature Notes* 27, no. 1 (1953): 2, NPSHC; Herbert Evison, Oral History Interview of Mildred J. Ericson, 1962?, Oral History Materials, NPSHC.

21 Ben Croft, "Carving a Legacy: Butter Sculptor Sarah Pratt's Journey from Apprentice to Master," *Farm Week*, August 16, 2023, www.farmweeknow.com/general

/carving-a-legacy-butter-sculptor-sarah-pratts-journey-from-apprentice-to-master /article_7bb7b52c-1b6c-11ee-817e-e3f5f69699cc.html.

22 *World Book* ad, *Maryland Teacher* 8, no. 8 (1951): 3; Sizer, *Horace's Compromise*, 9, 19; Daniel Moulthrop, Ninive Clements Calegari, and Dave Eggers, *Teachers Have It Easy: The Big Sacrifices and Small Salaries of America's Teachers* (New York: New Press, 2005), 7, 58–59; Gold, *School's In*, 220–221.

23 Liz Riggs, "The Myth of a Teacher's 'Summer Vacation,'" *Atlantic*, July 2, 2015, www .theatlantic.com/education/archive/2015/07/myth-of-teacher-summer-vacation /397535/.

24 Lortie, *Schoolteacher*, 10; John I. Goodlad, *Teachers for Our Nation's Schools* (San Francisco: Jossey-Bass, 1990), 70.

Index

About the Author

CHRISTINE A. OGREN is a professor in the Department of Educational Policy and Leadership Studies at the University of Iowa. She is author of *The American State Normal School: "An Instrument of Great Good"*; coeditor of *Rethinking Campus Life: New Perspectives on the History of College Students in the United States*; and has published articles in *History of Education Quarterly, Paedagogica Historica, Higher Education: Handbook of Theory and Research*, and other outlets. Ogren is a former president of the History of Education Society and member of the executive committee of the International Standing Conference for the History of Education.